Praise for *2052*

"This thoughtful and thought-provoking book will be inspiring, and challenging, for all who really care about our common future."

—Gro Harlem Brundtland,
former prime minister of Norway; leader,
World Commission on Environment and Development

"It's too late to wonder how different and refreshingly breathable the world would be if everyone had listened hard to Jorgen Randers forty years ago. The question now is if we'll heed him this time. Here's our chance. Please seize it, everyone."

Alan Weisman,
author of *The World Without Us* and *Gaviotas*

"A sober, cogent, and courageous assessment of a future not dictated by fate, or economics, or limits to technology, but by the most egregious leadership failure in history. But there is still time to change course . . . just enough time and no more."

—David W. Orr, Oberlin College,
author of *Down to the Wire: Confronting Climate Collapse*

"This is an extraordinary and profoundly important book. Randers' mastery of many fields is impressive, and he presents his 'best guess' future with clarity and force. As a result, he provides a challenging template against which we can judge our own expectations for midcentury."

—James Gustave Speth,
author of *America the Possible*

"Read *2052* and get the views of a great futurist—one with a fine track record of being right."

—Paul R. Ehrlich,
author of *The Dominant Animal*

"An unconventional and lucid explanation of the likely macro-economic developments of the world over the next forty years."
—Lord Nicholas Stern,
author of *The Stern Review on the Economics of Climate Change*;
chair, Grantham Research Institute on Climate Change
and the Environment, London School of Economics

"With clarity, conscience, and courage, global-systems pioneer Jorgen Randers and his distinguished contributors map the forces that will shape the next four decades. Their sobering but far from despairing insights will encourage all who strive in applied hope to build a society worthy of nature's legacy and humans' potential."
—Amory B. Lovins,
chairman and chief scientist, Rocky Mountain Institute;
senior author, *Reinventing Fire*; coauthor, *Natural Capitalism*

2052

A Global Forecast
for the **Next Forty Years**

2052

Jorgen Randers

A REPORT TO THE CLUB OF ROME
COMMEMORATING THE 40TH ANNIVERSARY OF
The Limits to Growth

Chelsea Green Publishing
White River Junction, Vermont

Editor: Joni Praded
Project Manager: Patricia Stone
Copy Editor: Cannon Labrie
Proofreader: Nancy Ringer
Indexer: Margaret Holloway
Designer: Melissa Jacobson

Printed in the United States of America
First printing May, 2012
10 9 8 7 6 5 4 3 2 1   12 13 14 15 16

Our Commitment to Green Publishing
Chelsea Green sees publishing as a tool for cultural change and ecological stewardship. We strive to align our book manufacturing practices with our editorial mission and to reduce the impact of our business enterprise in the environment. We print our books and catalogs on chlorine-free recycled paper, using vegetable-based inks whenever possible. This book may cost slightly more because it was printed on paper that contains recycled fiber, and we hope you'll agree that it's worth it. Chelsea Green is a member of the Green Press Initiative (www.greenpressinitiative.org), a nonprofit coalition of publishers, manufacturers, and authors working to protect the world's endangered forests and conserve natural resources. *2052: A Global Forecast for the Next Forty Years* was printed on FSC®-certified paper supplied by Thomson-Shore that contains at least 30% postconsumer recycled fiber.

Library of Congress Cataloging-in-Publication Data
Randers, Jorgen.
  2052 : a global forecast for the next forty years / Jorgen Randers.
    p. cm.
  "A Report to the Club of Rome Commemorating the 40th Anniversary of The Limits to Growth."
  Includes bibliographical references and index.
  ISBN 978-1-60358-467-8 (hardcover) — ISBN 978-1-60358-421-0 (pbk.) — ISBN 978-1-60358-422-7 (ebook)
1. Economic history—21st century. 2. Economic forecasting. I. Title.

HC59.3.R36 2012
330.9001'12--dc23

                    2012012065

Chelsea Green Publishing
85 North Main Street, Suite 120
White River Junction, VT 05001
(802) 295-6300
www.chelseagreen.com

FSC
www.fsc.org
MIX
Paper from
responsible sources
FSC® C013483

For my children and grandchildren

CONTENTS

PART 3: ANALYSIS

Acknowledgments

This book would not have seen the day of light had it not been for my great fortune in meeting, accidentally, in a physics colloquium at MIT in 1970, the father of system dynamics, Jay W. Forrester, just at the time when he won the contract to do *The Limits to Growth* study for the Club of Rome. That made me visible for the very able project leader Jay chose to do the project, namely Dennis L. Meadows, who further did the masterstroke of involving Donella H. Meadows, the great, diligent, and warm author of all of our joint publications. All three played central roles in my career, and Dennis and Dana became lifelong friends. I owe them a lot!

I would also like to present my thanks to:

- Toyota Norway AS, the BI Norwegian Business School, and the Norwegian Union for Academic Personnel ("Akademikerne"), for being the unconventional group of sponsors of this forecast;
- My old friend Ulrich Golüke, for creating the quantitative foundation (statistical data, spreadsheets, and other models) for this forecast;
- The forty-one professionals who enthusiastically contributed glimpses of the future to this book—and thereby showed that they are not only independent thinkers, but also able to write;
- All my close friends, for having persisted for forty years in systematically opposing my pessimistic views about the future;
- My wife, Marie, and daughter, Engelke, for enduring my sadness and encouraging me to continue the fight for a world where humanity will live in sustainable harmony with nature;
- WWF, for gathering into one global nongovernmental organization that small minority who really believe the planet is worth saving;
- The Club of Rome, who warmly welcomed this book as a report to the Club of Rome, as part of their commemoration of the first report to the Club forty years ago; and
- Chelsea Green Publishing, for their long-lasting dedication to the cause and for helping make the presentation readable.

Together we could create a much better world!

What Will the Future Bring?

President Vaclav Havel of the Czech Republic in front of an auditorium of journalists before chairing a crucial meeting to avoid war in former Yugoslavia:

"Your Excellency. Are you an optimist?"

Long pause.

"No, I am not an optimist in the sense that I believe that everything will go well. But neither am I a pessimist in the sense that I believe everything will go wrong. I am hopeful. For without hope there will be no progress. Hope is as important as life itself."[1]

Forty years ago, my colleagues and I spent two years working busily in our offices at MIT. We thought long and hard about the future and—under the leadership of Dennis L. Meadows and with the authorship of Donnella II. Meadows—produced what became the infamous little book called *The Limits to Growth*.[2] The book was a scenario analysis in which we tried to answer the question "What will happen over the next 130 years if humanity decides to follow certain policies?" For example, what will happen if global society continues to pursue economic growth without special emphasis on population control? Or what will happen if humanity decides to focus its immense technological skills (and some money) on developing environmentally benign agriculture at a global scale? We made several different pictures of the future. Some described futures where things went wrong; others described futures where the situation was much better for the human lot.

But we did not make a forecast. We did not try to tell what would actually happen over the century to come. The reason was that we did not believe this could be done with scientific rigor. So many things could conceivably happen over the long century from 1970 to 2100 that we felt unable to pick one possible future and defend it against the multitude of other possible futures.

Instead we made a scenario analysis. We tried to say something about the likely result of various sets of policies. We tried to describe the likely effect of using societal resources to accelerate the technological solutions to the obvious problems of the time: population growth, food shortages, scarce resources, and emerging environmental damage. We used a computer model to help us get ideas about what might happen if humanity decided to set an upper limit on per capita consumption, or on the number of children per woman.

We tried to make our various scenarios—our pictures of the future—internally consistent. We tried to make sure that population developments were logically consistent with our assumptions concerning desired family size, and that the desired family size was consistent with the levels of education and health available. We tried to make sure that technical solutions we assumed would occur did not appear spontaneously in our scenarios, but only after decades of research, development, and small-scale pilots. To avoid conflicting assumptions, we translated all of our assumptions into our computer model. That computer model also helped us refrain from drawing illogical inferences from the full set of assumptions.

The main conclusion from our exercise in the early 1970s was that, without big changes, humanity was poised to grow dangerously beyond the physical limits of our planet. This was a conclusion based on the observation (self-evident for us, but not for all) that it takes time for humanity to solve any pressing issue arising from the finiteness (obvious for us, but not for all) of the planet. It takes time to identify the problem, time to accept that it is real, time to solve it, and time to implement the new solution. The first part—the "observation and acceptance delay"—made it likely (to us, but not all) that humanity would allow itself to grow in size and physical impact beyond the sustainable carrying capacity of the global ecosystem. This long delay would allow—and even invite—what we called *overshoot*, especially if humanity was growing fast toward planetary constraints. Practically speaking, it is possible for humanity to remain in overshoot for a while (as when overfishing), but overshoot cannot and will not last forever once its foundations have been destroyed (when there are no more fish).

Will the World Collapse?

Once in overshoot there are only two paths back into sustainable territory: either *managed decline*, through the orderly introduction of a new solution (fish from fish farms), or *collapse* (you stop eating fish because there are none—and end the livelihood of the fishermen, as in Newfoundland after 1992). Overshoot cannot be sustained. If you try to sustain it, intractable problems will arise in the short term. These problems will provide strong motivation to identify and put in place new solutions. However, a new solution does not occur overnight, but only after a "solution and implementation delay"—which easily covers a decade. So even if you start before the foundations are totally gone, you run the risk of finishing them off while you are waiting for the new solution. This was the real message of *The Limits to Growth* in 1972.

In the decades since it was published, the sluggish human response to the climate problem has provided a first-class illustration of this message. The problem was first identified in the 1960s,[3] the Intergovernmental Panel on Climate Change (IPCC) was formed in 1988 to provide the scientific view,[4] and the Kyoto protocol was agreed in 1997.[5] Still—after forty years—we have not yet seen reduction in the annual emissions of greenhouse gases. Humanity remains in solid overshoot (emitting around twice as much CO_2 per year as is absorbed by the world's oceans and forests), and we can discern the early signs of the coming gradual destruction of the ecosystem—which provides a number of ecological services on which humans depend. Managed decline is being discussed in conference after conference, but with little effect on emissions.

In the scenarios of *The Limits to Growth*, overshoot and collapse were a future possibility that my colleagues and I really believed would be avoided through new, wise, and forward-looking policy. Once the potential dangers of endless growth and delayed solutions were understood, swift action would be taken. A rational warning, based on the most accurate data available, we thought, might heighten awareness, shorten delays, and change the dim outlook for the future.

Sadly, though, it is not obvious that the last forty years has given support to our youthful optimism. But at least *The Limits to Growth* defined the conceptual tools for an enlightened debate—although that debate never really took place.

An Educated Guess

In this book I will do something totally different. With the great help of my new friends ("new" in the sense that all the contributors to *2052*—except William W. Behrens—did not join in the first effort forty years ago) I will try to make a forecast of what will happen over the next forty years. This is partly to satisfy my own curiosity and partly an attempt to kick society into action. Making such a forecast is a daunting task, one that cannot be done with high precision. So many things could happen between now and 2052 that the outcome is not predictable in the scientific sense—that is, with a narrow uncertainty band. Numerous possible futures exist, many of which are likely and most of which are unlikely.

So I cannot make a scientific forecast—in the sense that it is possible to state authoritatively that this forecast is the most likely to happen. But luckily it is possible to make a guess. And even better, it is possible to make an *educated* guess, that, at a minimum, should be based on available facts and be internally consistent—that is, not contradict itself.

This book contains my educated guess. It is not a "scientific truth"—that kind of truth doesn't exist in the futures field. It is refined judgment, a well-informed judgment. Personally, I am sure I am right, although this cannot be proven. But neither can I be proven wrong until we are well on our way to 2052.

PART 1
BACKGROUND

CHAPTER 1

Worrying about the Future

I have lived my whole adult life worrying about the future. Not about my personal future, but the global future—the future of humanity—on its small planet Earth.

Now, at sixty-six, I see that I have been worrying in vain. Not because the global future looks problem free and rosy. My worrying has been in vain because it hasn't had much impact on global evolution over the long generation since I started worrying.

It all began when I arrived as a PhD student in physics at the Massachusetts Institute of Technology in January 1970. I had lived my prior life in little, safe, and egalitarian Norway, well shielded from global developments, focused on the mysteries of solid-state physics. Through a complicated sequence of events, by the summer of 1970 I was deeply involved in what was to become the first report to the Club of Rome on "The Predicament of Mankind," working as a researcher in the A. P. Sloan School of Management at MIT. The report—called *The Limits to Growth*—described various scenarios for world development to 2100. The scenarios were based on simulation runs from a computer model, my new field of expertise.

Within a few months, my worrying was in full bloom. Our research task was to consider what would happen if the global population and economy continued their recent developments for a hundred years or so. It did not take much quantitative skill to discover that our planet was much too small, and that humanity was facing serious trouble some fifty years down the line— that is, unless humanity made a conscious and unconventional decision to change its ways.

We published *The Limits to Growth* in 1972, with our recommendations about what should be done in order to promote sustainable well-being on our finite planet. I spent the 1970s and 1980s worrying about whether humanity would in fact be wise enough to heed our advice and change its global policies and behavior—in time. I used a lot of time and energy, in various roles, trying to convince people that changing would be much better than following traditional patterns. After 1993 I left academia and upped the intensity of my effort by working through WWF—the big influential nature-conservation organization that is called the World Wildlife Fund in the United States. Since 2005 I have focused more narrowly on stopping climate change.

But I never stopped worrying about the future of humanity on small planet Earth. My worrying can be traced through some of my writings over the last twenty years.[1]

Is there reason to worry? Are we facing a global future that makes it sensible to be concerned? Will the future be better than the present? Or will it be worse? Or is this simply a hang-up of an old man?

You are holding the book that is my answer to these questions. After four decades of worrying about a blurred future that I really did not know well, I decided it would help my pain to try to describe the next four decades as precisely as possible. I did not want a picture of an ideal world—one of the various dream societies pursued by idealists. I wanted a picture of the future that humanity is going to create for itself during the four decades ahead, the future that will result from the many human decisions of mixed quality and wisdom, the future that is most likely to happen, the future that will be written in the history books.

In short, I wanted a forecast of the most likely global roadmap to 2052 so that I would know what I am in for. So that I would know whether there actually is reason to worry on behalf of my children. Or the poor in Africa. So that I could possibly do what all other upper-middle-class people in the industrial world seem to do, namely, relax and contribute to societal development with an unworried mind.

Luckily my forecast of the most likely global future to 2052 will have other uses.

First, the forecast will enable you to give your *own* answer to whether there is reason to worry. Your answer may be different from mine. Different people draw different conclusions from the same picture.

Second, it will satisfy curiosity. Having worried about the future for so long, I am genuinely interested in knowing what it will be. On my fiftieth birthday, my fondest wish was to awake from the dead for a week in the year 2100, to learn what had transpired during the twenty-first century. I believe many share this curiosity about what lies ahead.

Third, some will use the forecast to help them invest profitably.

Fourth, the more socially inclined will use the forecast to clarify what new policies, legislation, and societal institutions will have the greatest effect in creating a better future, so they know where to put in their effort.

Others will want to know what the future holds in order to improve their chances for a better life during the next several decades, for example by moving to another city, country, or region before it becomes impossible, or by changing a profession before it becomes outdated.

Finally, some will want to adapt up front to the world of the future, to coming hot spells, sea-level rise, migration flows, more centralist government, and destruction of attractive tourist spots.

There are many motivations, and they are all valid. Our common interest is a desire to know how the world will develop over the next forty years.

Why Now?

In the middle of my worrying, a decade ago or so, my conviction grew that humanity, faced with great but mostly solvable challenges, is not going to rise to the occasion. I began to believe that the necessary change would not happen—at least not in time. Which does not mean, of course, that the world will come to an end. But it does mean that the global future will be less rosy than it could have been. In a way, this realization helped my pain. I started to accept my loss.

But this mental shift did not stop my worrying. It simply shifted its focus. Now I was worrying about how bad the situation would get before humanity resolved to change its ways. That probably would have been a better state of mind if I had been able to air the matter in the public arena. But I did not dare to make the shift public. Along with my small group of co-worriers—the avant-garde of the global sustainability movement—I worried that admitting that the human response was inadequate would be demotivating. I worried about reducing to zero the small ongoing effort to mend our human ways. Presenting my worries, however carefully, could trigger shouts of "Game over!" and "Game lost!" which in turn could become self-fulfilling. It could tempt the few who were hard at work on sustainable development to throw in their towels.

So I kept worrying behind closed doors, while observing continually rising emissions of greenhouse gases, increasingly dysfunctional global environmental governance, growing destruction of coral reefs, and the continuing loss of the remaining old-growth forests. I love old-growth forests—those quiet, timeless inventories of species, displaying the result of hundreds of millions of years of biological evolution.

Surprisingly the forests proved to be my salvation. One day I mentioned to a psychologist friend that I felt physical pain when I saw logging machines destroy, in one day, what nature would take centuries to repair—if that repair even occurred. She advised me in her quiet, professional tone that I had to learn to live with the loss. To express and accept that such-and-such particular forest was gone—permanently, with no resurrection possible. Actively handle the grief, as one should after the loss of a mother or good friend. Accept the fact that this old growth was gone, and that more would be going. Look the future straight in the eye and accept it. Get used to how things are. Stop worrying.

It took a long time to accept this wise advice. But over the years, it did help. Now I am genuinely happy whenever I see some remaining patch of undisturbed old-growth forest, in the middle of an ocean of clear-cut land. Regardless how small, it is much better than nothing. Before, I would have focused my attention on its messy clear-cut surroundings and been sad because it would remind me about how recently much of the Northern Hemisphere was covered by peaceful, deep, and undisturbed temperate and boreal forests. In Michigan this is less than one hundred years ago; in Russia less than fifty! And I would have grown even sadder when thinking about how fast the rest would go.

By analogy, I believe it will be calming to get to know the world that is likely to be our home in the future, rather than dreaming about the world that could have been. The first step down the road to mental peace is to obtain a precise description of what the future is likely to look like. Then to accept it. And finally to stop grieving.

Is a Forecast Possible?

But can this be done? Is it possible to make a forecast of global developments over a forty-year period? Clearly it is possible to make a guess—just like it is possible to guess who will win the soccer championship in 2016. And guessing is simple; it can be done without any knowledge whatsoever about the topic. There is a chance that your guess is right. And a much larger chance that it is wrong, as in all gambling.

In the normal use of the term, "forecasting" is a more ambitious exercise. A forecast is expected to have a higher chance of being right than wrong—ideally much higher. People understand that it is an advantage to know a lot about the system before one tries to forecast its future path. If rational players plan to rely on a prediction, they usually prefer an educated forecast over uninformed guesswork. Guessing is for the less informed.

My learned—and other—friends never stop pointing out that predicting the world future to 2052 is impossible. Not only in practice, but also in theory.

Of course they are right. I am the first to accept this, having spent a lifetime making nonlinear dynamic simulation models of socioeconomic systems. But my critics need to be more precise. They are right in the sense that it is impossible to predict individual events in the future, even with deep knowledge about the system. The weakness of weather forecasts beyond five days proves this to most outdoorsmen. But they are not right when it comes to forecasting broad developments. Technically speaking, it *is* possible to say something about trends and tendencies that are rooted in stable causal feedback structures in the world system.

The forecast in this book is of that broad nature. It is an informed guess tracing the big lines in what I see as the probable global evolution toward 2052. I will use numbers to make my case, but always in the most indicative sense. The most reliable aspects of my forecast are its general trends or tendencies.

But isn't this process disregarding human free will? Couldn't people suddenly make a decision in 2033 that completely derails the system from its expected path? Yes, of course they could. But my view—which is shared by many professional colleagues in the social sciences—is that such out-of-the-blue decisions are very unlikely. All decisions are made in a context, and the context strongly influences the decision. One might be tempted to say that decisions, at least the major ones, are formed by the context—as Marx did. Yes, I agree that decisions may come a year earlier or three years later if the right leader emerges at the right time. And yes, they may arise as an Internet campaign rather than as a resolution in parliament. Details are hard to predict, but forecasting the big picture is simpler. It is simpler to tell whether it will be colder next winter than this summer than it is to tell whether next week will be warmer or colder than today.

Let us take a simple but highly relevant example of human decision making, namely, the decision to have another child. One perspective is that this is a prime example of the operation of the unpredictable and free will, that the decision to have another baby is done on the spur of the moment and that success is determined by a number of local conditions at the time of the conception. Another perspective is to observe that women on average have fewer children if they are urban, educated, and lower middle class than if they are rural, illiterate, and poor. Thus I agree that it is impossible to predict that my daughter will have exactly one child. But it is still possible to say that the number of children per mother will decline as a country industrializes. This is the difference between event prediction and trend forecasting.

In the pages ahead, we will explore the broad trends that will influence our lives and those of our children. Here and there you will find an imaginary future event described, but that is only to bring the possibilities to life. It is simpler to prepare for the future if you start by imagining it.

My forecast does not eliminate free will, but rather is based on the belief that human decision making is influenced by the conditions under which the decision is being made. Smaller families result when the education level is higher. More social unrest occurs when income distribution is uneven. If there is reason to believe that conditions will develop in a certain manner, it is reasonable to forecast the decisions that will follow suit.

Why Forty Years?

Why not ten or one hundred?[2] The reason is boringly simple and personal. In 2012 it is forty years since *The Limits to Growth* was published, discussing how humanity could handle life on a limited planet over the next hundred years or so. Today we know what was done during the first forty years—and what was not done. We know a great deal about the rationale for the decisions made during these decades. And we have a fair understanding of the pressures that have locked us into nonaction on a number of fronts. We have experienced how fast technology can solve certain solvable problems, and how slowly humanity progresses on less tractable issues. Since we know so much about the first forty years, it seemed reasonable to extract lessons from those forty years, and try to look at the next forty. When studying a dynamic phenomenon one should start by looking as far back as one is planning to look ahead. If you want to say something about population growth from 2012 to 2052, it is helpful to know the population numbers from 1972 to 2012.

So my forecast for the next forty years is an educated guess at what I believe will happen, not a scenario analysis, and certainly not a description of what ought to happen. The latter has been done too many times. Global society knows very well what should be done to create a better world for our children. We need to remove poverty and address the climate challenge. We know that this can be done technologically and at a relatively low cost. But, sadly, as you will see, I don't believe this will be done. Humanity, as I had feared, will not rise to the occasion, at least not rapidly enough to avoid unnecessary damage. The complex and time-consuming decision making of democratic nation-states will ensure that.

Different societal groups will fare differently. The poor peasant in rural China in 2012 will have a much better ride toward 2052 than the upper-middle-classer of the postindustrial world, who will lose many of his privileges.

Bases for an Educated Guess

So how does one go about painting a picture of the most likely global future to 2052? Not only is the topic big, but it is broad, deep, and multifaceted. There is not one reality, there are many parallel realities. No picture can be complete; every picture will be a selection from the wonderfully rich reality that is the human condition. And then there are the dynamics. Evolution is not a straight line from a current equilibrium to the next. As the system evolves toward its next equilibrium, that equilibrium moves as a consequence of new conditions. Thus the path of development from here to there can take any form: a curve, a sine wave, a spiral, and much more. It is the classic "thesis, antithesis, and synthesis" evolving in parallel in multiple dimensions at the same time.

Here is what I did. I tried to handle the richness by calling on the expertise of a number of colleagues. I tried to handle the dynamics using my old friend, the dynamic simulation model. And I tried to maintain perspective by exploring new paradigms by deliberately avoiding being stuck in the current post–World War II paradigm, which imprecisely could be termed "happiness via continued economic growth based on fossil fuels." Let us take them one by one.

The Richness of the Global Future

To help me avoid tunnel vision, myopia, and the obvious limitations in my knowledge about most aspects of the world, I asked a number of my friends and colleagues—independent thinkers and writers—to tell me what they were absolutely certain would happen before 2052. Most accepted the challenge with enthusiasm, even when they were told to constrain their "glimpse of the future" to 1,500 words and to keep within a field they knew well. You will find nearly thirty-five of these glimpses—in full or excerpted—in this volume.

In those glimpses you will see what educated people from all over the world say when they are forced to do something they do not really like, namely, to make a prediction—without all the hedges and caveats that are normal in scientific, commercial, and governmental affairs. In sum, the glimpses give a multidimensional sketch of the future world. The collection is very broad in scope, but many common themes emerged and are included in my forecast.

Furthermore, the glimpses were surprisingly free from contradictions. That is indeed surprising, and might mean that "independent thinkers and writers" often do end up with the same general picture when forced to look ahead and honestly describe their view—and do not have to consider the consequences of what they are telling.

The Dynamics

Many global forecasts are inconsistent. This means that one part of the forecast contradicts another part of the forecast. Let me use a simple example to explain. Often a conventional forecast describes—in glowing terms—how total production (GDP) will grow at high rates over the next several decades. One central assumption behind such a forecast is normally a certain development in population, gleaned from the national statistical office or the UN. If that assumption is maintained it is likely that the forecast is wrong, simply because it has not taken into account the strong impact of higher income on the birth rate. People have fewer children when they get richer. Population growth will slow as GDP becomes higher. So a forecast that does not adjust the future population downward will be wrong. Such a forecast will tend to exaggerate the future birth rate, overestimate future population, and underestimate GDP per person. The future income per person will prove to be higher than in the initial forecast. The mistake does not only pertain to the end state. It leads to misleading dynamics—the description of the development path will also be wrong. Another example would be prior assumptions made about the speed of technological development over the next several decades. These assumptions may be contradicted if the forecast indicates rapid growth in the economy. A larger economy will afford more research and experience higher rates of technological development.

To help avoid this type of inconsistency, and help ensure that my forecast actually does follow logically from the assumptions made, I use a set of dynamic spreadsheets to check my results. The spreadsheets are (at least approximations to) state-determined equation systems that describe the world as a set of differential equations. In these models, the situation evolves over time from its starting state, in a logically consistent manner, through the operation of the causal relationships that are reflected in the equations that drive the models. The quantitative backbone of my forecast is most readily available to you in the spreadsheets on the *2052* website (www.2052.info). The spreadsheets are not fully dynamic, so I have used (although to a limited extent) two computer models of the world to make sure that major feedback effects are not omitted from my forecast.

If you did not understand the last four sentences, don't worry. They are there for those computer/mathematics aficionados who understand what they mean. What is important is that I am fully aware of the risk of internal inconsistency in a verbal forecast, and that I have used spreadsheets and computer models of the global system to try to reduce such inconsistency.

I also have relied on an impressive collection of statistical time series to ensure that I do not accidentally deviate from well-established tradition and behavior—which are of course reflected in historical data. The data is also available in the spreadsheets on the book's website.

The Paradigm

All this leads to my third helper—a conscious attitude to one's choice of paradigm. A paradigm is a worldview. There are many different worldviews. Marxism is one, religious conservatism another. None is right. Different paradigms simply highlight different aspects of reality. A paradigm is also a simplification that helps you distinguish the noise from significant trends (as defined by your own paradigm, that is). But it is most important to understand that your chosen paradigm—which is normally tacit, rarely described—has surprisingly strong impact on what you see. Let us take an example. The conventional macroeconomics paradigm assumes that the world's markets are in equilibrium. Hence most economists do see a world in equilibrium when they read their newspaper or walk down the street. The opponents to this paradigm, for example, the system dynamics school to which I belong, assume that the world is not in equilibrium. To us the world is careening from one turn to the next in a never-ending search for the next equilibrium, which always is on the move.

The important point is that you should be aware that you have your own paradigm, that is, your tacit set of beliefs and interpretations that help you live your life. Ideally you should be able to shift from one paradigm to another depending on the problem at hand. Most people are unable to do so.

The current Western world has a dominant paradigm. It includes basic beliefs like "the efficiency of market-based economies," "the self-correcting ability of democratic government," "benefits from continued economic growth based on fossil fuels," and "increased welfare through free trade and globalization." When trying to clarify the next forty years, it is important to include the possibility of a change in the dominant paradigm. At least one should avoid limiting oneself to analyses through one set of glasses, namely, the current dominant paradigm.

Yes, simplification is important to live a happy life in the current world. But when looking forty years ahead, it becomes important to choose the right simplification. And it may be safer to try many, in the hope of losing fewer babies with the bathwater.

Full Steam Ahead with a Peaceful Mind

It is important for me to end by emphasizing that this book is also written to encourage action. As mentioned, books like this one are normally not written, because socially conscious authors rightfully worry that their work might kill motivation and hinder ongoing and future action to improve the situation. I agree with this general view, but still have chosen to risk describing what is ahead of us. Hopefully my global forecast will act as an external enemy and kick humanity—or at least a few dedicated individuals—into action. In this way my forecast could play the role of the global environmental disaster that never seems to come suddenly enough to trigger wide support for coordinated political action.

Remember my endless worrying? And the advice from the psychologist to openly grieve and then finally accept the loss of my beloved old-growth forests? Instead of worrying diffusely about what might be in store for humanity over the next forty years, I now have (in this book) a description of what I see as the most likely future to 2052. I have gotten to know this future, grieved over the unnecessary suffering involved, and finally come to peace with the lost global opportunity. My mind is less tortured. The future is as it is. Whenever I now see a small sign of increased sustainability—or more precisely, a small sign of reduced unsustainability—I react with genuine happiness rather than with general sadness about the world that could have been.

CHAPTER 2

Five Big Issues toward 2052

So what will the future look like?

The simplest way to get an answer is of course to ask someone who knows. But if you want a reliable forecast for the future of the world over the next forty years, it is difficult—simply because there is no one who really knows. There are even fewer who pretend to know. And if you also insist that the scenario shall be complete and consistent, there is, as far as I know, nowhere to go. It is relatively easy to find prescriptions on how the world ought to develop (for example, the World Business Council for Sustainable Development *Vision 2050*,[1] which describes what must be done in order for us to have a sustainable world in 2050). But I do not know of a well-considered forecast of what will actually happen at a global level to 2052.

In the past, there were research groups working on broad-scope computer models of global development, seeking to produce consistent scenarios of the long-term future. But this fad peaked in the 1970s and early 1980s and then died out.[2] Today, long term models of the world are largely limited to macroeconomics and energy, with 2030 as the longest commonly used time horizon and with important variables (like population and productivity growth) kept exogenous. Of course there exist special-purpose models of the global climate with much longer time horizons, but these do not include socioeconomic variables. So the best offer available is sector perspectives on global development. The full picture is missing.

This lack of a complete picture of the future is the basic reason for my uncertainty and worrying. After a long life in the sustainability movement, and as a builder of world models, I know full well what ought to be done in order to have (what I see as) an attractive world by 2052. But at the same time, I am convinced that humanity will not put in place the full work program necessary to create an attractive world by 2052. So the real challenge is to estimate how much (or how little) of what needs to be done actually will be done.

The Sustainability Revolution

Luckily it is simple to sketch the big picture of global physical development over the last three hundred years. Before the 1700s, the world was thinly populated, largely agricultural, and using very little energy. This was a world run by slaves, horses, oxen, and some firewood—to use headline language. The advent of steam engines running on coal began the industrial revolution. The transition to the industrial age was characterized by a huge increase in the use of energy. Over the last 250 years this use of energy made the industrialized countries rich in material goods and ensured a less strenuous life for the masses. The less industrialized countries of today are following suit as fast as they can. The recent emergence of China is a vivid illustration of what industrialization of a country means. The rest of the world strives to follow suit.

By 2052, the industrial revolution will be complete in rich countries, like the agricultural revolution before it. The transfer of workers from agriculture to manufacturing will be complete as well, and the workforce will move onward to services and care. Only a few will remain in physical production. From then on, the focus will be on steady improvement in the supply of services and care to the common folk.

But there is another reason why the past focus on industrialization will wane. We know already (deep in our hearts) that there is little increased satisfaction in never-ending growth in the per capita consumption of food and manufactured goods. Once well fed, warm, safe, and comfortable, most humans yearn for more abstract satisfaction. Never-ending growth in material consumption and energy use may generate marginal improvements for some individuals but will be easily overwhelmed by the negative side effects for the masses when everyone tries to emulate the rich—because we live on a finite planet. Thus sooner or later, the industrial revolution will be followed by the sustainability revolution. This is the era when the main objective of nations will be to evolve a national society that can be sustained in the long run both physically and mentally. It will start in the rich countries and spread to the rest of the world later in this century. I can't tell you exactly what this future society will look like. But I am willing to bet that the overriding ambition will not be "fossil-fueled economic growth" but rather "sustainable well-being."

These two words—*sustainability* and *well-being*—carry meaning without being sharply defined. We don't know in minute detail what such a shift will involve. But we do know some main parameters. The future world will not have an expanding population. It will still use much energy per person, but that energy will be used wisely and be of the renewable sort. In the end the world will run on energy from the sun—either directly as solar heat or solar electricity, or indirectly via wind, hydro, and biomass. It will be a world that focuses on human well-being, not only on its material component.

The big question is how fast the transition to sustainability will happen. The sustainability revolution has already begun, that is for sure. The new paradigm already emerged forty years ago, or perhaps even fifty (with Rachel Carson in 1962)[3]. It has spread since, but it is still far from mainstream. We have evolved an increased understanding of the need to replace fossil energy, but we have not really embarked on the challenge. And some—even in high places—have started to talk seriously about the need to replace GDP growth with growth in well-being as the overriding societal goal. The best recent example is the report by Joseph Stiglitz, Amartya Sen, and Jean-Paul Fitoussi to President Sarkozy of France in 2009, in which these macroeconomists broke rank with traditional theory and started advocating an accelerated shift of emphasis from GDP to well-being.[4]

So the sustainability revolution has started but is still in its infancy. When will it be completed? I am sure that by the year 2100 we will have a world that is much more sustainable than the current one—for the simple reason that "unsustainability is unsustainable," to use the wonderful phrase of corporate sustainability expert Alan Knight. Current unsustainable ways—by definition of the word *unsustainable*—cannot be continued indefinitely; they will have to be replaced with systems and behaviors that can be maintained in the longer run. Whether the new sustainable world will be attractive or one with much lower well-being than today is hard to tell. It depends on what humanity chooses to do during the rest of the twenty-first century. As you will see from my forecast in this book, I believe the transition to sustainability will be only half complete by 2052, and may run into serious difficulties in the second half of the century. Global society will have to perform a miracle after 2052 if it is to end the century in a desirable and durable situation.

Five Central Issues Involving System Change

The transition to sustainability will require fundamental change to a number of the systems that govern current world developments. Not only will the energy system need to change from fossil to solar, and the ruling paradigm from perpetual physical growth to some form of stability that fits within the physical carrying capacity of the globe, but there will also be changes to the softer institutional guides like capitalism, democracy, agreed power sharing, and the human perspective on nature.

Luckily my ambition in this book is "only" to forecast global developments to 2052—not all the way to sustainability. It hugely simplifies the task, because (as you will see from later chapters) I expect the real crunch to be just beyond the time horizon of my forecast—that is, in the decades following 2052. Still there are many issues that will face humankind during the first half of the twenty-first century. I need to have an opinion on each of them in order to formulate a broad and consistent forecast.

After much pondering and initial work on early versions of my forecast, I believe that the next forty years will be strongly influenced by how we handle five central issues. They are all issues involving the intangible systems and concepts that influence our daily lives: capitalism, economic growth, democracy, intergenerational equity, and our relationship with the earth's climate. In each case questions are already being asked about the viability of current ways. In each case some kind of partial answer will emerge over the next forty years, followed by some change in concepts, values, and perspectives. But don't expect immediate progress. System change takes time. But the time following a paradigm shift is like the time following an earthquake: the new situation is both different and stable.

It's helpful to discuss these five central issues one by one. To deepen the discussion, I include for each issue the perspective of an expert who addresses possible world developments occurring in the years leading up to 2052.

The End of Capitalism?

Capitalism has done wonders for global wealth creation over the last centuries, and this system for allocation of human activity dominates the current world economy. Capitalism has successfully focused attention and capital on organizations that are able to provide goods and services to customers who are willing and able to pay. Whenever demand shifts, the capitalistic system reallocates, again and again, thereby contributing to a continuing restructuring and growth of the societal pie. But in the same process, uncontrolled capitalism concentrates wealth in fewer hands. So there is a growing group of critics who point to the inequitable distribution of success in the system. The defenders of capitalism have always responded that this is the task of the politicians. But since politicians, particularly in democratic societies, seem unable to tax and redistribute in a sufficient manner, capitalism normally ends with the blame.

Employment is the main tool of distribution in the capitalist economy. If you have a job, you get a share of the total pie. Not necessarily a fair share, but more than nothing. If you do not have a job, you don't get anything, unless you live in a country where the state ensures an income for those without work. But unemployment compensation is normally quite limited both in value and in the length of time it is available. This is why job loss is so much feared in all capitalist economies, and why capitalism comes under fire whenever unemployment rates increase.

In the aftermath of recent business downturns, and particularly after the downturn of 2008, unemployment has increased, and criticism of the capitalist system is once more on the rise. As a practical matter, the fundamental question is, Will there be enough new jobs? Or will we get accelerating unemployment, inequity, and finally rebellion against capitalism—at least in those countries where capitalism is not modified by a strong state?

"Glimpse 2-1: The Dark Decades: Privilege and Polarization," provides a colorful and useful perspective on what we are facing. Read it now, before I comment on the content and how it fits into my forecast. Also notice that there is a short author bio at the end of this glimpse and all the others that you will find throughout the book. The bio is at the end because the ideas presented, and their place in the total forecast, are more important for your understanding than who wrote them.

GLIMPSE 2-1

The Dark Decades: Privilege and Polarization

Carlos Joly

From a half century of progressive enlightenment and increasing well-being we are moving to a new Dark Age of hard times for the many and inordinate privilege and wealth for the few.

Upward social mobility was a general phenomenon from after 1945 until about 1990. In one and two generations, families moved from being poor or working class to middle class and upper middle class. In the United States, reindustrialization, economic growth, broad university access, labor union–negotiated benefits, Medicare, Medicaid, and health insurance did the trick. In western Europe, their equivalents in social democratic economies and European Union (EU) policies resulted in well-functioning welfare states providing a better life with expanding opportunities for urban workers, farmers, artisans, and small businessowners. Working hours shortened and vacations lengthened while purchasing power increased and healthy, youthful pensioners came to see retirement as a "golden age."

But in the past twenty years this has begun to change. People in mature economies no longer report increasing well-being. They have grounds for pessimism. They will be worse off.

As I see it, we are entering an age of increasing polarization economically, socially, culturally, and environmentally. In mature markets there will be more poor and more inequity—polarization between the pauperized many and the fortunate few. In emerging economies we will see less poverty—an economic and social evolution like we saw in mature markets after the Second World War. They are catching up, as the Western rich are falling back. However, common to both will be a general degradation of environmental conditions and an increasing frequency and severity of extreme weather events affecting economies everywhere, albeit in different ways. Emerging economies will have to learn to deal with emerging climate change, from soy and wheat affected by too much and too little rain in the Argentine pampas to pipelines and other infrastructure in Russian Siberia breaking up from sagging tundra.

Overall, I expect the international community will not put in place robust emissions-reduction limits until disaster is upon us, and probably then policies and money will go to emergency response and remediation, as prevention will be seen as no longer possible. Mature economies will fall behind as they fail to modernize and green their industrial infrastructure. China will win this game—in wind, solar, battery technology, and railways.

Oversimplifying the situation, the cause of the recurrent crises in the West is the triumph of financial capitalism, aided and abetted by its neoliberal institutions—the Federal Reserve, the US Treasury, the International Monetary Fund, the European Central Bank, international patent rights legislation—and coupled with the takeover of government by a corporate and financial oligarchy.[5] There are exceptions, noticeably the Nordic Model with its real social democracy, its work-life constitutions mediating in a fair way the interests of capital, labor, and government, its natural resource laws making sure the extractive industry pays proper taxes, and its welfare state institutions meant to create well-being for the many through incentivizing employment.[6]

Growth, Consumerism, Climate Change

People's closets, attics, and garages are full of stuff. Yet at the macro level, the world is driven to more material production. Governments promote traditional GDP growth to create jobs and take in more taxes, and they actively support financial capitalism because they falsely believe it is the only way. The GDP accounting system leaves environmental assets like water resources, soil fertility, quality of life, and a stable climate out of the calculations, while finance ministries, the EU, the Union of South American Nations, and the Association of Southeast Asian Nations design economic policy with environmental blinders. Globalization means more stuff gets shipped to the other ends of the earth at all times of the year, multiplying emissions.

At the corporate level, increasing volumes of stuff is what gives rise to the profit levels demanded by the stock markets. And, as in national accounting, corporate accounts are not required to internalize pollution and environmental degradation. Until the measurement and reporting systems used by markets take into account environmental degradation, we will continue to outpace nature's limits, by which I mean its assimilative and regenerative capacities to sustain civilization and other life.

New Accounting Rules

What is being counted has to change: in mature markets at least, the production and consumption of cultural, nonpolluting, and nonmaterial goods has to replace stuff, and their monetary value has to be repriced upward. In simple words, *what we do* to make money has to change. But the needed wholesale transformation of energy, agriculture, transportation, and manufacturing will not happen in time—that is, well before 2052—owing to successful political opposition by vested interests in the coal, oil, shale gas, petrochemical, and automobile industries and the utilities and related businesses that depend on them.

The result is that we are only forty years from disaster. In 2052 the concentration of greenhouse gases in the atmosphere will be moving toward levels that will trigger irreversible large-scale damage. To keep from reaching that level, the world would need to cut emissions by at least half by 2052. I do not expect that this will happen. Man-made greenhouse gases will grow beyond the tipping point.

New technology is not the barrier: 100% wind, water, and solar energy can be achieved with existing technology.[7] Nor is lack of money the real issue. War spending is over 2% to 3% of world GDP.[8] It would take much less than this to cover the cost of bringing greenhouse gas emissions down by 50% in twenty years and do the necessary adaptation to residual climate-change impacts.

From Mitigation to Adaptation

What I expect is that efforts will shift from emissions reduction to adaptation—from trying to avoid the disaster to vain attempts to soften the blow from storms, droughts, floods, heat waves, cold waves, and changing rainfall patterns of increasing frequency and severity. Not only will agriculture change, but so will the location of new cities and the localization of new infrastructure. Tourist destinations and all that depends on them will be affected. Some established places in the Mediterranean will be too hot and dry in summer, to be replaced by others, perhaps in the Baltics and Scandinavia, for example. Sustainability will come to be identified with survivability.

Corporate social responsibility, responsible investment, voluntary eco-efficiency, carbon trading, and romantic conservationism will be no more of a solution to the epic climate challenge than the Global Compact, Agenda 21, and the Millennium Development Goals are solutions to world poverty. Voluntary self-regulation by the markets is the failed dogma of the 1990s and 2000s. Nothing less than government-led efforts on the scale of Second World War industrialization and a Marshall Plan will do the job. We have to stop kidding ourselves with Band-Aid solutions when radical surgery is needed.

Capitulation in Decision Making

The problem in the developed world will continue to be political priorities, leadership, and will. Politicians and parliaments will continue to err on the side of polluting rather than green industries. Developing countries will understandably focus on growing their economies to provide basic housing, transportation, and health services to their people and not focus on the best environmental solutions in order to get there. They will be subject to the same short-term financial-market pressures as developed markets. Thus I believe that climate change disaster is inevitable during the twenty-first century. It will affect all countries, at different speeds and with different impacts, depending on their natural and social conditions, infrastructure, and adaptation resources. Society unfortunately seems to shift direction only under acute danger and high drama, whereas climate catastrophe comes in drips and drabs, not as a big bang but rather as the sum of a large number of small calamities.

With the stock market in the driver's seat, humanity will pursue continued economic growth. Governments will remain unable to imagine other ways to create jobs or raise taxes and thus will go along with this. The effect, by 2052, will be less poverty in developing countries, more poverty and inequity in the developed world, and more environmental degradation overall.

I sincerely hope I am wrong. As Romain Roland, nineteenth-century novelist and humanist, said: "The pessimism of the mind does not exclude the optimism of the will."

Carlos Joly (Argentinian, born 1947) has lived and worked in Europe for twenty-five years. He is an investment manager who over the years has pioneered various approaches to integrating environmental issues in portfolio management. He is currently chair of the Climate Change Scientific Advisory Committee of Natixis Asset Management in France.

As I see it, "Glimpse 2-1: The Dark Decades" describes a future that many of the critics of the current world believe in. This is a future where humanity is much too slow in responding to the combined challenge of distributional inequity and climate change, and as a consequence must endure decades of dysfunctional global development. It is interesting that the glimpse is written by a person with broad experience from within the financial establishment and still places much of the blame on the current use of the capitalist system.

I think the analysis is absolutely correct, but that the tone of the perspective is a little too pessimistic. The problems described in "The Dark Decades" will ultimately arise everywhere, but during the next forty years they will primarily affect the rich world. This minority (one-fifth of the world population) will experience a fall from former glory because of stagnating productivity growth and increasing tension from inequity. But at the same time the majority in the rest of the world will reap the fruits of increasing productivity and income. This will generate a feeling of progress for several decades and compensate for many of the increasing ills, like more inclement weather. The concentration of CO_2 in the atmosphere will certainly increase, but it won't trigger self-reinforcing climate change before 2052.

Slow and insufficient response to our challenges will dominate global developments over the next forty years. Overall, the human response will be strong enough to solve some problems, but not fast enough to solve other problems—as is typical of the current capitalist system. As an example, let's look at the issue of peak oil. The peak oil movement forecasts that global production of oil measured in physical units per year will peak (or has already peaked) and thus leave humanity with a declining annual availability of oil during the rest of this century. I believe it is correct that the production of *conventional* oil is very close to (or even past) its peak. But it is important to note how the capitalist system is seeking to counter this shortage: first, by developing various sources of unconventional oil (for example tar sands, shale oil, and biofuels); and second by shifting energy use toward non-oil sources like gas and renewables (such as wind, solar, hydro, and biomass). Figure 2-1[9] illustrates the result. As the production of conventional oil stagnated after the 1970s, different types of unconventional oils emerged to fill the gap. First oil from shallow offshore fields, then oil from deeper water, and lately the truly unconventional oils. The capitalist system has responded, as would be expected, to the shortage of conventional oil and the rise in oil prices. As a result the price peaks tend to be temporary—lasting for a decade or so—because in the end oil prices will be determined by the production cost of the newest substitute.

As a concrete example of the adaptive power of the capitalist system, it is worth noting that the United States within the last decade or so has been able to increase its production of biofuels (largely corn based) to cover one-tenth of all transport fuels, and the production of shale gas (largely domestic) to one-quarter of all gas use. Various drivers were involved, but this example show that unconventional sources can replace conventional sources rather fast when conditions are suitable.

The rise of unconventional oil blunts, but does not postpone forever, the decline in the use of oil. Thus, the capitalistic response to peak oil does solve some problems, but not all. Peak oil remains a problem for the poor, who can ill afford the higher oil prices in the transition period. It is a problem for businesses that rely on a rapidly growing supply of cheap oil. And most important from

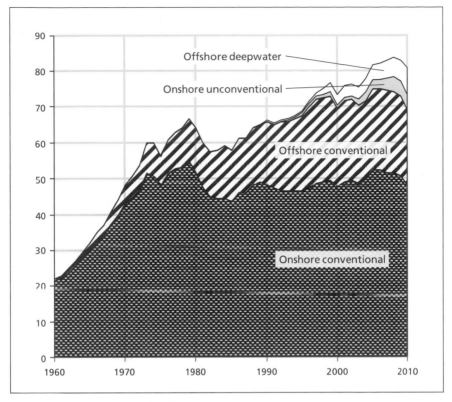

FIGURE 2-1 World oil production, conventional and unconventional, 1960–2010.
Scale: 0–90 millions of barrels per day. (Source: J. Grantham 2011)

my point of view, this "solution" creates a new problem: namely, the increased CO_2 emissions from unconventional fossil fuels, per unit of energy.

But it is true that the capitalistic response solves the problem for those who can afford to pay what it takes to reserve for themselves an increasing share of the limited availability of oil (and other limited resources, for that matter).

Figure 2-2[10] illustrates another success story for technology and the market economy, namely, the phenomenal drop in the production cost of solar panels since 1975. Attracted by the lure of a flexible, decentralized, and climate-friendly source of electricity, capital has poured into solar research and development (R&D) and pilot projects for decades. The cost has dropped to one-hundredth of what it was, and as a consequence we are on the threshold of grid parity, when solar power will compete with other sources of household electricity. The future eruption of renewable energy is a main topic in my forecast later in this book.

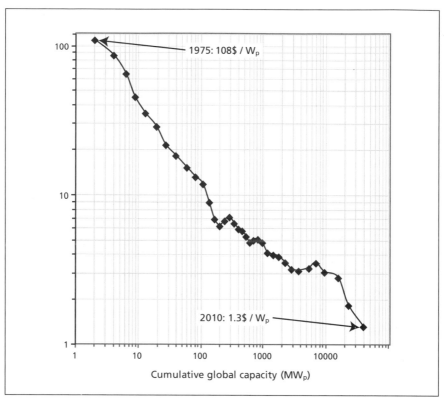

FIGURE 2-2 Average cost of solar panels, 1975–2010.
Scale: $1–$100 per Watt peak capacity. (Source: PV News 1982–2003 and Bloomberg *New Energy Finance* 2003–10)

Will capitalism also provide enough jobs? I believe the number of jobs will keep up with the workforce, most of the time and in most places, just as in the past. Interim periods of high unemployment will, in the end, trigger the necessary changes in the economic system. But the adjustments will not be perfect and they will come too late to avoid unnecessary suffering among the unemployed (and production loss to society). Some places will experience revolution, but in general I see little reason that the power struggle between workers and capitalists will have a different outcome over the next forty years than during the preceding forty years. So old-fashioned capitalism will survive in parts of the world but will be strongly modified elsewhere. We'll explore this more in later chapters.

The End of Economic Growth?

Let us then proceed to a perspective from the fastest-growing part of the developing world, namely, Southeast Asia. "Glimpse 2-2: Constraining Asian Consumption" addresses the issue of whether continued economic growth is possible on a physically finite earth. This is a debate that has been going since the early 1970s, and its resolution did emerge in the 1990s, when it became possible to give the answer: "Yes, economic growth can continue, but only as long as the accompanying ecological footprint remains within the carrying capacity of the globe." Clearly we can have continuing growth in the GDP (for instance by cutting each other's hair faster and faster, or at a higher price). But equally clearly we cannot have endless growth in physical assets on the planet (for instance an infinite number of polluting cars).

I believe that society will continue its effort to seek continued economic growth, among other reasons because this is the best-known method to create more jobs and facilitate redistribution. But as you will discover in my detailed forecast, I believe we won't succeed in maintaining the high growth rates from the last forty years. But we will try, and this will double the global GDP before 2052. But it won't quadruple, as it did during the last forty years.

Thus the proper question in my mind is the following: Will humanity manage to limit its ecological footprint to fit within the carrying capacity of the planet? Or will we continue to allow overuse of natural resources and the pollution-absorption capacity of the global environment? As you will see later, current lifestyles require roughly the support of 1.4 planets. Humanity has overshot. We see the result of the overshoot most clearly in the ongoing accumulation of CO_2 in the atmosphere.

"Glimpse 2-2: Constraining Asian Consumption" discusses this issue. Read it now.

GLIMPSE 2-2

Constraining Asian Consumption

Chandran Nair

In 2011, the world witnessed yet another convulsion of global markets due to US debt concerns and the unraveling of European economies.

Decades of mismanagement and denial were rooted in a misplaced belief that a consumption-led growth model underpinned by excessive borrowing would deliver prosperity for all and forever.

The turmoil in 2011 and the financial crisis of 2008 had their origins in the almost religious belief of the West in free markets that has gone on to dominate global financial markets for the past three decades. This long-held belief that markets, technology, and finance, coupled with democracy, can offer everyone every freedom and solve all the problems of the world needs to be reconsidered, to say the very least.

At the same time the unprecedented riots and looting that took place in England's various cities in the summer of 2011 was attributed to everything from the breakdown of civic values to weak policing, a sense of entitlement, and rampant consumerism. In 2011 even those on social welfare felt entitled to grossly overpriced Nikes made by cheap labor in Asia. None of the rioters were risking their lives for food as none were going hungry. Thus the UK riots were quite different from the unrest in the Middle East, where people in the streets were essentially demanding a better life with fair access to the bare basics that can only be provided by more equitable sharing of resources. The people did not call for some form of utopian Western democracy. Along with many of their brethren and sisters in the developing world, they increasingly believe that the consumption-led economic model that reinforces privilege and entitlement over contribution to the collective is not the template for them to follow.

While all of this is going on, Asia, with over 60% of the world's population, is left watching and wondering what it means for this most diverse of regions. No doubt, the shenanigans of global markets have played havoc with stock markets in the region. But it is one of the great lies of our times that the performance of stock markets reflects a nation's true health and affects the well-being of its common citizens. In reality, the stock market has hardly any effect on the vast majority of people in Asia, even those in the middle class.

What is actually having a real, negative impact on the majority of people, who do not own stocks or treasuries, is when many Asian governments pursue policies that continue to perpetuate the myth that they can all live and consume like Westerners. If there ever was an ideal moment to completely reject the propaganda of a

Disneyland worldview promoting the American Dream, the time is now. There is simply no capacity within our planetary boundaries for two or three more Americas. To this day, six billion people are being misled into believing that there are no natural constraints and they can have it all because human ingenuity will come to the rescue. The truth is they simply cannot, and the denial, by political leaders and those in business who stand most to gain from maintaining the status quo, must stop.

If in the next forty years Asians continue to aspire to live like present-day Americans or the slightly more parsimonious Europeans, and they successfully move toward this goal, the natural support systems needed to sustain human life will most likely collapse. The global carrying capacity is too small. It is unclear whether it is the Asians or the Americans/Europeans who will be forced to change their ways to the largest extent, but regardless a majority will still live in impoverished conditions. A minority, perhaps two billion, will be able to secure lifestyles (at huge cost to the rest) and inure themselves from the evolving strangulation of living conditions on the planet. The true impact will only be known in the second half of this century. For the first time in human history, human beings are at the height of a great technological leap forward and aware that continual progress (as it is now defined) will bring great suffering to many. Yet we plow on.

Let us take car ownership, which has sadly been seen in developing countries as a necessary engine of growth. If China, India, and other Asian countries aspire to ownership levels like those in the rich industrialized countries, which its citizens are told is their right, there will be as many as three billion cars in the world by 2050, almost four times the current number. This will be disastrous on many levels. Cities will become uninhabitable (many already are), and precious fuels that could be used elsewhere, including biofuels, will be directed toward driving. The health impacts of close to two billion cars in Asia will be the stuff of fiction. The same applies to everything from meat consumption and cheap cookies to air conditioners and iPads.

So what must Asia do to avoid such catastrophic outcomes? Above all, Asia must reject the blinkered view of those who urge Asians to consume relentlessly—be they Western economists and leaders who want the region to become a "motor of growth" to rebalance the world economy or Asian governments convinced that ever-expanding economies are what their populations want or need.

Instead Asian governments must find alternative ways of promoting human development. They will need to urgently reshape expectations and address directly the issue of rights, with clear focus on the following basic needs that must be accessible to the majority: food (safe and secure), water and sanitation, low-cost housing, education, and primary health care. They need to make clear, for example, that car ownership is not a right and that demand for goods and services must reflect true costs. They must stress that public interest takes precedence over individual rights, although this conflicts fundamentally with the core arguments of consumption-driven capitalism. They must stand up against the claim that allowing everyone to pursue their individual self-interest eventually will lead to benefits for all.

And they should call the bluff. They should state loud and clear that it is the obligation of the rich world to pare back, and to find less wasteful lifestyles.

Organizing such an economy will not be an easy task, especially in societies that for decades have been told that all limits can be overcome and prosperity can come only from conventional forms of consumption-driven growth. This will require strong government actions that will fly in the face of current Western orthodoxy about democracy and capitalism. In doing this they will have to take on a range of vested interests from global multinationals and local elites, including those Western governments and institutions that see large-scale Asian consumption as the savior of their economies.

A starting point will be to make resource management the center of all policy making, and then to put a proper price on greenhouse gases and resources via taxes, licenses, and even outright bans on certain forms of consumption. It is not that people must be poor, but rather that consumption must be redirected in ways that do not further deplete or pollute the already stressed resource base and put at risk the livelihood and health of hundreds of millions.

Asian nations will need fiscal measures, land-use practices, and new approaches to social organization that can create sustainable national economies. Measures constraining resource usage must be extended to every area of life. A key step will be fiscal and labor policies that strengthen local economies and reduce both poverty and mass migration to cities. Two key sectors are agriculture and energy. In the former, curbs on resource-intensive practices of industrialized agriculture will help distribute local income. So will a decentralized energy production system.

Will Asian governments take these bold moves and will they get support from the West?

It is very unclear, but being an incorrigible optimist I see the possibility of the second half of the twenty-first century being the era of cleansing and replenishing. This hope stems from my belief that during the next ten to twenty years Asian governments will realize the dead end of the current model and begin to change course. Hopefully at the same time some nations in the West will try to reduce their global footprints. This shift will be the biggest challenge of the twenty-first century, as it will require leaders willing to engage citizens in an honest debate about limits and therefore the changing expectations about how they live and what they need and want. It will be an almighty struggle, in more ways than one.

Chandran Nair (Malaysian, born 1954) is the founder and CEO of the Global Institute for Tomorrow based in Hong Kong. He also heads Avantage Ventures, a social investments advisory firm in Hong Kong and Beijing. Formerly he was the Asia-Pacific chairman of ERM, growing the company over a decade to become the region's largest environmental consulting firm.

"Constraining Asian Consumption" makes the point that it will be physically impossible to lift the material standard of living of all nations to that of the current West. For example, there simply is not enough raw material, fuel, and space available for everyone to have his own car. The glimpse argues that the leaders of the emerging world must internalize this fact and convince their populations to pursue sustainable increase in well-being, rather than brute material growth. But the glimpse signals uncertainty about whether these leaders will succeed.

I believe the analysis is correct, but that the real issue of overconsumption will not be solved through wise leadership. I do not believe it will prove possible to convince people to forgo potential consumption growth. Democratic society will pursue short-term satisfaction and choose their leaders accordingly. Thus success in limiting consumption will require an element of benevolent authoritarianism. This may work, for example, in China, but not everywhere.

In general, I believe that the brutal consequences of overconsumption will be softened by mechanisms other than wise leadership. Continuing technological advance will come to our partial rescue. Lack of cheap resources and space will force developments toward solutions with a lower ecological footprint (smaller chargeable cars; better-insulated homes closer to work; crops needing less fertilizer and water; bigger, more fuel-efficient and crowded planes). Increased demand for scarce resources will drive up real prices—also for the rich—and stimulate further technological advance.

Furthermore, I believe the future growth in global GDP will be lower than expected and hoped for. Thus the footprint will be lower than feared. And, importantly, before Asia reaches rich-world levels of consumption, the rich world (and particularly the United States) will have been forced downward, unable to maintain current levels of consumption. The gradual closing of the income gap between rich and poor countries will further add to the cost of maintaining current lifestyles in the West. Also, productivity growth in the rich capitalist world will lag because of continuing social friction and strife due to growing levels of inequity. As a total result, Western styles of consumption will wane, providing more room for the emerging world to catch up.

Finally, although all will try—and some, including China, will succeed—many will not manage to catch up with the West within the next forty years, in spite of trying. Their takeoff will not occur until after 2052, when declining national populations will provide more ecological space for each person. At this time more resource and climate efficient solutions will be well proven. But at this time humanity will also meet head-on a vicious global climate problem that will limit further increase in material well-being.

In summary, global average per capita resource consumption will never reach the level that Americans enjoyed around the year 2000. As a consequence the global overshoot will be less serious than feared. The technical solutions will come in time to soften much of the blow. The emergence of unconventional substitutes for conventional oil is one example of this.

It is useful at this point to make you aware of just how enormous current inequities are. The top part of figure 2-3[11] shows the differences in production (GDP) and consumption among five regions of the world—on a per capita basis. The numbers are in 2005 US dollars per person per year, adjusted for purchasing power parity (PPP), and this measure is further explained in appendix 2. To illustrate the regional disparities we divide the world into five regions, along economic lines. The first region is the United States, being the world's richest nation on a per capita basis. The second region includes the other most industrialized countries, defined as thirty members of the Organisation for

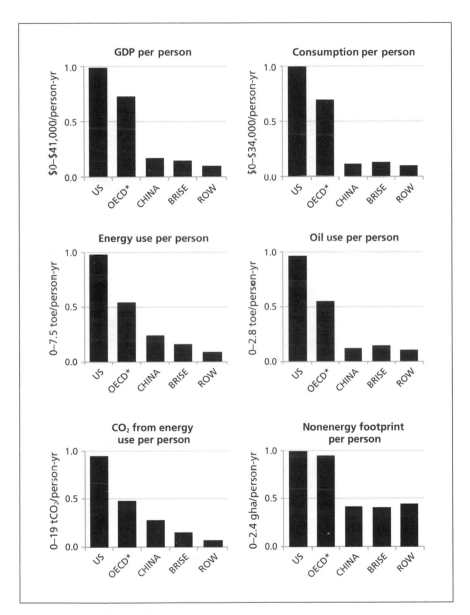

FIGURE 2-3 World inequity, 2010.
Definitions: OECD* = OECD-less-US; BRISE = big emerging economies; ROW = rest of world.
For details see appendix 2. **Population in billions**: US = 0.3, OECD-less-US = 0.7, China = 1.3,
BRISE = 2.4, ROW = 2.1. **Abbreviations**: toe = tonnes of oil equivalents; tCO$_2$ = tonnes of CO$_2$;
gha = hectares of average global productivity

Economic Co-operation and Development (OECD) outside the United States. The detailed list of nations is shown in appendix 2, and the region is denoted OECD-less-US. Our third region is China, which is big enough to constitute its own region. The fourth region consists of the biggest emerging economies, including Brazil, Russia, India, South Africa, and ten other populous economies like Indonesia, Mexico, and Vietnam. We denote this region BRISE, and once more the detailed list of countries is found in appendix 2. Finally there is the fifth region, the rest of the world (ROW), with a total of some 150 countries. Figure 2-3 shows the differences among these regions. For example, the average citizen of the United States produces and consumes roughly ten times as much as the average citizen of the ROW region. The OECD-less-US region is just behind. The middle part of figure 2-3 shows that the situation is similar—actually even less equitable—when it comes to per capita use of energy and oil. And the lower part of the figure shows that the each US citizen emits ten times as much CO_2 per person as each of the 2.1 billion people in ROW. At the bottom right you can finally see that the rich use two to three times as much land to supply their food and timber. China, in spite of its recent growth, is still closer to the poor than to the rich—when measured per person.

As shown by figure 2-3, lifting all people to the consumption level of US citizens would increase the human impact by five to ten times. As I see it, this won't happen on our finite planet, simply because there is not enough room. But humanity will try, and the extent of their future success is the main topic of the rest of this book.

The End of Slow Democracy?

Things take time. In many instances this is not a bad thing. By pondering and consulting one can help avoid action with unintended and undesirable side effects. But in other cases, as when racing toward a brick wall, decision delays are fatal. The world, as I see it, is facing a couple of issues in the latter category—first and foremost in the climate area. Here, action is needed now, not after another umpteen years of analysis. Others disagree, and hence the current decision-making procedures are excruciatingly slow.

Democracy has many advantages and often yields solutions that are more sustainable than top-down decisions. But speed is not one of the characteristics of democratic decision making. So the way I see it, the fundamental question in this domain is whether democracy will agree on a stronger state (and faster decision making) before it is too late—before we run into the brick wall of self-reinforcing climate change, irreversible biodiversity loss, and insufficient investment in forward-looking research and development.

"Glimpse 2-3: Shuffling toward Sustainability" tackles the issue of slow response.

GLIMPSE 2-3

Shuffling toward Sustainability

Paul Hohnen

Historians writing in 2052 will remark on three distinctive features of the first half of the twenty-first century.

The first will be in relation to the *physical environment*. They will note, with all the wisdom that hindsight and modern sensing and measurement technology offer, that profound changes occurred in the earth's biophysical systems over the previous four to five decades. These will include changes in the chemistry of the planet's atmosphere and weather systems; in the diversity and regenerative capacity of terrestrial, freshwater, and marine systems; and in the quantity and quality of natural capital, both nonrenewable and renewable. The combined consequence of these developments, they will note, had not only resulted in the greatest reduction the planet's capacity to provide ecosystem services since *Homo sapiens* began spreading out of Africa, but also precipitated a new era of climatic instability characterized by increased warming. They will conclude that the capacity of the species to adapt to the changing environment will increasingly determine what life on earth might look like by the end of the twenty-first century and beyond.

The second will concern the *scientific and sociological environments*. Future historians' review of scientific literature from 2012 onward will show that many of the trends noted above were well documented, understood, and discussed at a surprisingly early point in time. Examples will include declines (or even commercial disappearance) of stocks of many species of fish, increases in atmospheric concentrations of greenhouse gases and other pollutants, and the peak and decline in production of several important raw materials, such as oil. In many cases, the rate of change on the ground will be seen to have been seriously under- (and sometimes over-) estimated. Sociological studies will highlight wide differences (and even sharp disagreements) over the underlying scientific data and their implications. Sociologists and anthropologists will develop taxonomies to distinguish between social groups that, variously, denied there was a problem, thought there was a problem and tried to do something about it, or thought there was a problem but that it was ultimately intractable.

The third will concern the *policy environment*. Here future analyses will consider how systems of organizational governance—both state and private sector—responded to the information as it became available. By 2052, the changes in the biophysical environment will have forced decisions on a range of policy choices. Here are the policy issues that historians will document, and the conclusions they will draw in 2052:

- *The level of decision making.* Decisions had to be taken on global policy issues such as setting a price for carbon, commissioning large-scale projects to adapt to climate change, and reforming the international financial system. Options included collective decisions by nation-states in existing or new intergovernmental forums, decisions by individual nations or regions, or not doing anything at all. The historians will record that an intergovernmental approach was adopted because it was finally recognized that an "every country for itself" strategy was ineffective and counterproductive. Local wars over competition for resources had underlined this point.
- *The role of the state.* It was clear already in 2012 that governments—particularly when operating in groups of more than ten—were unable to make decisions at the speed needed to respond to many of the adverse trends mentioned above. Future historians will conclude that it became increasingly imperative to regionalize decision making. It proved impossible for 193 countries to agree on anything, as exemplified in the post-Kyoto negotiations. But smaller groups of countries proved able to move collectively. And there was progress in public-private partnerships. A blended model was chosen, with governments increasing state control

over business (similar to China's managed capitalism), but at the same time including business leaders in governmental decision making and implementation.

- *The role of the market*. In the decade 2010–20, future historians will note, it became apparent that development paths were taking the world further away from sustainable development, rather than closer. Capitalism was recognized to be undermining its own future. A debate ensued about just how "free" the free market should be in a resource- and pollution-constrained world. By 2022, the thirtieth anniversary of the Earth Summit, a series of weather-related commodity crises had convinced governments and businesses that adaptation to climate change was a permanent national security issue. Governments increased regulations and policies promoting investment in low-carbon, resource-efficient technologies and infrastructure—that is, a "green" economy. A decade after the failed 2012 Rio+20 conference, it was decided to prioritize the rapid transition from the old to the new economy, even when it required state interference with the working of the free market.

At a more detailed level, historians will also note that the business literature available in 2012 indicated that:

- "Business as usual" could not deliver sustainable development.
- Business was an important part of the solution, but needed help to prioritize the common good.
- Business leaders recognized that they needed a healthy ecosystem and a reasonably stable climate.
- Sustainable business practices were far from being mainstream.

Delving deeper, historians in 2052 will identify a complex set of issues that were identified already in 2012–22 as preventing efforts to put the global economy on a sustainable footing. They will conclude as follows:

- *Short-termism*. The need for quick returns, the rise of share-trading technologies that encouraged churning, and the expansion of the virtual economy meant that financial markets were shifting away from long-term perspectives and investments. To ensure the sustained growth of renewable energy and clean technologies, in the period 2012 to 2052 governments used a mix of instruments to encourage long-term investment in key sectors and domestic industries. A series of financial crises before 2020 eroded trust in the ability of existing financial models to ensure the public good.

- *Valuation methods.* By 2012, research had demonstrated that the commonly used national and business accounting tools presented a grossly distorted picture. In many cases, national "development" was in fact destroying economic value. The following decade saw concerted policy efforts to define and adopt indicators of human and ecosystem well-being and give these an economic value. By 2022, new definitions of societal value and company assets emerged, supplementing the old GDP, and a standard was developed for integration of corporate financial and sustainability reports.

- *Consumer inertia.* From the emergence of environmental concerns as political issues after the 1960s, a small and growing proportion of consumers helped drive the growth of "green" markets. By 2012, however, it was clear that the green consumer movement was still far from mainstream. This forced governments and business to reassess the mix of carrots and sticks needed to harness the power of consumer behavior. Despite opposition from trading partners and the World Trade Organization, many countries introduced policies before 2030 that favored the growth of domestic "green" markets, especially in the energy, agriculture, and waste sectors.

- *Technological innovation.* Responding to the realization that needed technologies were either not available or not sufficiently profitable, governments began intervening more directly to stimulate domestic strategic industries. Energy (including transportation), water, agriculture, waste treatment, and health were prioritized, along with infrastructure. Countries unable or unwilling to take this state-led approach continued to be reliant on resource-extractive industries. This led to a new global divide, based on access to clean technology.

- *Transition pain.* All developed countries suffered sharp social and economic pains as a result of the evolving shift from fossil-fueled growth toward sustainable development. Seen from 2052, it will be clear that those that transitioned most successfully to a green economy had used a combination of legislation and pollution taxes to subsidize and build support for the new economy. It had also proved important to confront noisy minorities pursuing their own short-term interests.

By 2052, it will be widely accepted that the second half of the twenty-first century will require even more adaptation to a changing planet. Much governance will be geared to that end.

Paul Hohnen *(Australian, 1950) is a consultant on sustainable development living in Europe. A former Australian diplomat, his career included periods as political director of Greenpeace International and strategic development director of the Global Reporting Initiative (GRI), which he helped found.*

"Shuffling toward Sustainability" describes in some detail the policy landscape over the next several decades, making the point that the intellectual basis for rational policy is already in place. What is wanting is decision making and execution. Democracy and capitalism both share an attraction for tradition. We know what needs to be done, but it will take time to implement. In order for the world to move briskly, there is the need to break with traditional approaches and form new partnerships that are able to agree within reasonable time limits.

I fully support this view. As you will see from my forecast in part 2, I believe that developments over the decades to come will be irritatingly slow (which also makes them simpler to predict). Global society will slide in the right direction, but at a speed that leaves much to be desired. We will remain stuck too long in the ideal that individual rights have priority over the common good, a view that will be increasingly unhelpful in an ever more crowded world.

Meanwhile tensions will build both socially and environmentally, and the release of these tensions is the fourth issue facing humanity toward 2052.

The End of Generational Harmony?

Every year a new cohort enters the labor, housing, and family markets of the world. Over the last hundred years or so we have gotten used to expecting that each generation enters the grown world in better shape. That means with better health, better education, more wealth, and better prospects. Needless to say, there are and have been great variations in this norm, but the generalization is useful because we may now be facing a situation where this march toward prosperity is starting to break apart.

Today's young, particularly in the rich world, are facing a new situation. They are inheriting a significant burden of national debt from their parents; they have to beat their way into markets characterized by persistent unemployment; they can ill afford housing at the same level as their parents; and they are expected to pay for their parents' pensions. On top of this, the prospects for a quick resolution of these issues are grim.

So the relevant question becomes: Will the younger generation calmly accept the burden bestowed on them by the older generation? Or will we get an aggressive and paralyzing confrontation between young and old, starting with confrontations with the baby boomers in the rich world? "Glimpse 2-4: Intergenerational War for Equity" provides an answer.

GLIMPSE 2-4

Intergenerational War for Equity

Karl Wagner

The next forty years will rank as one of the most crucial periods in the development of human civilization. The massive changes taking place will influence all people and countries, but there will be regional variations.

The Western world will see the most fundamental changes, and there will be one particular decade—the 2020s—that will carry the same monumental importance as the year 1848 did for the citizens of many European countries. That was the year that several centuries of struggle between the people and the ruling feudal class culminated in revolution. Suddenly Europeans had entered a new era.

Over the next forty years we will see the crumbling, first, of the old paradigm and, second, of the structures that build on this thinking—namely, the system that helps maintain the current wasteful, exploitative, and spiritually and emotionally underdeveloped civilization. The transition will be neither smooth nor peaceful.

The current, outdated paradigm will disappear faster than many think. Realities will change because of sheer necessity; there won't be room on the planet for enough business as usual. A new belief system will replace the old one:

- The culture of consumerism will be replaced by cultural elements that provide longer-term substantial satisfaction, increasing well-being, and fundamental happiness.
- The dominant interpretation of Darwin's theory, that life evolved through competition and survival of the fittest, will be replaced by an understanding that advanced life evolved through cooperation and not through domination.
- Cultures will come closer to each other, and the current clash of civilizations will not be the end point, but will turn out to be a chapter in the development of a higher level of global society.
- A new understanding of community will emerge, in the form of a modern blend of traditional community life and values and a more benign form of individualism, which grasps the value of collective solutions.

There will be many drivers behind this development. The main force for change will be disenfranchised young people. They are already now beginning to wake up to the fact that their parents and grandparents are in the process of leaving them an exploited planet with degraded life-support systems, indebted economies, few jobs, and no affordable housing. In developed countries they also inherit the responsibility of caring for an increasing number of retired people who plan to receive pensions and health care for the next thirty to forty years.

These youths rightfully want the opportunity to live a decent life and have a family. They do not want to spend their life paying off debt accumulated by previous generations. The analogy to the European revolutions of 1848 is unpleasantly close. As then, inequity will turn out to be a time bomb—but this time not only in Europe, but around the globe. During the next ten to fifteen years we will see emerging limits to popular patience. We will see young people lead in the fight for a universal right to a decent life and a decent job.

Other crucial drivers will be urbanization, climate change, peak oil, and declining population size. Together they will entirely alter land use, land distribution, and political decision making. People will live more densely. Transportation will become more expensive, and commuting by private car will become a luxury. The countryside will lose population. Cities will increasingly determine national politics and be the engine of societal evolution.

The biggest change, though, will be the increasing prevalence of electronic communications, the most powerful driver of globalization. The next decades will see a global consciousness emerging, an additional mind sphere, whose nature and true dimension is still unclear but will become evident within the next five to fifteen years. The world will move from cloud computing to cloud thinking and possibly even cloud feeling. Not only will something else—"the net"—derive logical conclusions for us, it will also set the agenda by constantly feeding back what everyone else thinks. And it certainly will influence the mood of the population. This explosion of continuous web access will not be without downsides. We already know that electronic communications is an ideal tool to gather and control personal information. We also know that it can be used to gather and inspire people, as in the Middle East uprisings in 2011. But the web can also be used to suppress and manipulate individuals and masses.

The resistance to change from those who are the beneficiaries of the current system will turn out to be more durable than many expect. Outdated governance systems that do not add to public well-being will be upheld by the sheer power and the will of a minority that wants to maintain the status quo that is serving them well in the short term. The result will be friction and conflict, which will play out in Western countries first and then, after a time delay, spread to other regions of the world. But before tensions are released, conditions for the majority in the industrialized world will deteriorate for years. The break will not occur until a critical mass of people have been pushed beyond their limit of patience.

Industry and business will play a major role on both sides. Smaller enterprise on a human scale will drive the community approach, while big multinationals will find it difficult, if not impossible, to abandon their quarterly-profit, shareholder-return, money-only thinking.

The transition will have many faces. There need not be massive and violent riots in cities by unemployed youth, but there will be. There need not be class warfare or terrorist units who bomb banks, nor cyber activists who publish hacked account details from tax havens, but there will be. Some people will lead the way by opting out from the old system and voluntarily joining a new one.

I believe the intensity of opposition will increase from now until a peak in Europe and the United States in the 2020s, then move inexorably toward some kind of revolution. This is inevitable, because the old system will not go away by itself. It will have to be forced out—by whatever action people take, and aided by factors such as new web technologies. This shift could happen through peaceful conversation in parliaments, but it won't.

The revolution will be global, but it will come first in Europe, the United States, and the other OECD countries, where tensions are already high and the older generations' high hopes for their future lie in starkest contrast with the low hopes of the current unemployed or overeducated youth. It will follow in Latin America somewhat later, and then after another twenty years in the then-dominant economies of China and the like. Africa might find itself facing a completely different set of challenges for many years to come and so is unlikely to be actively swept up in these global generational conflicts.

By the second half of the twenty-first century, the intergenerational war will be over. Humanity will find itself in a more equitable and sustainable world. The young will be better off, at the cost of the elderly.

Karl Wagner (Austrian, born 1952), biologist by education and environmental campaigner by training, has spent thirty years running environmental campaigns, nationally and globally, mostly for the World Wildlife Fund. He currently works for the Club of Rome.

"Intergenerational War for Equity" describes vividly what I would call a commonly overseen elephant in the drawing room. The old generation (my generation) has always held the perspective that we are toiling to leave a better world for our children. We have made sacrifices to work harder and more. Often we have saved for their education and paid for their room and board long after their physical maturity. We have done this in the perspective of the farmer who seeks to leave a better farm for the next generation. We have done this for so long and so automatically that we have not noticed that we no longer are being really helpful to our children. Many of them are ending up in an unattractive starting place.

"Intergenerational War for Equity" predicts—rightly, I believe—that the era of intergenerational harmony will come to an end. The new generation will not quietly take over the place prepared for them. The result will be a better life for the young and a corresponding loss for me (representing the old) and the banks (representing the capital owners). At the aggregate level this redistribution of wealth and opportunity will have a negative impact on productivity growth. Social tension and social strife do not aid the fine-tuning of the economy that is required to increase labor productivity by a percentage point or so every year. As a consequence, intergenerational conflict will lead to slower economic growth, a smaller pie to share, and even more tension. My hope would be that the redistribution takes place in a less violent and better organized manner than is likely.

Let me use the opportunity to highlight another intergenerational conflict. That elephant is even larger, but it will remain invisible, I am afraid, over the next forty years because there is no pressure group working to make it visible. I am speaking of the conflict of interest between the current and all future generations, meaning those that are not yet born. Humanity is in the process of making the world into a much less attractive place for its future inhabitants. It is true that we are continuing to invest in knowledge, institutions, and physical infrastructure with the intention of leaving a better world. But I am not sure that the unborn children will be satisfied with the extent of our effort. We will continue to optimize, but primarily for our own generation and that of our children. As a result, we will leave a difficult world for our grandchildren.

The End of Stable Climate?

The intergenerational issue as it relates to future generations is most obvious in three areas: anthropogenic biodiversity destruction, climate change, and entombment of radioactive waste. All will have consequences way beyond the lifetime of those who live today and their children. People are vaguely aware of this, but not to the extent necessary to give politicians the authority to do something that really matters.

The voter has rudimentary knowledge of the implications of living in a world damaged by global warming. He seems to understand what sea-level rise and more frequent heat waves might entail. But he seems unable to grasp what the loss of millions of species of plants and animals will mean to people in the year 2100, much the same way as he seems unable to comprehend what it will mean for someone to take care of others' nuclear waste for tens of thousands of years.

But the prime legacy issue in 2012 is humanity's big and growing emissions of greenhouse gases, which lead to global warming. We know very well what is going on, and figure 2-4[12] provides a summary.

Humanity emits significant amounts of CO_2 from three sources. The original source is deforestation, the removal and burning of forests to make room for cropland, roads, and buildings. Removal of the forest releases the carbon that was formerly held in the wood, which through burning or rotting converts carbon to CO_2. Luckily, the flow of CO_2 from forests has started to decline after a peak around 1990. CO_2 is also emitted in significant volumes when making cement, but the biggest source of human CO_2 emissions is our energy use. The carbon in coal, oil, and gas is converted to CO_2 and emitted when these fossil fuels are burned to generate heat or power. Figure 2-4 shows the dramatic increase in man-made CO_2 emissions since 1950. In addition, and not shown, are the emissions of other greenhouse gases, mostly methane from agriculture and landfills, which add perhaps one-fifth to the warming effect of CO_2. I use metric units throughout this book and use the long word "tonne" to remind you about this. Thus CO_2 flows are measured in billion tonnes of CO_2 per year.

But equally important, figure 2-4 also shows where the CO_2 ends up. The CO_2 is emitted as a gas into the atmosphere and quickly moves around the globe. It remains in the atmosphere for a long time while waiting to get absorbed in the ocean (as carbonic acid in the water) or in trees and plants (as plant material when they grow). Presently, very roughly one-quarter of the CO_2 flows into the ocean, one-quarter flows into new biomass, and one-half remains in the atmosphere. The long-run accumulated effect of these flows has been to lift the concentration of CO_2 in the atmosphere from 280 ppm in preindustrial times (circa 1750) to 390 ppm today (2010). The CO_2 flows also have increased the acidity of the oceans and created a more difficult life for shell-forming species.

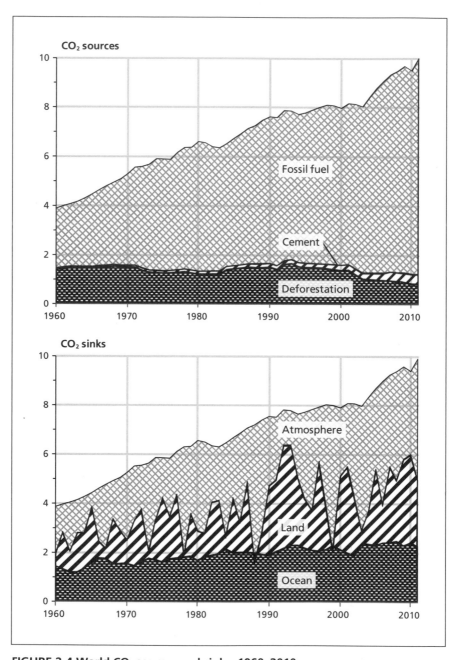

FIGURE 2-4 World CO₂ sources and sinks, 1960–2010.
Scale: 0–10 billion tonnes of CO₂ per year. (Source: Global Carbon Project 2011)

More CO_2 in the atmosphere accelerates plant and tree growth, but it also leads to higher temperatures on the surface of the earth. The global average temperature has increased by 0.7°C since preindustrial times. As one response to the observed warming, global society has agreed to try to keep the warming below plus 2°C. This is one of the few concrete results from decades of international negotiations, and it is necessary in order to reduce the risk of dangerous effects. And if we are to keep the temperature rise below plus 2°C we must keep the concentration of CO_2 in the atmosphere below 450 ppm (according to widely believed calculations). The concentration is currently going up by 2 ppm per year, so we do not have much time before we reach the danger threshold. 450 ppm less 390 ppm divided by 2 ppm per year gives us thirty years before we hit that ceiling.

"Glimpse 2-5: Extreme Weather in 2052" adds detail to this discussion. It provides a peek into the difficulties met when 194 individualistic countries try to agree on common action to limit human greenhouse gas emissions. It also tells us how far the process has come—or rather, how far we are still away from global commitments that will keep temperature rise below plus 2°C. Finally, the glimpse gives an overview of the damage that will result from insufficient action to cut human greenhouse gas emissions in time.

GLIMPSE 2-5

Extreme Weather in 2052

Robert W. Corell

In June 1992 heads of state from 108 nations, delegations from 172 countries, and 2,400 nongovernmental organizations gathered in Rio de Janeiro for the first "Earth Summit." They established the historic UN Framework Convention on Climate Change (UNFCCC)[13]—a formal international treaty[14] that went into full force in March 1994. It is the treaty within which international climate negotiations and protocols take place—involving the 194 nations that have ratified the convention. The UNFCCC sets forth a framework for addressing climate change, and its central goal is stabilization of greenhouse gas concentrations in the atmosphere at a level that would prevent dangerous anthropogenic interference with the climate system. Such a level should be achieved within a time frame sufficient to allow ecosystems to adapt naturally to climate change, to ensure that food production is not threatened, and to enable economic development to proceed in a sustainable manner.[15]

Since 1994, the UNFCCC has hosted sixteen Conferences of the Parties (COP) and succeeded in agreeing on a number of protocols, like the Kyoto protocol, and other formal agreements. The most recent were COP 15 in Copenhagen, Denmark, in 2009, COP 16 in Cancun, Mexico, in 2010, and COP 17 in Durban, South Africa, at the end of 2011.

The objective of the COP meetings is to negotiate an agreement to reduce global greenhouse gas emissions. As part of the negotiations, the 194 participating nations have periodically made public their current goals for emissions reductions and related climate change actions. These 194 publicly available goals are tracked by a number of organizations[16] and provide a possible starting point if one wants to forecast future emissions and the resulting global climate change.

In the following I describe the consequences if the current 194 national emissions-reduction goals were implemented. This may well describe the climate situation in 2052, although I hope not. I hope that the UNFCCC process will lead to much lower emissions in the next forty years, although the lack of recent progress makes this hard to believe.

Projections Based on IPCC's Scenarios

There are a number of analytical computer-based tools[17] for projecting the outcomes of different assumptions concerning climate gas emissions during the rest of this century. To bring some order to the plethora of forecasts, the UN Intergovernmental Panel on Climate Change (IPCC) in 2000 established a set of six standard scenarios for global socioeconomic-technological development to 2100.[18]

IPCC uses these scenarios to estimate the future climate gas emissions in each scenario and provide assessment reports that reflect the current knowledge about the resulting climate change in each scenario. The latest assessment, published in 2007, concluded that the global average surface temperature is most likely to increase by 2.5°C by 2100 in the scenario with the lowest emissions ("B1") and by 4.8°C in scenario with the highest emissions ("A1FI")—all relative to the temperature in preindustrial times.[19] The temperature increase by 2050 was estimated to be between 1.8°C and 2.2 °C. The current temperature is 0.7°C higher than in preindustrial times.

Projections Based on Current National Commitments
But instead of using the IPCC scenarios as a starting point, one can start from the 194 national emission reduction goals mentioned above and calculate the consequences if these goals were implemented. A central tool for doing this is a global climate simulation model called C-ROADS,[20] which tracks the publicly available national pledges and uses them as input to the model. A C-ROADS projection made June 29, 2011, concluded that if all 194 nations live up to their proposed goals under the UNFCCC process, the global average surface temperature will increase by 2.2°C by 2050 and 4.1°C by 2100. The uncertainty in the projections is large (plus or minus a degree or so), but the conclusion from C-ROADS is that the sum of current national commitments leads to a future that is nearly as warm as the "worst" IPCC scenario ("A1FI").

Our Recent Emissions Path and Future Implications
Of the six IPCC scenarios, A1FI is the one that projects the highest future emissions. Still, according to the Global Carbon Project, which annually reports carbon budgets and trends including global carbon emissions and atmospheric concentrations of global carbon,[21] the path of actual climate gas emissions over the last decade is almost identical to the emissions projected in A1FI. Actual global emissions followed A1FI rather precisely from 2004 to 2009 but did deviate temporarily in 2010, most likely due to the global financial crisis of 2007 and 2008, and are generally expected to be back on the A1FI trend by 2015.

A1FI portrays a future with high economic growth, continued globalization, rapid technological change, and an increase in the global average surface temperature in 2050 by 2.4°C and in 2100 by 4.8°C. As mentioned, the sum of current national pledges—if implemented—will lead to a future that closely tracks A1FI, at least until 2050. Therefore, it is possible to use the detailed global projections from the IPCC Global Circulation Models[22] database to make more detailed regional forecasts of the consequences of implementing the current national commitments. For example, the global pattern of increase in average surface temperatures in 2050 for A1FI is shown in figure 2-5. We see substantial increases in the temperature over much of the Arctic (more than plus 4°C) and considerable increases over land (between plus 2°C and 4°C), while the oceans are projected to warm little (less than plus 2°C). Notice that these increases are for the next forty years only.

Projected Impacts

The implications of this pattern of temperature change are described in detail in the literature.[23] The impacts are likely to be substantial. Projections state that many large-scale, terrestrial, and marine ecosystems will be unable to adapt to the rate of climate change. Water is likely to be a serious challenge, particularly for developing countries, with both availability and quality at risk, while precipitation changes are likely to increase droughts and, in other regions, floods. Glaciers by 2052 are likely to be melting at increased rates. Sea levels will rise largely as a consequence of thermal expansion of the surface layers. The only good news seems to be that there will be higher crop yields in some high-latitude regions, like Scandinavia, Siberia, and Canada, while food yields may fall in the developing world.

By 2052, the additional projected average sea-level rise is upward of 0.3 meters. But small islands in the Asian Pacific region may experience three to five times this average. The projections suggest an increase in weather extremes and changes in regional microclimate, such as increased intensity of hurricanes, poleward movement of thunderstorms, and increased intensity of rain. Coastal regions are likely to be at risk, with sea-level rise in lowland regions, such as Bangladesh, displacing millions of people. Vector-borne and water-borne disease will increase, especially in regions with inadequate health-care systems.

So these are the consequences in 2052 if the world implements the current national proposals for greenhouse gas reductions made by the 194 nations of the UNFCCC.

However, there are serious and credible analyses[24] that suggest that this will not be the course the world will take. These analyses suggest that technologies and sustainable energy resources are known or available today sufficient to perform the energy transition of the twenty-first century, and create a world in 2052 that is far brighter than that arising from implementation of current pledges.

Robert W. Corell *(American, born 1934), PhD, is an oceanographer and engineer who is actively engaged in research on global change and public policy. He formerly taught at universities in the United States and Norway and is now principal of the Global Environment and Technology Foundation in Arlington, Virginia.*

"Extreme Weather in 2052" describes the likely consequences if humanity does nothing more than reduce its greenhouse gas emissions by the sum total of all voluntary national commitments made by July 2011. If that becomes the case, annual emissions in 2052 will be around twice current emissions, and the temperature increase some 2.2°C. In other words, the world will already have surpassed the danger threshold of plus 2°C relative to preindustrial times.

Luckily, as you will see from my forecast, I believe humanity will do better than that. It will take time, but in ten years' time, in the 2020s, emissions reductions will start to systematically outperform current commitments. Many nations will reduce their emissions below the path of current commitments because the effort to increase energy efficiency finally starts to give results, because their economies are growing more slowly than anticipated, and because the voters are getting worried. Then, around 2030, emissions will peak and start a slow decline, so that they are back to 2010 levels in 2052.

The negative impacts will be significant—but not disastrous, at least not before 2052. There will be more droughts, floods, extreme weather, and insect infestations. The sea level will be 0.3 meters higher, the Arctic summer ice will be gone, and the new weather will bother agriculturalists and vacationers alike. Ecosystems will have moved some hundred kilometers toward the poles, or some hundred meters up the hillside. Acidic ocean water will bother shell-forming animals. Many species will have died out. And in 2052 the world will be looking with angst toward further change in the second half of the century. Self-reinforcing climate change will be worry number one—with methane gas emissions from the melting tundra leading to further temperature increase, which in turn will melt even more tundra. The world will still be operational, but with higher operating costs and scary prospects for the rest of the twenty-first century.

The regional variation will be huge. As an example, figure 2-5[25] shows the approximate distribution of global warming in 2050, if the world warms according to my forecast. The temperature rise from preindustrial times will be plus 2°C on average, but ranging from less than 0°C to more than 4°C. Hot spots will include Alaska, Canada, Siberia, the Arctic Ocean, and the Antarctic rim. Other more populated areas will also feel the heat: central United States, eastern Europe, northern Africa, central Asia, western Australia, and the tropical forests around the Amazon river. Other maps forecasting the regional distribution of future rainfall show other winners and other losers.

This last discussion illustrates the need for quantitative precision in a useful forecast. And so, in the following chapters, I present a consistent core that forms the backbone of my forecast of the global future. The core consists of measurable variables (population, workforce, GDP, energy use, CO_2 emissions, food production, nonenergy footprint) that evolve over time in response to causal pressures. Various soft issues—like the five questions discussed in this chapter—are treated qualitatively, as are questions like, "Will the passing of world leadership from the United States to China be peaceful?" Here my answer will depend on the regional variation in my forecast and can't be discussed meaningfully until you have read the forecast. But to make you ponder, remember that social unrest slows productivity growth—which in turn leads to more social tension and conflict. But at the same time slower growth means less depletion and pollution, and more time for us to plan for life within planetary limits. So the answer depends on the relative strength of the two effects. It requires quantitative precision and a system perspective, which is what you will get in part 2.

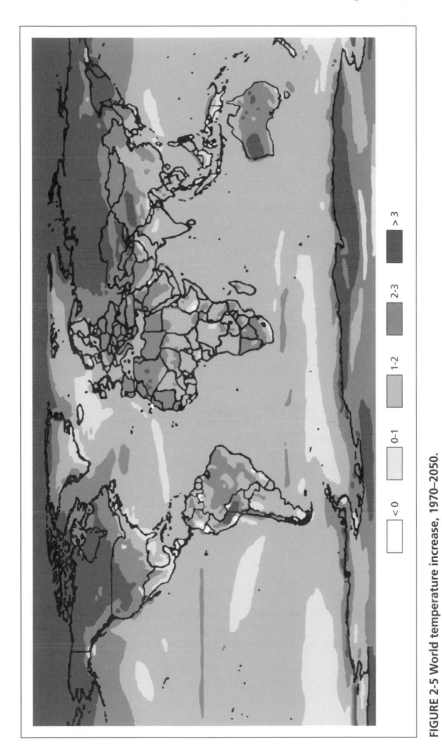

FIGURE 2-5 World temperature increase, 1970–2050.

Scale: Temperature change from preindustrial time in degrees centigrade. (Source: A. R. Ganguly et al. 2009)

PART 2

MY GLOBAL FORECAST

CHAPTER 3

The Logic behind My Forecast

C hapter 2 provided some selected perspectives on the next forty years—a look at five issues that will be fermenting behind the scene, influencing the detailed pattern of development during this generation. Part 2 of this book presents a fuller picture—my forecast of the broad lines of the global future to 2052.

That forecast is based on all information available to me: statistical data, anecdotal stories, impressions from traveling the world, and formal analyses of particular developments. As mentioned in part 1, my forecast also draws on the numerous "glimpses" of the future that I received from international experts in the summer of 2011, some of which describe broad trends and others that, in keeping with my request for them to go out on a limb and construct a sharp forecast of some event, provide a detailed portrait of a possible slice of life in 2052. But in the end I have relied on my own practical and scientific experience to choose what I believe are the most important drivers and causal relationships when trying to get a useful perspective on world development to 2052.

I have used a number of tools to make my forecast as consistent as possible. First, I used a statistical database describing global developments since 1970 in order to get the starting point—the current state of affairs—right. I also used statistics for past rates of change to ensure the right starting point for the rate of change in variables like population, productivity, and energy use. Second, as described in part 1, I used a dynamic spreadsheet (which is available on www.2052.info) to help ensure that my forecast is internally consistent, for example, ensuring that CO_2 emissions from energy use actually vary in correct proportion with changes in energy use and composition of energy sources. And finally, I used two system dynamics computer models to check that my forecast does not neglect the effects of well-known feedbacks, for example, ensuring that energy is not used without depletion of reserves and increasing production costs. These system dynamics models embody a lot of academic theory—drawn from economics, political science, sociology, engineering, biology, agriculture, and environmental science. But as with any set of projection tools, they still provide only mild assurance that my forecast makes dynamic sense.

Taken together, this diversity of sources and tools provides one perspective on the world socioeconomic-cultural-natural system. My forecast of the global future to 2052 is a reflection of this perspective. It is not the "complete truth." It describes some aspects of real-world developments, and neglects many others. This is unavoidable, but also desirable in order to avoid drowning in irrelevant detail.

The Guiding Star

But how do you decide what is relevant? System science tells us that in order to construct a useful world model it is necessary to start from a clearly formulated question. You cannot create a useful model unless you decide ahead of time what specific question you want to answer—what social phenomenon you want to elucidate.[1]

As skilled model builders know well, unless you focus, you quickly get lost in an ocean of detail.

I chose to let my forecasting effort be guided by two questions: "What will happen to consumption over the next forty years?" and "Under what conditions—in what social and natural environment—will that future consumption take place?" Besides keeping me on track, these questions have the additional advantage of being of general interest to many of today's global citizens, given the prevailing tendency toward materialism.

The two questions could perhaps have been merged into one: "How satisfied will I be with my life in 2052?" Which quickly translates into questions like: "Will I be richer?" "Will I be able to buy what I buy today?" "Will I be able to pursue my hobbies?" "Can I still go to the beach for summer vacation?" "How will my family fare?" Or slightly deeper: "Will there be a job for me in 2052? And if so, what type of job?" "Will I be able to live where I prefer to live?" "Will my children have the kind of comforts I have had?"

A Broad-Brush Picture

The broad-brush picture in the pages ahead will make it possible for you to answer for yourself whether you will be better off in 2052. Your answer will be highly dependent on who you are—influenced by your age, profession, and country of residence. Many global citizens will both be and feel much better in 2052, as a consequence of significantly improved living conditions. Others will not. One-third of us will be dead.

But it is important to remember that my aim is to describe the main aspects of the world you are going to live in—not the narrow details. It is more useful to know that the global population will peak around 2040 than it is to know that the population of Bangalore will continue to grow long beyond that date. It is more useful to know that solar heat and power will run more than one-third of the world in 2052 than to know exactly which countries will have a few nuclear plants left.

It is also important to remember that this is not the future we could have had. It is certainly not the future I would have liked. But it is the future that humanity most likely is going to create for itself

A Brief Summary of My Story

My forecast is built around a fairly simple set of cause-and-effect relationships that drive a number of global trends. These are worth sharing at the outset.

You will see that global population will peak much earlier than you thought, as will the workforce. The reason is the reduced desired family size in increasingly urban populations. Labor productivity (and hence production and GDP) will grow, but at an ever-slowing pace—because of problems with resource depletion, pollution, climate change, and rising inequity. As a result, global production of goods and services (the world GDP) will continue to grow but will peak much earlier and at a lower level than many expect. Energy use will continue to grow for a while, but at a slower rate than expected because of steady increases in energy efficiency. CO_2 emissions will at first parallel energy use—rising in tandem—but then gradually disconnect, as the share of renewable energy accelerates. The emissions will lead to higher concentrations of greenhouse gases in the atmosphere, higher temperatures, and more climate damage to planet Earth.

But my story also includes the societal response that will emerge in an attempt to solve the emerging problems of depletion, pollution, and inequity through increased investments (in both prevention and adaptation). This social investment will reach major proportions after a while and solve parts of the problem. But not the full problem, and in the process increased investment will require reduced consumption. Declining consumption and prosperity will cause growing inequity, tension, and social strife, which in turn will accelerate the decline in labor productivity. In bad cases, a negative spiral can occur.

My story differs for different parts of the world, and I describe developments in five regions: the United States; the other most industrialized nations, including the European Union, Japan, and Canada (OECD-less-US); China; fourteen big emerging economies including Brazil, Russia, India, and South

Africa (BRISE); and the rest of the world (ROW), containing the 2.1 billion people at the bottom of the income ladder.[2]

The world in 2052 will be one of huge regional and class differences. There will be global trade and migration, but not enough to eliminate big differences in material standards and quality of life between and within regions. There will be social friction, even armed conflict, because of distributional inequity. The world of 2052 will be exceedingly urban and virtual. There will be fewer children and more elderly, and some deeply held values about what is worth fighting for will have begun to give way to new ways of thinking. The world will have been through a tumultuous ride from 2012 and will be in less than perfect shape to handle an ominous second half of the twenty-first century. Many poor will be much better off, while the lifestyle of the former elites will have lost much of its charm.

On the other hand, the stage will be set for major transformations in the way we organize our politics, our financial systems, and even our lives. And, for the first time, an emphasis on well-being over financial growth will begin to gain broader acceptance, for individuals and for nations.

The Deterministic Backbone

My forecast takes as its foundation a selection of physical and ideological realities that have traditionally evolved in a sluggish manner with much inertia. These realities are simpler to forecast than most other phenomena because they change so gradually. In this category of variables you find population, GDP, energy use, climate gas emissions, temperature, industrial infrastructure, and many fundamental values (like the belief in the utility of democracy, scientific research, free markets, small government, and free trade, and the belief that nature is there for humans to use). Such realities take decades to change significantly. This rather sluggish reality constitutes what I call the "deterministic backbone" of my forecast. It is portrayed in figure 3-1, and the resulting development is described in chapters 4, 5, and 6.

Once I have described the workings of the rather tangible deterministic backbone, I proceed to add softer, less material aspects to this core structure—just as some add greenery and decorations to the stem and branches of their Christmas tree. But I try to restrict myself, adding detail parsimoniously, keeping in mind that the goal is to convey something about your life satisfaction in 2052. These nonmaterial aspects are discussed in chapters 7 and 8.

The regional specifics are discussed in chapter 10.

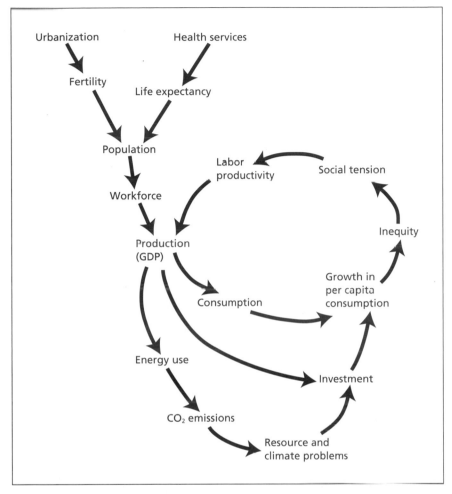

FIGURE 3-1 The main cause-and-effect relationships behind the *2052* forecast.

Linear Presentation of a Circular Maze

The presentation of my forecast is linear, from a (carefully chosen) starting point to a (carefully chosen) end point, and follows a (carefully chosen) path through the interacting intricacies of the world system. But it certainly was not developed in that way. It was developed in an iterative manner. Time and again I made a forecast, looked at the consequences, and had to conclude that the result was inconsistent with earlier choices I had made. So I had to revise, either the latter or the former, and try once again. After much trial and error I arrived at the forecast presented here.

The linear presentation starts from a forecast of future GDP—based on forecasts of future population and productivity—and then moves on to forecasts of future investment, consumption, energy use, climate impacts, food production, and land use. This structure was chosen in order to match the common intuitive perception of the direction of causality. The variables were chosen so that historical data exist all the way from 1970, not only for the state but for its rate of change. As mentioned above, I focus on variables that evolve gradually, so that trends are fairly stable. But there are feedback effects in the real world, which I have tried to handle through a process of iteration, revising my assumptions again and again until the forecast formed a consistent whole.

The Mathematical Formulation

To further simplify your reading of the next several chapters, I add the following guide to the mathematical formulation of the deterministic backbone of my forecast. This formulation is embedded in the spreadsheet that is available on the book's website, www.2052.info. There are individual sheets for each of my five world regions, plus one sheet providing the world total.

Chapters 4, 5, and 6 discuss the results for the world when applying the following logic, step by step:

1. The future global **population** is calculated based on forecasts of **fertility** (i.e., children per woman) and **mortality** (i.e., one divided by life expectancy).
2. The potential **workforce** is calculated as the part of the population that is between fifteen and sixty-five years of age.
3. Gross **labor productivity** is defined as GDP divided by the potential workforce, and is forecast based on historical trends and my assumptions about the future. All effects of capital, resource availability, technology, and labor-participation rates are included in this variable, which amounts to the economic value added per person between fifteen and sixty-five years of age and is measured in $\$^3$ per person-year.
4. Annual **production** (i.e., GDP) is calculated as the potential workforce multiplied by gross labor productivity.
5. The share of the production that is **investment** (i.e., not consumed during the year) is forecast based on historical trends and my assumptions about the future.
6. **Consumption** is forecast as production less investment. Society can consume only that part of total production that is not invested (i.e., spent in

order to support future consumption). In this vein I define as investment all future expenditure intended to counter negative effects of depletion, pollution, and inequity and to pay for adaptation to climate change. I do not distinguish between private and public investment.

7. **Consumption per person**—my guiding star—is calculated as consumption divided by population.

8. **Energy use** is calculated as production times the **energy intensity of production**. The latter is forecast based on historical trends and my assumptions about the future and is measured in tonnes of oil equivalents per dollar of GDP. All efforts to increase energy efficiency (industrial improvement, electric cars, insulated homes) help lower the energy intensity.

9. The **shares of energy** coming from coal, oil, gas, nuclear, and renewable energy are forecast based on historical trends and my assumptions about the future.

10. **CO_2 emissions from energy use** are calculated as the sum of the CO_2 emissions arising from the five forms of energy used. The **CO_2 intensity of energy use** is calculated as CO_2 emissions divided by energy use. The latter is measured in tonnes of CO_2 equivalents per tonne of oil equivalent. Introduction of renewable energy (wind, sun, nuclear, hydro) helps reduce the CO_2 intensity, as does carbon capture and storage (CCS).

11. The **concentration of CO_2** in the atmosphere is calculated (in a climate model outside the spreadsheet) along with the increase in **global average temperature** and **sea level**. The other Kyoto gases are included in the calculation.

12. **Food** production is calculated as **land** under cultivation times average **land yield**. Land (in billion hectares) and land yield (in tonnes of food per hectare year) are forecast based on historical trends and my assumptions about the future. The land yield includes the effect of all types of inputs (fertilizer, pesticides, water, seed, genetically modified organisms, and so on) and the effects of climate change.

13. The net **climate effect on food production**—which is the effect on land yield of higher temperature (which tends to lower yields) and higher concentration of CO_2 (which tends to increase yields)—is estimated based on a model outside the spreadsheet.

14. Finally, the amount of **unused biocapacity**[4] (i.e., land not used for food, wood, and cities) is calculated as **total biocapacity** (i.e., all land) less the **nonenergy footprint** (i.e., land used for food, wood, and cities). The two latter are forecast based on historical trends and my assumptions about the future.

These variables form the core of the forecast, while the various glimpses add depth and color to the discussion surrounding them. The glimpses also shed light on various things that the future has in store for us all: bigger cities, more solar power, ever-present Internet, more support for collective solutions, less nature, visible climate damage, and urban mining of metals, to name a few.

A Final Note on the Data Base

I have already told you that my forecast is based on a significant amount of data about the real world. For those of you who primarily trust numerical data, you will be delighted to find in the graphs in this book time-series data for some twenty independent variables, from 1970 to 2010, and not only at the global level, but for the five regions I use in my analysis. I have borrowed this huge amount of data from a number of credible sources, which have spent vast resources and many years to collect them. The sources are listed in appendix 2. Although the sources provide numbers with many significant digits, thereby giving the impression that they are very precise, you are well advised to remember that there is uncertainty in the second digit in most cases, and always in the third digit. Statistical data appear more precise than they are. You will find even more numbers in the spreadsheets on the book's website.

But my forecast is not based solely on data about the past. It is also based on knowledge about how the world works, and especially about how it is likely to work in the future. There is more uncertainty in this type of qualitative knowledge, and I often have had to choose which experts to rely on when making my forecast. The simplest way to summarize my many choices is to say that I generally hold views that are mainstream among educated and well-informed ecological economists in the industrial world of today. A more precise definition of what this means can be had by reviewing my bible on such matters, namely, a survey of the modern sustainability literature by Aled Jones and his colleagues at Anglia Ruskin University.[5] This is a very helpful and complete review of the recent and relevant reports on depletion, pollution, and climate-change issues, including their policy implications, and presented in a tone that very much mirrors my view on most matters. Thus throughout this book I simply state what I believe to be correct and do not give a concrete reference, except in those very few cases where my view deviates from the mainstream.

The third and final pillar under my forecast is that I basically believe that we will see the same rate of technological and societal change over the next forty years as we have seen over the last forty years. That is because the drivers will be the same and the organization of global society is unlikely to change discontinuously.

Let us now see what concrete forecasts this all adds up to.

CHAPTER 4

Population and Consumption to 2052

Those who, like me, have long worried about the future of life on Earth have fretted over one factor perhaps more than anything else, and that is population growth. Over the last several decades, we have wanted to know: How many people can the planet support? At what number is population likely to peak, and when? And how will that affect the world? It took all of human history for roughly three billion people to inhabit Earth by 1960, just forty more years for that number to double to six billion, and just over a decade more to reach the seven billion mark, around which we hover today.

Some of that early fretting paid off. Warnings issued by scientists inspired enough alarm to focus awareness on the issue and mobilize forces, at least to some degree. While our human numbers, and the associated consumption, do—and will—exceed the bounds of our natural resources, we could have been in an even worse situation.

Population Will Peak

So where will we go from here? My population forecast to 2052 is shown graphically in the right-hand part of figure 4-1, spliced onto historical data for the period from 1970 to 2010. The global population will peak well before 2052 (actually ten years earlier), because of a continuing decline in the number of children per woman. This decline will be only partly compensated by a continuing rise in life expectancy. As figure 4-1 shows, these two trends will cause the global population to reach a maximum of some 8.1 billion people in the early 2040s. Thereafter the global population will decline at accelerating speed.

This stagnation and decline in world population will be not (primarily) the consequence of starvation, pollution, or pests but the result of a voluntary decision in billions of urban households to have fewer children. Already more than half the people of the world live in cities, and that fraction will go up with continuing industrialization in the developing world. Most people will be urban and live under conditions where having many children is not an advantage. The desire to have small families will not be limited to two-career

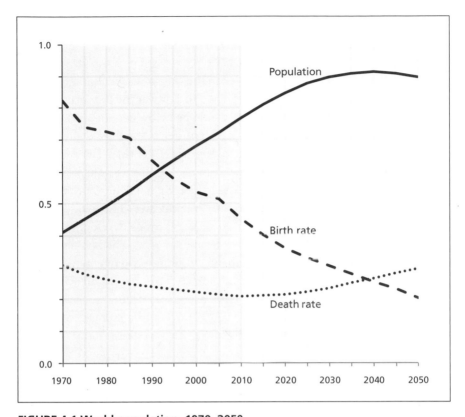

FIGURE 4-1 World population, 1970–2050.
Scale: Population (0–9 billion people); birth and death rate (0%–4% per year).

couples in the industrialized world. Billions of poor urban families in emerging economies will make the same choice, in an attempt to escape poverty.

The reasoning will be the same everywhere. Families will increasingly be able to have exactly the number of children they want—because of steady improvements in education, health, and contraception. And most will live in settings where another child is a burden. In the crowded megacity one more child is one more mouth to feed and one more person to get through school—not an additional farmhand. Better public health will ensure higher life expectancy and lower child mortality, thereby increasing the chance that the first child actually will live to be a continuing joy and pride for the family.

Systematic progress within medicine will help eliminate infectious disease, and in 2052 life expectancy will exceed seventy-five years all over the world, except during times of uncommon stress.[1] The number of children per woman (i.e., total fertility) will be approaching one. As a consequence, the global population will soon be declining at 1% per year and will be back to current levels (seven billion people) by 2075.

These tendencies can already be seen in the statistics. The average number of children per woman has declined from 4.5 to 2.5 over the last forty years. If this trend were continued, total fertility would be below zero in 2050. But this, obviously, will not happen. Instead the rate of decline will slow—toward an average of one child per woman in the middle of the century. The decline will be gradual but consistent. It is true that even urban parents want someone to take care of them in old age, but increasingly one child will be seen as enough, in addition to a state pension. Furthermore, one educated child will seem to be a safer bet than a number of uneducated ones. Spurious developments—like the current excess of boys in China after decades of a one-child policy and the subsequent de-selection of girls, and the increasing unwillingness of women to marry in societies where women traditionally take care of their in-laws— will strengthen the trend. Some spectacular drops may occur—such as the one that occurred in Libya between 1990 and 2010, when the average number of children fell from seven to two. But in general we are talking about a gradual decline in fertility, shown as a falling crude birth rate (i.e., annual births as a percent of the current population) in figure 4-1.[2]

Some pro-natalist governments will try to stem the decline. If they can afford to, they will provide cheap preschool options in order to free mothers and fathers to pursue careers in the formal economy. But this will not be the dominant modus operandi, because most governments will be unable to extract the necessary taxes from their citizens to subsidize child care. In these cases, it is simpler and cheaper for the government to help young urban couples choose a small family. Along the same lines, some of the world's religions will continue to work against the "Western hedonistic focus on self" rather than on children. But I believe negative practical experience from a crowded urban environment will win over old religious teachings that evolved when humanity was still puny and toiling on the land in a vast and wild natural environment.

The population will peak first in the rich world, where major populations like Germany's already would be declining today had it not been for immigration. This will happen around 2015. Next, just after 2020, population will peak in China, which is about to reap the benefits of the one-child policy of Deng. Russia's population is declining, in spite of efforts by the government to reverse the trend. Italy's fertility is among the lowest in the world in spite of the Pope and Italian macho culture. Other industrializing nations will follow the OECD and China. India and Africa south of the Sahara will be among the laggards. But in sum, the global population will peak, and much earlier than most people expect. By 2052 it will already be declining.

Workforce Will Peak a Little Earlier

Since I want to forecast the annual production of goods and services (i.e., future GDP), I am particularly interested in the subset of the world population that can actually work. I define this group as the number of people between fifteen and sixty-five years of age. Figure 4-2 shows the historical development of this age group. It has grown in all regions since 1970.

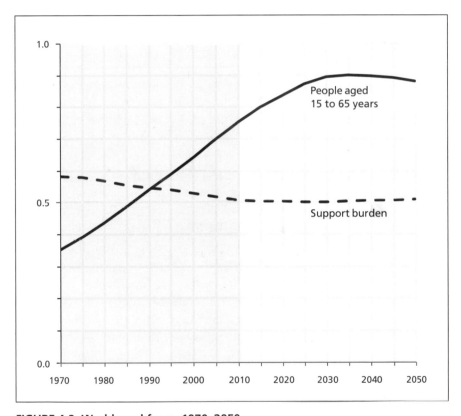

FIGURE 4-2. World workforce, 1970–2050.
Definition: Support burden = population divided by people aged 15–65 years.
Scale: People aged 15–65 (0–6 billion people); support burden (0–3).

This fifteen-to-sixty-five age group, then, is the *potential* workforce—the total number of people who could work if conditions were suitable. The *actual* workforce is smaller than the potential, often much smaller. Historically, the difference has lain first in the fact that women traditionally did not participate in the formal economy, and second that many of those aged fifteen to sixty-five were unemployed, sick, disabled, or not in a formal job for other reasons. But labor participation rates have grown over time, especially among women and especially in the socially advanced economies of the OECD. This is particularly true if one includes students in the actual workforce—as one should, since their effort is part of society's investment in future productivity. On the other hand, the group aged fifteen to sixty-five also excludes the increasing number of old people who not only are able to work but actually do so in the formal economy. In sum, the age group between fifteen and sixty-five years of age remains an approximation of the potential workforce, but good enough, I believe, for a broad-brush picture of the future.

What will happen to the potential workforce between now and 2052? The answer follows mathematically from the age distribution in my population forecast. The potential workforce will follow the pattern of the population: it will first grow, then peak, and then start to decline, as shown in figure 4-2. Interestingly, owing to population dynamics, the number of people aged fifteen to sixty-five will peak some five years *before* the peak in total population.

Many are concerned about this coming fall in the potential workforce. If you are among them, you ought to look closely at the other curve in figure 4-2, the one showing how the "support burden" will develop. The support burden is defined as the total population divided by the potential workforce. This burden—the number of persons supported by each person in the potential workforce—has been declining over the last forty years, as can be seen from figure 4-2. That historical drop is quite contrary to the impression given by the endless public discussion of the ever-increasing burden of the old on the younger productive population. The truth, though, is not that the burden is on a never-ending rise, as many erroneously assume. Rather, it's that the forty-year decline is just now about to stop. So, we are just reaching the point where changing age demographics will no longer lessen the burden of the workforce. Over the next forty years, the support burden will stay more or less constant. It won't change much, because the rise in the number of the elderly will be compensated for by a decline in the number of children. And if imbalances evolve, I believe societies will react surprisingly fast and increase the pension age—in spite of the opposition of those approaching pension age. They are, after all, a minority.

Productivity Will Grow, but Meet Obstacles

The potential workforce will continue to grow for decades, providing one basis for continued growth in GDP. For there is little reason to believe that labor participation rates (i.e., the fraction of those aged fifteen to sixty-five who work in the formal economy) will decline. In reality the opposite is happening. One of the reasons, among others, is that more and more women around the world are shifting from working for free in the household to paid employment. Thus growth in the potential workforce will lead to growth in the actual workforce, and more hands in the formal economy, which is what gets measured by the GDP. But what will happen to labor productivity?

Notice that I define gross labor productivity in this book as annual production relative to the *potential* workforce, not, as is common, relative to the *actual* workforce. So I divide total GDP by the number of persons aged fifteen to sixty-five, not only the number of people who work. The reason why I choose to focus on gross labor productivity is that this simplifies the statistical work. It is much simpler to find good time-series data for the number of people aged fifteen to sixty-five than to find time-series data for the number who actually work. It furthermore makes more sense to compare the gross labor productivity among economies that organize their labor markets in very different ways.

Gross labor productivity has increased over the last forty years, when you take the world average, as shown in figure 4-3. It has grown—albeit at a declining rate—through increased participation in the workforce and increased output per hour worked through the use of energy, machinery, equipment, computers, and other changes. The growth has been so rapid that it more than compensated for the gradual reduction in the number of hours worked per year by the average employee in many rich countries. From 1970 to 2010, gross labor productivity grew by some 90% on average, compared to 110% in the OECD countries outside the United States, and an astounding 1,200% in China. This worldwide growth in gross labor productivity reflects the intense desire in all nations to increase the annual production of goods and services, but it also shows that it is harder to lead (OECD) than to catch up (China).

To put this in perspective, it's helpful to consider the broad history of labor productivity. Starting in the 1800s increasing productivity in agriculture made it possible to produce enough food with much fewer people working on the land. In the end tractors (i.e., fossil energy), fertilizers, pesticides, and new seeds made most working people free to move into manufacturing. Here the process of impressive productivity rise repeated itself, through the introduction of energy, machinery, and economies of scale. As a result it became

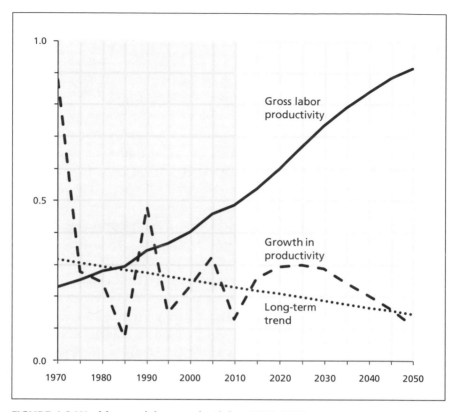

FIGURE 4-3 World gross labor productivity, 1970–2050.
Definition: Gross labor productivity = GDP divided by people aged 15–65 years.
Scale: Gross labor productivity ($0–$20,000 per person-yr); growth in productivity
and long-term trend (0%–7% per yr).

possible to satisfy the demand for industrial goods with a falling share of the
workforce in manufacturing.

In current postindustrial societies the majority of the workforce is free to
focus on the production of services and care. And labor productivity is growing
even in these sectors: computers are taking over accounting and administrative
tasks; robots are making tentative entries into the provision of care. We can
see the contours of a future economy where most of the workforce spends
its time in services, education, entertainment, creative activity, and that final
eater of time—care.

Different nations are in different stages of this development. The original
members of the OECD[3] led the way, posting solid growth in per capita
production in the post–World War II period. Later entrants, like Japan and
South Korea, caught up with the early movers within a generation, initially by

adopting much of their solutions and technology. Later, as the late entrants joined the front-runners, their growth rates declined to that of the leaders—for the obvious reason that they had to partake in the common evolution of new solutions and technology.

The historical shift toward higher productivity growth will continue over the next forty years. First, China will show spectacular growth rates while it catches up. Later a number of emerging economies will follow suit, with India somewhat further behind. Some of the poorest nations of the world will show little progress. So, gross labor productivity will continue to grow, but at very different rates in different regions. At one end of the spectrum will be successful emerging nations growing spectacularly for decades while catching up with the West. In the middle will be the stagnating rich world, which has already forced labor productivity to high levels and already has most of its labor force in services and care, where productivity gains are harder to achieve. Other nations won't be taking off at all, because they'll prove unable to introduce educational systems, courts, rule of law, and other elements that facilitate economic growth.

As a consequence, gross labor productivity in China will be getting quite close to that of the rich world in 2052. In my forecast China in 2052 will have a GDP of \$56,000 per person per year,[4] compared to \$73,000 in the United States and \$63,000 in the OECD outside the United States. This means that, from the time Deng Xiaoping opened the door for the market economy in 1978, it will have taken China just eighty years to (largely) catch up with the West. China will take more time to catch up than Japan and South Korea, who did the same in fifty years, because of China's weaker starting point.

Figure 4-3 shows how productivity growth has slowed since 1970 when we see the world as a whole. The historical data is very noisy, but the dotted trend line provides an indication.[5] Overall it reflects the fact that a region's growth typically stays high in the first several decades after takeoff, and then falls once the region catches up with the leading region—which during the last forty years has been the United States. The data also shows how the rate of progress in gross labor productivity has declined in the mature economies, for example, from 2% to 1% per year in the United States from 1970 to 2010—again as values on a trend line fit to very noisy yearly data. I believe this pattern will continue.

As figure 4-3 shows, productivity growth will first recover from the low value in 2010, then peak in the 2020s, and then decline toward the middle of the century. This development is the sum of my forecasts for the individual regions of the world. In 2052 GDP per person will grow at only 1% per year, and since the population will have started to decline, the world GDP will peak shortly thereafter and start to decline.

Not many have even entertained the thought that global GDP will ever plateau and start a systematic decline because of a decline in the workforce and stable or falling productivity. I believe this will be one of the central characteristics of the second half of the twenty-first century. But that is not until after 2052.

Production (GDP) Will Grow, but More and More Slowly

GDP is intended to be equal to the total production of goods and services in an economy during a year, valued at market prices. It is a generally recognized weakness that the the GDP normally disregards all production outside of formal markets (for example, in households). This disparity, though, will get smaller over time, as more activity is moved from the home and village into the monetized economy.

The world GDP is measured in trillions of dollars per year. One trillion is 1,000 billion, or 1 T (for Tera) in professional jargon. In 2010 the world economy produced goods and services worth $67 trillion, or 67 T$/yr. One-fifth of this was produced in the United States, one-third in the rest of the OECD, and one-seventh in China. The dollars used in this book are all 2005 dollars, and GDP numbers from different nations are converted from national currencies to dollars using purchasing power parity (PPP) exchange rates.

Global production of goods and services—measured as world GDP—has grown impressively over the last century, and particularly since 1950. The growth in output did result from a continuing increase in the workforce and from systematic increase in labor productivity. There was a dramatic rise in the number of hands and a spectacular rise in the amount of goods and services produced by each pair of hands. The workforce rose with the population. And productivity rose with the use of more energy, machinery, and technology, and as a consequence of increased specialization and division of labor.

So what will happen to production over the next forty years? Figure 4-4 shows my forecast, obtained by multiplying the future potential workforce with the future gross labor productivity. The result is a world GDP that stagnates and starts to decline just after the middle of the century.

By 2052 the world economy will be big—2.2 times as big as today. In other words, humanity will produce 120% more goods and services in 2052 than it did in 2010. This will enable higher average consumption rates, but it will also add to the human ecological footprint. There will be higher emissions and more rapid depletion of resources. But dramatic increases in resource and

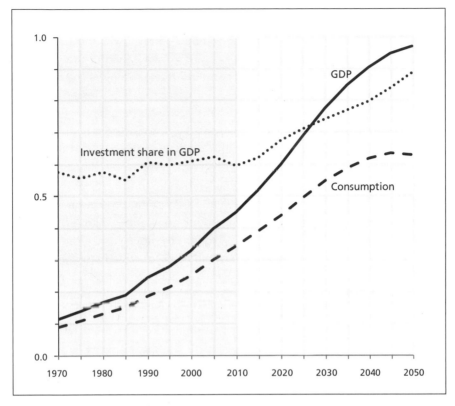

FIGURE 4-4. World production and consumption, 1970–2050.
Scale: Consumption and GDP ($0–$150 trillion per year); investment share (0%–40%).

energy efficiency over the next forty years will soften humanity's collision with global limitations. More about this later.

Meanwhile, GDP developments will vary among the regions. Some economies—particularly mature ones—will only grow slowly or perhaps not at all. China will show significant growth—as will many emerging nations. Parts of the poor world will still hover around their 2010 levels, as shown in chapter 10.

But even though the economy will roughly double in size, it will still be a lot smaller than many expect. That's because the workforce will be smaller and productivity will be lower than commonly anticipated. These factors, too, depend on others. The workforce will be smaller because the population will be lower; and population will be lower because fertility will be lower in our urbanized future. Productivity will be lower because productivity *growth* will be lower than expected; and productivity growth will be lower because the more mature economies of the future will have a larger share in services and care—which are harder to make more efficient. Furthermore, productivity growth will be hampered by erratic weather—which will make planning harder in agriculture and other sectors—and growing inequity—which will disturb the peace and calm needed for continuous fine-tuning of the economy.

Productivity growth relies on the orderly transfer of resources from less productive to more productive sectors. This is simpler in manufacturing than in services. It is faster if you are copying someone who did it before. It is helped by a stable legal environment. It is certainly not helped by external shocks, high unemployment, and social disorder. Sadly, I expect the latter to be part of the global future, but with significant regional variation. In some places unacceptable levels of inequity will cause conflict and an outright drop in productivity.

In mature economies with declining populations and shrinking workforce, the total result may be negative GDP growth. In other words, the total pie may shrink. Such shrinking makes it more difficult to redistribute income and wealth. In a market economy, slow growth generates unemployment and a skewed distribution of income. Over time this leads to more inequity, social tensions, friction, and protests against the current order. Unless the social order is changed to better handle issues of distribution, slow growth may create significant social problems and further reduction in the economic growth rate.

My forecast of world GDP in 2052 is significantly below the forecast one would make based on past growth rates in GDP. The average growth rate of the world economy from 1970 to 2010 was 3.5% per year. If we assumed the same growth rate over the next forty years, the world economy in 2052 would be more than three times as big as the current economy. The reduction from a trebling to a doubling of the human economy may perhaps not sound like much, but it may prove crucial, since it will reduce the total human activity on planet Earth by one-third in 2052. That amounts to lightening the planetary burden by the equivalent of all ongoing activity in the current global economy. This is a lot, especially since we are already beyond the physical carrying capacity of the globe.

It's important to note that my forecast is not based on an assumption that humanity will come to its senses and deliberately try to limit economic activity on Earth, in order to protect it from overload. What I am saying is that humanity will continue to try to create economic growth, but that it won't succeed as much as desired—for the reasons given above. And although we will fail in this sense, remember that my forecast says that we will add as much economic activity to the world over the next forty years as we did from the time of Adam and Eve. In that perspective a doubling is neither a small feat nor without significant global impact.

"Glimpse 4-1: The End of Uneconomic Growth" discusses the issue of continued economic growth on the planet, focusing on the composition of the growth. The message is that we may be moving toward a world where humanity will have learned to create economic value without destroying so much other (natural, cultural, and future) value in the process. The hope is that this learning will be more widespread by 2052—for instance, through systematic internalization of externalities in market prices supplemented with global bans on unacceptable behavior.

GLIMPSE 4-1

The End of Uneconomic Growth

Herman Daly

Will humanity come to its senses and deliberately slow economic growth in order to save the planet? I think not, but I do think there will be a shift in the composition of future economic activity, so it becomes less damaging to values that are currently not priced in the marketplace.

Forty years ago when I read *The Limits to Growth* I already believed that growth in total resource use (population times per capita resource use) would stop within the next forty years. The modeling analysis of the *Limits* team was a strong confirmation of that commonsense belief, based on principles going back at least to Malthus and earlier classical economists.

Well, it is now forty years later and economic growth is still the number-one policy goal of practically all nations; that is undeniable. Growth economists say that the "neo-Malthusians" were simply wrong, and that we should keep on growing as before. But I think economic growth has already ended in the sense that the growth that continues is now *uneconomic*; it costs more than it is worth at the margin and makes us poorer rather than richer. We still call it economic growth, or simply "growth" in the confused belief that growth must always be economic. I contend that we have reached the economic limit to growth but we don't know it, and desperately hide the fact by faulty national accounting, because growth is our idol and to stop worshiping it is anathema.

It is no refutation to ask if I would rather live in a cave and freeze in the dark than accept all the historical benefits of growth. Of course not. The total cumulative benefits of growth until today are in my view greater than the total cumulative costs, although some economic historians debate that. In any case, we cannot undo the past and should be grateful to those who paid the costs of creating the wealth we now enjoy. But, as any economist should know, it is the *marginal* (not total) costs and benefits that are relevant to determining when growth becomes uneconomic. Marginal benefits decline because we satisfy our most pressing wants first; marginal costs rise because we use the most accessible resources first and sacrifice the least vital ecosystem services as we grow (convert nature into artifacts). Are the marginal benefits of a third car worth the marginal costs of climate disruption and sea-level rise? Declining marginal benefits will equal rising marginal costs while net benefits are positive—in fact precisely when net benefits of past growth are at a maximum! No one is against being richer, at least up to some sufficient level of wealth. That rich is better than poor is a definitional truism. That growth always makes us richer is an elementary mistake even within the basic logic of standard economics.

As suggested above, we do not really want to know when growth becomes uneconomic because then we should stop growing at that point—and we don't know how to run a steady-state economy, and we are religiously committed to an ideology of "no limits." We want to believe that growth can cure poverty without sharing, and without limiting the scale of the human niche in creation. To maintain this state of delusion we confuse two distinct meanings of the term "economic growth." Sometimes it refers to the growth of that thing we call the economy (the physical subsystem of our world made up of the stocks of population and wealth and the flows of production and consumption). When the economy gets physically bigger we call that "economic growth." But the term also has a second, very different meaning. If an activity causes benefits to increase faster than costs, we call that an "economic" activity. In this sense, "economic growth" is growth that yields a net benefit or a profit. Now, does "economic growth" in the first sense imply "economic growth" in the second sense? No, absolutely not. The idea that a bigger economy must always make us richer is pure confusion.

That economists should contribute to this confusion is puzzling because all of *micro*economics is devoted to finding the optimal scale of a given activity—the point beyond which marginal costs exceed marginal benefits and further growth would be uneconomic. Marginal revenue = marginal cost is even called the "when to stop rule" for growth of a firm. Why does this simple logic of optimization disappear in *macro*economics? Why is the growth of the macro-economy not subject to an analogous "when to stop rule"?

We recognize that all microeconomic activities are parts of the larger macroeconomic system, and their growth causes displacement and sacrifice of other parts of the system. But the macro-economy itself is thought to be the whole shebang, and when it expands, presumably into the void, it displaces nothing and therefore incurs no opportunity cost. But this is false of course. The macro-economy too is a *part*, a subsystem of the biosphere, a part of the greater economy of the natural ecosystem. Growth of the macro-economy imposes a rising opportunity cost of reduced natural capital that at some point will constrain further growth.

But some say that if our empirical measure of growth is GDP, based on voluntary buying and selling of final goods and services in free markets, then that guarantees that growth always consists of goods, not "bads." The free market does not price bads—but nevertheless bads are inevitably produced as joint products along with goods. Since bads are unpriced, GDP accounting cannot subtract them—instead it registers the additional production of anti-bads (which do have a price) and counts them as goods. For example, we do not subtract the cost of pollution as a bad, yet we add the value of pollution cleanup as a good. This is asymmetric accounting. In addition we count the consumption of natural capital (depletion of mines, wells, aquifers, forests, fisheries, or topsoil, for instance) as if it were income rather than capital drawdown—a colossal accounting error. Paradoxically, therefore, GDP, whatever else it may measure, is *also* the best statistical index we have of the aggregate of pollution, depletion, congestion, and loss of biodiversity. Economist Kenneth Boulding suggested, with tongue only a little bit in cheek, that we relabel it Gross Domestic *Cost*. At least we should put the costs and the benefits in separate accounts for comparison. Economists and psychologists are now discovering that, beyond a sufficiency threshold, the positive correlation between GDP and self-evaluated happiness disappears. This is not surprising, because GDP was never meant as a measure of happiness or welfare—only of activity; some of which is joyful, some beneficial, some regrettably necessary, some remedial, some trivial, some harmful, and some stupid.

In sum, I think that we have reached the limits to growth in the last forty years, but also that we have willfully denied it, much to the harm of most of us, but to the benefit of an elite minority who keep on pushing the growth ideology, because they have found ways to privatize the benefits of growth while socializing the even greater costs.

The big question in my mind is, Can denial, delusion, and obfuscation last another forty years? And if we keep on denying the economic limit to growth, how long do we have before crashing into the more discontinuous and catastrophic biophysical limits? I am hopeful that in the next forty years we can finally recognize and adapt to the more forgiving economic limit. Adaptation will mean moving from growth to a steady-state economy, one almost certainly at a smaller scale than at present. By scale I mean physical size of the economy relative to the ecosystem, probably best measured by resource throughput.

I must confess surprise that denial has endured for forty years. I think to wake up will require something like repentance and conversion, to put it in religious terms. It is idle to predict whether we will have the spiritual strength and rational clarity for such a conversion. Prediction of the direction of history is premised on a determinism that negates purpose and effort as causative. And if we are really determinists, then it doesn't matter what we predict; even our predictions are determined. As a non-determinist I hope and work for an end to growth mania within the next forty years. That is my personal bet on the medium-run future. How confident am I that I will win that bet? About 30%, maybe.

Herman E. Daly *(American, born 1938) is professor emeritus in the School of Public Policy at the University of Maryland and a former senior economist at the Environment Department of the World Bank. His books include* Steady-State Economics *(1972) and* Ecological Economics and Sustainable Development *(2007).*

I agree with the message in "The End of Uneconomic Growth." There will be progress over the coming decades in the effort to shift economic activity into areas that do not create so much harm. And I agree that it is unlikely that humanity will have ceased all uneconomic growth by 2052. But the main step forward in my mind will be a huge increase in human spending on solving what the glimpse calls "bads." In macroeconomic terms, humanity will increase the investment share of the GDP and use all this money to solve problems of depletion, pollution, congestion, climate change, and biodiversity loss. As a consequence, consumption will be lower: the shift toward more focus on treating bads will necessitate a parallel reduction in consumption. This will be perceived as a decline in the material standard of living. But the shift will not reduce the GDP. Nor will it reduce employment. Employment follows GDP. Only consumption will be lower than it could have been.

It is also important that slower GDP growth over the next forty years will give us better time to undertake the shift toward a more rational economy, which does not systematically destroy future or non-priced values. The coming doubling of the world economy will lead to a smaller ecological footprint than a trebling would have. The smaller economy won't deplete resources as fast, nor generate as much pollution as the bigger economy would. The smaller economy will do less damage to the planet. First of all, in absolute terms, we will extract only two resource units instead of three, and emit two pollution units instead of three. But there is a second benefit of smaller size: we will crash into global limits more gently, so to speak. The lower growth rate will give us more time during the next forty years to observe the emerging damage and prepare remedial action. We will have more time to learn and more time to convert that learning into practical solutions that will avoid future damage—and repair past damage.

Finally, it is worth noting that my forecast implies that the *average* GDP per world citizen will grow by nearly 80% over the next forty years. This is more or less a repetition of what happened during the last forty years. But the regional distribution will be very different. The Chinese will become tremendously much more productive, while the Americans and Europeans will remain where they were in 2010. Many big emerging economies will see clear increases in their production, while the rest of the world will stay unpleasantly near their current GDP per person.

Investments—Forced and Voluntary—Will Increase

During the next forty years, humanity will find itself facing an increasing stream of challenges that basically arise from the fact that it is trying to undertake this huge expansion on a small planet. We will face increasing scarcity of various resources, unpleasant accumulation of various pollutants, imminent loss of selected species and ecosystems, growing needs to defend our buildings against new and scary weather patterns, time-consuming problems associated with congestion, and so on. In each case, society will respond. The response will follow the human tradition. It will not be a decision to pull back—at least not initially. Instead it will be a decision to throw money at the problem. Society will try to solve the problem by developing a new solution. Society will pay for a substitute, for a new production process, or, in general terms, for a new way of achieving the same result without the harmful side effect. In other words, society will try to solve the oncoming stream of problems through increased investment.

This increased investment will come from a mixture of private and public sources. But on the ground—in the "real economy" as the economists call it, not the financial economy—increased investment means that more people and capital are put to work to bring forth a solution that is more sustainable than the old ways. The investment response will be strong and fast if the new solution is cheaper than the old one. But if the new solution is more expensive than the old one, progress will be slower. For example, over the next generation humanity will replace cheap fossil-based gasoline with a more expensive solution, be it chargeable cars or sustainable biofuels. Such "uphill" shifts will be excruciatingly slow unless there is some form of government intervention: supportive legislation or allocation of tax money. If the state does not enter, the shift will not occur, at scale, until the market price of the old solution exceeds the expected cost of the new solution. But since it takes a lot of time—at least twenty years from an unsolved problem to large-scale implementation of a solution (think about the time it took to get mobile phones in place)—society may end up having to face an unsolved problem for a period, while waiting for the solution. During this period it will be tempting to use money on adaptation instead of a solution. It will seem better to invest in a dike (which will stop damage from a rising sea level in five years) than to invest in climate-friendly technologies like carbon capture and storage (which will at best stop the ocean rise in fifty years).

But irrespective of the exact form of societal response, in all cases emerging problems will mean increased investment. The added investment may be *forced* (ex post, as when having to clean up after a hurricane) or *voluntary* (ex ante, as when developing new low-carbon energy sources). In both cases a larger share of the GDP will be in the form of investment goods and services, and a lower share will be available for immediate consumption. My guiding star, as you remember, is to forecast future consumption. I do this by forecasting investment and subtracting it from forecast GDP. I forecast investment by multiplying the GDP with my forecast for "the share of GDP in investment." This investment share, and its rise during the next forty years, will play a significant role in our future.

World GDP includes both the production of "consumer goods and services" and the production of "investment goods and services." The first includes all goods and services that are consumed within a year; the latter includes everything society does in a year in order to maintain high levels of production in future years. Investment includes the construction of buildings, roads, machinery, equipment, power plants, mine shafts, cars, airplanes, trains, and more. Many think that expenditure on education should also be seen as investment, since it is crucial for future productivity, as is all expenditure on research and development. I share this view.

On average, humanity consumes 75% of what it produces in a year, while 25% is investment. Notice that it does not matter in my context whether consumption is "private" (such as when you buy a TV or a hamburger, or drive your own car to a privately financed hospital for treatment paid for from your bank account) or "public" (such as when you enjoy a military parade, receive food vouchers, or are taken to a publicly financed hospital in a state-owned ambulance paid for by your taxes). In this book I define both private and public consumption as consumption, since both contribute to your life satisfaction. They both satisfy immediate needs or desires. Similarly, I do not distinguish between private and public investment. As long as the activity is not consumption and is intended to secure consumption in the long run, I view it as investment.

I would have preferred to view government spending on education, research, and defense as investment, along with more conventional government investment in roads, hospitals, and other infrastructure. But this is difficult in practice because the available statistics[6] treat all government spending as one sum. In this book I have chosen to treat the sum as consumption. This leads to a systematic underestimate of society's effort to prepare for a better future, but as we will see below, the error is limited.

So, as societies around the world increasingly face resource depletion, environmental pollution, ecosystem destruction, and climate damage, I believe they will respond to these challenges by adding to traditional investments in two ways. First, there will be an increase in proactive *voluntary* investment done up front in order to avoid future resource scarcity or future environmental damage. And second, there will be an increase in reactive *forced* investment done after the fact to repair damage caused by untreated resource and environmental problems. An example of voluntary investment is to replace cheap conventional oil with more expensive renewable energy. An example of forced investment is to rebuild homes after hurricane damage or flooding. I believe that these investments increasingly will be done by the state, and not only in response to profitability signals via the market. The evolution toward increased governmental influence will be slow and gradual, held back by past traditions.

The big question is whether the sum of forced and voluntary investments will grow so fast in the decades ahead that consumption will fall. Will society choose to increase proactive, and be forced to increase reactive, investments so much that consumption will be pushed below its traditional track? Will society have to forgo short-term pleasure in order to ensure long-term sustainability? It is obvious that if society invests more, there will be less to consume. But it is equally true that if the GDP grows rapidly at the same time, this will soften the blow. If the economy grows fast, the main effect of higher investment will be lower *growth* in consumption.

Here and in the following I disregard the obvious possibility of consumption based on external borrowing. This is only a temporary solution in a forty-year perspective. A nation cannot forever maintain consumption levels based on borrowing, although the United States made a spectacular attempt at doing so after the year 2000.

Since 1970, the investment share of the world economy has been around 25%. One-quarter of annual production has been in the form of investment goods and services, made in order to ensure higher consumption in the future. This "normal" rate of investment has proven sufficient to replace worn infrastructure and add enough new infrastructure to enable continued economic growth.

In addition, world society has spent another 10% of the GDP on government. This is the fraction of the global GDP that has been controlled directly by the government. It is a mixture of consumption and investment, but as mentioned, I treat it as consumption. If I had not, the government would have added perhaps 5 percentage points to the investment share. Thus, societies have traditionally used nearly one-third of annual production to do things in order to maintain high consumption rates in the future. This third could be seen as the willingness of society to ensure "sustainability"—to maintain consumption in the long run, at the cost of lower consumption in the short term.

But countries have been willing to sacrifice much more in times of need. China is a current example. Here investments have constituted nearly 40% of the Chinese GDP for decades. And, to defend itself and its form of governance, the United States increased defense spending from 1.6% of the GDP in 1940 to a full 32% three years into World War II.

New Costs Will Emerge

Over the next forty years global society will need extra investment money to:

- develop and implement substitutes for scarce resources like conventional oil and gas and phosphorus;
- develop and implement solutions for dangerous emissions like CFCs, SO_2, NOX, and climate gases;
- replace ecological services that formerly were free, such as water from glaciers, or underground water for agriculture, or fish protein;
- repair accumulated damage from past human activity, which could include decommissioning nuclear power plants or removing offshore installations;
- protect against future climate damage by adapting to consequences like sea-level rise;
- rebuild real estate and infrastructure destroyed by extreme weather, and compensate for a shorter average lifetime for infrastructure; and
- maintain armed forces to fight off immigration, defend resource supplies, and provide manpower during more frequent emergencies.

It is a sad fact that few things will become simpler or cheaper over the next forty years, as a consequence of business as usual. The only exceptions seem to be the increased yields in agriculture and forestry north of 50°N, cheaper access to the seabed resources once the Arctic summer ice melts, and cheaper shipping from Europe to east Asia when using northern routes that were formerly blocked by ice. But such vessels require costly reinforcement to handle potential ice, and expensive insurance against oil spills in the ice. In addition comes, of course, the man-made benefits from the lower cost of new technologies like solar panels, windmills, or batteries for electric cars once they move down the learning curve.

I remind you that in my terminology, what I call extra "investment" to meet future challenges actually includes a number of expenses that will be booked as "consumption" in national accounts. These include the increased costs of fuel, irrigation water, environmental protection, military defense, and other needs that follow from straining planetary limits. I have chosen to do this because it is simpler to communicate the new costs as increased investment rather than as increased consumption. The academically correct alternative would have been to establish a new category, called something like "extra consumption that does not contribute to increased well-being but simply protects well-being from falling when global resource and pollution constraints get tighter." I have found it simpler to include this category under the heading of investment expenditure.

What will be the sum of new costs in the future? How much will investment have to rise to handle the new challenges? It is impossible to give a precise answer, but I can provide order-of-magnitude estimates for a number of different potential costs and add them up.

The answer I get, then, is that planned expenditure of around 1% to 6% of the world GDP will go a long way toward solving many of the current problems, like cutting greenhouse gas emissions by half, or replacing the fossil-based energy system with a renewable system based on solar, wind, and hydro, or helping the poorest countries develop. One percent seems to be a low estimate, while 6% seems to be on the high side. Since investments currently constitute some 25% of GDP, one will need to push the investment share in the GDP above 30% in order to solve the problems that we already know. If we add in forced investment to mitigate disasters or unrest, this might add an equal amount. So as a rough estimate, investment rates might increase by one-half, growing to 36% of GDP, which is the same as defense spending in the United States at the end of World War II and the voluntary savings of the Chinese since 2000. This would lead to a high investment share, but not impossibly high. And it would still allow us to use two-thirds of the world's productive capacity to maintain current consumption.

My forecast of the investment share in the GDP to 2052 is shown in figure 4-4. The *voluntary* investment spending will increase very gradually from 2015, in pace with the general public realization that the energy, climate, and resource situation needs to be handled. It will receive a sporadic boost whenever the public panics after a particularly bad disaster. The *forced* investment will follow a similar pattern, but somewhat delayed. Forced investments will first rise gradually, and then more rapidly as the rate of climate damage increases nearer the middle of the century. I repeat that in my terminology, the extra investment includes expenditure that will be booked as consumption in the national accounts, for example, the increased costs of fuel or of irrigation water made necessary because of the new challenges.

What kind of support can one find for my rough estimates of the future investment costs? What kind of past experience exists, and what kind of budget numbers have been prepared?

The best-known numbers are probably the many attempts at quantifying what it would cost to solve the global climate problem. The Stern Commission's estimate in 2006 is perhaps the most widely quoted, assessing the cost as 1% of world GDP, if done in the cheapest way.[7] This estimate was later, in 2008, increased by Lord Stern to 2% of the GDP. The cost of inaction was at the same time estimated to be a reduction in the GDP around 2100 of 5%–20%. In 2007 the US economist William Nordhaus estimated the total economic damages from climate change to be between 0% and 10% of the GDP, for temperature increases between 0°C and 6°C. The IPCC suggested damages in the range of 1% to 5% of GDP at a temperature rise of 4°C.[8]

Returning to the cost of mitigation, the famous McKinsey cost curve from 2006 gave an estimate in the range 0.8%–1.4% of the GDP in 2030, but the cost would be higher during the period in which the climate-friendly technologies matured. The follow-up study some years later translated the cost into an extra annual investment cost of 0.5–0.8 T$/yr in the years 2020–2030, over and beyond normal investments—again in the order of 1% of GDP.[9] The OECD, on the other hand, in 2011 estimated the cost of achieving a low-carbon future to be 4% of the GDP for its rich member states.[10]

In another area, studying the cost of sustainable development, the 1992 *Agenda 21* that emerged from the UN's first Earth Summit estimated the cost of creating a sustainable world. The tag ended at 0.5 T$/yr, around 2% of the world GDP at the time.[11] Another relevant number is the UN recommendation that rich countries should give 1% of their GDP in development assistance to help alleviate world poverty.

It has been suggested that the cost of securing clean water for all through desalination would be 19 T$. This amounts to 30% of one year's global GDP, and if spread over thirty years, again some 1% of GDP.[12] Interestingly, a more recent estimate of the cost of doubling global food production was much lower, 5 T$ over the next fifty years.

In the field of energy, the International Energy Agency (IEA) has recently estimated the cost of changing the world's energy infrastructure sufficiently to avoid dangerous global warming.[13] In 2009 the IEA compared the cost of their "reference scenario" (with continued traditional reliance on coal, oil, and gas) to what they call the "450 ppm scenario" (which is what could keep global warming under plus 2°C). The accumulated cost from 2010 to 2030 of the 450 ppm scenario was estimated to be around 10 T$ higher than for the reference scenario. This amounts to some 0.5 T$/yr, which is again somewhat less than 1% of world GDP. However, the fuel-cost savings once the new infrastructure is in place would compensate for a large fraction of the cost. The challenge, according to the IEA, is to entice society to make the up-front investments in order to get the long-term benefit of lower fuel costs and lower greenhouse gas emissions.

These are huge costs, but how big are they relative to the investment in energy infrastructure that needs to be made anyway? In 2011, the IEA estimated the total cost of energy infrastructure from 2011 to 2035 to be 38 T$.[14] That amounts to some 30 T$ during the first twenty years, which needs to be compared with the 10 T$ extra cost in order to make the energy system climate-friendly. Thus it appears that the extra cost of making the energy system climate-friendly is of the order of one-third. The energy bill will be one-third higher.

These macro estimates are supported by anecdotal evidence at the micro level. What will be the impact on the cost of electricity if utilities shift from coal to more climate-friendly gas? My educated guess: the cost of electricity will rise by 30%. What will it cost to move from conventional fossil gas to unconventional shale gas? My educated guess: a doubling of the gas price from the level in the late 1990s (but a reduction by half from the peak gas prices in 2006). What will it cost to add carbon capture and storage to big-point sources of CO_2? My educated guess: 100% in the cost of power initially, perhaps falling to a 30% increase in the long run. What will it cost to transition from gasoline guzzlers to more climate-friendly cars? My educated guess: a 30% increase in the cost of the car initially, much less later. It looks as if the cost of energy-related goods and services might increase by one-third. If energy expenditure amounts to 6% of the GDP, the increase will amount to 2% of GDP.

Finally, there is an important recent addition to the literature on what it will cost to restructure the global economy. This is the 2012 report from UNEP titled *Towards a Green Economy: Pathways to Sustainable Development and Poverty Eradication*.[15] The report is a study of what it will cost to achieve a transition to a low-carbon and resource-efficient economy, essentially seeking the same goal as the IEA, namely, to keep global warming below plus 2°C. The answer is that this goal can be achieved if 2% of world GDP is invested in ten key sectors: agriculture, buildings, energy, fisheries, forests, manufacturing, tourism, transportation, water, and waste management. The main message of the UNEP report sounds like mine: what is needed is simply to shift future investment flows away from damaging projects and industries toward greener alternatives.

My overall conclusion is that the cost of countering these new developments with proactive investments will be several percent of the world's GDP. If the rich world is to carry the bill, its citizens will have to pay a larger share of their GDP. If action is postponed, the cost will be even higher. Some of the increases in gross investment are already behind us, for example, the cost increase due to growing scarcity of oil. The cost of a barrel of oil went from a few dollars at the time when it flowed freely from the rich oil fields of Texas and Saudi Arabia to ten times this amount when the oil had to be lifted a hundred meters from the ocean floor in the North Sea at the end of the twentieth century. Measured in fixed 2005 dollars, the price of oil was around $20 per barrel for a hundred years to 1972 and has since increased fivefold or more. This implies an increase in the oil bill to consumers of 3 T$/yr.[16] This amounts to a full 5% of world GDP and follows from growing scarcity of one single resource. Gas is next in line, and European gas prices have increased at least fourfold since the 1990s.

What Does It Mean to Cost 1% of GDP?

Many costs in this book and in the public debate are expressed as $x\%$ of the GDP. It is important to understand what this means in real life, or on the ground, so to speak.

Allowing such costs means a shift in the organization of the economy so we end up producing more of something and less of other things. This is a win for those who will be making the new thing and a loss for those who must stop making the old thing.

Let's consider an example. Various studies have concluded that halving the climate gas emissions from rich countries will cost some 1% of the GDP. What does that mean? One percent of the GDP of the OECD countries amounts to some $0.4 trillion per year (0.4 T$/yr to use my compact unit). But that number is so huge that it escapes understanding for most. It gives much more meaning to say the same thing with different words. Solving the climate problem will require us to move 1% of the nation's workers from the production of gasoline-powered fossil cars to the production of electric and other low-emission cars; from the construction of coal-fired utilities to the building of wind farms; from the welding of gas pipelines to the building of power transmission lines. The shift of 1% of the workforce will also require a parallel shift in the equipment that these workers use, so they can make electric engines rather than gas turbines, or build small well-insulated homes instead of big uninsulated homes, or produce solar shingles (that convert the sunlight shining on a roof into electricity for the home) rather than ordinary tiles. Thus, spending 1% of the GDP on solving the climate problem amounts to shifting 1% of the workforce and 1% of the productive capital into climate-friendly activity.

If this shift were done over ten years, it would mean moving 0.1% of the workforce every year. That is not a big shift even under full employment, and it ought to be trivial when unemployment figures are in the 10% bracket. But although simple in principle, this shift to a green economy has proved nearly impossible in the real world. Not only because the new green products are more expensive than the ones they replace, but also because of understandable resistance to change among those who hold lucrative jobs in the old fossil economy and those own-ing fossil-based capital that may have to be scrapped if society became climate-friendly before the end of the useful life of the equipment.

And if this is not enough, there is a final obstacle. The costs will arise *before* the benefits. So even if the cost is 1% of GDP in the long run, during the investment phase costs could be several times higher. This is boomtown dynamics in reverse: first comes a short period of high costs, then a long era of small benefits. The reverse-boomtown dynamics will help delay meaningful action to solve the world's problems.

Adaptation and Disaster Costs Will Explode

While I forecast a gradual increase in *voluntary* investment from 0% to 6% of the GDP from 2015 to 2050, I don't expect this investment to be decided upon until after global society has experienced another decade of erratic weather and increasing social tension. Only then will there be a willingness to spend substantially up front in order to avoid future problems. This is how long it will take before the systematic damage from heat waves, floods, strong winds, and sea-level rise become sufficiently clear-cut to convince the voter.

Meanwhile global society will be facing a gradual increase in what will be seen as natural disasters, but in my mind will be early symptoms of climate change. My forecast is that world society will also face an increase from 0% to 6% of GDP in *forced* investment over the next forty years.

The insured loss from natural disasters appears to have increased threefold over the last thirty years. It currently runs at around $150 billion per year—0.15 T$/yr—which is "only" 0.2% of world GDP.[17] But the damage in 2011 was three times higher: a full 0.4 T$/yr. If the damage keeps increasing, we could be speaking of disaster spending of 1% of world GDP per year in the longer run. The reason is both that the weather will get wilder and that an increasingly crowded world will end up building expensive infrastructure in exposed places, like on the coast or on floodplains.

But it is true that current disaster costs are still low compared to the muscle of the world economy. Hurricane Katrina caused damage worth 0.1 T$ in 2007—five times the average cost of recent US hurricanes of 0.02 T$—or 1% of the US GDP in that year. Cleanup after the Fukushima disaster could cost twice as much as Katrina and amount to 4% of Japan's GDP in 2011. But the nuclear cleanup cost will be spread over a long period, perhaps twenty years, so the annual charge will be "only" 0.2% of Japan's GDP.

So while these costs are small compared to the world GDP, they are much higher when measured as a percentage of the GDP of the nation in which they occur.

Still, isn't my estimate of an increase in global investment from 24% to 36% of GDP overly dramatic? I think not. My estimate amounts to a 50% increase in the global investment rate. This is exactly what you would need if the average useful lifetime of infrastructure were to fall from 30 to 20 years, shortened by more extreme weather and social unrest. If the average lifetime of a road or building is reduced from 30 to 20 years, the investment rate necessary to maintain stable quality increases by a full 50% (that is, from 1/30 = 3.3% to 1/20 = 5% per year). If normal replacement investment was 24% of GDP, the new higher rate of destruction would lift replacement investment to 36% of GDP. These are huge hikes, and difficult to grasp, until one starts considering the cost of moving megacities and transporting infrastructure to safer grounds. One would need to pay for new settlements, stronger buildings, better air-conditioning, higher dikes, and flood-proof highways. And if one succeeds in making a climate-proof, green oasis in a world otherwise cursed by heat waves and floods, what additional military expenditure will be necessary to keep the oasis safe?

In sum, many future developments will carry a cost tag in the order of several percent of world GDP. The sum could easily exceed 10% in the long run in a badly handled future. And that is what I expect will happen. Not because it is unavoidable, but because slow decision making will expose us to damage before we obtain the answer from delayed investments in new solutions.

The State Will Get More Involved

So, if we need to increase society's investment rate from its traditional value of 24%, by a voluntary 6% extra investment to avoid future unsustainability and a forced 6% extra investment to repair damage from climate change and social unrest, where will the money come from, particularly if these increases include, as they do, expenditures on higher operational costs, extra education, extra research, and extra defense?

Society may try to finance such investment hikes by reduction in traditional investment programs, in order to avoid a fall in consumption. Or society may be in the lucky situation of having unemployed people and equipment suitable for the job, and hence be capable of increasing investments without reducing consumption. This was one of the ambitions of the "green stimulus packages" after the downturn in 2008, which were in the order of 1% of the national GDP. As an example, China decided to shove 0.3 T$ into "green low-carbon economy" in its 2011–16 five-year plan. This amounted to 3% of the Chinese GDP.

But if the investment hike is too urgent or too big, neither method will suffice. Society will have to move people and equipment from the production of consumer goods and services to investments. This can be achieved through increased taxation that collects the funds necessary to initiate and complete the extra investment activity. The same tax increase simultaneously reduces the demand for consumer goods and frees people from working in the companies that formerly supplied the consumer goods. The macro effect is simply to increase the share of the total economy that is engaged in the production of investment goods and services. Importantly, the number of jobs is not affected, only the after-tax disposable income. The jobs simply move from one sector to another.

Experience shows that it is hard for democratic, free-market economies to make proactive decisions to increase voluntary investments before they are unavoidable. It is much simpler after crisis has struck and there is an externally imposed threat of destroyed infrastructure and livelihoods. The situation is a little better in more socialist, higher-tax regimes, where the pattern of investment is more heavily influenced by the state. More authoritarian, state-capitalist societies are capable of the most rapid response—but run the risk of moving in the wrong direction.

This picture won't change fast, because there is an important ideological difference between private and public activity. In the eyes of the free-market liberal, government spending is inferior to private spending, simply because a big government is less attractive than a small government. And the ideal of the free market is well established in the ruling belief system in the current West. Like any other deeply held value, this ideal won't fade away easily. For many, the distinction between private and public investment will remain important, even in the face of crisis, and worth fighting for. As a consequence, the free-market ideal will survive much longer than one should think, even during the coming decades when society will be increasingly facing challenges that can't be solved by the unaided market.

The stability of deeply held values simplifies my task of forecasting. I base my forecast on the belief that there will be only very slow decline in the widespread resistance to the idea of a bigger state (read: higher taxation). This means that solutions will come on line much later than optimal—at least in those parts of the world where the majority favors the market. Collective solutions will not be used until it is overabundantly clear that private solutions (based on individual initiatives in an unrestrained market) will not suffice.

"Glimpse 4-2: Light Green Growth" describes how the OECD has looked at the cost to society of reducing climate gas emissions enough to keep temperature increase below plus 2°C. The OECD expects the cost to be some 4% of world GDP, and the author, a former deputy director general of the OECD, doubts that the world (read: voters and politicians) will choose to incur this cost up front. As a consequence he foresees a partly unresolved climate problem and higher temperatures. But the glimpse also foresees a future where there will indeed be some well-organized forward-looking economies that do decide to green their economies up front, in spite of the cost, and shift to activities that contribute to less depletion and pollution.

GLIMPSE 4-2

Light Green Growth

Thorvald Moe

Historically, economic growth has increased both consumption levels and the loads on the environment. The question now is whether consumption growth can continue while we reduce the human ecological footprint. And, especially, while we dramatically curtail climate gas emissions.

Today, in the framework of sustainable development, some argue that continued growth in GDP may be compatible with avoiding an environmental disaster. A recent example of this rather optimistic way of thinking appears in a report from the OECD.[18]

A green growth strategy is centered on mutually reinforcing aspects of economic and environmental policies. It takes into account the full value of natural capital as a factor of production and its role in growth. It focuses on cost-effective ways of attenuating environmental pressures to affect a transition toward new patterns of growth that will avoid crossing critical local, regional, and global environmental thresholds.

So, if this report proves true, good policies could save us from crossing "critical environmental thresholds" before 2052, even if we continue our quest for increased consumption. Yet is that likely?

The Climate Challenge

After the Rio conference in 1992, climate change gained prominence as one of the most important future threats to economic development and human welfare—the most critical environmental threshold, so to speak.

Since then numerous economic models have been developed to study the interaction between economic developments and emissions of greenhouse gases (GHG) under alternative assumptions. Among them are two alternative scenarios presented by the OECD and based on one of their economic forecasting models.[19]

One scenario, which charts business as usual, assumes no new climate mitigation policies over and above those already in place in 2010. With such assumptions, CO_2 concentrations would increase to about 525 ppm and overall greenhouse gas concentrations to 650 ppm CO_2 equivalents in 2052. The concentration would continue to rise thereafter, causing average temperature to increase by much more than 2°C by 2052, by at least 4° to 6°C by 2100, and more in following decades.

The other scenario assumes a binding global climate agreement that limits warming to plus 2°C over preindustrial levels. The scenario assumes this cap will be achieved in a cost-effective way, through global pricing of carbon and by other policy measures. According to OECD's calculations, the economic costs would be relatively modest. For instance, stabilizing long-run CO_2 concentrations at about 450 ppm[20] in 2052 would reduce world GDP by 4% relative to the business-as-usual scenario, which assumes no further agreement on climate policy.

But this cost should be seen in its proper perspective. The OECD expects world GDP to rise by more than 250% over the same period. But it still amounts to a reduction of the total pie by 4%, and in order to achieve this restructuring of the economy the price of CO_2 emissions must be increased tenfold: from less than 30 dollars per tonne of CO_2 in 2008 to around 280 in 2050.

My Scenario: Green Growth with Further Warming

My educated guess is that neither of these two scenarios will actually happen over the next forty years. We will get further growth, some shift toward a greener (less climate-intensive) economy, but not enough to cut emissions enough to get the world on a path toward plus 2°C.

A number of countries will certainly agree to and implement a number of policy measures. In the developed—and perhaps in part of the emerging economies these measures will lead to some decou pling of greenhouse gas emissions from GDP growth. In other words, the greenhouse gas intensity of GDP growth will decline—through technological change and gradual restructuring of the economies as they mature (and develop away from "dirty" industries toward services). This is already happening in a number of developed econo-mies. The result will be greener growth, with lower energy use and lower greenhouse gas emissions per unit of GDP. But absolute global energy use and absolute greenhouse gas emissions will continue to rise, so that the 2°C target is likely to be overshot by 2052.

Global negotiations to agree on coordinated climate gas reductions have been conducted under the auspices of the UN since 1992. So far relatively little has been achieved, and I do not expect much to happen soon. There are legal obligations to reach limited cut targets by 2012 through the Kyoto protocol. But there is not yet any agreement beyond 2012. The political system in the United States does not seem to be able to deliver a consensus on climate policies for a long time to come, and the US economy is presently characterized by weak growth and high levels of debt and unemployment. A number of European economies are in even deeper problems in the wake of the global financial crisis in 2008. GDP in China and India and other emerging economies may, on the other hand, grow by two-digit numbers for another couple of decades. This is good for poverty alleviation but will contribute to increasing global energy use and greenhouse gas emissions—despite ambitious plans for energy saving in these countries.

So although a climate agreement would be relatively cheap, and although it would be rational to implement a reasonably cost-effective global-climate agreement, my educated guess is that the global political system will not achieve such an agreement in the near future. We will muddle through, following a "light green" growth path toward 2052. The costs and benefits of this development will be unevenly distributed across countries.

Growth will become greener with relative, but not absolute, decoupling of energy use and greenhouse gas emissions from GDP in many countries. The jury is out on whether such a development path over the next forty years will prevent us from "crossing critical local, regional and global environmental thresholds," as the OECD green-growth report suggested.

Some well-functioning developed countries will further integrate sustainable development and climate policies in their long-term economic strategies and successfully develop low-carbon economies with high employment. A number of developing countries, on the other hand, will experience increasing problems as they try to sustain economic development and reduce poverty in the face of temperature increases and other environmental problems such as water scarcity, rising energy costs, and damage to ecological productivity.

Globally, the balance of economic and political power will continue to change toward the big emerging economies, notably China. Only a sudden and highly visible resource collapse or climate crisis will be able to kick the public and key politicians into believing in the need for strong action. This could lead to an ambitious and binding global climate agreement under the auspices of G-20 countries. But I remain doubtful that action will be soon or strong enough. As energy expert David Victor says, "Even with diligent efforts greenhouse gases will accumulate, the planet will warm, and climate will change."[21]

Thorvald Moe (Norwegian, born 1939) has a PhD in economics from Stanford University. He worked for almost forty years in the Norwegian Ministry of Finance as director general, chief economist, and deputy permanent secretary. He has been Norwegian ambassador (1986–89) and deputy secretary general (1998–2002) to the OECD in Paris.

I share the view expressed in "Light Green Growth." Most nations will not choose to spend 4% of GDP up front to avoid future climate damage. As a consequence we will see only a lightly greened economy. We will get a world that spends more on reducing the "bads" of climate change, making higher investments in reduction of greenhouse gas emissions and low-carbon energy. But we will not see a world that spends enough at an early point in time to eliminate the climate problem. And even this limited increase in investment expenditure will reduce the funds available for consumption.

Consumption Will Stagnate—and Fall in Some Places

My forecast is that investment expenditure will increase everywhere over the next forty years. The impact will vary tremendously among regions, but the impact on consumption will always be in the negative direction. The blow to consumption will be worst in the slowly growing, mature economies. And particularly in economies where there is a tradition of low investment rates—such as in the United States.

The United States must create room in its economy for gross (internally financed) investment of perhaps one-third of the GDP if the country is going to be able to handle future challenges. This should be compared to the traditional investment share of some 15% of the GDP. Even if the United States were to grow at 2% per year on a per capita basis—which I don't think it will—and all the growth was concentrated in the investment sector, it would take eight years to lift the investment fraction from 19% to 36%, if consumption remained fixed. My forecast is that the United States will be forced to move in that direction and, as a result, experience a long period of stagnant or declining consumption. For many Americans it will be a repetition of the recent experience of many US blue-collar workers who have not received a real wage increase over the last generation, and whose hopes for their children have fallen below their own hopes thirty years ago.

But back to the global level. Future consumption is easily calculated as future production less future investment. The result is illustrated in figure 4-5, which shows that global consumption will grow toward stagnation in the 2040s and begin to fall around 2050.

However, what matters for the average global citizen is his own consumption level, not the total consumption. His interest is in the annual availability of consumer goods and services *per person*: in how much there will be for him of everything from automobiles and public transportation to health care and concert performances; in what will be available for individual consumption,

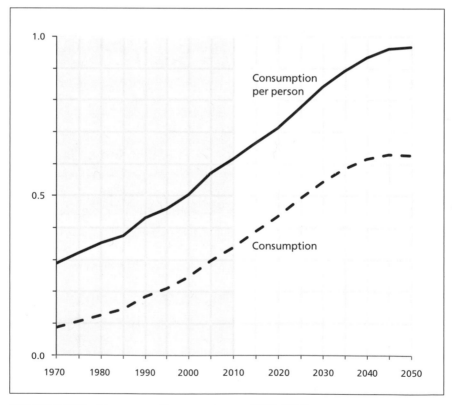

FIGURE 4-5 World consumption per person, 1970–2050.
Scale: Consumption per person ($0–$12,000 per person-year); consumption ($0–$150 trillion per year)

irrespective of whether it comes from private or public suppliers, and irrespective of whether it comes from the formal, monetized economy or is supplied by the family with no salary payments involved. Will it grow? Will it fall?

In other words: How will average consumption per global citizen develop over the next forty years? This simple question brings us straight into one of the most common confusions in the public debate on economics. This is the failure to distinguish between consumption *per person* and consumption *per country*. I focus on the former, because that is what matters directly for your life satisfaction. There is of course the indirect effect from the growth of the total economy: if it grows faster, it may be simpler for you to get a job. But still I think you ought to focus on per capita consumption, not the total.

And you need to understand that developments at the national and the individual level are distinct and should not be confused, as many do when pondering the fate of Japan over the last couple of decades. Most informed people "know" that Japan has done badly since "its peak" around 1990. They know that the CDP has grown slowly and believe that Japanese have become worse off during these twenty years. They are right on the first score: Japan's GDP grew by a meager 14% from 1990 to 2010, measured in inflation-adjusted money. But during the same time, consumption grew by 30% because the investment rate fell to a lower level more suitable for a slowly growing economy. And since the population was more or less stable (it grew by only 3%), consumption per person in Japan grew by a full 33% from 1990 to 2010. This is a high growth rate, and obtained because a slow-growing GDP was shared by an even slower-growing population. As a result, the average Japanese person is significantly richer today than in 1990, in spite of having lived for two decades in a stagnant economy. The current income per person is high, which in turn explains the explosion of labor cost in Japanese industry (and the yen). But it all happened without significant growth in the Japanese economy,[22] and below the radars of many analysts and commentators.

The case of Japan illustrates the fact that most media debates, political analyses, and news from the financial community focus on the national level, on total GDP. This is understandable. If one wants to estimate tax revenue over the next several years, it is best to look at the total economy, since taxes tend to follow total taxable income. If one wants to avoid inflationary pressure in the economy, it is also best to look at the total economy, since the remedy is to adjust total production to the productive capacity of the nation. And even investors are more interested in totals than in per capita figures, because the totals say more about how fast the market for the investors' companies will grow. Total GDP is most relevant for future share values.

But given my focus on your level of satisfaction in the future, it is more relevant to study per capita figures, and particularly to forecast consumption *per person*. The math is simple. If the population grows faster than total consumption, consumption per person will decline. You will be less well off. On the contrary, if the population grows slower than total consumption, consumption per person will rise. You will be better off. However, the important fact to note is that consumption per person will rise even when both population and consumption decline—as long as the population declines faster than consumption.

Figure 4-5 shows the result when I divide future consumption by future population. Consumption per capita will continue to grow from 2010 to 2050, but at a steadily slower rate. As you may remember from figure 4-1 (page 63), the world population will reach a flat peak in the early 2040s and by 2052 will be in slow decline. Global consumption will follow the same pattern, but with its peak slightly later. As a mathematical result, consumption per person will continue to rise, albeit slowly, even after 2050—because population falls faster than consumption.

Slowdown in the growth of global *average* per capita consumption will mean very different things in the five regions of the world. It will mean decline in per capita consumption in the mature and slow-growing economies of the world (like the United States and Europe) and rapid rise in the fast-growing parts of the world (like China, later followed by many big emerging economies). Many poor countries will remain in poverty, at the low levels of per capita consumption.

Still, the tendency to boost disposable income through population decline may accelerate during the second half of the twenty-first century, as discussed in the "Grocline—A Benefit from Population Decline" sidebar on page 97.

"Grocline" is a long-term possibility. It could bring us back to a sustainable planet. It could slim the human footprint until it fits within the carrying capacity of the planet. Grocline would be politically feasible because per capita disposable income would grow while the pie shrinks.

But I am afraid that grocline will arrive too late. Before contraction sets in, humanity will have emitted enough greenhouse gases from its energy production and use that the planet will be on its way toward runaway climate change in the last third of the twenty-first century.

Grocline—A Benefit from Population Decline

In the decades after the end of my forecast period, after 2052, average consumption per person will start to grow again. Not because of growth in total consumption, but because the global population will be in decline. So even if humanity at that time will do no better than to maintain total consumption at a stable level, the amount of goods and services available to each individual will be increasing. The situation will be an accentuation of the situation in Japan in the 1990s and 2000s: stagnant economy, falling population, and rising per capita income. Much to its own surprise, the world will discover that slow growth in total consumption no longer causes as much hardship and tension as during recent decades. Because when the population declines, there is more for everyone.

I do not say, however, that this epoch of declining GDP and population will be without its problems. After 2060, the rise in per capita consumption will take place in a world that is badly damaged by climate change and where biodiversity is squeezed into protected corners of the world. And there will be the tension from great regional disparities, with some nations living in relative luxury and others in deep poverty.

Later on—in the last third of the twenty-first century—I believe the world economy will have entered into an era where the combination of individual growth and societal decline has become the norm. Per capita consumption will be growing year by year, just as in the good old days. And at the same time the total economy—the GDP—will be in constant decline. This could be called "grocline"— simultaneous growth and decline. The grocline world is one where the individual situation improves while the total pie shrinks. It's good and bad at the same time—decade after decade.

This is confusing to minds accustomed to growth. Let me use a simple numerical example to explain what grocline will be like. Assume a population that is declining at 1.5% per year. Assume that the workforce is declining at the same rate. Assume furthermore that labor productivity is growing by 1% per year. This could perhaps be achieved in the long run through continuing fine-tuning of the postindustrial economy—for example, using robots to improve the flow of services and care per hour of human effort.

The result would be an annual *decline* in total production of 0.5%.[23] Total GDP would be half a percentage point lower every year. But production per person would still grow annually by 1% per year, since that is the rate of productivity growth. Every person would be better off, year by year, in spite of continuing decline in the total economy.

CHAPTER 5

Energy and CO$_2$ to 2052

The next two factors to consider in my global forecast are energy use and CO$_2$ levels. In broad terms, about 87% of today's global energy use is supplied by the three fossil fuels: coal, oil, and gas. They are the cheapest sources for electricity, heat, and transportation fuels. Of the remaining energy use, 5% comes from nuclear energy and 8% from renewable sources.[1] The renewable sources are biomass (providing much of the heating in developing countries), hydropower (providing much of the electricity where rivers exist), and finally the small but quickly growing supply of electricity from wind and solar panels.

Energy Efficiency Will Continue to Rise

We can expect—with a few caveats—that energy use will rise with the level of economic activity, that CO$_2$ will be emitted (largely[2]) in proportion to the use of fossil energy, and that the concentration of CO$_2$ in the atmosphere will rise and push up the average temperature.

At the outset it is important to remind ourselves that there is enough coal to sustain current human energy-usage rates for hundreds of years, a great deal of gas (particularly shale gas), and roughly one-half of all oil still left in the ground. In conclusion, there is more than enough energy available to keep the world running way beyond 2052.

But not at current cost. The remaining fossil resources are increasingly inaccessible—deeper down, in smaller fields, further to the north, in less friendly nations—and this will contribute to higher production costs. Another major challenge is the fact that the remaining fossil sources contain five times as much carbon as can be burned if the global temperature is to remain below plus 2°C relative to preindustrial times.[3] I believe that this fact sooner or later will dawn on people and lead to an accelerated effort to shift out of fossil energy—perhaps through the introduction of an extra fee (carbon tax or emissions quota cost) on fossil energy. But I am not optimistic about how fast this will happen. As you will see from my forecast, I expect the world to progress more or less at the same rate as over the last forty years.

The cost of fossil energy will go up, but not as high as many fear—or hope—and only for limited periods (say a decade). The reason is that there exist vast reserves of backstop technologies. For example, one can make synthetic oil from coal at USD 70 per barrel. Thus there is little reason to think that the price of conventional oil will remain high above USD 70 for decades. Recently we have seen the rather sudden advent of great volumes of cheap shale gas in the United States. This gas can be produced at a cost of some $3 per million BTU,[4] which is one-half the cost of gas in Europe, and one-quarter of the exorbitant gas prices in the United States in 2005 and 2008. It is true that these unconventional sources are less climate-friendly than conventional oil and gas, and that sooner or later they will be charged with quota costs. But once more I think this will take time. Fossil fuels will not be replaced by renewables at scale before the cost of climate-friendly energy has been lowered through technological advance and experience. As you will see from my forecast, even in 2052 more than one-half of world energy use will be from fossil sources.

But let me return to forecasting how much energy will be needed to drive the global economy in the future. It should not surprise anyone that total energy use will grow. Much of the historical growth in labor productivity and GDP was made possible through increased use of energy. Industrial man used ever more electricity to run his machinery and cool his southern homes, ever more heat to cook his food and warm his northern homes, ever more fuel to move his cars and trucks and to transport his raw material and finished goods without much human effort. Growth in GDP was growth in energy use. But not in total proportion. GDP grew faster than energy use over the last forty years. In fact, the energy used to produce one dollar's worth of GDP fell by some 40% from 1970 to 2010, as shown in figure 5-1.

I expect that this decline will continue at nearly the same rate in the future, and that we will get another reduction of one-third in energy intensity over the next forty years. The decline will be caused by the economic incentive to save energy, and by the continuing shift from physical production to less energy-intensive production of services and care, which will reduce the need for energy to drive the economy. The downward trend will continue, supported by the fact that it is both technically feasible and desirable from a climate point of view. Regional statistics will show surprising declines as physical production is moved from the OECD to China and other emerging economies, but these shifts will not influence the global numbers.

Energy intensity is measured as the number of tonnes of oil equivalents that are necessary to produce GDP worth $1 million. This number was 180 tonnes of oil equivalents per $1 million in 2010. That figure becomes much

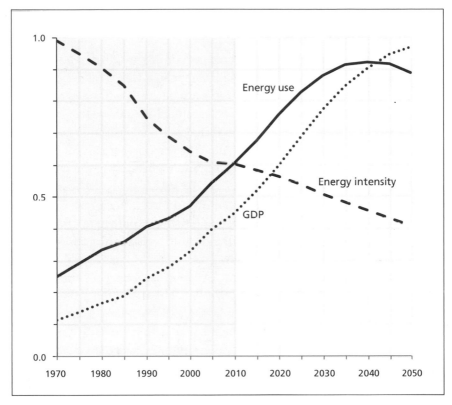

FIGURE 5-1 World energy use, 1970–2050.
Definition: Energy intensity = energy use divided by GDP.
Scale: Energy use (0–20 billion tonnes of oil equivalents per year); GDP ($0–$150 trillion per year); energy use per GDP (0–300 tonnes of oil equivalents per $1 million).

more understandable, and totally amazing, when you convert it to the number of kilograms of oil that are required in order to produce one dollar's worth of goods and services. The answer is 0.18—or for those of you who use US units, more than six ounces of oil for each dollar of GDP. We currently use a big milk glass of oil to produce something that sells for a dollar!

Energy is already so costly that it pays to reduce its use in many situations. If energy prices increase in real terms, the incentive to use less will become stronger. Political action, too, could drive costs up and usage down, but this is unlikely to occur. It seems most likely that popular opposition to tax hikes on energy will remain and make it difficult to raise energy prices enough to dent current usage. This is one of the reasons why I do not expect that we will see much more than normal progress on the energy efficiency front. Another reason is that if efficiency actually did increase significantly, that would reduce total energy demand and thus lower energy prices; that in turn would boost demand, all else being equal.

So, the 30% reduction in energy intensity I project by 2052 is more or less a surprise-free extension of history following the first OPEC oil-price hikes in the 1970s. A 30% increase in efficiency is not much. It is what you will easily achieve over some decades if you start paying attention to the fuel efficiency of your car, the insulation in your walls and windows, the localization and layout of your manufacturing plant, and the fuel consumption per passenger seat in your aircraft—and insist that you make improvements only at the end of the useful life of your asset.

In an ideal world with strong incentives in place, much faster progress would be achieved. It is interesting to note that the European Union (EU) formally decided in 2009—in its famous 20/20/20 legislation—to increase the energy efficiency of the EU by 20% by 2020; and that China, in the run-up to the Copenhagen climate meeting in 2009, promised to reduce the energy intensity of its economy by 40% by 2020. I hope that ambitions like these— proposed by well-meaning semi-authoritarian bodies like the EU Commission and the Communist Party of China—will dominate over the next forty years, but I do not believe so. I doubt that the necessary extra incentives (read: carbon tax or quota price) will be agreed to by the democracies involved. As a result, we will see progress more or less at the same speed as during the last genera-tion—let us call it "progress as usual."

There will be regional differences because of different starting points and because efficiency will grow faster in economies that are catching up than in countries that arc leading the way. The leaders will have to develop the energy-efficient solutions as they go along, while the followers are free to copy. Some of the efficiency increase will be paid for by the extra investments—forced and voluntary—that will arise over the years ahead.

Energy Use Will Grow, but Not Forever

I calculate future energy use by multiplying future GDP with future energy intensity.

Since I expect the global economy to grow by a factor of two before 2052, and energy intensity to fall by a third, my forecasted energy use in 2052 is higher than today's. As shown in figure 5-1 (page 101), energy use will grow by 50% from 2012 to 2052. But more interesting and surprising is the fact that global energy use will reach a peak in the 2030s and then start a slow decline.

The direct reason is that energy efficiency will grow faster than GDP. This does not mean that everyone will receive all the energy they need for decent life in the 2040s. But it does mean that demand will start a slow decline even though the world still will hold two to three billion people who can't afford to buy a reasonable amount of energy.

My forecast is below the IEA's business-as-usual scenario from 2010, which expects a doubling of energy use by 2050.[5] And it is way below IPCC's A1FI scenario from 2000, which expects *more* than a doubling of global energy use by 2050.[6] But my forecast for 2052 is only slightly higher than the energy use in the IEA's 450 ppm scenario, which shows what needs to happen if global average temperature is to be kept below plus 2°C. The difference is that my forecast is not a straight line from here to 2052. My forecast goes through an initial period of rapid growth before it peaks in 2030 and then declines toward 2052. Thus the accumulated energy use is much higher than in the IEA 450 ppm scenario. It is fair to say that my energy forecast to 2052 is lower than conventional thinking in the energy industry, but above what it will take to solve the climate problem.

This peak and decline is a logical consequence of my low forecast of world GDP (as a consequence in turn of lower population growth and declining productivity growth caused by problems with resources, inequity, and the climate) and my forecast of continued advance in energy efficiency. The combined effect is much lower demand for energy in the future than is normally expected. Few commentators seem to expect that global energy use will peak and decline during their lifetimes. But the signals are there for those who want to see them. For example, household electricity consumption in Norway has been declining over the last decade, in spite of rapid population growth and rapid growth in real disposable income. This is largely due to better home insulation and the use of electric heat pumps—in other words, increased efficiency.

Although global energy use will peak and decline in most of the world, it will not do so in the poorest areas. We will experience a shift of the world's energy use from the current rich industrialized countries toward the poor countries. China will be in a middle position; its energy use will peak in the 2040s.

Climate Intensity Will Be Reduced by Renewables

If humanity chooses to continue to rely on fossil coal, oil, and gas in the traditional blend, CO_2 emissions from energy production will grow by 50% by 2052. This would place the world on an emissions path that would lead to more than plus 2°C warming by 2052, and much more after that. Luckily I don't think this will happen. Instead we will continue our effort to reduce the climate intensity of our energy use.

Climate intensity will decline as a result of a continuing shift in the composition of the energy supply, as shown in figure 5-2. The use of coal, oil, and gas has grown significantly since 1970, but since 2000 the use of oil has started to level off, and I expect it to peak before 2025 and then decline. The use of oil in 2050 will be back to the level of 1980. Notice that this category includes not only conventional oil but all forms of unconventional oil, except biofuel (which is classified as renewable energy). The use of *conventional* oil probably has already peaked, as shown in figure 2-1 on page 21. I also expect peaks in both coal and gas use before 2040, as a consequence of slow growth in total energy use, but primarily because of very rapid increase in the use of renewable energy during the next forty years.

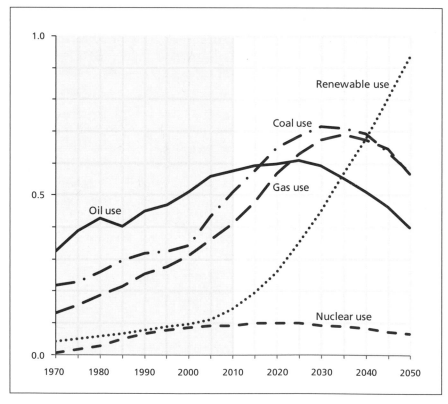

FIGURE 5-2 World use of different energy types, 1970–2050.
Scale: Energy uses (0–7 billion tonnes of oil equivalents per year).

The shift toward lower climate intensity (the amount of greenhouse gases emitted per unit of energy used) has been going on for a long time already. The climate intensity has fallen from three tonnes of CO_2 per tonnes of oil equivalents of energy use in 1970 to 2.7 tonnes in 2010. But this is a fall of just 10% in forty years, as can be seen from figure 5-3 on page 115.

The reduction in the climate intensity has been slow, even during the years leading up to 2008 when climate was central on the political agenda. I do believe, though, that the push for a low-carbon energy future will continue, and with increasing vigor after 2030, when the climate damage will be more visible and once more emerge as a political driver. Global society will accelerate the conversion from coal, oil, and gas to less CO_2-intensive energy sources like solar, wind, hydro, nuclear, biomass, plus gas, and possibly coal, with carbon capture and storage (CCS). Initially, this will happen because it's technically feasible and not very expensive, and later on, because there will be increasingly widespread worry about the consequences of unmitigated climate change.

I expect that the world's consumption of fossil fuels will be in steep decline by 2052. The contribution from nuclear will be declining. The real winner will be the new renewables—solar, wind, and biomass—which, along with hydro, will grow from 8% of energy use in 2010 to 37% in 2050. That is a huge increase and an average growth rate of 4% per year, which is, however, much below what we see in the wind and solar field these days.

The shift toward renewables will be slowed by the existence of a cheap intermediary solution, namely, replacing coal with gas. Changing the fuel from coal to gas in a power station reduces the amount of CO_2 emitted per unit of electricity by two-thirds, and it is a big step toward a lower-carbon future. But gas is not an ultimate solution: a world running on gas would still be emitting too much CO_2 and also facing an eventual depletion of the world's gas reserves. In this sense, shifting from coal to gas serves to postpone the ultimate solution. But the proponents in the fossil-energy industry will rightfully argue that "fuel shifting" from coal to gas does reduce emissions fast and is a practical and reasonably cheap solution in the short term. And they will be listened to. One additional reason is that gas-powered utilities are flexible and can serve as backup sources for power from future wind farms and solar installations, when the wind does not blow or the sun does not shine.

In a strictly rational world with a long time horizon, people would have aimed directly for the ultimate energy solution, which is the sun (directly as heat or power, or indirectly as wind, hydro, or biomass). The sun shines thousands of times more energy on planet Earth than we will ever use. Furthermore, the sun is a decentralized source that gives the user local control over his or her own energy supply. But we do not live in a rational world, with long planning horizons. We live, and will live, in a world dominated by short-term thinking and profit maximization. As a result, I believe world society will make a big swing to an era of gas, where fossil gas will be used much more extensively than in a strictly rational world. My forecast is supported by the recent upsurge in the use of shale gas in the United States, especially since shale gas seems to be available in all large energy-consuming regions.

In spite of this detour, the fundamental solution is on its way. The shift from the fossil to the solar age has started. Since 2005, the boom in wind and solar capacity has begun to add measurably to the renewable capacity of the world. This trend will accelerate: the technologies are well known, and the effort to lower the costs of windmills and solar panels is in full swing. The amazing success in the effort to reduce the cost of photovoltaic panels over the last forty years was shown in figure 2-2 on page 22. Much of the future voluntary extra investment will go in this direction.

The cost-reduction process in solar energy pertains to both solar power and solar heating. No fundamental technological barriers are yet in sight. The only obstacle is cost, which needs to come down to parity with coal or gas power. And this is happening, as explained in "Glimpse 5-1: The Road to PV."

GLIMPSE 5-1

The Road to PV

Terje Osmundsen

As we enter 2012, the prospect for renewable energy looks gloomier than it did a year ago. Particularly in Europe, the financial crisis has led to radical cuts in incentives and targets for renewables.

In the United States, and other markets, electricity prices are stagnating or even declining, not least due to abundant supply from the newborn shale-gas industry. The prospects for a global climate deal that could trigger the required investments in green energy seem depressingly far away. It is not surprising, therefore, that shares in clean-tech companies have dropped more than in any other industry sector over the last eighteen months.

But there are other signs of change. Despite the economic crisis, new solar capacity around the world increased by a staggering 54% to about 28 GW of installed capacity. Solar investment touched $140 billion during the year, up 36% relative to the year before. The misfortune of numerous equipment suppliers didn't deter the global oil company Total from entering the photovoltaic (PV) industry via the acquisition of SunPower and two other companies. And from Beijing, news came that China will follow the example of Germany and introduce a guaranteed tariff for solar PV to support its goal of installing 50 GW by 2020. Where is this heading?

From Nuclear to Gas?

The most important long-term trend shaping electricity generation is the urgent need to decarbonize the sector. This is taking place slowly, but irreversibly, despite the fact that coal appears to be the winner in the medium term: close to 40% of all new power-generation capacity under construction or planning in the period up to 2016 is coal-fired.

Pre-Fukushima, conventional wisdom had it that nuclear was the only low-carbon source that could be a real alternative to coal. Today, the outlook for nuclear looks grim. I predict that the majority of current plans to add nuclear capacity in the coming years will not materialize—particularly because a utility burning shale gas will be much cheaper. The projected costs of new nuclear plants have regularly been revised upward and will most likely be upped again to meet new safety regulations post-Fukushima. Already today, in the southern parts of the United States, developers are offering solar PV power at a lower cost than the calculated generation cost of a new nuclear plant.

There are many reasons to applaud a gradual phaseout of nuclear, but it does make fighting climate change even harder. How much harder depends on the outcome of the looming battle between coal and natural gas. One year ago, it looked like only coal was abundant and cheap enough to replace nuclear. But with the recent discovery of shale gas resources, many parts of the world will have an abundant supply of natural gas for several decades to come; the faster the shift from coal to gas, the better for the climate.

There will be regional differences. In Europe, North America, and Japan, stiffer regulations and the rising cost of carbon combined with competitive available gas will tempt most utilities to switch to gas. In emerging markets like China, India, and South Africa, coal-fired power generation will most likely remain the utilities' preferred choice to 2020. But even here there will be a gradual switch toward gas.

What are the implications for renewable energy? In the next five to ten years, I am afraid the natural-gas revolution combined with the deep financial crisis in the "old world" will lead to reduced support for renewable energy, particularly in countries with significant gas resources.

But in the medium and long term, the rise of gas will be good news for renewables, mainly because gas fits better with the intermittent power from wind and solar. Gas-fired power-generation plants can relatively easily be turned up and down, when there is need to supplement the variable flow of electricity from solar and wind plants. We will see numerous "hybrid" solar/gas or wind/gas power plants, offering continuous power to the network. This will be the case even if the current controversies around shale gas fracking will limit somewhat the new supply of unconventional gas.

As a result of these trends, the share of renewables in the world's electricity mix will grow from less than 20% in 2010 to more than 30% in 2030, equivalent to more than a doubling of electricity produced. Initially hydro and wind will be the biggest contributors of green power, but beyond 2025–30 solar PV will take the lead and become the principal source of electricity generation by 2050.

This transformation will be driven by dwindling costs and subsiding investment risk.

Dwindling Costs

The cost of electricity from PV has continued to fall by more than 10% per year. This impressive performance is illustrated in figure 2-2 on page 22. With every doubling of PV capacity, the cost of PV panels falls by 20%. There are two drivers to this rule of thumb: the cost of manufacturing the panels is declining, and the efficiency of each panel is increasing. Much R&D money is being spent on increasing efficiencies and learning curves in capturing solar energy, and advances could reduce the cost of solar power to one-tenth of current cost. But it will take time. Still I believe that the average investment cost per watt capacity will continue to fall by 5%–10% per year and that average performance of the panels will improve by 3%–4% per decade.

Even at today's prices, utilities can reduce costs by replacing diesel- and oil-generated power with solar PV at peak hours. In sunny regions (solar radiation above 1,700 kWh per square meter per year) the cost of electricity will approach 10 US cents per kWh in 2015, falling to 7–8 cents in 2020. This will make PV competitive with the cost of adding new nuclear, coal, or natural gas[7] capacity in 2020. By 2030, the cost of PV power will have dropped as low as 5 US cents per kWh in major parts of the world, making it cheaper than any other alternative. PV power will then have become the preferred choice for most utilities.

Subsiding Investment Risk

Massive investments are required, however, to reach these cost targets and to grow the industry from 0.1% to 20%–25% of the world's electricity production: more than $10 trillion (= 10 T$) in PV power plants only, according to IEA.[8] Several times more will be needed in the grid extensions and storage solutions needed. This amounts to around 1% of global GDP every year over the next forty years.

In this decade, the required investments will occur only if governments continue to provide support in the form of fixed tariffs, quotas, tax credits, or a real carbon levy on fossil fuels. The higher costs and perceived political risks of investing in PV mean it will remain a daily struggle to attract investors and lenders. But as we approach 2020, things will look different. No longer dependent on government incentives, PV power plants will suddenly look like the low-risk alternative, virtually a "safe haven" for long-term investors: zero technology risk, no fuel costs, no carbon risk, and—not least— the prospect of the amortized PV plant operating at almost no cost for many years beyond the guaranteed twenty-five-year lifetime. When this becomes reality in five to ten years' time, a whole range of cash-rich players will flock to the PV investment market: utilities, energy companies, pension funds, development banks, private investors, infrastructure investors, and energy-consuming industries, among others. Ideas and technology will meet capital, and the world will get disruptive innovation.

Terje Osmundsen (Norwegian, born 1957) is a former state secretary to the prime minister of Norway, with a varied career from international business (natural gas, engineering, telecom) to publishing and scenario-based consulting. Since 2009, he has been senior vice president of Scatec Solar AS, a leading developer and supplier of solar power plants.

I agree with the main message of "The Road to PV." Solar heat and power will be a major contributor to a world that will be 37% renewable in 2052. But there will also be contributions from wind, which is experiencing the same type of cost reductions, and for which current costs are much lower than for solar power. This applies first of all to windmills on land and windmills standing in shallow water, which are being built at scale in Europe. But the real potential, in terms of production volume, is deep offshore windmills on floaters. The deep offshore potential is enormous because of strong winds and huge areas. The North Sea is capable of producing perhaps 10,000 TWh per year of offshore power—enough to run all of Europe if the power could be distributed. But the cost is currently many times higher than that of wind power produced on land.

Renewables will supply the largest share of world energy in 2052. At that time the energy mix will be renewables (37%), coal (23%), gas (22%), oil (15%), and nuclear (2%). The decline of the relative importance of nuclear is described in "Glimpse 5-2: The Death of Nuclear."

GLIMPSE 5-2
The Death of Nuclear

Jonathon Porritt

In 2052, only two countries, France and China, will be generating any electricity from nuclear energy at all—and both will have decided to get out of nuclear altogether by 2065.

I suspect there are few people who subscribe to such a view today. Despite the Fukushima reactor disaster in spring 2011, the prevailing mood in many countries in autumn 2011 remained broadly supportive of some kind of nuclear renaissance.

However, even before Fukushima, this renaissance was not quite all it was made out to be. As energy expert Amory Lovins points out, "There are now 61 nuclear plants 'officially' under construction. However, of those 61 units, 12 have been 'under construction' for over 20 years; 43 have no official start-up date; half are late; 45 are in four centrally planned and untransparent power systems, and not one was a genuinely free-market transaction."[9]

The fact that such a renaissance has been talked up at many different points since the Chernobyl disaster in 1986, without any such renaissance materializing, is neither here nor there. Nuclear hopes never finally fade away, and the fear of accelerating climate change has fanned those hopes into an even brighter incandescence—even among the ranks of some leading environmentalists in the United States and Europe who would once have scorned any idea that a low-carbon future would be built on the back of nuclear energy.

Much of this twenty-first-century pro-nuclear advocacy adopts a "necessary evil" tonality; there's no particular enthusiasm for the technology itself, let alone for the nuclear industry. UK environmentalist George Monbiot sees no contradiction between "falling in love with nuclear" and describing those who work for the nuclear industry as "a bunch of arm-twisting, corner-cutting scumbags."[10]

In 2006 the Sustainable Development Commission sought to advise the UK government on the pros and cons of nuclear power. The pros are clear and important: very low operating costs; reasonable security of fuel supply; and a low-carbon source of electricity compared to fossil fuels.

For the commission, however, the cons substantially outweighed those pros: massive capital costs; no real solution to the problems of nuclear waste and decommissioning; concerns about proliferation and security; and major ethical issues about intergenerational justice (dumping the problems of nuclear on future generations) and "moral hazard," with the industry ruthlessly exploiting governments to bail it out when things go wrong. Which they always do.[11]

The advice was disregarded. The power of the industry within nuclear nations is enormous.

Given that, why might anyone be persuaded that the industry will be on its last legs by 2052? There are three main reasons.

The first is financial. However assiduously the industry works to obscure the true cost of nuclear power, investors understand what's going on. When the UK government pledged not to use any public money to take forward a new generation of nuclear power, investors just laughed. The subsidy-free nuclear reactor simply doesn't exist—anywhere in the world—and unless the level of government subsidy on offer sufficiently and very substantially "de-risks" their own investments, investors simply won't touch it.

Post-Fukushima, that de-risking challenge has become all but insurmountable. Uniquely, the nuclear industry is still exempted from covering the true cost of insuring their power stations—for the self-evident reason that no balance sheet in the world could bear that kind of liability.

To be fair, nuclear enthusiasts understandably argue that the Fukushima reactors were very old, and that today's new reactor designs will perform much more efficiently and much more safely. And, to be fair, they might. But we won't know for many years to come, and deep skepticism is the only intellectually robust response to those claims, given how flawed all such predictions have been over the last few decades.

The second reason why I believe the industry will be all but dead in 2052 is that the contribution it can make to the safe, low-carbon world is vanishingly small. Nuclear power now accounts for about 13% of the world's electricity, and just 5.5% of commercial primary energy. The role of nuclear was already declining before Fukushima, and that decline can only accelerate post-Fukushima. As of March 2011, there were 437 nuclear reactors operating in the world. Since 2008, 9 new reactors came on line, the majority of them in China, and 11 were shut down. The average age of today's nuclear plant is twenty-six years, and the industry was hoping—before Fukushima—to extend reactor lifetime to forty years or more. Post-Fukushima, that will now become much harder.

Here are the facts: we would need to see 260 new reactors coming on line between now and 2025 just to keep pace with the closure program if old reactors are to come off-line at an acceptable age.[12] You would therefore have to be a near-insane optimist to suppose that nuclear power will be contributing anything more than today's 5.5% by 2030, at a massive cost to taxpayers the world over.

Far greater levels of renewable generating capacity could be installed during the same time.

Prioritizing nuclear puts investment in renewables at risk. Ironically, it will substantially worsen the prospects for a low-carbon future by ensuring that fossil fuels will be used to fill the gap for far longer than needs to be the case. That's the "nuclear dream" for you in a nutshell: a very small contribution to our low-carbon energy future, at huge cost and great risk, exacerbating rather than diminishing our dependence on fossil fuels.

And there's one final reason why that nuclear dream will never deliver, and it relates to the vulnerability of nuclear facilities to terrorist attacks. It seems to me to be all but inevitable that there will be some terrorist attack on some nuclear facility somewhere in the world at some time over the next decade. Many security experts are astonished that it hasn't already happened.

The likelihood of this being a cyber attack of some description has been greatly amplified by the "success" of the Israeli and US governments' infiltrating their "Stuxnet worm" into the operating code of Iran's nuclear power system. But just as likely is a physical attack, not necessarily on a reactor itself, but on the "temporary" nuclear-fuel storage facilities sited next to many reactors. The level of protection for these facilities is significantly lower than for the reactors themselves. I can understand why people don't want to talk about this, as the sheer scale of the ensuing horror is hard to imagine. But the truth is that the entire industry is vulnerable to these risks.

So here's how I see it: post-Fukushima, the industry will struggle to make its case. Investors are already spooked by Fukushima and by the industry's continuing and massive cost overruns. When taxpayers realize the combination of threats together with the huge bill they will have to cough up for, the antinuclear movement will gain new momentum. The success of a nonnuclear Germany will persuade many that nuclear isn't even "the least worst option." Relatively few reactors will therefore be built over the next ten to fifteen years, and almost all of them will be in centralist regimes, such as China.

On top of that, imagine at some stage a proven terrorist threat to one of America's or Europe's older nuclear reactors (it doesn't need to be an actual attack; clear proof that such an attack is possible will be quite sufficient), inducing panic around the world. The share value of energy companies with nuclear capacity will fall like a stone—even before the investors manage to get out.

Governments will be compelled either to close down existing reactors immediately or to announce nonnegotiable closure programs, with no new builds ever again on the agenda. Even France and China will be obliged to follow suit. By that stage the arguments in favor of the nonnuclear alternative (driven by massive investments in efficiency, renewables, combined heat and power, and carbon capture and storage installed on all gas and biomass plants) will be overwhelming. End of story. End of nuclear.

Jonathon Porritt (British, born 1950), is founder-director of Forum for the Future (www.forum forthefuture.org), codirector of the Prince of Wales's Business and Sustainability Programme, and a former director of Friends of the Earth and chairman of the Green Party in the UK.

Although I am skeptical that we'll experience a nuclear renaissance, I don't go so far as believing that nuclear will be history by 2052. I think the number of reactors will go down by one-third—to some three hundred—and that the majority of them will be in China and other emerging economies. Since the total energy supply will have increased, this means that the nuclear share will be below 3%, and one-half of today's contribution.

At the other end of the spectrum of success will be renewables, which in 2050 will provide fifteen times as much energy as nuclear. This is a lot, but much less than the 95% viewed as feasible by the World Wide Fund for Nature (WWF).[13] On the other hand, the less radical IEA has renewables covering 14% of energy supply in 2050 in its baseline technology scenario and 38% in its progressive "BLUE map" scenario.[14] In other words, my forecast of 37% in renewables implies that humanity will choose a middle road, doing a lot, but not all that is possible and all that is required to solve the climate problem. I expect spectacular growth in renewables, and a gradual decline in nuclear. The fossils will shift from oil and coal toward gas and be in joint decline in 2052.

I agree that 37% is well below what could have been achieved in a rational world that actively wanted to become low-carbon. But short-termism in democracy and capitalism will limit the extra investment that is necessary for a rapid transition from fossils to renewables. There will be time-consuming opposition against most types of "infrastructure investments" (read: siting of new wind farms, damming of new rivers, harvesting of new forests for bio-mass, establishment of new transmission lines), similar to the even more intense opposition against the siting of new nuclear plants. As a result much of the growth will have to come from wind turbines that are placed offshore and solar panels that are placed invisibly on rooftops or in the desert, supplemented with biomass from special-purpose plantations on land that was already degraded. These obstacles will ensure that the growth in installed capacity is constrained to what it takes to reach 37% by 2052. It will then take another generation or so before the renewable fraction will have risen to its ultimate goal of 100%, through the widespread use of solar energy in its various forms.

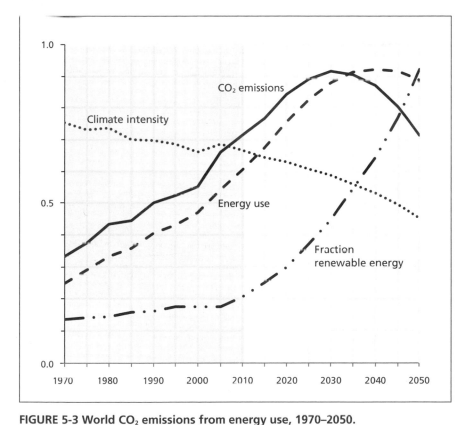

FIGURE 5-3 World CO₂ emissions from energy use, 1970–2050.
Definition: Climate intensity = CO₂ emissions divided by energy use.
Fraction renewable energy=use of renewable energy divided by total energy use.
Scale: CO₂ emissions (0–45 billion tonnes of CO₂ per year); energy use (0–20 billion tonnes of oil equivalents per year); climate intensity (0–4 tonnes of CO₂ per tonnes of oil equivalents); fraction renewable energy (0%–40%).

CO₂ Emissions from Energy Will Peak in 2030

My forecast of future emissions of CO_2 from energy use can be seen in figure 5-3, which shows that the emissions will increase to a peak in 2030 and then decline. This forecast is achieved by multiplying the future use of each energy type (measured in tonnes of oil equivalents of energy used per year) with the average CO_2 emission from the use of that type of energy (measured in tonnes of CO_2 per tonnes of oil equivalents of energy used).[15] My forecast for climate intensity is achieved by dividing these emissions with my forecast of global GDP. The result shows that the climate intensity will fall more over the next forty years (−32%) than over the last forty (−12%).

In chapter 10 you will see that decline in CO_2 emissions will start first in the rich world, around 2015, followed by China in 2030, the big emerging economies in 2040, and finally the rest of the world sometime in the second half of the twenty-first century. Emissions will grow outside the OECD while these countries seek to catch up with the material standards of the industrialized world. The non-OECD emissions will also grow because climate-intensive production will be moved away from the more expensive countries.

In 2052, as per my forecast, world CO_2 emissions from energy use will still be a full 40% above global emissions in 1990. Emissions will be falling year by year, however, and could happen to be identical to today's emissions in 2052. But there is no doubt that the world will have lost its chance to keep global warming below the internationally agreed goal of plus 2°C. This is despite the existence of technologies that could have accelerated the emissions cuts significantly. One of them is carbon capture and geological storage, as described in "The Potential in CCS" sidebar.

The Potential in CCS

It is worth noting that carbon capture and storage (CCS) is capable of reducing the emissions of CO_2 dramatically. By capturing the CO_2 from the exhaust emissions from coal- and gas-fired utilities and other point sources of CO_2, and storing it permanently underground, one can reduce CO_2 emissions from power production and manufacturing by more than 80%.

As usual the problem is cost—and psychology. People seem to have concluded that CCS is impossibly expensive—and also fear potential leakage from underground storage—in spite of the expert view negating both. It therefore appears unlikely that CCS will be used aggressively, at least during the next decade or two. But it is also worth noting that the IEA is suggesting the use of CCS to remove a full eight billion tonnes of CO_2 per year in 2050 in its New Policies scenario. That would require between four thousand and eight thousand big CCS plants.

So although I would have wished for larger use, I believe that we will see only one thousand CCS plants in 2052, capturing perhaps one billion tonnes of CO_2 per year. In the longer run I believe in a bigger role for CCS in the fight against climate change. It will be used to remove CO_2 from the atmosphere and stick it back into the ground, closing the carbon loop. This will happen in wood-fired power stations with CCS.

There are few other methods available to actively remove CO_2 from the atmosphere. In wood-fired power stations, it works as follows: When wood (or any other type of biomass) grows, it sucks CO_2 from the atmosphere and converts it into plant material. When the material is burnt, the CO_2 is released into the exhaust gas. When the exhaust is sent through a CCS plant, the CO_2 is captured. It is then compressed into a liquid and injected into deep underground reservoirs. In this way a power station fueled with biomass and equipped with CCS will move CO_2 from the atmosphere and back into the ground, generating electricity in the process.

In my forecast, in 2052 the use of fossil energy will still generate nine billion tonnes of CO_2 per year, more or less the same as today. If one-quarter of these fossil-fired power plants were retrofitted with CCS, reducing their emissions by 80%, global emissions would fall by some two billion tonnes of CO_2, or 20%. This would require two thousand big CCS plants. The cost would be around $1 billion per retrofit (my estimate), so the total investment cost would be $2 trillion (2 T$), or 1% of the world GDP in 2052, which is really not much, and why I believe CCS will be a part of the long-term future.

But in the next forty years, CCS will have a limited role in reducing CO_2 emissions, dwarfed by increases in energy efficiency and renewables.

Temperature Increase Will Exceed Plus 2°C

The curve for CO_2 emissions from energy use in figure 5-3 on page 115 represents the essence of my forecast on the climate front. It is my summary of what humanity will do over the next forty years in increasing the world GDP, decreasing the energy intensity of that GDP, and decreasing the climate intensity of the resulting energy use. The curve does not at all resemble the often-heard recommendation that greenhouse gas emissions must be cut by 50% in 2050, and that the peak in emissions must take place before 2020. My forecast peaks fifteen years too late, and the cut in 2050 is only 0% relative to emissions in 2010. So how will my forecast compare with the internationally agreed goal to keep the CO_2 concentration in the atmosphere so low that the average temperature does not increase by more than 2°C relative to preindustrial times?

Before I give you the exact answer, it is interesting to make some "back of the envelope" calculations to increase your understanding of what challenge we are facing. Scientists have calculated that in order to keep temperature rise below plus 2°C, humanity must keep within a "remaining carbon budget" of some six hundred billion tonnes of CO_2 from energy use. This is the additional amount of CO_2 we can send into the atmosphere from fossil fuels without exceeding the 2°C goal. Six hundred billion tonnes is less than one-third of our accumulated CO_2 emissions since we began using fossil fuels in the 1700s.

In 2010 humans emitted thirty-two billion tonnes of CO_2 per year from energy use. So this could continue for another twenty years, that is to 2030, before the budget is used up. But then emissions would have to stop completely, and we would have nothing left to cover the long tail as we gradually reduce our emissions to zero during the second half of the twenty-first century. A better strategy could be to reduce emissions now, in order to have part of the budget left after 2030. But if we want the budget to last for forty years, annual emissions would have to be halved, to sixteen billion tonnes of CO_2 per year. And that is certainly not on the agenda, if we are to judge from the slow progress of the climate negotiations.

My forecast happens to use up the remaining carbon budget before 2030. So there is no chance that it will keep global warming below plus 2°C.

To verify this conclusion, I asked Climate Interactive[16] to run their C-ROADS computer model to calculate the effects of the CO_2 emissions path illustrated in figure 5-3 on page 115. The result is shown in figure 5-4, and it verifies our back-of-the-envelope calculation. By 2052 humanity will already have reached the danger threshold: the temperature will already be plus 2°C over preindustrial times. The C-ROADS model also shows that the CO_2 concentration in the atmosphere will be 495 ppm,[17] and a full 538 ppm CO_2 equivalents if we also include the effect of the other greenhouse gases. The average sea-level increase will be 36 cm over the level in 2000, which equals 56 cm over preindustrial times. Ocean acidity will have increased from a pH of 8.05 to 7.97.

In summary, my forecast is that the world in 2052 will be much warmer than today, and it will face further warming over the following generation. There will be visible climate damage and growing worry about the future. The world in 2052 will be knee-deep, literally—remember that the oceans will have risen by more than one foot between now and then—in a self-inflicted climate problem. Most likely they will be talking about a climate "crisis" in the media.

The crisis could become catastrophic if self-reinforcing climate change is triggered. This is a possibility in the latter half of the twenty-first century, when the temperature might go so high that it starts melting the tundra,

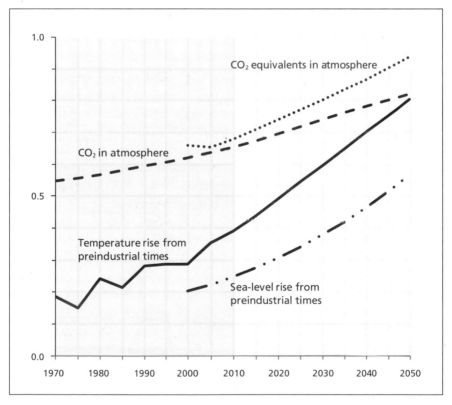

FIGURE 5-4 World climate change, 1970–2050.
Scale: Temperature rise from preindustrial times (0°C–2.5°C); sea-level rise from preindustrial times (0–1 meter); CO_2 in atmosphere (0–600 ppm); CO_2 equivalents in atmosphere (0–600 ppms).

thereby releasing vast amounts of methane gas that is currently locked in the frozen ground cover. Methane is a powerful greenhouse gas that, once released, will further increase the temperature, which in turn will melt more tundra in a process that won't stop until all tundra has melted and all methane has escaped. On the other hand, self-reinforcing climate change can be avoided if humanity chooses to actively extract CO_2 from the atmosphere—in time. For example, by using biomass as fuel in power stations with CCS (see "The Potential in CCS" sidebar on page 116).

But it will take a long time and a dedicated effort to achieve significant deviation from the trends in figure 5-4. This is because of the huge inertia in the climate system. It takes a lot of change over a long period of time to change the average temperature of the globe. And this is simple to understand: it takes a lot of energy to heat or cool an ocean. You don't get far with your kettle cooker.

Plus 2°C Will Cause Real Difficulties

As a consequence of the increase in the average global temperature of plus 2°C by 2052, humanity will experience an increasing number of bothersome climate effects over the decades to come. These will be extreme weather events like untypical floods, recurring droughts, landslides in new places, and uncommon trajectories for tornadoes, hurricanes, and cyclones. And there will be coral bleaching, forest death, and new insect infestations. Each event will lead to public outrage and create fear for the future. But in most cases the short-term costs of action will be seen as unacceptably high and lead to a "well-considered" decision to postpone significant action. Only very slowly will the unending sequence of extreme weather events create a political majority in favor of real action. Only after decades will society vote in favor of the extra voluntary investment that is necessary to cut emissions significantly.

Global warming to above the 2°C target will be enough to cause significant change to our normal surroundings. The most obvious effects will be the melting of the Arctic summer ice, the reduction of most glaciers outside the Arctic, the 1-foot rise in sea level (caused primarily by thermal expansion, not by melting ice), the 100-kilometer poleward motion of climatic zones, deserts encroaching on new areas in the tropics, and the accelerating melting of the northern permafrost. Global warming will even destroy aesthetic values: one result could be an ugly mixture of dying ecosystems (for example, bleached coral reefs and evergreen forests decimated by bark beetles) and biotopes perturbed by invaders from nearer to the equator (for example, watercress in temperate regions).

"Glimpse 5-3: Troubled Arctic Waters" gives an illustration of how global warming will lead to surprising effects at the local level.

GLIMPSE 5-3

Troubled Arctic Waters

Dag O. Hessen

The key actors in this story are small, typically just a few millimeters. In fact, planktonic *Calanus* (relatives of crabs and lobsters) remind us that the big players are not always large in size. But in the Arctic seas, *Calanus* are large in numbers, and they play a vital role. They are among the noble group of organisms that definitely earn the title *keystone species*. And understanding what could happen to *Calanus* as Arctic waters warm tells us much about the future of life in high-latitude seas.

Ecological and economic systems share several properties, including the fact that predicting their future is difficult because everything in them depends on everything else. They are both characterized by multiple interacting feedback loops—cause-and-effect cycles that now and then produce counterintuitive responses. Sometimes, change is gradual. At other times, seemingly small impacts can trigger a big reaction and possibly set in swing irreversible large-scale change.

By 2052 the northern marine waters will be in the midst of such a transition period, and no one can really tell how far it will go. This is partly due to the nonlinearity of biological systems, meaning that the ecosystem response to a given change (like temperature) may not be gradual and simple to predict. Beyond certain points or thresholds, there may be sudden, dramatic, and apparently random changes due to species shifts or shifts in key ecological processes with cascading effects on the entire system. Part of this is due to the fact that a food web is exactly that—a web. For example, species B may very well tolerate elevated temperatures, but if its prey A does not, B may suffer a heat-induced collapse due to loss of A—possibly with cascading effects to species C, D, E, and more. Or consider the other potential feedbacks of an oceanic temperature rise: increased heat absorption due to reduced snow and ice cover, permafrost melt with subsequent release of CO_2

and CH_4, ocean acidification causing reduced biological fixation of CO_2, and so on. I really don't know where this will take us, but from 2052 and on it will be terra incognita—or rather *mare incognita*.

I do know, though, that by 2052 the temperature in the North Sea will most likely be on average 1.5°C higher than today. Surface water in summer may be elevated by more than 2°C. The same trend will go on all the way up to the Arctic Ocean, which by 2052 will be completely devoid of ice during summer, with higher summer temperatures to match. So why will *Calanus*—our phytoplankton-eating copepods—and its fellows suffer when the cold northern waters heat up to what would seem more pleasant temperatures? Do not high temperature go along with high productivity?

Not necessarily. First of all, some species simply do best at low temperatures because they are evolutionarily adapted to them. But, secondly, elevated temperatures have some surprising side effects on phytoplankton. We expect that the productivity and average size of phytoplankton will *decrease* substantially when the ocean warms.

This is at least partly because the nutrient-poor surface water will heat up more rapidly, making it less able to mix easily with the nutrient-rich deep waters that contain phytoplankton. And so higher temperatures mean less food for *Calanus*—because there will be less phytoplankton mixed into surface water where the copepods feed. It also means smaller food, partly because smaller species do better than larger ones under strong nutrient limitation, but also because cells tend to get smaller at elevated temperatures. Oh sure, *Calanus* may be small, but the algae are even smaller, and smaller algae mean less of a mouthful for *Calanus*.

Perhaps even worse, these Arctic waters will by 2052 also experience a drop in pH from a historically very stable level of around 8.2 to 7.9. This is not a trivial change. We will see that crustaceans like *Calanus* and other calcifying organisms, both plants and animals, start to suffer since they have a hard time constructing their exoskeletons.

But let's not be to Calanocentric. The Arctic warming will by 2052 affect the entire system via cascading effects. New species will appear. Not only new species of copepods and algae, but also new fish species. Cod, mackerel, and herring typically found there will move northward. A wide range of bottom-dwelling flora and fauna will invade from the south, partly replacing old inhabitants. Some for the better, presumably, but many for the worse. Jellyfish of various kinds will proliferate at the expense of fish. And then I almost forgot the birds. You probably won't see auks and puffins hatch on the west coast of Norway. By 2052 they will be gone, moved to more northern areas.

One would perhaps have expected that when the ice retreats over the polar sea, it would open up vast new areas not only for oil and gas exploration, but also for marine productivity. Well, I am afraid that this optimistic idea is naïve. First of all, the very deep oceans are not at all as productive as the more shallow and coastal upwelling areas. Second, the peculiar under-ice ecosystem that is an important part of this high-arctic marine ecosystem will have vanished. During the polar spring you now find green carpets under the ice floes. These are ice algae, rich in polyunsaturated fatty acids and very nutritious. Relatives of our *Calanus* time their reproductive peak to graze on these under-ice meadows. But when the ice starts to melt earlier in the year, there will be an increasing mismatch in blooming periods and reproductive efforts of our *Calanus*. And scarcity of *Calanus* means scarcity in a key food for fish—affecting seabirds, seals, polar bears, and others. The cascading effect again. By 2052 there will be only faint remains of this quite remarkable food web.

More news awaits, though, for the second half of the twenty-first century when the increased meltdown of the Greenland ice sheet will cause other unpleasantries. The Gulf Stream conveyer belt is to a large extent driven by salinity gradient caused by the density differences of fresh and more salty waters. If the freshwater input disrupts this circulation after 2052, I would say: "You haven't seen anything yet."

If fate fares me well, I will be able to witness the world by 2052 as a very old man, but it will give me no pleasure on my last days to realize that I, along with numerous other scientists, were right when we vocalized these worries long before the year 2000. I am a biologist, and the trajectories humanity has followed over the past twenty-five years, despite very clear warnings, makes me wonder about human rationality. To be more precise, I wonder about the apparent victory of our selfish, evolutionarily short-sighted reasoning that maximizes personal goods at present over the intellectual or moral rationality that would have been able to avoid the crisis.

Luckily, I can end on a more positive note. We will not, at least by 2052, experience an ecosystem collapse (a popular term that I actually dislike, as ecosystems can change radically and in unpleasant ways, but do not collapse). This globe has been through terrible bottlenecks before and life has always found its way, but clearly at the expense of most of the existing forms of life. Apparently there will always be bacteria, algae, and even cockroaches around. I believe the *Calanus* species will survive in some habitat or other, and humans are rather robust too. My real worry is the self-reinforcing feedbacks—they are probably already starting to kick in. By 2052 I am sure that even the most wholehearted optimist will realize that humanity is facing a serious challenge, but I also believe that we will still be socially, technologically, and psychologically locked into "business as usual"—the old paradigm.

Thus I may feel lucky in 2052 that my time on Earth soon will be over—but seeing my great-grandchildren playing in the yard, that will give me little comfort.

Dag O. Hessen *(Norwegian, born 1956) is a professor of biology. He has published a large number of scientific papers about evolution and ecology, including climate-change issues. He has also published several popular science books and papers and is active in the public climate-change debate.*

I have no reason nor the competence to disagree with the vision of "Troubled Arctic Waters." What really worries me when reading this description of the many surprising effects of global warming in that specific ecosystem, the Arctic, is that such surprises probably are also lurking in all the other earthly ecosystems that I do not know well.

For there will be huge regional differences in the effects of climate change. At one end of the spectrum will be "the New North"—northern Canada, Alaska, Siberia, northern Russia and Scandinavia—which will benefit from a warmer climate, new trade routes, and faster agricultural and forest growth. At the other will be low-lying island states that will literally be underwater, with no place to move their populations. Intermediate cases will be breadbasket regions that lose their formerly stable pattern of rain and sunshine—some drying out, some getting too wet.

All along there will be the urban-rural split. The process of urbanization has been driven for generations by people seeking the increased opportunity and the better services of densely populated areas. This process will continue but will be strengthened by the increasing threat to rural life from violent weather extremes. People will feel safer in the company of others, as described in "Glimpse 5-4: The Flight to the City."

GLIMPSE 5-4

The Flight to the City

Thomas N. Gladwin

From now until 2040 the world's urban population will grow from 3.5 to about five billion. The scale and speed of this urban growth will exceed anything witnessed before in human history. This increase of 1.5 billion will absorb virtually all of the world's population growth during the time. Most of the growth in city dwelling will occur in what is currently called the developing world, principally in Asia and Africa. China and India alone will account for more than one-third of the total increase.

Much of the growth will result from natural increases—higher birth than death rates—within existing cities. But a significant minority will come from rural to urban migration and urban area reclassification. The migrants will be motivated by both the pull of better employment opportunities and social services and the push of displacement caused by rural environmental and economic degradation. While about 70% of the natural increase will occur in informal settlements (read: crowded slums), over 95% of the migrants from the countryside will begin their urban dwelling in these slums, typically situated in dangerous floodplains, river basins, steep slopes, or reclaimed land, and plagued by poor governance, inadequate infrastructure, and unhealthy living conditions. The number of urban slum dwellers in developing regions will grow from about one billion in 2010 to over 1.5 billion in 2030, given the economic inability or political unwillingness of urban governments to make slum alleviation a priority.

The urbanization process of the early twenty-first century will thus concentrate the bulk of world poverty into cities. About half of the growth will be situated in the world's low-elevation coastal zones that possess less than 10% of global renewable freshwater supplies and suffer from severe ecosystem degradation. Following the persistent pattern of urban de-densification, the 2010–30 period will witness a huge increase in the spatial extent of urban built-up area, adding to the loss of farmland, forests, open space, and biodiversity.

But the big cities will also offer the best hope of escape. An estimated 0.5 billion people will shift out of slums into more secure living conditions during the next twenty years. The rapid urbanization will generate substantial economic growth. It will foster economies of scale and agglomeration, face-to-face networks of creativity and collaboration, specialization, lowered transaction costs, and entrepreneurship, all generating huge productivity gains. With eighty million new people urbanizing each year, more than $35 trillion (35 T$!) will be spent between 2010 and 2030 on infrastructure including housing, transportation, sanitation, water, electricity, and telecommunications. Trillions more will be spent on the expansion of services such as education and health care. Over one billion new jobs will be created. Rising per capita incomes will lift over two billion people into the global middle class, most significantly in Asia.

The period between 2030 and 2052 will witness more substantial global warming. By 2052, the planet will be on average 2°C warmer than in preindustrial times, with temperatures in central parts of the continents (Canada, United States, Siberia, China, the Amazon) even higher. This warming will radically alter urbanization patterns. Climate-induced deglaciation, freshwater scarcity, drought, rain-fed crop failures, sea-level rise, tropical cyclones, forest fires, seasonal flooding, and extreme temperatures will cause massive population displacements, adding to the already substantial flow of migrants moving from rural to urban locations. Climate change will also motivate people to shift out of cities highly vulnerable to climate risks toward safer established or entirely new cities with more reliable precipitation, higher elevations, and cooler temperatures. Most of this human movement will initially occur within nations or regions where migration is permissible. Later there may be growing demands for long-distance migration toward more inhabitable regions such as northern Canada, Scotland, Scandinavia, and northern Russia— already called "the New North."

Also between 2030 and 2052 well-governed cities in the wealthiest parts of the world (China, Brazil, United States, northern Europe) will increasingly invest in climate-change mitigation and adaptation. Greenhouse gas emissions will be reduced, particularly in the urban environments, via energy-efficient technologies, low-carbon energy sources, mass transit, promotion of nonmotorized transit, green-building retrofits, mixed-use development, congestion charges, and other measures. These eco-cities will become superefficient through the application of pervasive computing, sensor networks, smart grids, and broad-based fiber-optic and wireless telecommunications. Resource scarcities will be addressed through high-rise hydroponic farming, desalinization, bio-based building materials, massive waste recycling, and water-use/irrigation efficiency. Adaptations to climate variability will include distributed infrastructure systems, construction of sea walls and storm-surge barriers, disaster-response capacities, and solar/wind-powered cooling and air-conditioning systems. Escalating energy, water, material, and housing costs will drive hundreds of millions of people from the suburbs and other nations into this safer and lower-cost urban living.

The 2030–52 climate-urbanization story will be very different for highly vulnerable cities with low adaptive capacities, most prominently in Africa and Southeast Asia. Still plagued by weak governance systems, corruption, insufficient international assistance, constrained investment capacity, political instability, infrastructure deficits, youth bulges, and massive poverty, cities in these regions will be unable to substantially reduce or adapt to the impacts of climate-related hazards. Water supplies will be falling due to reduction in river flows, falling groundwater tables, and saltwater intrusion into groundwater. Heavy precipitation events will cause extensive flooding and landslides, leading to disruption of public water, electricity, sanitation, and transportation systems. Sea-level rise will increase coastal erosion and subsidence, causing substantial damage to residential and commercial structures. Temperature, precipitation, and humidity will boost the range, life cycle, and rate of transmission of infectious diseases. Higher temperatures and extended heat waves will greatly boost heat-related mortality. Hundreds of millions from the countryside, where adverse effects of climate change will be even more horrific, will nonetheless be streaming into these climate-troubled cities. At the same time, employers, jobs, and wealthier residents will be fleeing these same cities in search of more secure places to live and to do business, often in newly developed cities or distant places. The adverse effects of climate change will thus fall disproportionately on those without the resources to move. Climate-vulnerable cities will be entrapped in a vicious cycle of increased harm, reduced adaptive capacity, and thus ever-greater vulnerability.

By 2052, our species will truly be *Homo sapiens urbanis*. The urban share of total global population will be approximately 80% (compared with 50% in 2010), with the currently industrialized countries at about 90% and less developed countries at 75%. These percentages exceed earlier projections, which failed to account for increased migration to the city because of erratic weather, resource scarcity, expensive commuting, and the general move from climate-vulnerable to climate-resilient cities.

The world will also be a very dangerous place, with the Global North spending trillions of dollars on security to prevent unwanted immigration and to guard against threats posed by criminal gangs and terrorists controlling cities increasingly afflicted by climate chaos in the Global South.

Thomas N. Gladwin (American, born 1948) is the Max McGraw Professor of Sustainable Enterprise and associate director of the Erb Institute for Global Sustainable Enterprise at the University of Michigan. His teaching, research, and consulting focus on system dynamics, global change, and sustainable business.

The picture painted in "Flight to the City" is, sadly, a likely development. More people will seek shelter inside modern city walls, leaving a small rural population to fend for itself, against increasingly violent weather and ecosystem change.

This and other negative effects of global warming will become increasingly apparent during the next twenty years, but in such a gradual manner that they are not likely to trigger the type of warlike action needed to reduce greenhouse gas emissions. If there is any free money, I expect that it will be spent primarily on adaptation to the damage that can already be observed. As a long-term consequence, rich countries will become better prepared to withstand the vagaries of the new weather. London will have its enhanced barrier on the Thames. Germany will have an even stricter building code and housing built to these exacting standards. The poor countries are less likely to have any free funds at all, and hence more likely to take the full brunt of climate-induced damage.

In the longer run, in the 2030s, awareness about what is going on will grow sufficiently to provide broad support for stronger measures. And if I am right, by 2052 the voters in the well-governed part of the world will have seen enough damage to be genuinely concerned about the possibility of self-reinforcing climate change in the last half of the century. A tremendous effort—and further increase in the extra investment—will finally be under way to reduce emissions, for the benefit of all, rich and poor, urban and rural, in parallel with an extraordinary effort to adapt to the new climate, for the benefit of those who pay the bill, which will be primarily the urban rich.

CHAPTER 6

Food and Footprint to 2052

All conversations about global forecasts eventually lead to questions about food security. We've been asking these questions ever since our population began growing ferociously. And what we want to know is this: as time marches on, will we be able to feed ourselves?

Food Production Will Satisfy Reduced Demand

I believe the answer is yes—at least until 2052. This is partly because food production will continue to grow over the decades ahead, and partly because demand will not increase as much as many expect. By 2052, the negative impact of global warming on food production will only just have started to bite. The population will be only one-third larger than it is today, and although many poor will eat much better, many rich will eat much less red meat. Rich man—*Homo affluensis*—will have moved down the food chain to less refined foods requiring less agricultural output. Average food consumption will be four times what is needed to survive—the "subsistence level"—and more than enough for a healthy and palatable diet. But the food will be unevenly distributed, then as now. Sadly, many will still starve.

Food production has grown spectacularly over the last forty years. Measured as the annual production of food in millions of tonnes per year, it more than doubled from 1970 to 2010. This was achieved largely through the use of capital and technology, not by an increase in the area of cultivated land. New seeds, more fertilizer, more pesticides, and more irrigation boosted average land yields from 2.4 tonnes of food per hectare-year in 1970 to 4.6 in 2010, which amounts to 90%. Meanwhile the area of cultivated land increased only 15%. Land that was built upon or degraded was more than compensated for by an inflow of new land, often obtained by slashing more forest or irrigating new savannah.

The trend toward higher food production will continue. Significant land reserves exist, in the former Soviet Union, in Brazil, and in sub-Saharan Africa. New irrigation water can be mustered, and in almost endless amounts if the user is able to pay for desalination of seawater. And as long as there is energy, there will be fertilizer. On top of this comes the likely further development of genetically modified plants—at least outside Europe. Although I fear that GMOs will prove unsustainable in the long run, and ideally I feel they should be avoided, I believe their use will increase in the decades ahead. GMOs will help boost yields in regions that are too dry or too wet, or unsuitable in other ways. Humanity will accept their risks, because their benefits arise in the short term, and their potential ecological costs arise in the long run—in terms of resistance or gene flight.

But as we get closer to 2052, agriculture will be increasingly affected by climate change.[1] There are two general effects, which work in opposite directions. First, plants tend to grow faster when there is more CO_2 in the atmosphere. Second, plants tends to grow slower when the temperature increases (the exception being in northern climes, where cold is the limiting factor on plant growth). Since the CO_2 concentration in the atmosphere will grow steadily over the next forty years, it will help boost agricultural yields everywhere. But at the same time, the ever higher temperatures will work the other way. It is not clear what the net result on yields will be, but it is not expected to be very big by 2052, perhaps plus or minus 5%.

My forecast is based on the assumption that the net effect on yields will be small, minus 5% by 2052, relative to yields if there were no global warming. The effect would be bigger if the crop composition was kept constant, but I do not believe this will be the case: farmers will gradually shift toward crops that handle the new climate well.

But I do forecast a decline in the land area used for cultivation. This is not only because of the expansion of urban land, but also because desertification and sea-level rise will increasingly make some land unusable. This effect will become much stronger after 2052, outside the time horizon for my forecast, but already in 2052 the land area used for cultivation will be 6% below the peak value in the 2030s.

In sum, we will have a situation where the land area used for cultivation will not increase much over the next forty years, but where the intensity of the use of that land will increase. So much attention will be put into increasing yields that the global average yield in 2052 (4.6 tonnes per hectare-year) will reach the same level as the land yield in the OECD countries in 1982. This means two things: yields will grow, and there will still be room for more yield growth. But growing climate effects will be lurking in the background.

Figure 6-1 shows my forecast in quantitative detail. Annual food production in 2052 will be ten billion tonnes of grain equivalents per year, up by around 50% from today. As a consequence the average per capita daily grain consumption will be 27% higher. The average global citizen will have at his or her disposal some 1,300 kg of food every year (up from 1,000 kg today). This is four times subsistence level.

My forecast implies that there will be enough food around to satisfy all of us who can afford to pay. The more we pay, the better we will eat. Continued trade will limit regional differences in per capita food consumption for people with the same purchasing power. Basic foods will remain relatively cheap, and the number of kilograms of food per person-year will go up. But this does not mean that there will not be starvation. Among those who cannot raise their own food in sufficient quantities and do not have sufficient money, there will remain a lasting element of persistent hunger. Hopefully the share of hungry people in the global population will decline, but if it does not, this will result more from lacking economic development than from lacking agricultural potential in the world.

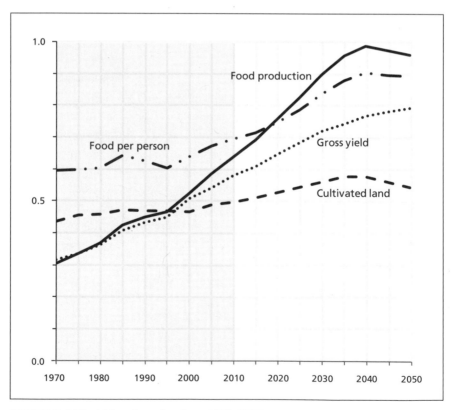

FIGURE 6-1 World food production, 1970–2050.
Scale: Food production (0–10.5 billion tonnes per year); cultivated land (0–3 billion hectares); gross yield (0–8 tonnes per hectare-year); food per person (0–1.4 tonnes per person-year).

Biofuels and White Meat Will Advance

Some land will be used for the production of biofuels. I believe the area will be limited, as a percentage of the world agricultural capacity, but biofuel production will create an upward pressure on food prices, and some unnecessary suffering among the poor—but higher food prices will also lead to higher food production. "Glimpse 6-1: Expensive Oil = Expensive Food" discusses this issue.

GLIMPSE 6-1

Expensive Oil = Expensive Food

Erling Moxnes

Will it be possible to feed the world population in 2052? The UN Food and Agriculture Organization (FAO) certainly hopes so. But the answer, I believe, is both yes and no. Sufficient volumes of food can be produced, but I think the price of the food will be so high that the poor of the world will not be able to afford a decent diet. This will hold even more true if the world decides to considerably scale up the use of biofuels, which will be bought by affluent drivers at prices determined by the price of fossil fuels. And this is more, per unit of grain equivalent, than the poor can pay. The result could be famine among the poor as the world's agriculture sector fuels cars rather than feeding people.

Food Markets If There Was No Biofuel
Even without scaled-up biofuel production, the world today is unable to feed its population. The FAO estimates that close to a billion people are unable to pay the price for all the food they need; they are chronically hungry. But this is primarily a question of distribution. There is enough food around to feed everyone adequately, but the poor cannot afford to buy their fair share.

Population growth leads to increasing demand for food. Likewise, economic growth allows people to increase per capita food intake and to replace cheap staple foods such as grains, tubers, legumes, and seeds with meat. Increasing demand stimulates increases in production. Under such conditions, the FAO expects the supply of food to increase up to 2052. But determining how much the food will cost compared to today is not so easy.

The land area now used to grow crops could probably increase by 30%. However, marginal costs will increase with the use of less productive lands and increasing losses of biodiversity. Those increasing marginal costs imply that one cannot simply extrapolate the declining food prices of the past. Traditionally production costs declined as labor productivity increased in agriculture. This explains the recent long historical period where food prices declined relative to wages. New agricultural technologies, new plant varieties, aquaculture, and education will help prolong this green revolution. Pulling in the opposite direction, though, higher energy prices will increase the costs of fertilizers, pesticides, plowing, irrigation, and transportation.

Which of the above factors will dominate in the future is hard to predict. Potential climate change adds uncertainty, both because the weather influences yields and because mitigation policies could lead to higher energy prices and restrictions on emissions of methane and nitrous oxide from agricultural production.

Markets for Fuel and Biofuel

While there are limits to how many calories each of us can eat, demand for fuel—such as petroleum liquids, alcohol, biodiesel, and other types of transportable energy—tends to increase endlessly with income. For a long historical period fuel prices declined relative to wages because of discoveries of giant oil fields, increased scales of operations, and technological progress. Again, one cannot extrapolate this historical decline to future prices, because we will soon have depleted the cheapest oil resources. Conventional oil production has probably peaked. The availability of fossil-based fuels may still increase for some time, through new discoveries and because it is possible to convert coal and gas into liquid fuels. But conversion adds costs, and eventually costs of coal and natural gas will increase as these energy sources have to be brought in from less accessible locations. Probably the world will see a major transition from oil toward methanol produced from shale gas and conventional natural gas in remote locations.

Thus, in the coming decades there will be long periods with high oil prices. High prices will be needed to finance costly capacity expansions and structural change, and to force consumers to reduce their dependence on fossil fuels.

The Impact of Biofuel on Food Prices and Hunger

First-generation biofuels are made by converting normal agricultural outputs like corn, sugar beet, and sugarcane to ethanol. Over the last twenty years, research, development, and experience have led to efficiency improvements and cost reductions. Estimates suggest that biofuel costs range from around USD 45 per barrel for the cheapest sugarcane in Brazil to around USD 100 per barrel for corn and sugar beets in the United States, and around USD 120 per barrel for the more expensive wheat-based ethanol in Europe. More experience and larger scales of operations will lead to further cost reductions. Similar to petroleum, considerable use of fuel in the production process makes costs escalate with fuel prices.

Many users of fossil fuel can use biofuels with no or limited adjustments. Therefore prices of biofuels are strongly coupled to prices of oil. Note, however, that demand for fuels is much larger than demand for food. Measured by energy content, current world oil production is about five times larger than world agricultural production. Assuming that the conversion of food to biofuel involves a loss of some 40% of the energy content of the food, the entire world food production could not replace more than 12% of current world oil production. New plant species could raise the percentage somewhat, but if more than 12% of current world oil production were to be replaced, hardly any food would be left for human consumption.

Future biofuel expansion will depend on the difference between fuel prices and biofuel production costs. Long periods with fuel prices exceeding costs will lead to a long-term buildup of biofuel production capacity. In periods when fuel prices drop below biofuel production costs, investment in new plants will stop, while production in old plants will go on as long as current fuel prices cover operating costs. Increasing biofuel production will cause feedstock and food prices to rise, and this will eventually stop the growth in biofuels. Even though biofuel production is and will remain a small percentage of world fuel production, it certainly can cause higher food prices. The potential for increased agricultural production is considerable compared to human food demand, but small compared to the potential for increased biofuel demand. As limits for agricultural production are approached, marginal costs will increase and lead to high food prices also in the long run. Many poor people will not be able to pay the higher prices for the staple foods they rely on for survival. Hence, biofuel production could easily expand at the expense of food consumption.

Enter the Government

What could keep this prediction from coming true over the coming decades? Development of new ample sources of fuels could limit fuel prices and prevent biofuels from taking off. However, it takes decades to develop new technologies, reduce costs, and expand operations. It also takes decades to improve energy efficiency and to foster cultures where energy is less important. Energy-consuming machinery, buildings, and infrastructures have long economic lifetimes. Much of the man-made capital of 2052 has already been produced.

International agreements to reserve agriculture for human consumption and to prohibit production of biofuels from agricultural products will require major changes in people's attitudes toward land as private property and toward the institution of the free market. Such attitudes will be particularly hard toward change in nations that are more than self-sufficient in food while they depend on imports of increasingly costly petroleum.

Nations with limited agricultural production are more likely to prohibit local production of biofuels. China has implemented restrictions on the use of corn for ethanol, and Indonesia has raised export duties on palm oil to secure local supplies of cooking oil. However, such policies will not always be enacted in time to be effective. In previous food crises, poorly managed countries have exported cash crops out of regions with hunger.

A redistribution of incomes to enable poor people to compete for food is also unlikely at the international level. But it can be done nationally, to avoid revolution caused by hunger.

Perhaps the greatest reason for pessimism is widespread misperceptions among journalists, politicians, and voters. Focus tends to be on current-day problems with current-day perspectives. Most people do not understand how energy and food markets work, and they underestimate the time it takes to change course and the need for precaution. They do not realize fully that we have more resources to prevent future hunger today than we will have tomorrow.

Erling Moxnes (Norwegian, born 1952) is a professor in system dynamics at the University of Bergen (Norway). He has a PhD from Dartmouth College (USA). He has published on resource management and economics with a focus on misperceptions of dynamics and on policy.

I agree with the main point of "Expensive Oil = Expensive Food," namely, that biofuel will exert an upward pressure on the price of food. But I think the effect will be limited because we will not choose to use much food for biofuel purposes. This is because most food-based biofuels are not particularly climate friendly, and the cost of making oil from coal is so low (USD 70 per barrel of oil) that it will hold back the production of more expensive biofuels. It will also help that shale gas appears to be available in great quantities at the equivalent price of USD 13 per barrel of oil.

Furthermore, the effect on the price of food will be counteracted by the tremendous reduction in the use of grain for feed that will occur when the rich populations of the world finally choose to reduce their consumption of red meat. Or to be more precise: once the economic and cultural elite decide it is no longer in their own interest to emulate the US ambition of huge amounts of red meat for every meal. I believe this rejection will come—because of health reasons, concerns about animal welfare, sustainability, and sheer cost. It will be seen as more refined to eat less.

When rich man shifts from red meat to chicken, pork, and grain-fed aquaculture, many more can be fed from the same agricultural base. It takes some 7 kg of grain to produce 1 kg of red meat, while it takes only 2 kg to produce 1 kg of chicken. After such a shift, the same amount of grain can feed 3.5 times as many people. The shift toward lower-quality proteins will also result from the limited supply of high-quality protein. "Glimpse 6-2: The Limits to Protein" provides more detail.

The Limits to Protein

David Butcher

Scarcity of high-quality animal protein—partly from land-based animals and partly from fish and other products from salt or freshwater—will confront us over the next forty years.

Total world protein production will likely remain similar to present-day levels. The catch of marine fish has already stagnated and may decline dramatically toward 2052. But the decline will be compensated for through aquaculture production, as long as there is enough feed. The availability of feed, too, will determine supplies of land-based protein such as beef, chicken, and pork.

The production of plants for feed is highly susceptible to unexpected variations in the weather. Land-use change, degradation from poor management practices, desertification, and inundation from sea-level rise will all add pressure to the world's arable land. Improved irrigation practices will help, but water availability will remain critical, especially in international river basins where tensions and outright conflict will erupt over it.

On the positive side, science will provide some relief through the development of improved plant strains, more efficient irrigation techniques, effective fertilizer use, and efficient pyrolysis of vegetation in order to increase soil carbon. Improved genetics and animal husbandry will produce more productive flocks and herds.

But feeding the animals used for human protein consumption will be in direct competition with human needs for grain crops and also for animal protein. Ruminants will continue to use nonarable lands, transforming low-quality herbage into high-quality protein. But the production of pork will decline because pigs compete directly for human-grade carbohydrates and protein. Poultry products will become the mainstay because these birds convert feed into protein with high efficiency. Furthermore, poultry populations can be rapidly expanded and contracted to take advantage of fluctuations in feed availability.

Aquaculture is widely seen as the natural supplement to the stagnating catch of wild fish. But aquaculture requires a steady flow of high-quality—usually fish—protein to feed the captive fish. A number of freshwater species have great promise because of their lower protein requirements, but they are usually less popular in the marketplace. So aquaculture will remain a competitor for protein-rich feed by 2052.

The distributional effect of the limited supply of protein will be ugly. The affluent will force up prices and consume what high-quality protein there is. The poor, especially in urban areas, will get less, and signs of protein deficiency will reappear, with resultant disease and a lowering of the quality of life for those affected.

David Butcher *(Australian, born 1941) is a veterinarian with particular interests in epidemiology, wildlife diseases, and biodiversity conservation. He is a former CEO of WWF Australia and Greening Australia (NSW) and now lives on an Illawarra property that is 30% subtropical rain forest.*

I agree with "The Limits to Protein" that there are many threats to the continued supply of cheap, high-quality protein. So the price will be high, even after the rich have constrained their consumption of red meat way below past US norms.

Commercial Fish Stocks Will Be Confined to Regulated Fisheries

The world catch of wild fish stagnated in the early 1990s at around ninety million tonnes of fish per year. But that did not stop the growth in human consumption of fish. Fish from aquaculture has quickly filled the gap and now constitutes more than a third of global fish consumption. Some fish farming is sustainably based on vegetable feed, but much is based on a highly unsustainable use of wild fish as fodder.

Lately global society has made progress toward limiting the natural tendency to overfish unregulated stocks. The Marine Stewardship Council has established a label for well-managed fisheries, and an increasing number of fisheries are being certified—and hopefully will remain protected against overfishing. For areas outside such systems there appears to be less hope. Fishermen are bent on taking what catch they can lay their hands on, and often with the financial support (via so-called perverse subsidies) of their governments. The tragedy of the commons syndrome is much too strong to be resisted by poor people seeking an extra meal or high-seas trawlers looking to boost their catch.

So fish in the long-term future will likely come from two sources: certified fisheries and fish farms using vegetable feed. High-quality fish will be expensive and go to the wealthier part of humanity. The sidebar titled "Fish Futures" gives more detail and, importantly, describes why it is near impossible to establish rational regulation of individual fisheries even if one intensely wants to do so.

Fish Futures

It is near impossible to predict what will happen to world fisheries over the next forty years. The annual catch of wild fish has been stagnant for two decades. Will this trend continue? There are three reasons why oceans present such a tough challenge to manage and predict.

- *Volatility*. The long-term future of the oceans cannot be foretold because of the natural volatility of marine fish populations, and the inability of most predictive approaches to handle nonlinear, massive change.
- *Weak signals*. Signs of economic and biological trouble tend to be weak, delayed, and distorted, making change-as-you-go adaptation not a viable management method.
- *Knowledge gap*. The science on some of the most dangerous trends is still in its infancy; we simply don't know enough.

Volatility

Let me begin with the problem of volatility. Fish stocks are famously fickle. In the ocean, the forces of productivity and predation seesaw back and forth on a scale unimaginable on land. Biomass can swing wildly, driven by changes in currents, nutrients, and temperature. This makes fisheries notoriously hard to manage, and even the ancients, with their primitive gear, inadvertently wiped out their near-shore stocks, unable to manage a resource so unreliable that today's sustainable harvest is tomorrow's death blow.

Now imagine trying to go beyond single stocks and predict the interaction between stocks, in a food-chain system so complex as to completely defy not only our current understanding, but possibly the limits of computation itself. So far, we have not been able to answer even some basic questions: Does overfishing lead to a general impoverishment of the lower parts of the pyramid of life in the ocean? Do stocks recover from collapse? What level of disturbance can ocean systems absorb?

Weak Signals

Let me turn next to the problem of weak signals. Fishery yield curves are typically quite flat. In other words, it is possible to increase fishing pressure quite dramatically for several years before catch levels decrease to a level that is discernible in the noise of normal yearly variations. In some cases, this can already be too late—the damage is done, the stock has been damaged and is headed for a crash. A similar problem occurs when the cost of fishing does not increase as the stocks decline. This is particularly true for schooling fish, which are easily detected with modern fish-finding technology, and whose strong local concentration falsely suggests overall abundance. The fisherman who caught the last major school of codfish on George's Bank came home and told his wife that all was well: his boat was filled to the brim. The problems of weak and noisy signals abound in the ocean, and this lack of systematic feedback makes prediction and adaptation so difficult.

Knowledge Gap

Some of the most disconcerting threats remain outside of our ability to reliably quantify them. Ocean acidification, for example, is a major wild card—we understand neither its expected intensity nor its potential impact. Research on its effects is in its infancy. While we have some initial work indicating that zooplankton has declined significantly in the last fifty years, the all-important trend lines and causalities are lost in the enormous volatility of zooplankton abundance. In the worst case, this could be a crisis that threatens the very foundation of life on our planet. In the best case, it could simply involve a slight recalibration of the ocean's food chain. We simply do not know at this point.

Lacking Precaution

So, we are dealing with a poorly understood complex system with weak feedback loops and limited opportunities for adaptation. This is a classic case for the application of massive levels of precaution, but, of course, this is not what is happening. What we can say with some better-than-even chance about aquatic life in 2052 is this:

Most fisheries without effective mortality controls will eventually collapse, with unknown chances for recovery. However, the oceans will not be empty. The United States, Oceania, Japan, and the EU will have intervened in time, and their fisheries will have recovered by 2052. The same holds true for large industrial fisheries, such as anchovy and tuna, except for Atlantic bluefin tuna, which will have been hounded into collapse by 2020 and will be largely extinct. All in all, those massive fisheries, which account for the majority of the volume of landed fish, will have been put on solid footing.[2]

This is emphatically not true for the smaller-scaled fisheries in the tropics. It will prove to be impossible to impose effective mortality controls on most coastal commercial fisheries of Asia, Africa, and South America—there are too many boats catching too many types of fish with too great a variety of gear, and the managerial capacity will simply not be in place. Many of these fisheries will collapse at some point in the next twenty years, and it is entirely unclear whether they can biologically recover and, if so, whether they will be allowed to do so by a completely reformed fishery management system.

Ocean habitat will be a mixed story. The impact of industrial bottom trawling has been enormous in some places (although not all), and often self-defeating. With the increase in fuel pricing, decrease in subsidies, new bottom-fishing technologies, and strong international pressure, we can expect this situation to improve for the large industrial fleets. However, the tropical coastal and estuarine systems will suffer immensely to 2052 as mangroves disappear, rivers are dammed, and swamps are drained. These are the prime breeding habitats for many tropical marine fishes, and their destruction will further contribute to the impoverishment of coastal fisheries.[3]

The parallels between the ocean and the global greenhouse issues are striking. Both present potentially life-threatening long-range problems, largely invisible at the current time; both tend to provide weak, delayed, and noisy signals; both require levels of coordination that are entirely unchartered territory. It is not a comforting picture.

Planetary Ecosystems Will Suffer

Grossly simplified, my forecast to 2052 says that there will be enough energy, grain, and chicken, plus some fish—with some exception for the poor. And there will be much too much CO_2. What will be the total effect on the planet? And on nature? That is, on that diminishing fraction of the planet that is not used by humanity?

Global society is exerting an increasing burden on planet Earth. It has been discussed for decades whether the human burden is sustainable or is in the run-up toward some form of environmental collapse. After a long stalemate in the struggle between the two views in the 1970s and 1980s, this debate was brought a huge step forward during the last fifteen years through the invention of ways to measure the burden—"the ecological footprint"—so it can be compared with measures of planetary carrying capacity.

There are different ways to measure the human ecological footprint. The ambition is always to measure the resource and pollution impact of the human economy; or, in other words, to measure the amount of resources used and the pollution generated in one year, using current technology. One starting point when trying to quantify the ecological footprint is to measure the land area needed to produce the food we eat. One then can improve the measure by adding the land area used for grazing of human animals. And then improve again, by adding successively the land area used for timber production, for cities, for roads, and for other infrastructure. In order to include the impact of fisheries one can add the acreage of fish banks in use. And finally, in an attempt to quantify the impact of human energy use, one can add in the amount of forest that would have been necessary to absorb (through plant growth) the annual CO_2 that is emitted from energy production. The land masses involved are measured in "global hectares," that is, in the number of *hectares of average biological productivity* that it would take to bring forth anually the output that humans use. The Global Footprint Network has been a leader in this effort and is publishing national time-series data for its version of the ecological footprint.[4]

Measured this way, the ecological footprint of humanity has doubled since 1970. This would not have mattered if the footprint were small relative to the size of the planet. But that is not the case. The ecological footprint in 2010 was some 40% higher than the carrying capacity of the globe. In other words, humanity was, and is, using 1.4 planets to supply its current use of grain, meat, timber, fish, urban space, and energy. And notice that this applies even when we use a very conservative measure of the human impact. Our measure does not include all the land area necessary to generate freshwater, to absorb other types of pollution than CO_2, or for that matter any land area for the other creatures with which we share our beautiful planet.

So the human ecological footprint has overshot the carrying capacity of the earth. How is that possible? How long can it last? The current overshoot is possible because the footprint includes the amount of forestland that would have been needed to absorb all the CO_2 that we emit from energy production. This land does not exist, and the CO_2 is not being absorbed fully in tree growth. The rest is accumulating in the atmosphere. Furthermore, the amount of forest needed to do the trick is roughly twice as much as the remaining forest area on planet Earth. As a consequence, we experience a gradual and unsustainable warming of the planet. So overshoot will last until climate change forces us to pare back emissions until what is emitted can be absorbed sustainably by the remaining forest.

As I have stated before, there are only two ways out of overshoot: managed decline or natural collapse. Currently humanity is seeking the first alternative, a planned and orderly program of reductions of greenhouse gas emissions, in time to keep global warming below plus 2°C. But since I do not believe we will act fast enough to achieve this goal, we will get increasing climate damage throughout this century.

When it finally starts to dawn on people and politicians that the world is in planetary overshoot and headed for trouble, there will begin a race to secure one's own future interests. The most visible moves on that front lately have been the Chinese purchases of agricultural land in Africa, and the attempts of Pacific islanders to buy flood-proof land in Australia and New Zealand. Both actions reflect a way of thinking that will become increasingly prevalent over the decades ahead. "Glimpse 6-3: The Race to Lose Last" explores this aspect of the future.

GLIMPSE 6-3

The Race to Lose Last

Mathis Wackernagel

At a private lunch when I recently asked one of the world's highest-ranking international diplomats what, among all the possible scenarios for Pakistan, was the most positive vision she held, everyone around the table laughed nervously.

This diplomat was surprisingly honest. She admitted that she had not one positive vision for Pakistan. She was candid about a view that leaders widely hold but seldom acknowledge: humanity is on a slippery slope of resource depletion. It is unlikely leaders can do anything about it. Hence, their job is to make sure their people will lose last. This means securing for their people enough resources from the globe's diminishing resource pie to ensure that their nation will float even if others sink.

From this vantage point, money shields a population from losing first. Leaders beholden to this view therefore embrace even more vigorously GDP growth as their key objective; the financial advantage will allow their constituency to stay just a bit further ahead of the others in the resource race to 2052.

From a resource perspective, the projections for Pakistan do not look rosy. Their tiny bio-capacity of less than 0.6 global hectares per person (or about one-third of the global average) is facing a rapidly increasing demand.[5] Pakistan's demand already exceeds the country's bio-capacity by 80%. It does not take a mathematical genius to draw the conclusion that with current trends of growing populations and increasing material expectations—in a context of a limited bio-capacity and rising fossil fuel costs—Pakistan will run out of resources well before 2052. Most likely, the lack of bio-capacity will manifest itself through heightened levels of internal conflict. The conflict will come with a high price tag, including a significant drop in the population's longevity. Of course, such decay could have disastrous global ramifications, not least due to Pakistan's nuclear arsenal. By 2052, Pakistan could well be a devolved, failed state, with hundreds of fiefdoms, medieval levels of child mortality, and very low literacy.

Pakistan could of course try to import the needed resources. But in a world of global overshoot—where global demand for bio-capacity exceeds the available biological space—it is unlikely that a financially weak Pakistan could successfully outcompete the economic demands of other countries for those same resources.

But Pakistan could take a different turn. It could publicly recognize the significance of lacking resources for its residents' current and future well-being. It could seek a societal consensus among Pakistanis on how to handle the social implications of tightening physical constraints. This would be tough—particularly since it would require a totally new vision of development, including a central role for women. But if well done, it would ensure much better and more prosperous living conditions for Pakistanis within the existing ecological and financial limitations.

Unfortunately, Pakistan, like most countries in the world, is unlikely to act in this manner because it is blinded by two misconceptions: first, nothing can be done about the slow but cumulative ecological trends, neither on the demand side nor on the supply side; and second, if anything could be done, it would be too costly, and achievable only through global consensus.

Both misconceptions are paralyzing, and deeply misinformed. Yes, resource trends have an enormous inertia. But they are built on past and present societal choices. Resource consumption is largely driven by population size and the infrastructure already in place—cities, power stations, roads, and airports. By reversing population trends and reshaping infrastructure, the dependence on imported resources can be turned around. But how? Pakistan, or any country, could start to manage its ecological assets as one would run a good family farm.

A good family farm produces more, in net terms, than the farm family consumes. The good farmer has secured enough land to grow crops and support his or her livestock. The extra production beyond the farm family's own consumption can be sold and traded for other goods and services—TVs, clothes, books. Some countries are like good family farms, with more bio-capacity than what it takes, in net terms, to provide for their inhabitants.

Compare this with a weekend hobby farm, with honeybees, a rabbit, and an apple tree, where most resources have to be bought from elsewhere. Presently 80% of the world population lives in countries that are like hobby farms. They consume more, in net terms, than what the ecosystems of their country can regenerate. The rest is imported or derives from unsustainable overuse of local fields and forests.

In fact the world as a whole has become a hobby farm, using 1.4 times what the biosphere can regenerate.[6] The difference between what nature provides and what humanity takes comes from liquidation of natural capital. It is grabbed from future generations, at a very cheap price.

If we looked at the world like good farmers, we would recognize that it is in our interest to look after our farm. We would see the danger in becoming increasingly a hobby farm when there are ever fewer good farms available to provide us with what we need. Countries would know to look after their farms and curb their resource demand in order to be strong and independent—and this would stabilize the global situation as well.

In such a world, we would maximize not the throughput (as suggested by growth in GDP) but our per capita wealth, and we would use the sustainable returns from this wealth to maintain well-being into the future.

Perhaps the wisdom will come once resource prices start creeping up more rapidly than economies expand. Once that happens, it is going to feel like climbing up a downward-moving escalator. But will this feeling generate more insight among decision makers, and quicker and more decisive action?

I fear not. As incomes tighten, governments may rather cease to invest, even in education and infrastructure maintenance, leaving their populations fending for themselves as they face ever-higher food and energy bills. National bankruptcies may become more frequent.

In other words, resource constraints will produce social upsets way before producing ecological collapse—the menu includes currency decay, runaway debts, insolvency, social unrest, civil wars. All these events will obfuscate the underlying resource drama, as it did in the "Arab Spring" of 2011. While the uprising against repressive leaders was largely seen as a positive development toward democracy, the underlying circumstance was that rapidly expanding populations in the region were meeting rising food and energy prices. Such potent social dynamite cannot be contained even by cynical dictators.

Now consider China. China's leaders have understood the resource race for decades—far better than any large nation. They have actively prepared themselves in order to access resources from abroad. They have limited their population growth, reforested devastated areas, and carefully managed urbanization pressures. They have begun to secure access to resources abroad, although their ultimate goal is a self-sufficient China—a continuation of the age-old Middle Kingdom.

China is not a democracy, but it features a governing system in which the population expects its leaders to deliver. Delivery has been the government's continued license to operate. China's leaders have successfully used economic growth as a way to lift millions out of poverty, and to keep a vast portion of its population excited and loyal. The growth has created opportunities for many and generated a sense of progress for a large majority.

Expanding budgets and economies simplify politics. Rather than having to tackle challenging redistribution conflicts, growth provides more all around, allowing Chinese decision makers to please one constituency without having to take from another one. More *is* better.

But how long will it be physically possible for China to extend this growth? If its energy consumption was half that of the United States in 2000, and exceeded that of the United States by 2009, how can this trajectory be sustained? Already today, China has the largest bio-capacity deficit of all nations—it would take the equivalent bio-capacity of 2.2 Chinas to support the country's current domestic demand.[7]

The big difference between China and other nations is that China is fully aware of the problem. The "farmer's view" is present even in the highest places. China has for millennia striven to be independent of the outside world. It is wary of its growing dependence on outside resources and is putting considerable efforts into building a national resource base and an economy based on domestic consumption rather than on resource-intensive exports to the rich world.

The "farmers" in Beijing are seeking to uphold their present growth rate, but their goal is to decouple it from its ecological footprint. Without economic growth, economic disappointment will rattle Chinese society, and thereby the world economy. Without massive decoupling, China will not make it to 2052. Is it physically possible to decouple their economy? Yes. But we have not yet seen the physical evidence that China is acting fast enough. But I hope they will, because China, like our big banks, is "too big to fail." If China coughs, we will all get a severe flu.

Mathis Wackernagel *(Swiss, born 1962) is cocreator of the ecological footprint concept and president of Global Footprint Network, an international sustainability think tank, with offices in Oakland, California; Geneva, Switzerland; and Brussels, Belgium.*

I believe that "The Race to Lose Last" makes a valid point about national policy. But the advice is not easy to follow in practical politics. This is bad for the affected nations' future, but it makes it much simpler for me to forecast what will actually happen: namely, little deviation from recent trends.

Unused Bio-capacity Will Plunge

In order to study the consequences of overshoot, it is clarifying to split the ecological footprint in two parts: the energy footprint and the nonenergy footprint. The energy footprint consists of the CO_2 emissions that we discussed at length in chapter 5. These emissions are so high that they lead to accumulation of CO_2 in the atmosphere and higher temperatures. The nonenergy footprint, on the other hand, takes the form of human use of physical land: it is the number of hectares used to raise food, graze animals, grow trees, and rear fish. So how has this area developed since 1970? And how does it compare with the available land—with the available biological capacity of the planet?[8]

The nonenergy footprint has grown slowly from 1970 to 2010, from 60% of the carrying capacity in 1970 to 70% in 2010. So if we disregard the energy footprint, humanity is still operating in a sustainable fashion, inside the land area available on the planet. But disregarding the energy footprint is, of course, a totally unsustainable assumption: even if we do so, climate gases will continue to accumulate in the atmosphere. The point I am trying to make is that we are currently using less land for food, meat, wood, fish, and cities than is available on the planet. That is the good, although myopic, news.

The bad news is that the growth in the nonenergy footprint has led to a significant reduction in the amount of unused bio-capacity (defined as total bio-capacity less the nonenergy footprint), as shown in figure 6-2. The unused bio-capacity is the amount of land that we have not yet occupied for food, meat, wood, fish, and cities. The unused part of the world has declined significantly, from 40% to 30% of the total availability in the last forty years. If we divide by the population, we see that the spare capacity per person has fallen even more dramatically, from 1.2 to 0.3 global hectares per person. There is now only a tiny reserve of unused, biologically productive nature behind each of us.

The nonenergy footprint has been growing much slower than world population over the last forty years. This means that we need less land today to support a global citizen than we did in 1970. The reason is improved technology: we have increased dramatically the annual output from each hectare of land, for example, through the use of fertilizer, genetic improvement, and fish

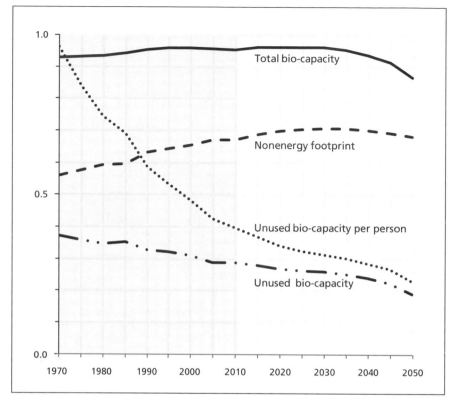

FIGURE 6-2 World biological capacity, 1970–2050.
Definition: Unused bio-capacity = total bio-capacity less nonenergy footprint.
Scale: Total bio-capacity, nonenergy footprint, and unused bio-capacity (0–12.5 billion global hectares of average biological productivity); unused bio-capacity per person (0–1.3 global hectares of average biological productivity per person).

farming. I expect this trend to continue, albeit at declining speed, as shown in figure 6-2. By multiplying my forecast for the nonenergy footprint per person with my forecast population, I get the future nonenergy footprint (not shown). And when I subtract this from the total bio-capacity of the world, I get my forecast for unused bio-capacity over the years to 2052. Some of the decline is caused by a decline in the total bio-capacity itself.

The total bio-capacity of the world sits in its areas of biologically productive land. The total bio-capcity has held up amazingly well over the last forty years, and I expect it to remain stable for some decades before it starts declining after 2040. The drop will result from global warming and all the other human onslaughts on nature's productive capacity. The Millennium Ecosystem Assessment,[9] which presented its final report in 2005, gave all the reasons for this assumption through its description of the accelerating degradation of most of the ecosystems on Earth. The drop would have started much earlier, had it not been for the significant effort humanity will put in place in the years to come to counter negative effects on important ecological services.

The ecological-footprint data that I use do not include the land area needed to produce metals and minerals; nor the land needed to collect water; nor the productive land needed to absorb and neutralize other pollutants. This means that the actual human footprint is larger than the one reflected in my numbers, and that the remaining unused bio-capacity—the buffer so to speak—is even smaller than indicated in figure 6-2. How much smaller is difficult to say, but there is little reason to doubt the general conclusions that humanity is overextending its use of the planet, and that current behavior is not sustainable in the long run.

Anything that can be done to reduce the human footprint will help to increase the buffer. One such thing will be to shift the mining of metals from mines in the wilderness to urban dumps. The megacities of the world will increasingly close their material loops in order not to drown in garbage. Recycling of metal waste will increase, and this trend is already visible, in both rich and poor countries. Used products and landfills will increasingly be used as sources for new material, as will effluents collected at the end of pipes. This will reduce the need for new mines, and "Glimpse 6-4: Urban Mining of Metals" makes the additional point that consequently few things are likely to run out.

GLIMPSE 6-4

Urban Mining of Metals

Chris Tuppen

By 2052, for many materials, and especially metals, urban mining will exceed extractive mining. That is to say, it will become more economically attractive to recover and recycle than to dig and refine. This transformation will be driven by a combination of three key factors.

First will be the increasing scarcity of some naturally occurring metal ores. Second will be high level of societal stocks for many of the more common elements such as iron and aluminum. And third will be ever-higher processing costs associated with ore refining.

Scarcity

There are several interrelated factors to consider in predicting specific metal ores for which demand may soon exceed supply.

The first is natural abundance. For a metal ore to be economically recoverable it needs to occur in a concentrated fashion. Natural abundance, in either the earth's crust or its oceans, gives a clue to its overall availability, but not the full story. For example, although the world's oceans host around 15,000 tonnes of dissolved gold[10] valued at ~USD 750 billion, it's in such low concentrations that it's simply not worth recovering. (At least not yet!)

Second, consider reserves. At any point in time the metals industry has good knowledge about untapped, economically viable, proven reserves and a reasonable estimate of undiscovered resources. Both of these figures continually change as new discoveries are made and existing mines are depleted. Some elements are sufficiently common for scarcity not to be a problem for decades to come. In those cases the total resource is ample and new reserves are likely to be found whenever the old ones are depleted.

Finally, some of the rarer metals are often recovered as a by-product of other metal extraction. For example, only 30% of new silver is mined directly; the remaining 70% is a by-product of lead, zinc, copper, or gold production.[11] The indium used for LCDs and touchscreens, for instance, all comes from lead and zinc smelters.

Societal Stocks

Over the centuries large quantities of metals have been transferred from underground rock to aboveground products. There are now substantial stocks of metal in manufactured items[12]—over fourteen billion tonnes of steel and in excess of two hundred million tonnes of copper, to take two examples. Major infrastructure development, especially in the emerging economies, will further increase societal stocks, and when population growth levels off, this will mean larger fractions of primary demand can be provided through recycling.

The recycling rates of many heavily used metals are already high: around 80% for steel,[13] for example. If one assumes that around 4% of societal steel stock reaches the end of its life every year, and that recycling rates remain high, one can predict that urban rather than extractive mining will be the dominant source of new steel before 2020.

Ore Processing Costs

Most metals have to be chemically extracted from their ores using large amounts of energy, often emitting significant quantities of CO_2 and other pollutants in the process. The increasing cost of energy and carbon will be reflected in the economics of the metal industry.

The processing of ore also often requires resources from other scarce natural systems, especially the provision of water. For example, even though Chile's water demand is already six times greater than water renewals,[14] the water consumption of the Chilean mining industry is still expected to increase by 45% by 2020.

Other Influences

But these key factors don't tell the whole story. The advent of urban mining will also be influenced by geopolitics. Some elements are concentrated in just a few places, and access can be restricted by conflicts and/or trade barriers. For example, the Democratic Republic of the Congo is rich in minerals, but links to human rights abuses has led to campaigns for such minerals to be avoided. From a different perspective, Europe is highly dependent on imports for many crucial metals, and the European Commission, concerned about future availability, has recently highlighted that China produces 95% of all rare earth concentrates, Brazil 90% of all niobium, and South Africa 79% of all rhodium.[15]

The distribution of metal usage also changes as demands change. For example, the introduction of the digital camera has seen a large reduction in the use of silver in conventional photographic film. But this has been more than compensated for by the use of silver in everything from contacts in PV panels to thin fibers in socks to counteract odors.

Efficiency matters, too. Metal stocks will last longer if the amount used per unit of production can be substantially decreased. This has already happened in a number of instances, such as the thickness of metal in beverage cans and the miniaturization of electronic equipment.

When a suitable substitute exists, it extends the reserves of a metal. But the availability of suitable alternatives varies considerably and is dependent on the chemical and physical properties required for any specific application.

Metals to Watch

Taking all these factors into consideration, it is quite straightforward to predict which metals will be in good supply for years to come. Fortunately these include the industrially critical elements aluminum, iron, silicon, and titanium. Metals[16] frequently listed on "endangered" lists include indium, silver, and some of the rare earths.

Indium is inherently scarce; estimates place its economically viable proven reserves at around 11,000 tonnes, which represents a fifteen years' supply at current consumption rates.[17] Even the most optimistic estimate of predicted global resources comes out at a mere 50,000 tonnes.[18] Over the past fifteen years indium production has increased more than tenfold. This has been due to its increasing use in optically active compound semiconductors and the use of indium tin oxide as a transparent electrical conductor across the front of computer, smartphone, and TV screens as well as thin-film solar panels. Fortunately these applications require only small amounts per unit of production, with a typical screen needing only around 50 mg of indium.[19] The downside of this frugalness is that societal stocks of indium are highly dispersed, making recovery for reuse very difficult. As the prices of screens and PV panels continue to fall, and demand thereby increases, it will be increasingly difficult to supply—and recycle—sufficient indium. There are prospects of carbon nanotubes offering a substitute for transparent conductive films, but this could be a long way off.

Silver has economically viable proven reserves of around 500,000 tonnes,[20] representing seventeen years of current consumption. It is widely used in industrial applications as well as for jewelery, silver plate, and coins. Some uses are growing very rapidly; in particular the solar industry has emerged as a significant industrial user. Silver demand for this sector grew 30% in 2009 and is expected to show a further tenfold increase over the next several years.[21]

The rare earths neodymium, dysprosium, and terbium are all used to make strong, lightweight magnets that are particularly effective in wind turbines and electric cars. The rare earths (also known as the lanthanides) are notoriously difficult to separate from each other.

From a natural abundance perspective they are not that rare. However, viable sources are scarce. China not only hosts the biggest reserves of usable rare earth ore but completely dominates its processing.[22]

Based on proven and projected reserves, projected consumption levels, and current recycling rates, indium, silver, dysprosium, and quite a few more metals could well have "run out" by 2052. Some will undoubtedly be "saved" by technological developments and substitutions, while shortages of others will prompt greater recovery and recycling to take place.

Ultimately this analysis leads me to conclude that over the next forty years there will be major increases in urban mining—in some cases because reserves are no longer available, and in others because large societal stocks will make it more financially attractive to recover and recycle than to dig and refine. So, at least for metals, the dream of circular material flows will eventually happen—but through conventional economic drivers rather than philosophy.

Chris Tuppen (British, born 1954) has been involved in sustainability for over twenty years. He runs Advancing Sustainability LLP and is an honorary professor at Keele University. He was previously BT's chief sustainability officer.

I think the main message of "Urban Mining of Metals" is correct: humanity will gradually reduce its dependence on mining "in the wild," and not only of metals, but, in the long run, also for fossil fuels—and primarily coal. This will lessen the footprint some.

Still, the amount of land not used by humans will drop dramatically, to less than 20% in 2052. The per capita availability of wilderness will fall from 1.2 global hectares per person in 1970 to 0.3 in 2052. That is a reduction by 75% in one lifetime—a momentous change. Humanity will be using practically all biologically productive land for human purposes. Undisturbed nature will be constrained to protected areas. Here nature will try to survive as well as it can. But not even inside the fences of a national park will flora and fauna be able to defend themselves against climate change, which inexorably will be shifting the ecosystems toward the north in the Northern Hemisphere and toward the south in the Southern. Once enough time has passed, the ecosystem will have moved beyond the fences of the park. Or up the hill above the park.

Over the next forty years, temperature zones will move poleward at (very roughly) 5 kilometers a year, and up mountainsides at (very roughly) 5 meters per year. In forty years that means 80 kilometers northward and 200 meters upward. Ecosystems will be following—in an attempt to escape from uncommon heat. Consider what this will do to your pet forest, park, or garden. "Glimpse 6-5: Nature Limited to Parks" will get your emotions going.

GLIMPSE 6-5

Nature Limited to Parks

Stephan Harding

Biodiversity is the diversity of life at various levels of organization, ranging from genes to species, ecosystems, biomes, and landscapes. As far as we can tell, the earth just before the appearance of modern humans was the most biodiverse it has ever been during the 3.5 billion years of life's tenure on this planet, and before we began to upset things it hosted a total of somewhere between 10 million and 100 million species. The fossil record shows us that there have been five mass extinctions in the last 400 million years or so, all due to natural causes such as meteorite impacts or flood basalt events, or possibly because of drastic internal reorganizations within biotic communities, but the greatest and fastest mass extinction is happening now and is entirely due to the economic activities of modern industrial societies.

We are currently hemorrhaging species at a rate up to 1,000 times the natural rate of extinction, or, more prosaically, every day we are losing a hundred species, mostly in the great tropical forests because of our endless desires for timber, soya, palm oil, and beef. Coral reefs and the marine realm in general are not exempt from our destructive attentions—they too are experiencing catastrophic species declines. The list of atrocities that our culture has perpetrated on the living world makes for chilling reading. We could have eliminated a quarter of all the organisms on the Earth by 2052. Even by the year 2000, about 11% of all bird species, 18% of mammals, 7% of fish, and 8% of all the world's plants were threatened with extinction. According to the Living Planet Index, in the period from 1970 to 2000, the population sizes of forest species declined by 15%, those of freshwater species by a staggering 54%, and those of marine species by 35%. By 2052, we may well have increased the overall rate of species extinctions to around 10,000 times the natural background rate.

The plight of biodiversity in the modern world came home to me recently when I took my nine-year-old son on a visit to our local zoo. What we found there epitomizes the likely relationship between humans and the rest of the biological world in 2052. A sea of humans obsessed with mobile phones, cameras, and a whole plethora of planet-destroying consumer goods seethed and swarmed in a pulsing, chattering crowd around small islands of carefully managed artificial habitat, each containing an exotic species either doomed to extinction or under heavy stress in its dwindling wild home.

The world in 2052 will be a zoo writ large, only far worse, for by then we will have reduced all of the planet's once vast, unbroken terrestrial ecosystems to tiny islands of habitat surrounded by agribusiness fields crisscrossed with roads, pylons, and sprawling cities, while climate change will have made a great deal of the planet almost uninhabitable for most species, including ourselves, owing to extreme weather events and sea-level rise.

The major drivers of the mass extinction will, by 2052, have revealed themselves far more evidently than they do today. Perhaps the most visible of them all is the destruction and fragmentation of habitats, which I think by then will have laid waste to all of the world's wild places, most notably the tropical rain forests, which will survive only as a few pitifully small and severely degraded remnants within national parks and reserves.

Another major driver of the mass extinction is the introduction of exotic species, which by 2052 may well have wiped out more species than some of the other major drivers, such as pollution, human population pressures, and overharvesting. Even by 2006, about 4,000 exotic plant species and 2,300 exotic animal species brought to the United States alone had threatened 42% of species on the endangered species list, causing about $138 billion of damage in sectors such as forestry, agriculture, and fisheries.

But perhaps the most pernicious of all the drivers of the mass extinction will have become well entrenched by 2052. I refer of course to climate change. By 2052 the planet will have warmed by 2°C and possibly more, with many disastrous consequences both for humans and for our planet's biodiversity. One such effect could be the irreversible dieback through wildfires of the Amazon forest. The carbon dioxide released into the atmosphere from such burning could increase the warming to 10°C by the end of the century, a pace more rapid than any other previous episode of natural warming.

Climate change will force species out of their home ranges in search of new habitats. Each species has its own very specific range of tolerance for temperature and moisture, and species are even now moving in an attempt to live within their climatological comfort zones as the climate changes around them. The general trend in a 2003 study of 1,700 species is a poleward movement of 6 kilometers per decade, and a 6-meter-per-decade movement up the sides of mountains.[23] Virtually the whole biosphere is being uprooted in unprecedented ways. Examples are legion, including the northward march of the boreal forest at the expense of open tundra vegetation; the northward expansion of red foxes in Arctic Canada and the simultaneous shrinking in the range of the arctic fox; the upward movements of alpine plants in the European Alps by 1 to 4 meters per decade; the increasing abundance of warm-water species among the zooplankton, fish, and intertidal invertebrates in the North Atlantic and along the coasts of California; and the extension of lowland Costa Rican birds into higher areas from lower mountain slopes because of changes in the frequency of dry-season mist. By 2006 in Britain and North America thirty-nine butterfly species had moved northward by up to 200 kilometers in twenty-seven years.

By 2052, many terrestrial species will have died out, as the changing climate obliged them to find new homes, yet their forced migrations were made impossible by the severe fragmentation of habitats. In the marine realm, huge numbers of cold-adapted species will have died out in the high latitudes, leaving precious little space for poleward migrating species from the far vaster tropical and subtropical oceans. Ocean acidification—a direct result of the additional carbon dioxide in the atmosphere—will have killed off many species that secrete calcium carbonate in their body parts, such as the corals and coccolithophorid marine algae. Many of these species play essential roles in climate regulation by sequestering carbon and by seeding planet-cooling clouds, so their demise will further warm the earth.

By 2052 ecosystems globally will have been literally torn apart by climate change as the delicate synchronization of events within them is disrupted. The once carefully ordered sequencings of leaf burst, caterpillar emergence, chick hatching, and so on will no longer mesh together as seamlessly as they did, and so these "phenological decouplings" will lead to further collapses of biodiversity in some ecosystems. Since biodiversity is intimately connected to the effectiveness of vital ecosystem functions such as nutrient cycling, water flow regulation, and climate modulation, these losses will make ecosystems less resilient—far less able to buffer the changes thrust upon them by climate change and habitat fragmentation. As a result, by 2052 some land masses in the low and mid latitudes will be well on the way to becoming inhospitable deserts or semideserts.

By 2052, biodiversity loss will have made life very difficult for billions of people who rely directly on the ecosystems around them for their well-being. And those privileged humans in the "developed" world—the people my son and I joined in the zoo that day—what of them? They will also suffer from the consequences of climate change and biodiversity loss, but by 2052 it is possible that technology will have shielded them, for a while at least, from the worst effects. Perhaps for them the initial consequences of the mass extinction will be an immense psychological diminishment—for the wild animals, both large and small, that molded the human psyche with their awesome presences since the dawn of our species will by then have become nothing more than flattened images on those scintillating screens that so fatally disconnect us from the world of nature.

Stephan Harding (British, born 1953) holds a doctorate in behavioral ecology from the University of Oxford. He is currently head of the master's in holistic science program at Schumacher College, Dartington, Devon, UK. He is author of Animate Earth: Science Intuition and Gaia, and the presenter of a documentary film of the same name.

The vision of "Nature Limited to Parks" is not only spot-on and very sad, but also an ideal transition from the physical future that has been the topic of chapters 4, 5, and 6 to the nonmaterial future, which will be the topic of chapters 7 and 8.

CHAPTER 7

The Nonmaterial Future to 2052

It took a long time to finalize my forecast of the material future to 2052, which you have now seen. I made many starts and pursued many lines of reasoning. Most of them ended in impossible contradictions or in unlikely breaks with recent history and traditional human behavior.

To my great surprise the end result is quite different from what I expected at the outset. I expected to uncover a bleak, even catastrophic, future, ending in some kind of environmental collapse before the middle of the twenty-first century. This would have been in line with what I have been worrying about all my life.

Instead I found a future world that will be much more diverse: some regions doing quite well and others having failed miserably and fallen into anarchy, and all of them toiling in increasingly erratic weather, and looking forward with alarm to an increasingly violent climate in the second half of the twenty-first century. I also found a future dominated by urbanization: people seeking opportunity, safety, and strength by gathering in huge cities. I found a world that will be poorer on a per capita basis than I had expected, and with a culture that I do not particularly like—but that I believe many others will like. That culture will be marked by artificial urban living, well insulated from the vagaries of a disappearing natural world, and well equipped with virtual edutainment. I did not find large-scale resource shortage, because the future world will be materially smaller and poorer than I originally expected. Finally I concluded that although things will go relatively well until 2052, the world of 2052 will be well established on a path that I really fear—the path toward self-reinforcing climate change and climate disaster in the second part of the century. I certainly did not find a world on a well-planned path toward sustainability.

I don't know how to assess this future. It will be much better than a global cataclysm where population and production drop dramatically as a consequence of natural disaster and war. But it will be much worse than the now common expectation of continuing growth in GDP and disposable income. It will be good for me as an old Norwegian living in the New North, which will fare well over the next couple of decades. But it will be surprisingly bad for all my good friends in the United States, who will have to endure gradual and seemingly never-ending stagnation from the peak years of their empire in the twentieth century. And much worse for the two billion earthlings who will remain poor.

Thus, it is impossible to pass one general judgment about the global future to 2052. The best, I believe, is that I continue to elaborate on what lies ahead and allow you to make the final judgment. Therefore I will turn to the less material aspects of the future, to the things that cannot easily be captured in numbers in my spreadsheets.

Smaller GDP: Milder Push against Global Limits

Although I had indeed expected to find an early peak in the global population, having followed population questions with interest and an open mind for the last forty years, I was genuinely surprised to discover that the global economy will grow much less than I had expected. The fact that world GDP would be only about twice as large as today was a big surprise. Like many others, I had expected that world GDP would grow briskly during the next forty years, moving billions from poverty to middle-class life, and making the rich even richer. And—like all environmentally concerned people—I had worried that this would push humanity far beyond the carrying capacity of the planet and trigger environmental collapse. If world GDP were to grow at 3% per year for another forty years, this would add two new world economies on top of the one we already have. Intuitively that did not—and still does not—seem sustainable.

As we've seen in prior chapters, global production in 2052 will be very close to peaking, and preparing for decline in the second half of the twenty-first century—resulting from the combined effects of a declining workforce and the gradual slowing of productivity growth as economies mature. One result will be stagnation, or even decline, in the average disposable income per person. Energy use will be declining. Climate gas emissions will still be high, but falling, and the nonenergy footprint relatively stable. In sum, the human footprint on the planet will be much lower than I had expected, largely because so many more will remain poor. But the footprint will still be in overshoot, and more than high enough to cause serious damage to global biodiversity.

A main consequence of this forecast of "half-slow" GDP growth to 2052 is that the world economy will not bump as hard into the planetary limits as would otherwise have been the case. The speed at impact will be lower, the overshoot smaller. For example, global energy use in 2052 will be declining and only 50% higher than today—in spite of the halfhearted global effort in the intervening decades to increase energy efficiency. Climate emissions will be much lower than they would otherwise have been. This does not mean smooth sailing: average temperatures will be 2°C higher than in preindustrial times, and still rising. Biodiversity will be badly damaged. Some areas will have become desert or flooded. But the situation will be much better than if the planet had had to carry three additional world economies rather than the two that I forecast.

Slower Growth in Productivity

The lower-than-expected GDP in 2052—which is a saving grace from the point of view of planetary health—will occur not because people and nations will want to stop growth. It will occur because there will be fewer hands (as the population ages and then declines) and, particularly, because of slower productivity growth (as the economies mature and increasing inequity and social friction take their toll).

As more economies mature, they move their production into services and care, see their labor participation rates saturate, and no longer reap the emerging-economy benefits of copying methods and technology from front-runner nations.

Additionally, we are also about to experience some waning of materialism as a driver in a materially rich society. This might reduce the push for further economic growth, although I think the effect will remain weak. People will always maintain the dream of being able to buy their way out of the gray world of the masses. This dream will probably become increasingly more intense, not less, when the world becomes more crowded. Still, there will be those who make a conscious shift away from the more-is-better mentality.

The total result will be continuing decline in productivity growth, which in turn will contribute to stagnation and then decline in world GDP. Bear in mind that this is the global snapshot: rises and falls in growth and productivity will occur at different times in different places, all contributing to this overall trend.

Tensions from Declining Consumption

The stagnation and subsequent decline of the global economy is a huge advantage from the point of view of planetary limits. If we are lucky, the damage created during overshoot (the climate damage, the biodiversity destruction, and the dousing of the global environment with toxics) will be repairable in the second half of the twenty-first century, through huge installments of extra investment. But this assumes that climate change does not become self-reinforcing.

This beneficial peak and decline in the "total pie" will have another consequence: it will uncover a totally different pattern of distribution among the regions of the world. Average consumption per person will be higher in 2052. But that is the average; the details of my forecast show that this will result from some rich getting poorer and many poor getting richer over the next forty years. The average global consumer will have some 70% more to spend in 2052 than today. But since incomes in China will be growing briskly, this means that others will have less—relative to today. The prime losers will be the OECD countries, with the United States in the lead.

One reason why per capita consumption will stagnate is that forced and voluntary investment will rise. Faced with increasing threats from pollution and depletion, nations will allocate an increasing fraction of societal production to fight these ills. And when crisis strikes, as it will increasingly frequently after 2030, investments will have to be further increased to repair the damage. As a result, the production of consumer goods and services will be reduced while people work to undo environmental damage and extract scarce resources. The situation will resemble the Soviet Union in the 1950s and 1960s, focusing on "heavy industry" at the expense of "consumption goods."

Consumption will also take a hit from lower productivity growth. And sadly, here is a feedback effect: stagnation leads to lower productivity growth. Not immediately, since firing a worker normally increases the profit per each of those who remain, but in the long term. When the growth of the economic pie slows down over a period of years, the distribution of income and wealth normally becomes more uneven. The poor lose out, and the gap between rich and poor increases. This in turn normally leads to social tension and in unlucky cases to conflict—which unavoidably slows productivity growth. Slow productivity growth in turn leads to slower growth in GDP, a smaller pie to share, more conflict, and even slower growth. Until the spiral is stopped by wise politics or redistribution of some kind—at least redistribution of opportunity—society locks itself into a slow-growth syndrome.

I am afraid this syndrome will characterize the rich nations over the next generation or so. The effect will be particularly bad in free-market economies with low tax rates and weak traditions for redistribution. Here unemployment and inequity will slow the growth in gross productivity. The situation will be better in economies with a solid safety net. Here it is simpler to avoid turbulence through transfer payments and thereby maintain productivity growth. This is illustrated by the high growth rates of the social democratic (many would say socialistic) economies of Scandinavia—with high tax rates funding ample social safety nets that help out on everything from health care to unemployment, childbirth leaves, education, and elderly care and catch people expelled from the workforce.

So, this long period of stagnation or slow decline in per capita consumption in the rich world toward 2052 will be bad. I repeat my suggestion that you ask a Detroit autoworker who has not gotten a real wage increase for the last thirty years, how he would feel extending this period by another forty years. But the indirect effect is worse: slow growth will cause more inequity, which in turn will lead to friction, which in turn will make it even more difficult to fine-tune labor productivity and achieve GDP growth.

Prevalence of Short-Termism

The negative effect of stagnation on productivity growth is not a necessity. It can be avoided, at least in principle. Redistribution of income and opportunity before problems arise can dramatically reduce the likelihood of social unrest. But peaceful redistribution has been rare in the past and will continue to be so in the future. This is because most societal decision making is governed by its short-term effects. Society—in both democratic and authoritarian regimes—is rather blind to long-term advantages. Humanity is blatantly short-term, and hence organized redistribution before needs become critical has been rare.

So although society can in principle decide to make dramatic shifts in the distribution of income and wealth and in the composition of the economy, in the amount and type of energy used, and in the emissions of greenhouse gases, I (regretfully) do not think society will do so. At least not at scale. This is because most such decisions are associated with up-front costs. And up front it is difficult to see the benefits that will arise further down the line. People shy away from such solutions. They want the advantage first, and grudgingly accept to pay the bill afterward.

My assumption that the short-term perspective will win out in future decision making is crucial, and one that I would have not dared to make so strongly when I was younger and had less experience with the real world. But forty years of practical experience and forty years of fighting for sustainability have convinced me that society—and particularly democratic society—indeed tends to choose the cheapest solution. This is the solution where the ratio of benefit to cost is the highest—when disregarding the costs and benefits beyond a time horizon of five years, give or take. This is what the economists call the cost-effective solution, the solution that gives most bang for the buck, so to speak, in a normal human perspective, which rarely extends beyond five years. The short time horizon is a serious challenge if society needs to spend now in order to avoid a problem in the distant future. Short-termism works actively against wise policy in such situations. And since short-termism tends to dominate among the voter mind-set, it also tends to dominate the mind-set of politicians.

Short-termism also dominates in the marketplace. The market uses a discount rate of 10% per year (or more) when comparing costs now with benefits in the future. This means that a benefit that lies twenty years ahead will be valued at one-tenth of its real value. In other words, a problem twenty years in the future will be worth solving only if the cost of the solution is less than one-tenth of the value saved. It comes as no surprise to those who know economics that it is "cost efficient" to allow the world to collapse from climate damage, as long as the collapse is more than forty years into the future. The net present value of reducing emissions and saving the world is lower than the net present value of business as usual. It is cheaper to push the world over the cliff than to try to save it.

The political world is not much better, given the short tenure of political appointments. Politicians can rarely spend time on agendas that yield a positive result only after the next election—which is normally less than four years away.

So both modern democracy and capitalist markets are amazingly short-sighted. This is a problem for a world facing a long-term climate threat. But it is an undisputable advantage for us in the forecasting business. Short-termism makes it unlikely that we will see strong deviations from the cost-effective (read: cheapest) solution, which can often be calculated ahead of time. Human short-termism keeps society on a relatively narrow path, with few sharp bends. When I forecast that the world will choose the cheapest solution, I will normally be proven right.

Luckily (for the world) there are exceptions. Some of these are the result of forward-looking actions of wise leaders. Others are forced upon society because there is an enemy at the door, because crisis already has struck, or because all other escape routes have been closed. But these exceptions are few; normally the cheapest solution will win. And cheap means cheap in the short term. Which is less than five years.

Prevalent short-termism is the basic reason why I forecast with conviction that humanity will choose to solve only part of the climate problem, although they could have easily solved it all. And this is the reason why I believe humanity will postpone serious action until climate damage is clearly visible on most doorsteps and parliamentary stairs. The exception will be forward-looking authoritarian regimes that have the liberty to consult more rarely with their populations.

Stronger Government

Many argue that fighting climate change and alleviating world poverty are the real challenges of our times. This fight should be given priority over more traditional tasks like reducing inflation and debt, creating enough employment, providing education and health care, avoiding nuclear war, and cleaning up local air pollution. I tend to agree, but I doubt that this will ever happen.

One common denominator of the climate and poverty challenges is that neither is easily solved by the market. The reason is obvious: the benefits of climate stabilization and poverty alleviation are too far in the future for business to find it profitable to invest in the project today. Little will happen unless someone—and this is most likely the state—enters the picture and changes the conditions under which the market works. The most obvious state intervention would be to introduce new legislation or pricing of externalities as necessary. Many progressive firms would welcome governmental initiatives that create even and profitable playing fields in new arenas, for example, in the form of all-encompassing carbon taxes or compulsory water fees. But new legislation requires a majority in the legislature, at least in democratic society. And since broad-scoped legislation is certain to bother some stakeholder group in the short term, it often fails to be passed, even though it would benefit the major-ity in the long term. As a result business does not receive the necessary help from new legislation or new prices. The climate and poverty challenges will remain unprofitable for the private sector, and hence unsolved in the short run.

But when a problem reaches sufficient proportion and has lasted long enough, the state normally enters the scene anyway. For sooner or later the voter does accept the need to get something done and does accept the taxation necessary to finance the operation. This has been the case in poverty alleviation for generations: the global job has become the task of new institutions that handle governmental development assistance and are financed by taxation in the donor countries. Similarly, the state will ultimately become a major player in the war on climate change. But that will only be after one has given up on the idea of a global quota trading system for greenhouse gas emissions and replaced that fancy, but impossibly complicated, system with a straight tax on fossil fuels, the income from which will be used to develop and implement climate-friendly technologies like renewable energy, energy-efficient building and transportation, and carbon capture and storage. We see the beginnings in the global fee on international airline travel that is intended to fund climate and energy investments, in both the rich and the poor world.

In the terms of my forecast, society will increasingly accept "voluntary investments" to reduce future climate emissions and find no way around accepting the "forced investments" that will become necessary to repair climate damage after the fact, and defend against new threats.

All in all this will mean bigger government in the decades ahead: a larger role for the state, higher taxes, and a larger share of investments in the GDP. The mirror image is less room for consumption and a smaller role for the market, which is good for those who trust the state, bad for those who worship the market.

Forced Redistribution

When reviewing the world scene anno 2012 it is hard to escape the conclusion that differences are growing. An elite group is getting richer by the day at incomprehensible speed. Others find themselves in the same situation year in and year out. And some are losing their jobs and sliding down the hierarchy. One result is increased inequity and social tension.

While there was rapid growth, some of the tension was released by the fact that everyone was progressing—if not by leaps and bounds, at least upward and in pace with colleagues and neighbors. But when per capita consumption slows and then stagnates during the next forty years, and worse, begins to decline, the tensions can no longer be released through distribution of new pieces from a growing pie. The only solution will be to redistribute the existing pie. To take from the rich and give to the poor.

It is difficult to forecast exactly where and when such relaxation of the accumulated tension through forced redistribution will occur, much like it was difficult to forecast the exact dates of the Arab Spring or the collapse of the Soviet Union. But the fact that it is hard to forecast the details does not make it less likely. It is only a question of time and circumstance.

There are a number of imbalances that will be addressed sometime during the next forty years. Some of them are so intensely unjust that it is hard to believe that they could exist for generations. But a quick look at history shows that inequities often remain for hundreds of years—like during czarist Russia—or even thousands—like during the Chinese dynasties—when the emperor and his family lived in a fantasy world extracted from the sweat of tens of millions of peasants. So even if things are bloody unjust, and stagnant, they do not necessarily lead to revolt. Particularly if the elite is willing to defend its prerogative with violence.

The exploding wage differential between senior management and ordinary workers in rich-world corporations is an interesting case. There is nothing except tradition that makes boards and owners think they have to pay CEOs and chairmen the exorbitant salaries they currently receive in order to get the work done. CEO and chairman work can, of course, be done by a great many individuals, if they were asked to. Furthermore, they would do the work for far less money if there was not the tradition of paying so well. Some argue that these are salaries determined by the market. If so, it is a great example of market failure. There is no doubt that social utility would increase if CEO and chairman compensation were reduced.

It will be difficult to correct this market failure, namely, to organize a decline in senior executive pay. This will require collective behavior from a group who is not used to organizing, namely, owners. But the fox is already in the henhouse, in the form of institutional owners and sovereign fund managers who have much looser emotional ties to the insider group of senior executives. On the other hand, this fox may not work well when the focus shifts to exorbitant pay in the financial sector. Here inequity is as great, but here our fox gets part of the profit.

Then there is the other glaring gap between the suffering of the unemployed minority and the well-being of the employed majority in all parts of the world. This gap was partly closed during the last forty years—through improved unemployment benefits in the industrial world—in my mind, a wise decision made by the employed majority. But still being unemployed is a major burden for those affected, and this burden will affect a larger group when growth rates decline over the next forty years. As a consequence unemployment will soar and there will be the need for higher and more lasting benefits, which translates into a need for higher taxes for those who have a job. A democratic parliament has perhaps no obligation to solve the problems of any minority—in this case the unemployed—but my forecast is that the unemployed will create enough turmoil (to use that word) to win a significantly greater part of the pie, even if they do not take part in making it. The protest of the Greeks against the cutbacks in 2011 was a case in point.

Then there is a new issue that is likely to intensify over the years ahead: namely, the fact that the current generation is asked not only to pay for the national debt accumulated by their parents, but also to pay for their parents' pensions. This pill is made even more bitter by the fact that the young are asked to do this while at the same time being faced with house prices so high that they cannot afford the type of dwelling in which their parents reside. I will be very surprised if this tension is not relieved through some form of "forced redistribution"—which simply means that someone who lent money won't get it back and someone who had expected a reasonable pension won't receive it. Again it is very hard to tell when and where the revolt will take place—but I suggest you start looking where debts are high, pension rights ample, and the support burden growing.

These revolts will not be limited to the rich world; one can see emerging tensions among the masses and the newly rich Chinese millionaires, the Russian oligarchs, the Saudi kings, the Colombian and Mexican drug barons. Some elites will be willing to fight back to keep their unfair share, while others may give in piecemeal. But many of these imbalances will decline before 2052, driven by the accumulated frustration in the masses as their consumption declines. The effect will be temporary disruption and a further slowing of the growth in labor productivity.

Megacity Environment

Let me then turn to the issue of daily life in the next forty years.

Many material aspects of life will follow traditional tracks: The majority will move into increasingly better housing—bigger and with a better indoor climate. They will eat better—more and in some places more healthily. They will become more mobile—through either car ownership or more public buses, planes, and trains. They will have access to better health services—private or public. Their gadgets will be more energy efficient than today, but easily recognizable: refrigerators, cars, digital communications devices (i.e., the future TV, PC, and smartphone implant). This majority will include the populations of China and the large emerging economies. Being better off in 2052 does not mean that they will have attained the lifestyle of the current West, but they will be much better off in 2052 than they were in 2012.

But I do not think this general improvement will apply to the current global elite. I very roughly define this group as those who reside in the OECD countries, whose average consumption is $28,000 per person-year, which is four times the global average. This group will experience material stagnation or even decline, particularly after 2030. They will not live in ever bigger and better houses, they won't eat ever more, they won't travel ever farther, and they are likely to be sicker—not from infectious disease or worn hips, but from lifestyle sickness like obesity, diabetes, and cancer. The basic reason, once more, is the steady decline in labor productivity over the years ahead, and the need for extra investment to handle the societal challenges of pollution, depletion, climate change, and inequity.

However, there is one thing most global citizens will have in common, and that is urban living. Life will no longer be village life in contact with land, animals, and nature. Home life will largely be conducted in high-rise apartments in big cities. Work life will be in an office, shop, or care center. And recreation will be increasingly virtual (via the future version of the TV including participatory games), though I doubt we'll see the end of having a beer in the local pub. Every couple of years there will be the vacation trip to a famous tourist spot, which will be crowded with package tourists queuing to see the sights, buying souvenirs, and taking (the future equivalent of) photos.

The fact that 80% of the world's population will live in cities will have an impact on the political agenda, which increasingly will focus on the problems of the urban dweller: traffic, air quality, noise, sewage, water, and power. And urbanization will drive one of the most important developments of the next forty years, namely, the reduction in total fertility—that is, the number of children per woman.

The trend toward more urbanization will be strengthened by climate change in two ways. First, per capita greenhouse gas emissions are lower for megacity dwellers than for people living in the periphery, because of the reduced need for personal travel. The climate cost of shipping huge quantities of food and water to the city is lower than the climate cost of long commutes from rural homes to city work. Second, it is cheaper (per person) to defend one megacity against the vagaries of extreme weather than to protect many individual settlements spread throughout the countryside. One city dike can protect millions of people against sea-level rise.

Humanity will be retreating into its cities partly because people prefer big city life over rural tranquillity, partly because cities are simpler to defend against enemies natural and human, and partly because much of the outlying territory will be damaged or at least disturbed by climate change. Some areas will have dried up, while others will be frequently flooded. Some areas will look ugly because they recently burned. Others will be less attractive because the original harmonious ecosystem is being replaced with a new one, as part of the incessant drift of temperature zones toward the poles—by 2052 they will have moved some 200 kilometers north in the Northern Hemisphere.

The future world will be a more urban world, with more urban values and more urban perspectives. It will be more like New York than California, much more like Chongqing than Tibet, more like Paris than Cote d'Azur, much more like Johannesburg than the Garden Route. Both physically and spiritually "Glimpse 7-1: Megacity Living and Externalization of the Mind" gives a feel for the situation.

GLIMPSE 7-1

Megacity Living and Externalization of the Mind

Per Arild Garnåsjordet and Lars Hem

City of the Future

In 2052 most of the world's population will live in big cities. Many of these cities will be very big (ten to forty million people). Furthermore, many of the smaller cities (one to five million) will be surrounded by huge urbanized areas closely connected to the infrastructure of the city. In the industrialized world, the infrastructure will be well developed so people can easily move and meet. In the less industrialized societies, the big cities will be divided into two kinds of communities, as they are today: The center (or multiple centers) will be part of the industrialized world, with adequate infrastructure. The periphery will be huge shantytowns basically without infrastructure. There will be "cities of gold" on a "planet of slums."

However, the slums will be more integrated in the economy than presently. A new division of labor will develop within the megacity. Parts of the slum may, for instance, specialize in recycling, as we can observe in some of the large Indian cities today, while other parts may do intensive agriculture. Thirty percent of the food consumed in Kampala today is produced in the metropolitan area.

The huge populations in the megacities of 2052 will be part of the global community. Still, most people will live their lives as part of a local community that will form the stable frame for their daily lives. The local community will gain importance for most people as the main source of their collective identity, rather than the megacity itself. The multi-center structure will facilitate the cultivation of specific cultural traditions and help create a community for children, who need a recognizable social world to take them through the transition from childhood to citizenship.

The megacity will differ from current cities in two important ways. One will be the very magnitude and cultural diversity of the city and the fact that there will be only small remnants of a rural world to counterbalance them, politically and culturally. The megacity will constitute the social world for the overwhelming majority of people. The megacity will frame the societal existence of the human species and will be more important than the nation-states in which they are located. We can already perceive this: you don't move to the United States, but to New York or Los Angeles.

Externalization of the Mind

The other main difference from present cities is that the Internet will be within easy reach for all megacity dwellers, along with traditional infrastructure like sanitation, roads, and power. The societal needs and aspirations of the city dwellers will be framed by the externalization of human intelligence implied by ever-present access to the Internet.

Steady access to the Internet will reduce the general illiteracy in the megacity. As a result, the number of talented people will increase, and their Internet access to a world community will contribute to the economic growth and the acceleration of local societal change. But the most radical, and unpredictable, change will be in the mentality of the majority who will live their lives continually connected to the Internet. Many of us already do, but as an acquired habit in adulthood. Growing up with the externalization of one's cognitive capacity through permanent Internet contact is another matter. It will change people's sense of self and their emotional makeup, their basic cognitive orientation, and their coping strategies.

We believe that over the next forty years there will be a parallel evolution of the megacities and the human minds continuously connected via the Internet. The megacity will become the paradigmatic living space for humans, and constant web contact will frame how people psychologically cope and thrive in this space. Let us look at some consequences.

EDUCATION OF CHILDREN

The societies of the Western world have been in constant and accelerating change through all their history, but not until the second half of the twentieth century did the change reach a pace so fast that most parents now know that their children will live in a world profoundly different from their own. Parents know that they are ignorant about much of the world their children will live in. But we can only teach children what we know. A main agenda in today's pedagogic discourse is teaching children to take responsibility for what they need to learn and know.

ALWAYS TRACKED

The traditional psychological and epistemic abyss between what is written and what is spoken is already blurred—and new norms concerning trust, privacy, and emotional sharing are under development in response. The informal electronic communications in text messages, e-mails, and social media are different because they are recorded—and can always be traced. The polite and "white" lies in informal communication risk constant exposure if they are digitalized. And a paradox: what is "on record" electronically is less stable than what is on record in paper. The latter lasts for centuries, while the former must be refreshed every ten years or so.

A GLOBAL REALITY

The Internet is a medium without borders, and communication through it is from anywhere, not from any specific location, which implies a profoundly different notion of self. One's belonging to a physical place is blurred by one's belonging to various virtual networks.

Conclusion

The megacity will be the social and physical environment for the lives of the majority of people in 2052. This will be an environment that is diverse and fluid, without clear borders between locations and without stable social structures and ideologies to give guidance as to how one's life is supposed to be. It will be an environment with few stable necessities and of open-ended and undefined opportunities. Megacity dwellers will be shaped by constant connection to the Internet, which also has few stable necessities and is completely open-ended as to opportunities. Their mentality will be different from ours in profound ways.

Per Arild Garnåsjordet *(Norwegian, born 1945) is a geographer and senior researcher at Statistics Norway. From 1995–2006 he was managing director for Asplan Viak, a major consulting firm in urban and regional planning.*

Lars Hem *(Norwegian, born 1945), PhD, is an associate professor of clinical psychology, Department of Psychology, Aarhus University, and a specialist and supervisor in psychotherapy. He has written books on the theory of science, social psychology, dreams and REM sleep, and psychotherapy.*

Omnipresent Internet

"Megacity Living" highlights the continuation of another essential trend toward 2052: the omnipresence of the Internet. Everyone will have access to all human knowledge at the touch of the fingertip (or perhaps simply by thinking about it, thereby sending a signal to some type of implant). Ideally this should increase gross labor productivity: the right answer will always be at hand. But that applies only when the bottleneck is lack of knowledge—for instance, when you want to know what type of seed to use when the climate is changing so fast that you do not have the time to accumulate your own experience through controlled experiments year after year.

But the bottleneck in human endeavor, and especially in democratic society, is not lacking knowledge but lacking the ability to agree. It is not obvious that access to ever more information will facilitate agreement. It may equally well galvanize the opposing fronts. And experience seems to indicate that people are not strongly influenced by information that they do not like: Many kept smoking long after it had been proved that it damages one's health. Some—like myself—keep eating organic meat even if it can't be proven that this is better than eating steaks from the feedlot.

Forming a consensus will become harder. In the past there was one national newspaper (or at most a few) that set the agenda; now there is a forest of blogs. Formerly there were a handful of national broadcasters (or perhaps just one); now there are hundreds of local ones, catering to special tastes. Formerly there were just a few encyclopedias; now there is the ever-changing Wikipedia and numerous others. Sifting the essentials from the noise is becoming increasingly difficult. Forming a majority view is becoming impossibly time-consuming.

And this is in spite of the fact that the web already makes it much simpler to gather those who have a common agenda. Thus it is simple to predict that future society will consist of an impenetrable jungle of special interest groups. There will be groups for and against everything. If the leaders try to move forward they will be opposed; if they try to move backward they will also be opposed. There will be well-organized pressure groups pushing right, and equally strong and eloquent groups pushing left. And if the tired government tries to stand still, there will be groups calling for action. The effect on productivity growth is obvious: the pace of advance will slow down because it will take longer to agree. The fuller the world, the stronger the effect. In a crowded world any action affects someone else's interest—or at the very least the view from his window.

So I don't think that the omnipresent web will accelerate gross productivity growth. The braking power of NIMBY ("not in my back yard") will be stronger than the acceleration from more knowledge.

I also expect another effect from the always-on-web culture; namely, a more direct public hand on the policy rudder. Public opinion will be well known at all times (through continuous polling) and will have to be considered in political decision making. This means that the short-termism of the majority will dominate even more strongly than today. Future society will increasingly choose the solution that is cheapest in the short run. This will simplify life for us forecasters, but it will be bad for those who must endure the long-term consequences of shortsighted policy.

Finally, the omnipresent Internet will result in wonderful/horrible transparency. It will be increasingly difficult to do anything in hiding, and the digital tracks of your actions will last longer than your physical footprints on the street. What this will do for criminality I do not know, but it seems like it would make it harder to get away with white-collar crime. It is interesting that some are already discussing whether to ban money and shift all payments to debit cards—so there will always be an electronic track, simplifying the work of the police. I doubt that traditional privacy will survive in an increasingly crowded and transparent world, where the Internet is always on.

Disappearing Charms

Thus the Internet may be the end of a long-standing desire to protect the charm of privacy. Soon everything will be in digital form somewhere, and once transferable will be transferred. WikiLeaks is only a precursor. But the loss of privacy may be so gradual that it will not be perceived as a serious loss. Most Norwegians do not object to the fact that the tax authority fills in their tax returns *before* they send them out—based on information in their files. Physical privacy may survive, but the world is gradually and inevitably becoming more transparent, so everything will be known.

But the bourgeois charm of privacy will not be the only value that will be threatened over the next forty years. In a richer and more populous world with less undisturbed nature, many of the past and current luxuries of the elites will disappear, or at least get increasingly scarce. The process may be so slow that it does not cause significant remorse. Examples abound—from the comical to the truly sad. We have all come to accept that it is no longer possible to experience an expedition to a white spot on the map. And for those few who still legally hunt the big five (lion, leopard, elephant, rhino, and buffalo), this can probably nowhere be done without paying a fee. If you want to climb Mount Everest, you must plan for enough time to handle the traffic jam when descending from the peak. To ski untouched snow you have to get up early in the morning, walk up big hills, or book helicopter flights months in advance in those few skiable regions that still allow helicopters in spite of the noise they create for all the other tourists. Real caviar is rationed through protection of the sturgeon. Good French wine is impossibly expensive because tens of millions of new customers suddenly exist in east Asia. French champagne will gradually disappear and be replaced by new champagnes coming from the sandy hills of south England. Glacier climbing or viewing will disappear as the land-based ice melts. You will need to book years ahead to see the museums in the Hermitage or Florence.

All in all, elite tourism—one of the real charms of the upper classes of the past—will receive a double whammy, from climate change and an explosion in the number of tourists.

The urban dweller of the future will be rather distant from nature and may not miss these amenities. She or he may not be feeling the call of the wild and may not be bothered by having to line up in order to see the famous paintings in Europe. She or he will have grown up in the Internet age and may well be more interested in new modern urban culture and virtual reality. In 2052 there will be, beyond doubt, great consolation prizes for couch potatoes in the form of absolute first-class virtual nature and museums. The homebody will be able to see and experience anything from the living room—history, present, and future all included. And if one wants to go somewhere special, there will be the totally artificial, polished luxury of five-star hotels and cruise ships. The hotels will be destinations in themselves—with no external sightseeing spot, but great indoor shopping and entertainment. Or one could choose the floating version: the huge cruise ship that never enters a port but entertains its visitors with a new spectacular show on board every evening of the week.

So perhaps the loss of the bourgeois charms of privacy and exclusivity will not be among the great losses over the next forty years. But I for one—as a representative of the old elite—will miss the opportunity to visit undisturbed old-growth forests or snorkel the biodiverse reefs of the tropics. These still-existing charms are likely to be gone after another couple of decades of income growth and global warming.

The observant reader will have noticed that most of the amenities that will go are of little interest to the ordinary citizen, since these attractions have never been within his spending power anyway. That is true and it is one of the main reasons why I do not think there will be a democratic majority in favor of early action in order to save these charms.

Better Health

The issue of future health has not been mentioned thus far, except indirectly in my population forecast—which depends on lower infant mortality, higher life expectancy, and widely available contraception. In short, the global population will peak earlier because of modern medicine, which will have progressed even further by 2052. Obesity is likely to rise as increasingly Westernized societies transition away from traditional diets, or declining wealth in OECD nations means people have less money to spend on quality food. It will eventually be rolled back through medical innovation or a general desire to look good and feel well, and I do think that the rollback will be well under way in 2052.

Over the next forty years, medicine will be characterized by tremendous technological advance. In 2052 the medical profession will be capable of doing far more than people will be able to pay for. And that will be so irrespective of how we resolve the discussion about how you should pay: directly for what you get or via taxes. That discussion will be a long-drawn-out one, since the solution involves important distributional issues. For there are only those two alternatives: either the individual pays in proportion to her own needs, or the individual pays in proportion to the average need. The first would come out of the patient's funds when she is sick; the second would be based on an annual premium paid as tax to a public system or an insurance fee to an insurance company with the obligation to insure all citizens. Whether employers act as intermediaries does not matter, in principle.

"Glimpse 7-2: Individual Health from Public Care" provides a more detailed picture.

Individual Health from Public Care

Harald Siem

It might seem foolhardy to try to forecast the development in health and medicine in forty years to come. Looking back explains why. Unpredictable discoveries changed medicine.

Just one hundred years ago, there were hardly any really effective interventions in medical practice. Granted, we had caregivers and surgeons, and chloroform and ether had been known for fifty years. But modern anesthesia didn't arrive until the 1940s. X-ray imaging emerged in 1901. Later came contrast angiography, then computerized imaging, followed by ever more advanced methods of making pictures of the human interior. The last forty years have brought spectacular progress, in the real sense of the word.

The medical armamentarium has advanced from bloodletting, enemas, and leeches to antibiotics, effective drugs, and other treatments against mental illness, heart disease, certain cancers, parkinsonism, and unwanted pregnancies. Heart transplantation was considered impossible when I graduated from medical school; today it is routine.

This wave of new effective treatments gave a boost to the status of physicians, who were increasingly let in not through the kitchen, but through the front door. But then patients rights started to constrain the physician. And medical ethics started its move from paternalism to consumerism.

Emerging Trends in Medicine

Technological gains will continue, and two areas are moving especially fast. One is the growing use of stem cells. These undifferentiated, pluripotent cells have the ability to change, or develop, into any one of the 200-odd types of cell that compose the human body—meaning they can grow into different kinds of tissue and possibly repair damage. The other is the use of genetically tailored medicines—drugs that alter, or compensate for, defunct genes. Both areas will see huge advance in forty years.

A number of infectious diseases will be eradicated. Likely candidates are polio, measles, encephalitis, a couple of worm diseases, and possibly AIDS. At the same time, it is likely that new strains of influenza virus will evolve, and that new communicable diseases will emerge, often from animal reservoirs. Road accidents will be reduced; mental illness and violence in close relations will increase.

As a consequence the disease burden of future populations will change. The industrialized countries will lead the way, but the trend is global. The health challenge in the future will be primarily chronic, lifestyle-related diseases. Obesity, diabetes, and Alzheimer's disease will dominate the hospital wards and the nursing homes, first in the rich and later in the poor, or not so poor, countries. In the transition, some rapidly developing countries may have to live with the double burden of infectious diseases and chronic ailments.

The shift in the disease burden will force a shift in medical practice. Traditional practice was tailored for episodic illness—like pneumonia or appendicitis—where the patients perceived symptoms, the doctor diagnosed and treated the illness, and that was it. The chronic ailments require a different approach. They require a longitudinal organization of medical care, where the patient is being followed over time—also before she or he turns ill. Health-service providers will encourage people to monitor and manage their own health.

As people become more affluent, they will have fewer children, consume less tobacco and less fat, and have more time for leisure activities. This again will shift the disease burden. And so will climate change, most directly through extreme weather, disease vector increase (or change), and coastal flooding and forced migration.

Medical intervention will become even more effective, and life expectancy will grow rapidly, adding a year every five years in most countries. Few countries will have a life expectancy of less than sixty years in 2052, and many will be as high as ninety years. The exceptions will be countries that have been severely hit by AIDS, former communist states in transition, and failed states. Exceptions may arise from a devastating flu pandemic or similar catastrophic setback. Better nutrition, education, and living conditions and safe environments will account for much of the progress where it occurs. Maternal and child health and vaccinations will also play an important role.

So in general there will be progress on a broad front. The high burden of chronic ailments needing long-term care will usher in computerized care programs and monitoring. Automatic sensors and computerized lifestyle coaches will modify behavior and manage illnesses like diabetes. Such programs will dominate medical practice in 2052 but will meet much resistance. The clinical freedom of practitioners will be under attack; the growth of bureaucratic medicine will be resented. On the other hand, concerns about quality of care and liability will ensure that programmed care adopts the latest of best practices faster than any single doctor.

Rising Medical Costs

So expenditures for health care in all societies will rise. One might ask whether there is a ceiling beyond which spending for health cannot grow because of the needs in other sectors of society. If so, it is not yet easy to discern: in the United States, residents spend 18% of the GDP for health care. It is simpler to predict that there will be limits for tax-financed national health expenditure. Most likely, the public coverage will be supplemented with private health expenditure, where individuals use their own funds to buy additional health services.

So there will be a development toward universal health coverage, even in today's poor countries. The coverage can take two forms: national (tax-based) health systems or compulsory insurance schemes. Since medical needs for an individual arise in unpredictable ways, there is a logic for pooling risks, which means third-party payment at the point of consumption of treatment and care. But in all cases, the coverage will have to be limited in some way, in order not to bankrupt the system. The system will not be able to cover any condition or treatment. Costly treatment will be counted out, after bitter discussions of priority. One will not be able to avoid the question of who shall live. In other words, one will agree on what will be covered by a collective system, and what must be paid for by personal funds.

There are three competing forces in health: the demand from patients and patients' organizations, the interest of health-sector staff and professions, and the need for cost control by the authorities or the insurance companies, representing the common purse. Health politics will remain about patients, providers, and payment.

So, by 2052, we will see life expectancy grow in most, if not all, regions of the world. We will also see infectious diseases decline and chronic diseases increase, along with our reliance on automated care. And there will have been a partial answer to the question of who must use his or her private funds to live.

Harald Siem (Norwegian, born 1941) is a medical doctor with a master's in public health, trained in Basel, Oxford, Oslo, and Harvard. He has worked as a district medical officer then at the University of Oslo, and for the Oslo city health administration, International Organization for Migration, and WHO in Geneva, and now works in the Norwegian Directorate of Health.

I agree with the view presented in "Individual Health from Public Care." There will be general progress in the medical arena over the decades to come—albeit much, much slower than could have been, because of the major redistribution issues involved. Technological ability will lead regarding what is delivered to the masses, but there will be enough progress to ensure continuing increase in life expectancy. Increasingly, I believe, the state will enter the picture and finally will put in place the large-scale, collective solutions that are clearly more efficient and much more equitable than a heterogeneous mixture of individualistic solutions.

Armed Forces Fighting New Threats

Another aspect worth mentioning is the changing role of the military over the next forty years. The military will not disappear but will fight new enemies. The real threat to a nation will increasingly be extreme weather and the resulting damage—and in some places, a potential flood of climate refugees. Military man- and machine-power will increasingly be used to clean up the mess after hurricanes and to bring in emergency rations when drought strikes. The military will help keep borders closed. Real combat will increasingly be the task of robots and drones. "Glimpse 7-3: The Future of War and the Rise of Robots" describes this development.

GLIMPSE 7-3

The Future of War and the Rise of Robots

Ugo Bardi

It is an easy prediction that, forty years from now, human beings will have little place on the battlefield. They will be replaced largely by robotic weapons—a trend already in motion with the rising use of remote-controlled military drones or "UCAVs" (unmanned combat aerial vehicles). We can expect the term "unmanned weapon" to become as odd as the term "horseless carriage" is today. However, it is more difficult to predict how robotic weapons will affect warfare and the structure of society. Future wars may be more frequent but probably also smaller in scale and less destructive. It is possible that robotic weapons will make the concept of a nation-state obsolete, to be replaced by structures akin to present-day corporations. These developments will occur first in rich countries with low levels of corruption and high manpower costs.

To examine the future of warfare, we can use the simulation methods used in *The Limits to Growth* study in 1972[1]—methods that predict behavior within a given system and, specifically, that describe how the world's economic system transforms natural resources into waste, or pollution.

The military sector is part of the industrial system. Typically, during the past few centuries, the military sector has been drawing around 5%–10% of the GDP of most strong states, while in wartime this fraction may rise up to 30%–40% and even more.[2] In wartime, military activities generate an enormous amount of pollution in the form of infrastructure destruction. With the development of more and more destructive weapons, and especially of nuclear ones, the cost of war in terms of pollution may reach values several times larger than the pollution arising from the GDP of any state. So, while the military sector is expected to follow the size of the global economy, wars may accelerate global decline because of the large amount of pollution they generate. A nuclear war might make the most pessimistic *Limits to Growth* scenarios unfold almost instantly. Unfortunately, starting a war costs much less than cleaning up afterward.

Robotization may negate these trends by reducing the pollution cost of war. Robotic weapons are inherently precision weapons. They can be controlled to reduce collateral damage and, hence, pollution. In this respect, twenty-first-century robots are enormously better than the iconic weapon of the twentieth century: the nuclear warhead. There are other potential advantages as well. Present-day command-and-control systems are based on models developed during the eighteenth and nineteenth centuries to convince human beings to perform activities that are not natural for them: obey orders, march under enemy fire, and stand still while shelled, to name a few. The methods that accomplish these results are called "drilling." But drilling is not only a slow and expensive process; it is also very difficult to undo. So, once fighting has started, it is very hard to convince people to stop. Because of this inertia, wars often tend to continue all the way to the near-complete destruction of the weaker side. On the contrary, robots don't need propaganda. They can be easily reprogrammed, and therefore the decision to engage or disengage in a conflict can be very quick. If wars can be easily stopped as soon as it is clear who is winning, the result can be a great reduction in damage and, hence, pollution.

Overall, wars will become less costly with the use of robots, but that doesn't mean a reduction in their frequency. New major wars—even nuclear ones—cannot be excluded for the future. Future wars may become more frequent even in the face of a progressive decline of the world's industrial system caused by resource depletion. We may see war becoming endemic, and dispersed in a large number of small conflicts. Also, the low cost of war may make the distinction between "peacetime" and "wartime" disappear. Future wars may often be classified as police actions against groups defined as "rogue." These are, clearly, already ongoing trends.

We can expect, therefore, drastic changes in the way wars will be managed and conducted. National armies may be replaced by private contractors deemed more suitable for managing high-tech robotic weapons in the kind of small-scale conflict that may become common in the future. These contractors need not be limited to serve a specific national government and may well sell their services to the highest bidder, as is already happening. Nation-states, then, may also decline and perhaps disappear, as there will be no need for propaganda to convince people to sacrifice themselves in battle. In addition, nation-states have evolved specifically with the purpose of "defending the borders" when the main source of wealth was agriculture, and hence territory. In recent times, however, the focus of war has been more on the control of mineral resources, with several recent wars described, correctly, as oil wars. It may be possible that the structure considered best adapted to managing war and resources, in these conditions will be not the nation-state but something akin to modern corporations—more effective, perhaps, than states in employing high-tech military contractors for small-scale conflicts.

The reduction of the destructive power of war is an improvement on the present situation. When human fighters become hopelessly outmatched by robots, most humans will simply cease to be interesting targets, while robots will be used mainly to fight other robots. Certainly, that doesn't mean that war will not involve human victims any longer; military and political leaders will remain at risk, and the decision of targeting civilian infrastructure might still be considered an option. Terrorism, that is, military actions purposefully aimed against civilians, may turn out to be an especially suitable task for drones, which might easily be programmed for the extermination of specific ethnic, religious, or political groups. On the other hand, the fact that the actions of robots are recorded and traceable could create a barrier over their indiscriminate use against civilians—a plus when considering the violence, torture, rape, and other typical excesses of human troops. So even if war may become more frequent, it need not become more violent. Indeed, the trend of avoiding as much as possible collateral damage to civilians is already ongoing. It is a positive development after the emphasis on carpet bombing in the twentieth century.

War is so deeply embedded in the global economic system that we can expect it to exist as long as there are natural resources to compete for. Robots won't change that, as long as they are controlled and programmed by humans. In a more distant future, however, the battlefield experience is likely to give robots increased capabilities to act autonomously and a chance to become something much different from what the term "drone" implies. That doesn't mean that robots would take over their human masters. But it does mean that humans would not be needed as fighters. How such a society could develop is impossible to say at present. The only certainty is that wars are among the most unpredictable of human activities and that the future is, as always, full of surprises.

Ugo Bardi *(Italian, born 1952) teaches physical chemistry at the University of Florence, Italy. His interests cover the depletion of mineral resources and peak oil, nanotechnology, and robotics. He runs the Italian section of the Association for the Study of Peak Oil and blogs on www.cassandralegacy.blogspot.com. His most recent book is* The Limits to Growth Revisited.

The trends described in "The Future of War and the Rise of Robots" seem likely, but I think they will take time to become reality. Meanwhile, the military will not disappear but increasingly will be used to fight the consequences of inclement weather. What we will not see, I am afraid, is the large-scale use of the military in a constructive war against the *root causes* of climate change. The military will remain in the business of ex post repair, and possibly in ex ante adaptation. The world currently uses around 2% of its productive capacity on defense. This is about the level of effort that would have solved the climate problem. If the military capacity were used to increase energy efficiency (by, for instance, building better housing and better cars) and to build renewable energy sources (by building windmills, solar panels, and CCS plants) for a number of decades, the CO_2 emissions of the future world would drop precipitously. It would take a little longer than winning World War II but would be the thoroughly beneficial climate equivalent to the military response to the attack on Pearl Harbor in 1942.

"Glimpse 7-4: Military for Sustainability" provides the detail.

GLIMPSE 7-4
Military for Sustainability

John Elkington

With honorable exceptions, when most of us in the sustainability field list economic sectors and corporations to target and influence, the military-industrial complex routinely falls into a collective blind spot.

This is dangerous. It's not just that we invest a great deal of money here. Global military expenditure rose in 2010 by 1.3%, reaching a record USD 1.6 trillion, or 2.4% of world GDP, according to the Stockholm International Peace Research Institute.[3] But even though that figure represented the lowest growth rate since 2001—and a marked slowdown from the spending increase of 5.9% in 2009, thanks to the financial crisis—the impact of military expenditures on our economies and societies remains substantial. Like other major industries, the defense sector will (because it must) mutate and evolve over time, which raises the question of what role the military will play during the next forty years.

I am intrigued to see where cyberwarfare, "smart dust" sensors, miniature drones, or exoskeletons will take the military—and the rest of us—by the 2030s and 2040s, but I think it will take time before robotic systems replace humans in the field of war. As has so often happened in the history of conflict, however, many of these emerging technologies will likely find new applications outside the battlefield. By 2052, though, I expect significant focus on a new core business of the armed services: namely, recovering from natural disasters and fighting a growing range of unsustainabilities, including the destruction of key natural assets like fisheries, forests, and watersheds.

Only a wild optimist—or a fatalist—can believe that nation-states will disarm, following the example of Costa Rica. Indeed, that small Central American state can be seen as the exception that proves the rule. In addition to the ubiquity of death and taxes, we are guaranteed to have armed forces for the foreseeable future—but increasingly with the new purpose to deal with the consequences of large-scale environmental change.

For the armed services—and the defense industries—to legitimately play this new role, they will need to go through the same sort of transparency and sustainability revolutions that have hit a broad range of other sectors in recent decades. Think, for example, about the endemic corruption in so much of the defense world—and of the extent to which the military controls the economies in countries like Iran and China.

The only general to be elected US president in the twentieth century, Dwight D. Eisenhower, warned Americans against "plundering for our own ease and convenience the precious resources of tomorrow" and about the perils of underestimating the often-malign influence of the military-industrial complex:

> In the councils of government, we must guard against the acquisition of unwarranted influence, whether sought or unsought, by the military-industrial complex. The potential for the disastrous rise of misplaced power exists and will persist. We must never let the weight of this combination endanger our liberties or democratic processes.[4]

Among the initiatives designed to view the future of security, defense, and the armed forces through lenses other than those typically used by right-wingers, I like the work of the US Truman National Security Project. I buy into their thesis:

> Today's world is a dangerous place. Our security is at risk from terrorists, belligerent states, and the proliferation of weapons that can cause unimaginable, massive destruction. We are also threatened by less obvious foes such as pandemic disease, weak and corrupt governments, and the spread of anti-Americanism.
>
> The conservative strategy to meet today's threats is bankrupt. They have missed crucial opportunities. Their rhetoric has squandered world sympathy and support. Allies we need to conquer terror have been alienated. Poor strategic planning has weakened military morale and capabilities. Ideologically based Pentagon-focused policy-making is breeding instability abroad, exacerbating the conditions that make us vulnerable. The conservative strategy is making the world less safe.[5]

And what is true of Americans is true of the rest of us. If we must continue paying for the military, we must ensure it does what we need to get done. We must learn in the coming decades how to reboot and repurpose military operating systems. By 2052, if we succeed, the armed forces of many countries will have specialized in helping their economies and societies adapt to natural disasters—particularly those caused by advancing climate change. This will still mean fighting wars, managing border disputes, and coping with refugees, but I think we will also look back on Mikhail Gorbachev's "Green Cross" as an idea before its time.[6]

Environmental regeneration, augmentation (including various forms of geo-engineering), and conservation will become a key part of military training—extended to a growing proportion of young people, partly as a means of educating, training, and disciplining populations. Ground forces will be tasked with protecting key elements of the biosphere from human depredations. Naval forces will be redeployed to protect the remaining wild fisheries, and the growing number of fish-farming and ocean-ranching operations. Air forces will be used for a range of related surveillance tasks, including future generations of smart-sensor networks and drones, the latter often evolved on the principles of biomimicry.

Intelligence services—including the satellite remote-sensing branches—will police eco-crime and intervene where there is evidence of the new crime of ecocide.[7] The potential for "Big Brother" misuse and abuse of such systems is considerable, which is why transparency, accountability, and sustainability agendas will become central concerns for a growing number of countries.

Meanwhile, you can already see evidence of another trajectory in the military, with growing numbers of zero-impact goals being announced in relation to carbon, waste, toxics, and even fossil fuels. Consider the US Army's Net Zero Initiative.[8] By the 2020s, sustainability versions of Lockheed Martin's "Skunk Works"[9]—which gave disruptive innovators the space and resources to create transformative solutions—will be commonplace, with growing interest in spin-off technologies. This won't be confined to lead-free bullets or biodegradable landmines but will be open to suites of technologies designed to support populations in low-energy, low-footprint ways. Some exotic swords will be beaten into plowshares, like the NATO bunker transformed into a zero-energy data farm.[10]

Leading intelligence services have been adapting for some time, including the Central Intelligence Agency.[11] By 2052, however, we will also have seen a deeply unwelcome explosion of interest in "environmental weapons." These started with cloud-seeding attempts aimed at causing landslides in Vietnam and Cambodia, soon expanding to attempts to make incisions in the ozone layer.[12] As a result of bitter experience, new treaties will be drawn up to regulate the development and use of such weapons.

The history of conflict shows that every form of technology can be press-ganged into uniform. Our challenge is to press-gang the military into the sustainability business.

John Elkington *(British, born 1949) is cofounder of Environmental Data Services (ENDS, 1978), SustainAbility (1987), and Volans (2008), where he is executive chairman. He has written seventeen books, sits on over twenty boards or advisory boards, and blogs at www.johnelkington.com/journal.*

I believe the shift of military capacity into "green operations," perhaps alongside the peacekeeping blue berets of the UN, will occur much faster than expected. It will be a physical reflection of one of the major nonmaterial shifts over the next forty years: namely, the shift in the enemy picture. The "enemy" will shift from being the closest neighbor with a deviant view on what is the best system of governance and religion to man-made climate change. It will be a shift from being someone else to being our collective selves. To quote a poster from the first Earth Day in 1970: "We have met the enemy, and he is us."[13]

CHAPTER 8

The Zeitgeist in 2052

The rapid changes over the next forty years will have deep impacts on our cultures, our political systems, and our general frame of mind. So, what will the mood be like in the middle of the twenty-first century? By examining some core developments, we can explore the zeitgeist—the spirit—of 2052.

Fragmentation: More Focus on Local Solutions

Over the last decade or two many have come to believe that "globalization" would continue forever and ultimately create a "flat" world, with few differences across national borders. This development has been helped by institutional developments such as the World Trade Organization reducing trade barriers, and the European Union ensuring the free flow of labor and capital within Europe. But we may be seeing the limits to such flattening when the world's more than 190 countries prove unable to reach agreement on cutting greenhouse gas emissions—in spite of nearly fifteen years of effort to replace the Kyoto protocol. Similar lack of progress characterizes the Doha trade talks on liberalization of service flows.

Although I believe globalization will wane, it won't result in an outright decline in global trade. Trade will just grow less rapidly than optimal from a purely economic point of view. But trade will remain sufficiently free to help harmonize labor costs in the long run; free enough to continue shifting much production to low-income nations, thereby boosting their labor cost and disposable income in the longer run; and free enough to ensure that low-income countries gradually catch up with the rich countries. But as incomes rise, people will become more willing to protect the status quo. They will be more willing to sacrifice trade gains in exchange for protection of cultural traditions and national identity. Free trade will always have its enemies. And they will always have their say; not dominant, but always there, enough to weaken the invisible hand and slow economic restructuring.

The drift away from a purely economic focus in rich society is also important because it will add to all the other forces that are slowing productivity growth in these societies. Less trade means less use of comparative advantages and lower productivity growth—all else being equal.

The increased focus on cultural values in rich societies will reduce the support for common markets and the continued merger into ever larger economic units. Increased focus on soft values may even lead to fragmentation of existing institutions. The possible split of the European Union—as a consequence of very different attitudes toward life, work, and happiness in its southern and northern parts—is a case in point. At the opposite end of the income spectrum the east Asian countries are moving in the opposite direction, trying to form a Southeast Asian common market of much poorer nations.

And, on an even smaller scale, forward-thinking regions within some nations will increasingly focus on managing their inevitable degrowth. They will try to build regional resilience in the face of global economic unrest and dwindling access to cheap energy. And to do so, they will organize systems that rely on local food, local energy, and programs that strengthen regional and local economies.

"Glimpse 8-1: Scotland Joins New Europe" presents a thought-provoking forecast of how a desire for local control may play out in Europe over the next forty years. It is an indicator of the speed of global change these days that the ideas in the glimpse have moved far toward being commonplace within the short year since it was written in the summer of 2011.

GLIMPSE 8-1

Scotland Joins New Europe

Catherine Cameron

I believe that in forty years the balance of power will move further north in Europe. The countries in the ascendant will be Scandinavia, Germany, Benelux, and the Baltic states. Scotland will complete its separation from the UK to join this group, called "the New Europe" and established after the "resetting" of the EU in the late 2020s. The southern states of Spain, Portugal, Greece, Italy, and the Balkans will suffer temperature increases and water shortages leading to food shortages, ill health, and unrest. Population movements will follow, including migrants from North Africa. Below I describe the future of the UK, and Scotland in particular, with a backdrop of key events elsewhere in Europe.

2012

In the UK, mean temperature is almost 1.1°C above the preindustrial mean.[1] The high temperatures adversely affect rail transportation in the southeast of England.[2] It is exceptionally wet in Scotland, with over 250% of the average recorded rainfall. Drought conditions continue to affect southeastern England, with less than 30% of normal rainfall recorded.[3]

The UK produces 60% of its own food—and more than 74% of all food that can be produced domestically. Two-thirds of food imports into the UK are from other EU member states.[4] On the energy front, prices increase in the winter: gas by 18% and electricity by 16%. The increase is partly attributed to the unrest in the Middle East, the earthquake in Japan, and the rapidly growing Asian economies driving up demand.[5] The UK population is 62.2 million, of which Scotland is 5.2 million.[6]

On the political front, Scotland has had a devolved parliament and executive since 1999. In 2010 it pulled back from having a full referendum to devolve entirely from the UK.[7] A further referendum is due to be held before 2016. In the EU, Greece exits the euro. Italy receives a bail-out package amid furious Eurozone debate.

2022

South and central England suffer maximum summer temperatures at the extreme range of projections. Drought conditions are a problem in the southeast, with water rationing commonplace. Scotland continues to get higher rainfall, prompting investment in more hydropower.

Food imports from the EU become more expensive as countries prioritize domestic needs. England produces less cereal, vegetables, and fruit in the south, east, and west, while crop production in northern England and Scotland increases.

The UK is importing the majority of its gas and more than half its oil.[8] Scotland has scaled up wind power and is investing in more hydro and tidal power. Norway and Scotland sign the Tromso Agreement in 2022: Scotland provides wind power to Norway in exchange for oil and gas as part of a wider plan to collaborate on shared wind-power resources as deeper-water wind power becomes technically possible for both countries. Scotland votes to be a nuclear-free state after the Sizewell B accident in England, where a combination of tidal surge, coastal erosion, and poor maintenance led to the collapse of the reactor, land unfit for food production, and an exodus of the population.

Scotland's population reaches 5.5 million, partly because of in-migration. Many migrants are from England, with a marked increase of people over age sixty (for the health service and subsidized elderly care) and people moving away from the congestion, heat, and water scarcity.

The euro collapses in this decade following the exit of Portugal, Italy, Spain, and Ireland. A two-tier setting is agreed for Europe in the Stockholm Agreement in 2023. New Europe (the northern states) and Europe II (the southern states) agree to a preferential trading agreement, but border requirements are amended, reflecting the breakdown of the Schengen area.[9] Italy reverts to two states, an industrial north and an agricultural south, the latter with the same territory as the Kingdom of the Two Sicilies in 1860. The new border is heavily guarded in an attempt to deter migrants. Fascist policies are on the rise in Europe II in response to food-price rises, water shortages, and increased number of migrants from the Maghreb states.

2032

Temperature extremes continue, resulting in widespread disruption to working patterns, health, and transportation in southern England. Flooding has become a problem in western and central England, with insurance coverage difficult to obtain.

Food production in eastern, western, and central England has plummeted owing to the Sizewell accident, temperature increases, water shortages, and flooding. Imports from the EU are now scarce and expensive. Scotland is self-sufficient in basic foods.

Scotland's wind-power provision accelerates into deep water with Norway, using shared technology, staff, and installation platforms. Denmark, Greenland, and Iceland join this partnership later in the decade to form a clean-energy coalition, sharing research and development of tidal and hydropower, skills, resources, and resulting energy in the Keflavik Agreement signed in 2035.

In part from English moving north and in part from a relatively liberal immigration policy, Scotland's population reaches 6 million. As in the Scandinavian countries and Canada, immigration policy is heavily linked to the skills of the migrants.

The two-tier setting for Europe is more stable in this decade. Scotland devolves fully from the UK with little public debate. The focus in England is on energy, food, and water access. Scotland's distinctive energy policy and water abundance change the nature of the relationship between the two nations.

2042

The temperature extremes of 2003, when thousands of Europeans died in the heat, now occur every second year or so.[10] Water scarcity in southeast England continues, with rationing for four to six months of the year. Coastal erosion on the east coast accelerates, with the government policy of managed retreat overtaken by the collapse of some cliffs. Flooding in western and central England is worse than predicted.

Production of champagne and some soft fruits like apricots increases in southern England, while production of traditional cereal crops and vegetables continues to move north. Households are more and more self-sufficient, with their own power from solar panels, water collection from rainwater, and cottage gardening with some poultry and goats. There has been a significant decline in consumption of beef and lamb.

Scotland is wholly self-sufficient in electricity from wind power. This powers the transportation system and a large portion of domestic housing stock. The Keflavik Agreement is working well, with Finland and Sweden as new members and Canada as an associate member.[11]

Population has grown to 7.5 million in Scotland, up 50% in thirty years. Northumbria and the Lake District are the boom areas of England. Scotland puts in place restrictions on immigration.

Political turbulence continues across Europe II. Renewable power and water have become key trading commodities, as gold and oil were fifty years before.

2052

Temperature spikes in the summer ahead of the climate-model predictions.[12] In Scotland water continues to be plentiful.[13] Food production is a national priority for England. Cereals are now an important trading commodity. And Scotland has a 100% renewable energy supply consisting of wind, wave, and hydropower.

The population in Scotland has stabilized at a little over 8 million, with eligibility restrictions and border controls making it difficult for new migrants from outside New Europe to enter.

New Europe and Europe II no longer share any of the old EU structures or status. New Europe is now closely allied with the New North in the Thule Agreement signed in 2052.[14] There is some talk of an ever-closer union between these two groups given the high degree of common membership.

Catherine Cameron (British and Guyanese, born 1963) was a member of the core team behind The Stern Review: The Economics of Climate Change. She is now director of Agulhas: Applied Knowledge, helping companies and organizations respond to the additional challenges to sustainability posed by climate change. She is a visiting fellow at the Smith School of Environment & Enterprise at the University of Oxford.

As illustrated wonderfully by "Scotland Joins New Europe," climate change can be a driver of the desire for regional independence—as exemplified by Scotland and the northern part of the EU. The new weather patterns won't necessarily follow national borders. Some regions will be climate winners (like the New North), and others climate losers (like the low-lying Pacific islands). The climate effects may even differ within a nation and create new conflicts between winners and losers. But they may also make new bedfellows across national borders.

"Glimpse 8-2: The End of Mediterranean Disparity" shows how the warming of the Mediterranean may actually work to create a new regional unity around that inland sea. The dominant culture in that future region may end up resembling that of hot North Africa rather than that of balmy southern Europe.

The End of Mediterranean Disparity

Thymio Papayannis

Deep social and economic disparity has characterized the countries around the Mediterranean basin for a lengthy period of time. Those at the north of the basin, all members of the European Union, benefit from high incomes, decent social services, high educational standards, and rather stable democratic systems, but they face demographic problems with low fertility rates and aging populations. At the other extreme, in North Africa and the Middle East—with the exception of Israel and partly Turkey—populations are still rising rapidly, incomes are low, and political instability reigns.

Recently, however, a number of significant trends and changes are appearing in the Mediterranean, which seem at first glance unrelated.

Key Trends and Changes

Strong political unrest in the Muslim countries of the basin has led to toppling of the regimes in Egypt, Tunisia, and Libya and violent demonstrations in Syria. It appears that in all these countries there are growing demands for improved living conditions and for greater participation of local societies in governance.

In parallel, a serious financial crisis has seized Greece and Portugal and is menacing Spain and Italy. At the symptom level, the crisis is due to excessive national debt, resulting from high public-sector deficits and the inability of governments to borrow further funds. However, the root causes are low productivity, weak governments, uncontrolled public and private consumption, and corruption in almost all sectors. Measures to alleviate the problem imposed by the IMF, the European Union, and the European Bank have averted national default up to now, but the actions taken to decrease government spending and drastically increase taxation will prolong a spiral of depression and rising unemployment, until the root problem has been solved. The gravity of the ensuing financial and social problems poses threats to the stability of this part of the Mediterranean.

But in spite of these dire developments in the north of the Mediterranean, illegal immigration from Africa and Asia has been exploding, mainly toward Italy and Greece and to a lesser degree to Spain, Malta, and Cyprus. Greece, with a population of around 11 million, has a large number of illegal immigrants—perhaps a million strong—mostly unemployed and impoverished, conditions that fuel uncontrolled criminality. Most of the illegal immigrants are motivated not by political reasons and persecution, but by the desire to improve their income and living conditions.

In addition to the immigration, there is the environmental challenge. Serious drought has been affecting many parts of the Mediterranean basin and especially the Middle East. Cyprus in particular is suffering, with water resources dwindling and rationing for domestic freshwater becoming necessary. Desalination has been considered as a partial solution, but it is expensive and energy-consuming. Throughout the island, there are visible impacts of climatic change, desertification phenomena, and shrinking vegetation. Agriculture is suffering, with irrigation-dependent cultivation being abandoned as government policies seem to favor tourism facilities (including golf courses). Similar phenomena are appearing in other parts of the Middle East and are predicted for the south of Greece.

Throughout the basin, resources are being exploited unsustainably. Fish catches in the Mediterranean are dropping, and marine desertification has been expanding in many areas. Soil resources are being overexploited by intensive agriculture and polluted by agrochemicals, and thus they are losing their productivity. Natural areas, especially coastal, are disappearing as spreading human land uses—mainly urbanization and tourism—and the construction of major infrastructure modify them dramatically. As a result, the biodiversity of the Mediterranean eco-region is dwindling.

Projecting Future Developments

Immigration flows and environmental change will continue to affect the region in the next forty years.

First of all, it is clear now that effective measures to mitigate climate change will not be taken in time, and the Mediterranean will be highly affected. Sea-level rise will affect coastal areas. Measures to protect the areas, adapt to climate change, and combat its effects will be combined with urbanization and tourism investments and will result in a complete artificialization of most of the Mediterranean coasts. This in turn will degrade the attraction of the coastal areas and will undermine the tourism industry. Distortion of the water cycle and desertification will become realities that will negatively affect the use of natural resources throughout the basin.

The most striking developments, though, will happen at the income level. The economies of the European Union countries in the Mediterranean will have to accept a dramatic drop in per capita income over the years to come. As a result, a large part of their population will end up living near the poverty level. This will lead to social and political unrest and to intense governmental efforts to accelerate economic growth. It is safe to predict that this will cause major environmental damage. It is less likely, however, that these attempts will have lasting positive impacts on income; thus resignation and low consumption levels may prevail.

But this sad state of affairs will not stop the migration flows from the southern rim of the basin. The new democratic regimes in North Africa and the Middle East are creating expectations among their citizens for a better quality of life, which they will not be able to satisfy. The northern Mediterranean countries will retain their attractiveness for immigrants from the south. In fact, the immigrants will be better suited to cope with the impoverished conditions and the scarcity of natural resources in the European parts of the basin. Conditions there will be similar to those of today's North Africa. So—after a period of intense internal conflict—immigration will become tacitly accepted, and in 2052 the European countries of the Mediterranean will have nonnative-European majorities. A merging of practices and cultures will result.

This will necessitate new systems of governance. The Mediterranean has been dominated for millennia by empires—Macedonian, Hellenistic, Roman, Byzantine, and Ottoman—under which different communities lived in the same places, maintaining to a large extent their social structure, culture, and religion. Historic cities such as Constantinople, Alexandria, Thessaloniki, and Aleppo were truly cosmopolitan and played key roles in the birth of civilization. Thus, in the middle of our century, the Mediterranean may rediscover the arts of coexistence, this time in a democratic framework.

The fusion of peoples and cultures that will result may have positive side effects—namely, the smoother acceptance of the loss of affluence, less consumption than in the north, and a wiser use of natural resources—especially water and space—and energy. The people from the south and east may not be today as affluent or educated as the Europeans; they have, however, much better understanding of natural limitations, since they depend on them for their current subsistence. This will be their great contribution to the new integrated Mediterranean.

Four decades may not be sufficient time. It is probable, however, that by 2052 a new Mediterranean civilization will be visible, vibrant, and creative, with the disparity of the past between the south and the north rapidly disappearing.

Thymio Papayannis (Greek, born 1934) is an architect-planner. A graduate of MIT, he has been involved for the past thirty years in the conservation of natural and cultural heritage in the framework of the Ramsar Convention and its Mediterranean Wetlands Initiative (MedWet), WWF International, IUCN, and the Mount Athos Holy Community. He is president of the Society for the Protection of Prespa.

Climate change and economic development will drive geographic restructuring in the decades ahead. Those with a common fate will be pulled together—like the people around a warming Mediterranean. Those with very different prospects will be pushed apart—like the people of Scotland and England, and the two parts of the European Union. I think it will feel more like fragmentation than the formation of new unions, but in reality it will be both.

Another form of fragmentation is also possible: namely, the emergence of new cooperating groupings inside a national border. "Glimpse 8-3: Slum Urbanism in Africa" provides a fascinating example; namely, the anticipation that the slum dwellers of Africa, with no hope of help (read: economic development) from outside their township, will ultimately succeed in their own internally driven process of betterment.

GLIMPSE 8-3

Slum Urbanism in Africa

Edgar Pieterse

It is difficult to look across the next forty years and not be haunted by the past forty. According to the recent *African Futures 2050* study, "Over the entire half-century [1960–2010], Eastern Africa gained only about $150 per capita and Western Africa about $130 per capita, while [annual] GDP per capita in Central Africa has remained almost unchanged since 1960."[15] This is an astonishing accomplishment of economic, political, and social failure. Looking ahead to 2052, an even larger and more dramatic process of systemic exclusion will occur in African cities and towns.

UN-Habitat points out that almost 62% of urban residents in sub-Saharan Africa live in slum conditions. Roughly 280 million urban dwellers are regarded as income poor.[16] Forward-looking speculation suggests that Africa will double its population by 2052, from 1.1 billion in 2011 to 2.3 billion. The urban share will grow from 40% in 2011 to some 60% by 2052. One reasonable question is whether the majority of the urban population will continue to dwell in slums. Another is what the cumulative impacts of slum urbanism will be by 2052.

Africa is the only world region that will continue to have robust population growth throughout the next forty years, particularly east and west Africa, which will more than double. Over that period, Africa's share of the global population will grow from 15% to 23%.[17] In spite of this dramatic increase, Africa will remain peripheral in economic terms, contributing less than 5% to global trade.[18]

The limited economic performance is attributable to numerous factors. The most critical ones are severe infrastructure deficits, governmental inefficiencies, dramatic market failures, and the inability to forge effective regional trading blocs across the continent. And the perpetuation of slums can be attributed to a lack of infrastructure and maintenance investments to ensure affordable access to reliable and safe energy, safe drinking water, and sanitation. Investments will remain small because the formal part of the urban economies will remain relatively small. As a result the available tax base for large-scale public investments will remain inadequate. This is often compounded by pervasive administrative inefficiencies, enhanced by malfeasance and corruption—the lifeblood of many patronage systems that propel dominant political parties and elite systems across African countries.

Some recent reports suggest a rosier future, following from the observed economic growth over the past decade. From 2000 African GDP grew by some 5% per year, less than in Asia, but much faster than in the OECD. Furthermore, much of this growth stems from Africa's cities. However, cities need adequate infrastructural capacity to foster economic growth. And here I foresee problems over the next decades and a possible solution in the longer run.

During the past five years much effort has been expended to understand the infrastructural deficit in Africa. This question goes to the heart of Africa's prospects by 2052. If the infrastructure challenge is not adequately addressed, large-scale poverty rooted in structural economic exclusion and economic underperformance will persist. The World Bank has pegged the overall infrastructure deficit at $93 billion per year—less than 0.1 T$ per year. This is the level of annual investment required to address the current backlogs and cope with future growth.[19] According to the same report, a massive shortfall is likely.

In the competition for limited finance, particular kinds of infrastructure get prioritized—for example, connective economic infrastructure such as roads, ports, and airports, which ensure that primary commodities get to destination markets as quickly as possible. There are of course also intimate connections between the infrastructure financiers from China, India, and the United States and the pathways that products from mines and fields need to travel. Essential infrastructure to channel power, water, waste, and data follows a strange, patchy geography along the contours of where the middle classes and formal firms are located. The net effect is splintered urban territories and a pattern of fault lines that follow social lines of distinction, discrimination, and oppression, predictably encoded by ethnic, racial, and class bases of power.

At the core of this unequal and unviable spatial patterning is the question of cost recovery, or more crassly, money. Or in other words:

Affordability may be a barrier to further expansion of access. Most African households live on very modest budgets and spend more than half of their resources on food. The average African household has a budget of no more than $180 per month; urban households are about $100 per month better off than rural households. . . . In most countries, between one- and two-thirds of the urban population would face difficulties in covering the cost of service.[20]

In summary, given slow GDP growth, continued income inequality, and systemic political dysfunction, I believe that slum urbanism will remain a predominant feature of African cities. It is more uplifting to reflect on what kind of response this sad future will trigger in the hundreds of millions of urban households that fall below the poverty line.

The answer rests in a series of socioeconomic-cultural dynamics that is beyond the purview of economic forecasting models. I predict the emergence of a self-organizing movement to try to solve the problem. Slum movements organized under the global federal umbrella of Slum Dwellers International, for example, have been preparing a "social operating system" for urban slums. They seek to address the profound material and economic needs in the slums through empowerment and collective action. And since they work against a backdrop of long-term political and market failure, a sense of local *autonomy* is encouraged. Nothing is expected from the state. Nothing is anticipated from the formal private market. Instead, residents club together in various configurations to try to make their minimal incomes stretch further by leveraging each other's support, intelligence, and labor to gradually, but systematically, move everyone forward. At the core of this social operating system is a capacity for cannibalizing, subverting, appropriating, and recasting the resources and expectations of the formal city outside the slum.

I believe that these social technologies and capabilities will deepen through continuous cross-country and cross-settlement learning. They will be characterized by a healthy dose of suspicion of professional and governmental knowledge. They will create an alternative basis for flourishing, especially as an adept youthful population brings the benefits of digital technologies and mobile money (cell-phone-based transactions) into the equation. These movements will install and maintain their own decentralized infrastructural solutions at scale from around 2025 onward. These organic experiments and solutions will then become the entry point for the state, massively decentralized, and new kinds of businesses, steeped in social entrepreneurialism, to engage the urban majorities on their terms.

Thus, even though the infrastructural deficit, poverty, and GDP per capita trend lines are dismal for urban Africa in most forecasting models, I am quietly confident that a social revolution will produce a much more complicated, differentiated, and somewhat less unjust future.

Edgar Pieterse (South Africa, born 1968) is holder of the NRF South African Research Chair in urban policy. He directs the African Centre for Cities and is professor in the School of Architecture, Planning and Geomatics, both at the University of Cape Town. In 2008 he wrote City Futures: Confronting the Crisis of Urban Development.

Despite recent progress, many areas of Africa face rapid population growth, continued poverty, and massive resource depletion, making the scene portrayed in "Slum Urbanism in Africa" relevant for a large number of urban Africans. It has long been incredibly complex to achieve economic growth in an urban slum—and even to provide basic services to the people who dwell there. Thus it is heartening to know that potential solutions might be found in and by self-organized slum movements. This is another example of the bottom-up solutions that will characterize our always-connected future.

A New Paradigm: Less Fixation with Economic Growth

Once income levels exceed a certain threshold, noneconomic aspects of development are more important to the citizens of a state. Or so motivational theory says. But in practice, this shift away from economic goals is hard to observe. The nations of the current world appear to be as dedicated to their economic-growth goals as when they were much poorer.

I believe the search for higher income will remain a central driving force over the next forty years, not only in poor but also in rich countries. It is not surprising that poor countries will seek growth; they need it to remove poverty. It is more surprising that rich countries will continue to seek ways to increase their national incomes, even when their voters know well that higher income does not really increase life satisfaction. Growing the GDP has been the number-one goal for generations, it has made a number of countries rich and influential, and it won't be dropped easily. But more important is the fact that economic growth is the only proven way to increase the number of jobs. And new jobs are truly important, not primarily because they increase the output of goods and services, but because they allow more people to obtain a share of the economic pie. New jobs create fuller employment. New jobs enable redistribution without revolution. Finally, new jobs generate additional tax income. This makes the life of politicians simpler and more pleasant.

If high employment, and redistribution of the added value, could be achieved in other ways, without economic growth, I believe voters would be more willing to support cultural independence, protect national traditions, and favor local control—even at the cost of reduced GDP growth. But such mechanisms for redistribution have not been found. The simplest solution, to tax the rich and give the money to the poor, does not capture a majority in most parliaments.

Thus, growth in GDP will remain a central ambition in most countries for many decades. But over time there will emerge an ever louder critical chorus arguing that continued growth is not sustainable and must be replaced with a new goal for society. Many reasons will be given: insufficient resources, excessive greenhouse gas emissions, eroding soils, disappearing groundwater, reduced biodiversity, and so on. Other voices in the chorus will follow a different line of thought and argue that continued growth is not desirable, even if possible, because never-ending materialism won't lead to true life satisfaction.

The "growth versus no-growth" debate has already raged for forty years. It can be simplified as a conflict between traditionalists—the "pro-growthers" who want continued economic growth based on fossil fuels—and the sustainability crowd—the "hesitators" who seek enduring life satisfaction within planetary limitations and doubt that continued economic growth is the right tool. The clash between the pro-growthers and the hesitators is an interesting example of a paradigm conflict—a conflict between two incompatible worldviews. The available data from the real world is not yet sufficient to decide which paradigm will serve humanity best, although the climate challenge is starting to tip the scale in favor of the hesitators. The fact that the world's output of conventional oil production seems to have reached a plateau, and is declining in many regions, adds further support to the thought that humanity is approaching planetary limits.

But the sustainability crowd is still a tiny minority, and the paradigm shift is probably several decades into the future. One would perhaps expect the rich world to lead the way. But the rich countries are the most democratic, and hence, as I see it, the most short-term. In fact they are so short-term that it may well be that more authoritarian states are the first to move. Current developments in China are interesting. The authorities are experimenting with the idea of a harmonious society (in other words, a society in harmony with nature) seeking adequate well-being for all, rather than maximum disposable income. A problem may be that the Chinese leadership is too far ahead of its people.

But by 2052, the new paradigm—"sustainable well-being based on renewable energy"—will be exerting increasing influence on policy making. Not only because of the ominous threat from the approaching climate disaster in the second half of the twenty-first century, but also because the energy sector by then will have completed one-half of the transfer from a fossil to a solar base. It will feel much less threatening and much more realistic to aim for a world economy running on solar power. Simultaneously, the starting population decline will make it appear more realistic to achieve sustainability through reduction of the ecological footprint. It will be possible to reduce humanity's collective footprint, even if the per capita footprint is not reduced

My forecast is that by 2052 global society (and this time led by its wealthier parts) will increasingly be seeking sustainable well-being based on planet-friendly energy and resources. The narrow focus on material gain for the individual in the short term will be replaced by a wider perspective, as explained in "Glimpse 8-4: Valuing the Whole."

GLIMPSE 8-4

Valuing the Whole

Peter Willis

I predict that by 2052 a new paradigm will be strongly emergent. Leaders in both government and business will be expected to prioritize the well-being not just of their particular constituency, nation, or shareholders, as now, but also of the wider ecological and social systems that support them. I expect a generation of leaders to emerge who are skillful systems thinkers, who routinely consider the whole and work from a base of more inclusive values than have been the norm hitherto. This new leadership paradigm, I predict, will prove itself more effective in enabling society to meet its needs under the highly constrained circumstances that will characterize the next forty years.

I see three major trends that will drive this development. The first is the mounting stress and turbulence that will manifest in all the systems—particularly ecosystems and natural resources—that support our current, complex global civilization. The second is an increasingly rapid development and rollout of new, more viable forms of commercial and social organization, designed to replace the dysfunctional systems and institutional relationships associated with the causes of the first trend. And the third trend is the evolution of human values, which has been going on since the earliest times, has been accelerating dramatically over the last century, and looks as though it will continue to accelerate over the next forty years.

First, I believe the next forty years will bring crises to most regions, even sporadic catastrophe, triggered by various causes. Temporary shortages of energy, food, water, or minerals and erratic impacts of a warming climate will pose increasingly frequent challenges to our systems of well-being.

This will create a world where increasing proportions of our energy and attention will be directed at adapting our systems to fast-changing physical circumstances. It will become clear that we are in the "Anthropocene" epoch where, consciously or not, humanity is responsible for triggering planetary-scale change. In such a world the negative consequences of decisions and actions taken on a too-narrow understanding of the way the global system works will rebound more and more quickly, making it increasingly clear to voters and consumers that only skilled systems thinkers have a chance of making decisions that will actually improve people's well-being.

My second trend is less obvious than the first. Less ecologically damaging technologies are currently gaining momentum, but less damaging systems of commerce and economy are still the territory of narrow interest groups. Plenty of new and appropriate models exist—for example, alternative money systems, employee ownership of firms, and the sharing of assets usually considered private, like cars and homes—but so far few have been prototyped at sufficient scale to draw serious attention as viable alternatives. We can be hopeful that these innovations will gather momentum and popular appeal in the coming years, driven by the increasingly frequent breakdown of conventional systems.

A defining characteristic of these new institutions will be that they are founded on an ever-broadening sense that all parts of the global system, both human and nonhuman, need to be included if satisfactory decisions and outcomes are to be achieved. This does not translate into a simplistic extension of the scope of stakeholder engagements, so that all voices are heard. That way lies paralysis and unacceptably slow decision making. Rather, I see these social and institutional innovations being automatically designed with a view to benefit the widest possible number of stakeholders, since it will be obvious that in a hot, disparate, and crowded world[21] no group can secure sustainable well-being at the expense of its surrounding systems.

The third trend—the evolution of human values—is currently perhaps the least visible. It concerns the answer to the question "What really matters?" It must have been beyond the imagination of early hunter-gatherers moving in small family units to argue about the inalienable rights of the individual to self-determination or the idea of codified laws. What mattered most was the survival day by day of one's nearest kin. But once survival was assured for a large minority, as in Europe in the Middle Ages, the predominant concern became man's eternal soul and direct access to an almighty, overseeing God.

From this era there grew a strong focus on the rule of law, initially prescribed by God and his earthly agents, later by democratic vote. Next came the freedom to seek personal financial advancement, regardless of religion, and rooted in science-based knowledge of one's world. And now the twentieth-century "me-obsessed" epoch has itself begun to be challenged by the emergence of a globalized "we" culture. The whole environmental and social justice movement has as its central value (not always observed, it must be admitted) the idea that no solution can work only for a minority of members of a system—the whole system matters and must be taken into account.[22]

Luckily there are currently younger people who think of themselves as citizens of the world and for whom the notion of going to war to defend one's nation or religion is simply absurd. Yet simultaneously there are plenty for whom national pride matters supremely. What seems clear is that, despite sometimes high levels of local variability, the perspective of the human population is inexorably changing in the direction of a widening, more inclusive sense of what matters. I therefore predict that by 2052 there will be a number of influential people who will take it for granted that the well-being of the whole system is just as important as their personal well-being. By definition these leading lights will be the most flexible in their thinking and thus more likely to provide effective leadership in turbulent times than those stuck in earlier value sets.

What will be central elements of the new paradigm?

In the sphere of government, we will need leaders who are both highly rational and committed to the good of the whole system under their care. But rationality has limitations when faced with fast-moving, turbulent conditions, and leaders with a well-developed intuition and a willingness to act on it will be best able to achieve system-wide benefits. Partisan and sectional politics will be less well suited, and there may arise greater willingness to accept what we today consider authoritarian government, seeking collective well-being over individual rights. This may not be an easy transition to make, as the ecological and economic crises will in some quarters stimulate strong regressions into partisan, narrow interests for survival's sake.

In the world of business, we will need entrepreneurial businesses—perhaps collectively owned—to solve many of tomorrow's problems, created and run by people for whom self-aggrandizement or large personal wealth is simply not a driver. Hopefully it will be increasingly understood that great wealth distances one from other parts of society, and that wealth is a dysfunctional basis for genuinely successful leadership. These people's organizations will be flat or hierarchical as the situation demands.

Finally, we won't see continuation of the pattern in which those who lead remain in "leadership positions" until they retire. The baton of leadership will be passed easily and often, sometimes returning many times to the same hand, as the need arises.

Peter Willis *(South African, born 1954) is the South African director of the Cambridge Programme for Sustainability Leadership and regional chairman of the Prince of Wales's Business & Sustainability Programme. After a history degree from Oxford he worked in government and started various enterprises before emigrating to South Africa in 1993.*

I have hoped for forty years that we will see the full shift toward a holistic perspective as described in "Valuing the Whole." I am not convinced that it will occur in my time. But one practical way to assist consumers in automatically taking a holistic view is to help ensure that they cannot easily buy things that hurt the planet, as explained in the sidebar "Choice Editing."

Choice Editing

Alan Knight

Choice editing is a practice that ensures consumers do not get the opportunity to choose environmentally and socially damaging products and services. The environmental problem facing the world today reflects how inefficient our current supply chains are at meeting today's demands and how unfit they are to supply tomorrow's needs. We need to make interventions in the way we do things currently. One way of doing this is to remove the most damaging choices.

The good news is that many examples of such interventions exist. Labeling of good products is one way. By avoiding unlabeled products, consumers can reduce their footprints. The Forest Stewardship Council (FSC), which will celebrate its twentieth year in 2013, has already certified 150 billion hectares of forests. The FSC-inspired Marine Stewardship Council had by 2010 certified over 187 fisheries. We have the Roundtable on Sustainable Palm Oil and another body for biofuel. There are over sixty similar schemes looking at products as diverse as toilet tissue to the granite in my kitchen.

There are too many schemes for the consumer to embrace, but this should not be a problem, because already many companies are choosing to use these schemes in their own procurement policy rather than using them to offer choice to their customers. This is the really efficient form of choice editing.

For example, home improvement retailers such as the UK's B&Q make timber certification mandatory across their entire inventory. B&Q customers are not able to choose unsustainable timber. The schemes were originally adopted to ensure nothing damaging was happening in the companies' supply chains. This original reputation-protection goal is now being replaced by a sustainability goal. The timber retailers now need the FSC to ensure they will have enough wood to supply their customers in the long run.

Choice editing amounts to highlighting for people what they can do right, rather than telling them what they are doing wrong. It helps shift sustainability from a moral choice to a simple, practical, and exciting behavior.

Alan Knight (British, born 1964) specializes in corporate sustainability and product-centric sustainability for big brands (e.g., Virgin, Kingfisher, B&Q, SABMiller) and public policy (in UK government think tanks on sustainability, eco-labeling, and consumption). See www.dralanknight.com.

Modified Capitalism: A Stronger Role for Wise Government

I do not believe that capitalism will survive unchanged over the next forty years. The name will remain, but the working of capitalist society will be changed in two ways: investment flows will no longer be determined solely by what is profitable, and corporations will be forced to report not only on their financial performance, but also on the environmental and social consequences of their actions.

In chapter 4 I discussed the future need to enhance and redirect societal investment flows. Global society will be facing a number of waxing challenges over the next forty years, challenges that will require extra investment in order to be solved. In an increasing number of cases it will be necessary to act before these investment projects become profitable from a business point of view. Ideally the state would solve such problems by a change in relative prices ("internalizing external costs and benefits"), but this may prove so difficult in practice that it will be much faster to increase taxes and invest the proceeds directly in what society needs to get done.

One good example is the German decision to establish significant wind and solar capacity in Germany during the 2000s, and forcing the consumers to pay the bill. In principle it worked as follows (although the actual procedure was much less transparent, possibly deliberately so in order to gather sufficient support for the solution): The state decided that a certain fraction of the power should come from wind and sun. They established a feed-in tariff that made it profitable for homeowners to install solar panels on their roofs and for companies to build wind farms. And then they instructed all German electricity users to share the bill. Capitalist firms were allowed to bid for the contracts and deliver the goods, but the direction and volume of investment was decided outside the market, by the state. The result was much higher investment in wind and solar capacity than if Germany had left the investment decision to the market. Expensive wind and solar capacity was established and now constitutes some 20% of German power. This happened in spite of the fact that it would have been much cheaper to build additional gas-fired utilities. Through its decisions the German parliament significantly interfered with investment flows, with long-term effects on the profitability of the conventional (fossil-based) energy industry: once the wind and solar capacity had been built, its operating costs were so low that the power easily outcompeted fossil-based power. No further subsidies will be necessary during its lifetime.

In the future we will see many cases like this. The world will not thrive during the next forty years, I believe, if capital is allocated only to the uses with the highest short-term returns. In order to achieve a meaningful reduction in the human ecological footprint, and particularly in CO_2 emissions, society will have to allocate capital to projects that are less profitable than the most profitable project. To reiterate the German case, it will be necessary to build windmills and solar capacity even if doing so is more expensive than building another gas-powered utility. In other circumstances it will be necessary to insulate dwellings even if it is cheaper to run the gas heater or coal-fired air conditioner. These will be the cases in which short-termism doesn't win the day.

As you have seen from my forecast, I believe that global society will interfere, to some extent, with the operation of the free market to ensure that investments flow toward what is publicly needed, rather than toward what is most profitable. But only to "some" extent. And certainly not to the extent necessary to obtain a problem-free future for the generation living from 2052 onward. Most of the capital will still be governed by the market, and most of it will be allocated to purposes that are not particularly helpful in light of the great global challenges of the twenty-first century. But an increasing share of the money flows—what I call forced and voluntary extra investment—will be allocated by public decision making and not by the market, just as we choose to invest in weapons even when the economic return is way below zero.

I expect that global society will increase annual investments from 24% today to 36% of the GDP in 2052. Much of this investment will be in energy-efficient goods that are more expensive than old-fashioned stuff designed for an era of cheap energy. Another share will be invested in the shift from coal to more expensive fuels, like conventional gas. Some will go into the construction of new renewable energy supply, even during the years before it becomes competitive. And a lot will go into repair of climate damage or adaptation to future climate damage—for example, investing in new dikes along the coast to keep the rising ocean back.

These huge increases in investment would not come about if investment was left to the market. They will happen only through state intervention, based on parliamentary decision. State intervention will be either direct, when the government invests the tax dollars in whatever capacity it deems to be most necessary, or indirect, when the government passes legislation that makes the desired activity more profitable; for example, by legislating emissions standards on cars, a certain share of biofuels in all gasoline, a cap-and-trade system, or the simplest (and politically least feasible), an outright tax on CO_2 emissions.

There will be great regional variation in this type of state behavior. There are obviously very clear limits to how much governmental interference will be accepted in the Western democracies, particularly in the United States. And hence capitalism will survive in a purer form there than in Europe, where the government is more often seen as the good helper, not only as a burden to be kept at a minimum. By 2052, China will have shown the world how a strong government is much better at solving the type of challenges humanity will face in the twenty-first century. China will easily redirect the 5% of their GDP that is required to solve the oncoming barrage of problems. And they will do so while the market economies are dithering about whether to use another hundred billion US dollars (less than 0.1% of their GDP) to support climate-friendly technology.

This shift to modified capitalism will work best in countries with a wise leadership and a competent ministry of finance and planning that can orchestrate genuine competitive bidding for state-financed projects.

Do we still have capitalism if 30% of the money flow is governed by the government and 70% by the market? Most diehard capitalists would say no. I would say yes. There is still the central role for the privately owned capitalist corporations to execute the grand projects decided by the government, just as they partake in the building and running of the Olympics every second year. But to avoid a futile definitional debate, I suggest we name the modified system, where a significant part of the investment flows is governed by political decision and not by profitability, "modified capitalism." This should not insult anyone and will still provide the signal that things have changed. Modified capitalism will be a system wherein collective well-being is set above the return to the individual. The public part of the economy will be larger. And there will still be a major role for the private firm.

Another form of modified capitalism would arise if capital flows were governed by pension-fund managers who were intent on their real task, namely, to obtain secure pension income for their customers thirty years into the future, rather than tracking indexes that seek to maximize profits in the short run. In principle such pension-fund managers (suitably incentivized) could perform the job of a farsighted wise government. But it would require them to deviate from the straitjacket of monthly reporting and bonuses connected to quarterly results. This is, sad to say, unlikely to happen at scale. Most shareholders, I am afraid, are more interested in short-term profits than long-term vision. But a few privately held corporations and a few genuinely long-term pension funds could conceivably go the narrow path and invest (along with the Chinese Communist Party) in long-term solutions, like carbon capture and storage or clean water supply in the slums, and hope to get a stable income some decades ahead. But the return on investment will be lower. So, once more, I find this unlikely to happen.

Thus, I agree with those who argue that a corporation working within the brutal constraints of pure capitalism has little to no chance to contribute significantly to the solution of the main challenges of the twenty-first century. Stopping climate change and alleviating poverty are activities that have much lower return on investment than production of most consumer goods and services. Hence the socially good projects won't win in the internal fight for capital in the firm. The competing firm can of course conduct gestures of corporate (social) responsibility to signal its concerns about the long-term future. But only to a fairly limited, and costless, extent. If the corporation does too much more, it will not be around long enough to enjoy the fruits of its expensive bragging. Telling the public that one cares is an important part of what little real good the company can do within the constraints of the free market. But to really do good, the large corporation needs the state to invite tender for the socially good projects.

Those corporations that end up with the wise government as their customer will of course be producing the right thing (and be praised for that, like the firms in the solar industry). But they will be living dangerous lives, because of the tendency for quick shifts in public opinion and changing views of what is politically correct.

Furthermore, it will become increasingly dangerous for high-profile corporations to deviate from acceptable behavior—as defined by civil society. Over the next forty years society will impose a system of transparent and meaningful sustainability reporting on a somewhat resisting corporate world. It will become a normal obligation of the large corporation not only to report along commonly agreed principles on its financial progress, but to do the same concerning its environmental and social impacts. This won't happen overnight, nor all over the world at the same time, and not without serious opposition from many quarters. But the direction is clear and the speed connected to the emergence of the sustainability paradigm. "Glimpse 8-5: Systemic CSR, or CSR 2.0" provides more detail.

GLIMPSE 8-5

Systemic CSR, or CSR 2.0

Wayne Visser

Corporate sustainability and responsibility (CSR)—which also goes by various other proxy terms, such as corporate social responsibility, corporate citizenship, corporate sustainability, and business ethics—is the way in which business seeks to create shared value in society through economic development, good governance, stakeholder responsiveness, and environmental improvement. Put another way, CSR is an integrated, systemic approach by business that seeks to build, rather than erode or destroy, economic, social, human, and natural capital.

Today, companies tend to practice one of four types of CSR, depending on their level of maturity, namely, defensive CSR (compliance-driven, risk-based), charitable CSR (altruism-driven, philanthropy-based), promotional CSR (image-driven, PR-based), and strategic CSR (product-driven, code-based). All four of these types of CSR—which I call CSR 1.0 collectively—have failed to reverse the most serious negative social, environmental, and ethical consequences of the "free" market.

In this sense, CSR to date has failed. The failure of CSR 1.0 has three basic causes: it has promoted an incremental approach to social and environmental improvements; it has remained a peripheral function in most companies; and customers and the markets have not consistently rewarded responsible and sustainable corporate behavior or punished irresponsible and unsustainable companies.

Hence, what is needed—and what is just starting to emerge—is a new approach to CSR, which I call systemic CSR, or CSR 2.0. This is a purpose-driven, principle-based approach, in which business seeks to identify and tackle the root causes of our present unsustainability and irresponsibility, typically through innovating business models, revolutionizing their processes, products, and services, and lobbying for progressive national and international policies. This leads to my first forecast.

Forecast 1

By 2052, we will see most large international companies having moved through the first four types of CSR (defensive, charitable, promotional, and strategic) and practicing, to varying degrees, CSR 2.0.

But what will CSR 2.0 look like? How will we know it when we see it? The first test is creativity. The problem with the current obsession with CSR codes and standards is that it encourages a checklist approach to CSR. But our social and environmental problems are complex and intractable. They need creative solutions, like Freeplay's battery-free and off-grid windup technologies (for flashlights, radios, and computers, for instance), or Vodafone's M-Pesa scheme, which allows the unbanked to perform basic financial transactions using mobile phones.

Forecast 2

By 2052, reliance on CSR codes, standards, and guidelines will be seen as a necessary but insufficient way to practice CSR. Instead, companies will be judged on how innovative they are in using their products and processes to tackle social and environmental problems.

Another shift that is only just beginning is taking CSR solutions to scale. There is no shortage of charming case studies of laudably responsible and sustainable projects. The problem is that so few of them ever go to scale. We need more examples like BYD making small electric cars in China or the Grameen Bank microcredit movement.

Forecast 3

By 2052, self-selecting "ethical consumers" will become less relevant as a force for change. Companies—strongly encouraged by government policies and incentives—will scale up their choice editing, ceasing to offer "less ethical" product ranges, thus allowing guilt-free shopping.

Forecast 4

By 2052, cross-sector partnerships will be at the heart of all CSR approaches. These will increasingly be defined by business bringing its core competencies and skills (rather than just its financial resources) to the party—as Walmart did when it used its logistical capability to help distribute aid during Hurricane Katrina, or as the Corporate Leaders Group on Climate Change did when they urged the UK and EU governments to set bolder climate policies.

Forecast 5

By 2052, companies practicing CSR 2.0 will be expected to comply with global best-practice principles, such as those in the UN Global Compact or the Ruggie Human Rights Framework, but simultaneously to demonstrate sensitivity to local issues and priorities. An example is mining and metals giant BHP Billiton, which has strong climate-change policies globally, as well as malaria prevention programs in southern Africa.

Forecast 6

By 2052, progressive companies will be required to demonstrate full life-cycle management of their products, from cradle to cradle. We will see most large companies committing to the goal of zero-waste, carbon-neutral, and water-neutral production, with mandated take-back schemes for most products. We need a cradle-to-cradle approach, ensuring that products and processes are inherently "good," rather than "less bad," as Shaw Carpets does when taking back its carpets at the end of their useful life.

Forecast 7

By 2052, much like the generally accepted accounting principles (GAAP), some form of generally accepted sustainability principles (GASP) will be agreed upon, including consensus principles, methods, approaches, and rules for measuring and disclosing CSR. In addition, a set of credible CSR rating agencies will have emerged.

Still, the role of government in the next forty years will be crucial. Many of the issues that CSR is currently trying to tackle on a voluntary basis will be mandatory in the future, especially with regard to emissions reductions (toxics and greenhouse gases), waste practices, and transparency. There will also be a gradual harmonization of country-level legislation on social, environmental, and ethical issues. However, CSR will remain a voluntary practice—an innovation and differentiation frontier—for those companies that are either willing and able, or pushed and prodded through nongovernmental means, to go ahead of the legislation to improve quality of life around the world.

Forecast 8

By 2052, corporate transparency will take the form of publicly available sets of mandatory disclosed social, environmental, and governance data—available down to a product life-cycle impact level—as well as Web 2.0 collaborative CSR feedback platforms, WikiLeaks-type whistleblowing sites, and product-rating applications (like the GoodGuide iPhone app).

Forecast 9

By 2052, the way that companies manage CSR will also change. CSR departments will most likely shrink, disappear, or disperse, as the role for a CSR generalist is confined to small policy functions. By contrast, more specialists in various aspects of CSR—such as climate, biodiversity, human rights, or community involvement—will be required throughout many departments of a corporation. And employees' performance on CSR issues will increasingly be built into corporate appraisal systems, affecting salaries, bonuses, and promotion opportunities, as is already the case at Arcor, the confectionary company in Argentina.

Collectively, these forecasts reflect my belief in an increasingly widespread adoption of CSR 2.0 over the decades ahead. By 2052, CSR 2.0 reporting will have exposed the total impact of large companies on global sustainability. This will act to push the companies toward becoming part of the solution to the sustainability crisis.

Wayne Visser (South African, born 1970) is an author, poet, social entrepreneur, speaker, researcher, and lecturer in sustainability, corporate social responsibility, and purpose-inspired business. He is founder and director of the think tank CSR International and a part-time academic at the University of Cambridge.

Collective Creativity: A Web of Inspired Individuals

The always-on Internet of the future will have significant impact on most social processes—both expected and unexpected, known and unknown, desirable and less so. The web clearly will shape the world of entertainment, as it already does via music, shows, and gaming. It will change tourism from being less travel and more (virtual) experience. It will simplify science because all information will be available in real time at the scientist's fingertip. And so on.

One area that will benefit is human creativity. We have already seen the potential in the explosive growth of Wikipedia—the continuously evolving encyclopedia that was created in a few years by a self-recruiting group of individuals with very little organization and no (substantial) budget or system of governance. Wikipedia in essence created itself, and it set the tone for an endless sequence of similar ventures. The wiki way of using the web makes it practically possible to draw on the collective competence of humanity, for whatever inspiring task there is. It makes it possible to sum the voluntary effort of individuals into huge edifices that formerly could only have been ordered by the church—or achieved by successful social movements.

Such collaborative ventures, I believe, will be important in the future. They will help decentralize initiative and power. In the era of the pervasive Internet, anyone can start a movement or a collaborative effort for or against anything. Success will depend on whether she or he hits a resonance among other web users, not on what some overlord thinks about the project.

"Glimpse 8-6: Harnessing the Wisdom of the Crowd" describes how collaborative innovation will affect product development in business. The pace of innovation will increase when innovators learn to harvest interactively from the incredible amount of information out there.

GLIMPSE 8-6

Harnessing the Wisdom of the Crowd

Elisabeth Laville

Whether they like it or not, companies are part of an ecosystem and, increasingly, will not be able to survive unless they acknowledge that they are interdependent with other "species"—including their customers, suppliers, partners, NGOs, start-ups, universities, and academics. They will need to cooperate with these and other organizations or individuals in a social and environmental context that will become even more complex in the next forty years. And they will be faced with new problems: adapting to, not just mitigating, climate change; decoupling economic development from resource consumption; increasing well-being while decreasing material possession; and protecting the rights of indigenous peoples. In order to succeed, corporations, and human organizations in general, will need to open up way beyond what they can imagine today.

This transition will not be an easy one, since most companies today are still focused on getting their message out, rather than really harnessing what they can get back from their stakeholders. But let's face it: companies are already confronted with problems—especially social, environmental, and cultural ones that they do not fully understand and cannot really address. In response, leading firms have started to turn to external sources of ideas. A good example is Unilever, which chose to proactively address the issue of overfishing and resource depletion in the 1990s by collaborating with the World Wide Fund for Nature (WWF). At the time, Unilever was the world's largest single buyer of fish, and Greenpeace had started to plan a campaign against Unilever in Europe to highlight the unsustainable nature of European fisheries. In response Unilever engaged with WWF to set up the Marine Stewardship Council (MSC), which is now the worldwide reference label certifying a sustainable supply of fish. This was an innovation that would not have existed if it had not been for the conservation expertise of WWF coupled with the market power of Unilever.

In 2052 this new paradigm of open and collective innovation will be key to building corporate resilience—a healthier approach to economic adaptation than competition on all fronts. The fittest—the survivors—will be those who integrate the ability to cooperate in their governance. Most companies and organizations need to improve their capability to cope with resource scarcity, disruptive competition, or NGO campaigns affecting their reputation. Most need to continuously reinforce strengths and resolve weaknesses so they can recover more quickly from mistakes. By 2052 most surviving companies will have these skills.

There is much more to sustainable innovation than technical innovation. Society will also need low-tech soft innovation in order to effect change in individuals' behavior, culture, and habits. Already, we are finding that the effort to produce high-tech, low-energy buildings for social housing does not in fact always generate the expected reduction in energy consumption, because occupiers have not been taught how to use their new buildings.

Another example of fostering sustainable lifestyle without high-tech innovation will take place through collaborative consumption, where individuals will be swapping, sharing, bartering, trading, and renting in peer-to-peer marketplaces. Looking back from 2052, we will most likely wonder why we owned so much stuff, most of the time unused in cupboards or self-storage facilities.

Finally, societal innovation will spontaneously harness participation and collaboration toward common goals. Immediately following the Haiti earthquake, some 2,000 online volunteers in just two days created a complete digital map of Port-au-Prince, later used by the NGOs in the relief effort. We now know that when it comes to creativity and intelligence, the whole can indeed be greater than the sum of its parts. The collective intelligence of a group exceeds the cognitive abilities of the individual group members. The high-tech Internet will help us solve ordinary, daily, low-tech problems in ways and on a scale never possible before. But let us not be mistaken: the real innovation here, the one that makes a difference for the planet, is that coming from the people, not from the Internet.

Collective innovation is a real revolution that is just starting. The open-source movement in software development has demonstrated during the last twenty years that it is not only possible, but also very effective, to design complex systems through the collaboration of thousands, and sometimes of tens of thousand, each bringing his or her own contribution to a common work. Hundreds of thousands of others can contribute as guinea-pig users, giving feedback or suggestions for improvement. The success of Mozilla Firefox software (a free and open-source web browser that has become the second most widely used) shows the absolute efficiency of this collaborative approach, as does Wikipedia (the free, web-based, collaborative, open-source encyclopedia written by volunteers and now available in 282 languages).

Interestingly, in both cases, the organizations behind these open projects are not conventional corporations. They are not-for-profits owned in novel ways and flowering on noncapitalist values. The result is often lower prices and sometimes even free products, with high quality.

Over time, collective innovation will extend to other industries. Already we are seeing new initiatives like Freebeer, an open-source beer whose recipe and branding elements can be used by anyone for pleasure or profit. Or consider Apple, which is leveraging its iPhone and iPad sales with thousands of apps made by non-Apple volunteers.

Nearly 40% of global CEOs already expect the majority of innovation in the future will be codeveloped with partners outside the organization.[23] Instead of the old-fashioned model of in-house innovation, which was about standard internal R&D and secret and aggressive control of intellectual property, firms will commercialize external as well as internal ideas by deploying outside as well as in-house pathways to the market.

The boundaries between the ideas of a company and the ideas of its surrounding environment will become more porous. In 2052 the "not invented here" syndrome that restricted the use of external ideas will be outdated—at last. Who knows, this might even turn capitalism upside down by 2052, with companies increasingly becoming vehicles for bringing the fruit of collectively owned ideas to the individual user, and for harnessing the power of individual users to improve ideas for the common good.

Elisabeth Laville (French, born 1966) is one of Europe's leading experts in sustainability strategies and corporate responsibility. She is the cofounder and chief entrepreneur of Utopies (1993) and Graines de Changement (2005).

I agree that businesses will obtain competitive advantage in the future by "Harnessing the Wisdom of the Crowd" through web-supported collaborative efforts. "Glimpse 8-7: Peak Youth Gaming for the Public Good" moves one step ahead and points to the likely positive impact on collaborative behavior from extensive experience in web-based gaming.

GLIMPSE 8-7

Peak Youth Gaming for the Public Good

Sarah Severn

Kagiso[24] was born in Soweto, South Africa, in 1994, the year Nelson Mandela became president of South Africa. She grew up in poverty but through a series of early interventions was able to stay in school, became part of a girl's soccer league that included education about HIV prevention, and ultimately gained a university scholarship to study computer science. By 2014 Kagiso was studying Chinese, with many of her courses delivered online. She was already clear that she was going to set her sights on completing some of her graduate studies in China, as she wanted to immerse herself in the culture of a country that was making huge land and natural resources acquisitions in Africa. She obtained a scholarship to North Carolina State in the United States, which in turn enabled her to study at the China Agricultural University, a partner university. An extensive internship at Oxfam enabled her to look at sustainable intensification farming practices in sub-Saharan Africa. During her graduate studies Kagiso became a huge fan of EVOKE, the social-networking game designed to unleash solutions to global problems and foster social entrepreneurs. She won seed funding for her idea and returned to Africa to establish her own business delivering access to agricultural extension services through mobile technology. Kiva investments provided further start-up capital, and the business was established as a cooperative. By the time she was thirty Kagiso had over two hundred employees and the business was expanding into other countries across Africa. By 2052 Kagiso had developed and sold several businesses, primarily related to the deployment of mobile technology and the use of social networking and gaming to solve many of the most pressing environmental and social problems facing the African continent.

In the first decade of the twenty-first century we reached an era of peak youth, a time in history when the share of youth in the world's population was almost 29%. By 2025 there will be 72 million more, but the share will have been reduced to 23%.

In 2012 most youth live in developing countries. More of them are educated and fewer of them live in poverty. Their life expectancy is higher, and they are more connected to each other and the rest of the world, having grown up as "digital natives." Their educational opportunities have improved. Still they live in a world of growing inequity, increasingly scarce resources, and human-induced climate change. Roughly 12 million of those aged fifteen to twenty-four are living with AIDS, three quarters of whom live in sub-Saharan Africa, where the life expectancy is now only forty-six years. On top of all this unemployment levels among youth are increasing globally.

Amid all the narrative of tragedy and breakdown, however, there are signals from the influences shaping the world and values of youth today that give us reason for hope. In 2052 today's youth will have assumed leadership roles in government, business, and civil society. Many of them will not have waited this long to usher in a new future, however, but will have broken through with social and environmental innovation through their own start-up enterprises.

In general this youth cohort, often referred to as the Millennials, appear to be:

- **More connected:** A recent Accenture report on Millennials' use of technology showed that Chinese youth spend an average of thirty-four hours each week using real-time communications and social media/networking tools. This is almost triple the average of the other twelve countries profiled in the report. Additionally, the percentage of those using mobile phones is rapidly growing worldwide.
- **Demanding of transparency:** Millennials' use of digital technology shows that they are prepared to share a great deal about themselves, and they expect a similar degree of transparency from business and government. They have less trust in business and public institutions than previous generations. The age of the Internet and Wikileaks has given this generation the opportunity to see through the emperor's clothes, and they don't necessarily like what is revealed. With prospects for traditional forms of employment very weak, an increasingly educated and globally connected youth will continue to become more politically active through necessity.

- **More supportive of liberal and progressive agendas:** In the United States it is clear that youth are politically more progressive, and the youth vote was largely credited with Obama's success in 2008. The Egyptian uprising and other movements across the Middle East in 2011 also represented well-educated youth movements choosing to change repressive regimes that do not serve their needs, and organizing through the use of mobile technology and social media.

- **More flexible:** This is a generation in which many don't expect to have a lifelong career in the traditional sense. High levels of unemployment and good levels of education mean they will create their own livelihoods out of necessity. The key challenge is for them to find meaning and hope in their lives, through belief in themselves, connection with each other, and linkages to systems that can support rather than exploit them.

- **Community oriented:** Millennials have grown up in a world defined by terrorism, September 11, economic turmoil, and environmental degradation. Their connectivity enables them to witness every major natural disaster from tsunamis to earthquakes and every example of geopolitical instability. Their own stability comes from family, friends, and their digital community, and they are more team oriented and collaborative than other generations and seemingly more compassionate. The Pew Center remarks that "civic trends have always risen with age. This generation is now emerging as being much more involved at a much younger age."[25]

- **More spiritual:** In 2052 recent discoveries in the fields of quantum physics, human consciousness, and noetic science will be considered mainstream. Patricia Auberne in her book *Megatrends 2010* points to the emergence of spirituality in business as a key trend for the next decade. We live in turbulent times and the search for meaning in life is becoming a powerful driver. While Millennials are less likely to be engaged in formal religion, the physical context within which they are developing (high levels of connectivity and collaboration) and the implications from value-system research like that of Spiral Dynamics[26] all indicate that the human species will continue to develop the capacity to deal with greater levels of complexity and alternative realities.

The Role of Social Gaming

So how might the value systems of the Peak Youth generation change the world of 2052? One of the more surprising contributors to young people's sense of community and collaboration is the advent of gaming—particularly social gaming, which has become all the rage on social networks such as Facebook. Jane McGonical is at the forefront of thinking regarding social gaming. At her TED talk in 2010 she made a case for how a vast increase in gaming could solve some of our most systemic challenges such as climate change, hunger, poverty, and obesity.[27]

The average young person today in strong gaming cultures will have spent 10,000 hours playing online games; this correlates to the level at which cognitive science research suggests mastery is achieved. McGonical notes that when playing games players tap into their best qualities: to be motivated, optimistic, collaborative, cooperative, and resilient in the face of failure. The joyful emotions players feel in games actually start to spill over into real life, which also has the benefit of enhancing creativity.

It also appears that gamers love to be tied to human, planetary-scale stories, and McGonical has already created several games that aim to model a better world. For example, World Without Oil, developed with the World Bank Institute, was piloted in 2007 with 1,800 players. EVOKE is another social network game designed to help empower people all over the world to come up with creative solutions to our most urgent social problems.

The expansion of games and gamers will have profound implications in that we can potentially accelerate the future that we desire by collaborating on existing problems in a virtual setting. The potential for games to be created about themes like global food supply is substantial. Engaging large numbers of youth in these types of activities will also create more awareness of the political and institutional barriers that are blocking forward movement and could in turn lead to their increased engagement in political advocacy.

Sarah Severn (British, born 1956) has spent the last seventeen years at Nike working on sustainability in numerous roles, now as director of Stakeholder Mobilization, Sustainable Business and Innovation. For twelve years she has led Nike's efforts in climate change and is now working on activating system-level innovation, based in Beaverton, Oregon.

"Peak Youth Gaming for the Public Good" is an attractive vision, but I suspect that this development will be more visible in China and BRISE (the emerging economies) than in the rest of the world, since they do not already have other well-established institutions for political communication.

Intergenerational Equity: Widening the Lens

With the advent of increasing climate damage over the decades ahead, thinking people will become increasingly concerned with what type of world they are leaving for future generations. Since the advent of stationary agriculture, it has been a tacit understanding between generations that the current farmer could harvest as much as he could, as long as he left a better farm for his children. This great tradition will be broken for the first time at regional scale during the next forty years. It will become obvious that the current generation is adding problems to the shoulders of the next generation that far exceed the power of the new tools, which are also part of their inheritance.

I hope, although I am not convinced, that our respect for the these generations—not just our children and grandchildren, but well beyond—will increase as we observe the increasing ravages caused by erratic weather and biodiversity loss. John Elkington (whose glimpse, "Military for Sustainability," is on page 185) is more optimistic:

> I don't know what weapons World War III, let alone World War IV, will be fought with. But it seems a sure-fire certainty that future wars will ensure we have a World Court of the Generations by 2052, where governments, companies, and other actors are arraigned and prosecuted for ecocide and gross damage to the interests of future generations.

I hope he is right.

PART 3

ANALYSIS

CHAPTER 9

Reflections on the Future

I would not say the future I've just described is anyone's goal. It is not where I, nor the contributors to the book, or likely you as a reader, would want to go. Therefore it is important to repeat that we won't go there as a result of consciously bad intent. Rather, we will go there in a forty-year-long marathon during which global society will try to create a better life for everyone—mainly through continued economic growth. The effort will succeed in some places, but not everywhere. Billions will be better off in 2052 than in 2012, and some will reach Western lifestyles. The poorest two billion will be stuck near where they are today.

That effort to raise material standards will involve increasing energy use, and we'll rely on fossil energy longer than is good for the climate. So, in 2052 the world will be looking back at forty years of accelerating climate damage, caused by continuous global warming, and bracing itself for the possibility of self-reinforcing, and therefore runaway, climate change. At the middle of the twenty-first century a huge effort will finally be in swing to reduce the human ecological footprint, based on collectively agreed upon and state-financed proactive investment seeking to reduce the chance of climate disaster. Democracies, formerly dominated by short-termism and delay, will have begun to copy the faster and more centralized decision-making style of more authoritarian regimes.

The road to 2052 will not be smooth. There will be increasing inequity, tension, and social strife. Some nations will collapse. Many will fray at the bottom. But in 2052 a new urban and virtual civilization will be discernable, far distanced, however, from our natural human roots. A paradigm shift toward more holistic and sustainable values will be well under way. But temperatures will be rising, ecosystems will be in retreat, and the world of 2052 will not be an optimal starting point for the ensuing forty years.

The Main Drivers

We have walked through the main drivers of these coming shifts: global population and the size of world GDP. We've seen that there will be a rise and eventual decline in global population, peaking at about 8.1 billion in 2040 and returning to present-day levels by 2052. We've seen, too, that the downward-sloping long-term trend in labor productivity growth that characterized the past forty years will continue. And, to my surprise, it appears that by 2052, growth in the world economy will be petering out. Not because humanity won't try to maintain growth, and not (primarily) because of the lack of oil or some other resource, but because of slower population growth and because of slower productivity growth. The effects of depletion will help slow productivity growth.

Yet resource constraints will not be the main brake on the world economy to 2052. The Stone Age did not end because of lack of stone. Similarly, the fossil age will not end because of lack of fossil energy. Much fossil energy will be left in the ground after the human fossil age, simply because humans won't need it. Our use of energy will never become as high as we originally thought—because the economy will never grow so big as we once expected. We will use less energy because we will (grudgingly and as late as possible) economize on the use of this resource. And our use of fossil energy will never become as big as we once expected because we will (grudgingly and only once alternatives become competitive) shift toward renewable energy. But the shift away from fossil energy will not be fast enough to avoid dangerous warming, and we will have to live with the resulting damage, which will trigger large-scale and expensive investment in adaptation measures.

My forecast can be translated into macroeconomic terms, for the benefit of those who prefer to see the world in such terms: In a rational attempt to solve the onrush of problems from depletion, pollution, climate change, and biodiversity loss, humanity will seek to increase annual investments in protective measures. More money will be put into repair (e.g., of hurricane and flood damage), adaptation (e.g., new dikes against sea-level rise), and the development of new technologies (e.g., solar energy, carbon capture and storage). These investments will help reduce damage, help postpone the long-term decline in productivity, and help boost world GDP. The higher activity level will ensure higher employment but—importantly—won't lead to a similar increase in consumption. The reason is obvious: the consumers will have to limit their consumption to what is left of the GDP after the (huge) investments in repair, adaptation, and new technology. Sadly, lower consumption growth will exacerbate tension and social strife, which in turn will reduce productivity growth, because the pie available for sharing will be smaller than it could have been.

The "fact" that the world economy will be much smaller in 2052 will have one large and unexpected advantage: the lower growth rate will soften humanity's crash with global limits. That doesn't mean that there won't be significant damage. Extreme weather, sea-level rise, floods, and droughts will create problems that our children would have been happy to live without. Wild nature will be pushed poleward and into national parks at rates that will make it difficult to maintain natural beauty and ecological balance. But the damage will be less than if global society had peaked at 9.5 billion people and an economy four times the size of the current one, as is the current standard expectation.

The Future in Graphs

This forecast, and the data that drives it, can be summed up visually, as seen in figure 9-1. This graph shows world developments from 1970 to 2050: historical data for the last forty years extended by my forecast for the next forty years.

Figure 9-1 consists of three parts and illustrates the development of fifteen variables. These illustrate what I call State of Affairs, Production, and Standard of Living. The State of Affairs graph provides numbers for the size of the population, GDP, consumption, CO_2 emissions from energy use, and temperature rise as they evolve over time from 1970 to 2050. The Production graph shows the development of five indicators of human activity on Earth: energy use, food production, fraction renewable energy, investment share of GDP, and remaining unused bio-capacity. The Standard of Living graph shows various aspects of the human condition: GDP per person, energy use per person, food per person, consumption (of goods and services) per person, and finally sea-level rise. All fifteen variables are presented as average values for the world at large.

The resulting overview portrays a global society that expands toward limits before it starts to contract. Most variables follow historical trends toward 2030. But then various variables start to stagnate and decline. The only exceptions are temperature rise, sea-level rise, and the share of human energy use coming from renewable sources, which all keep growing, and unused bio-capacity, which keeps falling. The climate impacts continue to rise, nature is forced to retreat, while renewable energy is gaining market share.

Global CO_2 emissions peak first, in 2030. By 2050 they are back down to the level of forty years earlier. The population peaks in 2040 and then starts a very slow decline—it is down 1% by 2050. Energy use peaks next; according to my forecast the world will never use more energy in a single year than in 2042. But the energy peak is also flat; in essence global energy use will be constant for twenty years from 2030 to 2050, before it starts a slow decline. The fourth variable to peak is global consumption—the annual expenditure, private and

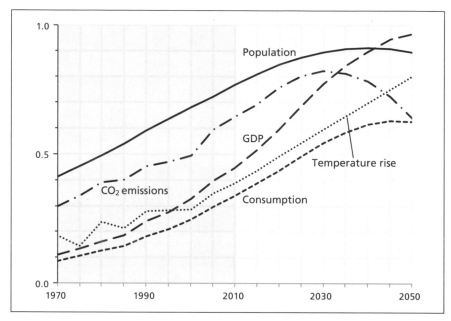

FIGURE 9-1a World State of Affairs, 1970–2050.

Scale: Population (0–9 billion people); GDP and consumption ($0–$150 trillion per year); CO_2 emissions (0–50 billion tonnes CO_2 per year); temperature rise (0°C–2.5°C).

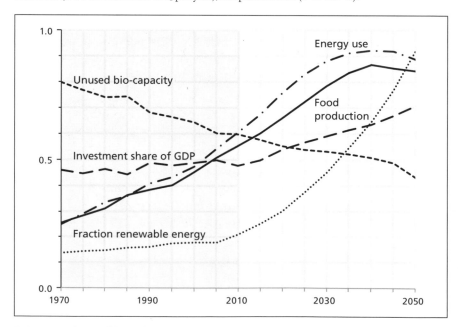

FIGURE 9-1b World Production, 1970–2050.

Scale: Food production (0–12 billion tonnes per year); energy use (0–20 billion tonnes of oil equivalents per year); fraction renewable energy (0%–40%); unused bio-capacity (0%–50%); investment share of GDP (0%–50%).

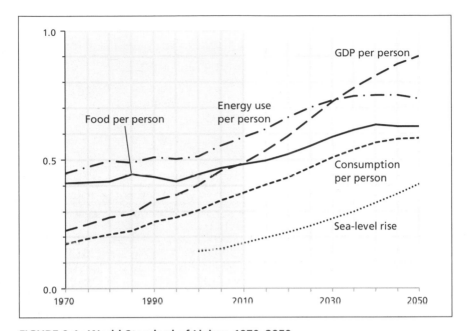

FIGURE 9-1c World Standard of Living, 1970–2050.
Scale: GDP per person and consumption per person ($0–$20,000 per person-year); food per person (0–2 tonnes per person-year); energy use per person (0–3 tonnes of oil equivalents per person-year); sea-level rise (0–1.4 meters).

public, on goods and services—but this can't be seen from the graph since consumption reaches its maximum just at the end of the graph and starts its decline in the following decade (after the end of the graph). And, finally, world GDP keeps growing throughout the whole period from 1970 to 2050, but at a slower rate at the end, toward a peak that occurs in the second half of the twenty-first century, outside the end of the graph.

The global temperature also keeps rising throughout, from plus 0.5°C in 1970 to plus 2.0°C in 2050. Calculations not shown in the graph, and done using the C-ROADS model based on my assumption that global CO_2 emissions will fall linearly from 2050 to zero in 2100, indicate that the global temperature will reach a maximum of plus 2.8°C in 2080, in a lagged response to the peak in CO_2 emissions fifty years earlier.

In the Standard of Living part of the graph, GDP per person keeps rising throughout. Each global citizen increases his or her annual production of goods and services, year after year. But the fraction of GDP allocated to investment starts to rise after 2015, first because society decides to defend itself against depletion, pollution, climate change, and biodiversity loss, and later because it has to repair damage from insufficient efforts to this end. As a result, the production of consumer goods and services per person stagnates around 2050—and continues into decline outside the end of the graph.

Food availability peaks around 2040, as climate change starts to reduce the amount of land that remains suitable for agriculture. At the same time the negative effect of higher temperatures start to slow the rise in land yields, overwhelming the fertilizing effect of more CO_2 in the atmosphere. Food production peaks in 2040 at a level near 60% above current levels, when measured in tonnes of food per year. Food per person stagnates at one-third above the per capita availability in 2010, which means that many are still hungry. Energy use per person declines gradually after a peak in 2035, as the investments in energy efficiency bear fruit.

But the impact of this continued expansion of human activity from 2010 onward takes its toll. The ecological cost of growth can be seen not only in the continuing increase in the average temperature, but also in the continuing fall in the amount of unused biological capacity (in the Production graph). By 2050 nearly half of what little land was not used for human purposes in 2010 will have been grabbed for human use (buildings, infrastructure, forestry, and agriculture). And meanwhile the sea level will rise by 36 centimeters between 2010 and 2050, to a total of 56 centimeters relative to preindustrial times.

The source of the data is provided in appendix 2, and readers who want to know more can visit the spreadsheet model on the book's website, www.2052 .info, which provides data on a number of other supplementary variables, for example, on demographics and the composition of the energy sector.

The Cliff-Hanger

Looking at the very big picture, the good news is that my forecast does not show a sudden and abrupt fall in living standards over the next forty years. It is true that some social groups—especially among the current elites—will have to live through what will feel like collapse. But it won't be collapse. It will "only" be decades of continuing stagnation in disposable income. In some rich regions the stagnation may deteriorate into declining per capita consumption, but not into collapse.

My forecast does not foresee unsolvable problems concerning oil, food, water, or other resources. One reason is that a large fraction of the world's population—two to three billion people—will remain poor. A second reason is that I believe temporary shortages (affecting those who can pay) in the end will be solved by global society throwing enough money at the problem—solving it through brute force. The world economy is an enormous muscle, if society finally decides to use it.

Thus the main challenge in our global future is not to solve the problems we are facing, but to reach agreement to do so. The real challenge is to have people and capital owners accept short-term sacrifice, roll up their sleeves, and do the heavy lifting. The agreement to act will arise, sooner or later, but it will come late in the day, and the resulting solution even later. As a consequence humanity will have to live with the unsolved problem longer than if the action had been started at once. Waiting for "the market" to give the start signal will lengthen the temporary period of forced sacrifice. Forward-looking political leadership could kick-start the societal response but may be kept from doing so by the democratic majority of voters with a short-term perspective.

As I am writing this (in 2012), humanity is well aware of the climate challenge, and the negotiations to agree on a global response are in full swing. Actually, the talking has been going on for more than twenty years. When will a conclusion be reached? My forecast is a quantitative estimate of what will finally be agreed to and when. It says, interestingly, that the human response will be just so strong (or weak) that it is impossible to conclude whether it will trigger self-reinforcing climate change in the second half of the twenty-first century. If the human response during the next forty years ends up being somewhat stronger than I forecast, global warming might keep below plus $2°C$ throughout the twenty-first century. If so, science believes that self-reinforcing warming is unlikely. But the CO_2 emissions in my forecast will produce a maximum temperature of plus $2.8°C$ around 2080. This is above the threshold that is deemed as safe by the climate scientists.

So we have a cliff-hanger! Will humanity mend its ways faster than my forecast predicts—and, if so, save the world from unstoppable climate change?

Self-reinforcing climate change is a process wherein current warming leads to more future warming, which in turn leads to even more warming in an unstoppable causal feedback loop. The simplest example is melting of the southern rim of the tundra. This will release methane, which is a strong greenhouse gas, which will lead to higher temperatures, which in turn will melt more tundra. This will release even more methane, which will lead to higher temperatures, and melt more tundra. The process will not stop until there is no more tundra to melt. Calculations indicate that if the process were allowed to go to the bitter end, the released methane effect could double the warming from CO_2. Self-reinforcing warming is different from other problems because it is impossible to stop once started. I should have said "near" impossible.

Stopping self-reinforcing warming can be done by cooling the earth (and particularly its oceans) enough to get back into safe territory. But this has to be done with sufficient strength to counterbalance the effect of the concurrent self-reinforcing change. It would require a powerful refrigerator indeed.[1]

The fact that my forecast tells the tale of a world that will move very close to the edge of the abyss—very close to triggering self-reinforcing climate change—should act as a great inspiration for us to do more than what we are likely to do.

My Own Reactions

So what are my own initial reactions upon reading the summary of my forecast of global developments to 2052?

My first reaction is one of relief. I am genuinely happy to see that there will not be total Armageddon within my lifetime. The sky will not fall in, at least not in my part of the world (the New North), and at least not before I leave for new hunting grounds (at age eighty-five in 2030)—where I hope to find more equality and less climate damage than in the place I will be leaving.

Global conditions over the next forty years will be much more difficult than they needed to be. But human civilization will be changing, not disappearing. It will be on a path—toward an urbanized, mechanized, and computerized world—that I do not particularly like. But it will not be dying.

The only things that may disappear are some of those beautiful landscapes that I love. The coral reefs, the endless uncut taiga, the biodiverse rain forest, may succumb during the next doubling of human activity on planet Earth. But humans will live on.

So my first reaction is actually relief. This is a much better future than I have been expecting during my four decades as a worrier.

My second reaction is: Am I right? Is my forecast likely to come true? Will the world really be stupid enough *not* to do what is perfectly doable, namely, to allocate enough money and manpower up front to solve the climate crisis as it emerges over the next several decades? I am sad to say that my answer is yes, I believe the world will be sufficiently stupid to postpone meaningful action. Simply because it is in the short-term interest of those that run the world—democratic majorities and the capitalist system. I had only one personal motivation for writing this book, and that was to find the most likely answer to my question about what will happen to my world in my future. To respond to this challenge I have built my answer as meticulously and consistently as I can, and I am afraid my answer is correct.

There is of course great uncertainty in my answer. My forecast is written in a much more blatant form than the normal scientific approach would allow. Instead of saying that the population in 2042 will be 8.1 billion people, I could have been more precise and said it will be between 8.0 and 8.6 billion sometime in the early 2040s. Instead of saying that the global GDP in 2050 will be 145 T$/yr, I could have said it will be between 120 and 160 T$/yr in the middle of the century. Instead of saying that the temperature will peak at plus 2.8°C, I could have said it will reach a maximum of between 1.5 and 4°C. These ranges indicate the true uncertainty in the forecasts, which is big. But I have based my forecast on average values, that is, to where we are likely to end in the uncertainty band. This is where I depart from strict science and venture out on that limb I described earlier: the one where one is forced to make an educated guess. In most places it would not matter if I used the highest or lowest estimate instead of the average. The only exception is in the forecast temperature increase. If global warming peaks in 2080 at plus 1.5°C (the lower estimate), we may be spared self reinforcing disaster. If it reaches plus 4°C (the higher estimate), I am sure we won't. At the average value of plus 2.8°C it is give or take.

Let me return to the question: Is my forecast likely to come true? The systems approach to that question would be to ask another question: What are the most sensitive assumptions? What are the pillars on which the forecast is built, and which of these pillars are least robust? The two pillars most vulnerable to change are the drop in urban fertility and the downward trend in productivity growth. The forecast is based on a number of other pillars that do not matter much or for which I am convinced that the foundation is sound: increasing life expectancy, sufficient reserves of fossil energy, the technological feasibility of large-scale and cheap renewable energy, sufficient capacity to produce food, and the short-term nature of humanity, democracy, and the market.

Let me take the two crucial pillars, one by one. If fertility does not drop as fast as I expect, the world population will peak at a higher level. So will the GDP, and so will energy use. Accumulated CO_2 emissions will be higher, as will be the peak temperature. The consequence will be a higher likelihood of self-reinforcing climate change after 2052. But at the same time, the higher population densities will trigger more pressure on resources and more conflict from crowding. Which in turn will ensure that the GDP does not actually grow as much as expected, with lower energy use and lower emissions as a result. This feedback will move us toward a world that has the same total GDP, but lower income per person. My important point is that there are a number of compensating feedbacks in any social system, and that they tend to reduce the consequences of external shifts. In this case, higher fertility may not influence the global future as much as many would expect.

On to the second pillar—the long-term downward trend in productivity growth. Here the same kind of feedback thinking applies. If productivity grows more slowly than expected, production will be lower, and this will be an advantage because the conflict with global limitations will be milder. The problem will be that poverty will take longer to disappear. But what if productivity grows faster than forecast? Then world GDP will grow faster than forecast and reach higher levels. So will energy use and climate emissions. Fossil fuels will be depleted more rapidly. But on the other hand, the economic muscle available to solve the problems of depletion and pollution will be stronger. And if the crash with planetary limits becomes more violent, perhaps the democratic awakening will happen earlier, so the bigger muscle is actually put to use at an earlier time. Once more the effect of alternative assumptions may not be as radical as expected: faster growth in GDP may trigger an earlier societal response to reduce the resulting damage to the planet.

My forecast rests on a number of other assumptions, for example, that cheap oil won't derail the gradual shift from fossil to solar energy; or that soil erosion will not terminate the growth in world food production; or that world poverty will not completely stop economic development. What if the problems of scarce oil, soil productivity, and poverty are not solved as part of "normal progress"? Here my answer follows a somewhat different rationale. If these problems are not solved now, they will be solved later. Meanwhile the problem will become more acute and finally release the sufficient amount of money for its solution. Meanwhile there will be unnecessary suffering. That suffering matters much to those who experience it, but in the long run it will not cause destruction of the carrying capacity of the globe.

My third initial reaction to the summary of my forecast—following relief and initial disbelief—is despair. Fear of losing it all. It really depresses me that I believe that humanity is not going to rise to the occasion and solve the climate problem before it may become self-reinforcing and unstoppable. As mentioned, this is not fear for loss of my own well-being. I am comfortable now, and will be long dead when crisis strikes. It is more intense anxiety about the fact that humanity will voluntarily destroy the wonderful world as we know it—reducing age-old biological diversity and man-made cultural diversity in the process. In short, I am scared on behalf of what it has taken nature hundreds of millions of years to create. I am also scared by the unnecessary suffering humanity will cause to itself, but I must admit that this takes second seat. I am convinced that the human species will survive the second half of the twenty-first century (along with the *Rattus norwegicus* and the common fly—to use the oft-quoted and deliberately insulting role models). The human being is incredibly adaptable. She or he most likely will not find the post-crisis world as detestable as I would.

Eight Straight Questions about the Future

I will discuss how we can potentially change the future in chapter 12. But first let me answer some of your likely questions about the next forty years as I expect them to unfold.

1. Will I Be Poorer?
Some of us will, others will not.

In order to give a clearer answer, the question must be asked more precisely. The question must be: Will I be poorer compared to *x*? And you must decide whether *x* should be (*a*) today, (*b*) what you would have been if humanity rose to the occasion and ran a rational world, or (*c*) relative to your peers.

Furthermore you must be precise about what future time you are asking about. Is it 2052? Or the halfway mark, 2032? You do remember, I hope, that the average income path to 2052 will not be a straight line. Per capita consumption in my forecast grows to a peak sometime within the next forty years and is in decline in 2052—details depending on where you live.

If we're willing to sacrifice some precision, though, I can provide this general answer: As long as you are not a citizen of the United States, you will be richer in 2052 than you are today. But only slightly so, unless you live in China or BRISE. I can add some detail: you will be much poorer than you would have been in 2052 if a benevolent dictator took control in 2012 and forced through the necessary investments to keep everyone employed and global warming below plus 2°C.

And I can add: Unless you do something very stupid (or very unconventional) during the next forty years, you will be in the same position vis-à-vis your neighbors and peers as you are now. Both you and your peers will experience the same parallel development over the next forty years. The only exception is if you are presently very affluent. Then it may be that your social rank will have declined through the processes of redistribution, which I believe will occur during the next forty years in order to reduce some of the tension implicit in the rapid increase in inequity in the capitalist world.

Finally, I will give you a piece of uninvited advice: Yours is the wrong question. You should not ask, "Will I be poorer?" You should rather ask, "Will

I be more satisfied?" Whether you are satisfied with life is more important (for you) than whether you are somewhat richer or poorer. Empirically, for some, income is the sole determinant of life satisfaction. But for the majority, a whole host of factors influence our well-being—job, health, family, community, prospects for the future—in addition to income. It is the sum total of all aspects of life that determine your well-being, both now and in the future.

So when you privately assess the implications for yourself of my global forecast, try to judge what it will mean for your well-being, not only what it will mean for your income.

2. Will There Be Enough Jobs?

Yes.

Or to be slightly less flippant: there will be as many jobs in the future as there have been in the past—relative to the workforce, that is. Or to be more scientific: there is little reason to expect that underemployment will be much higher (or lower) in the future than it has been over the last generation. This means that 10% of those who would like to get a paid job won't get it overnight. The number will be closer to 5% during business upturns and closer to 15% during downturns. In the future, like in the past.

The reason is simple. A job is absolutely crucial from the point of the individual in industrial and postindustrial urbanized society. It is the only way in which the individual can get part of the societal pie—without engaging in theft. Since a job is crucial, the individual will do his utmost to obtain one. And society—at least in the long run—will do its utmost to ensure there are jobs, typically by seeking rapid economic growth. But we know from recent history that this is a taxing task, and that politicians often fail. As a result we do experience lengthy periods of excessive unemployment, even in the advanced economies. And the task of securing full employment may become harder in the future, since I forecast lower growth rates in GDP.

But given the importance of employment for societal peace and order, and given the real fear among the elite about a reshuffling of the cards, the necessary effort will be applied—sooner or later. The reason why I am willing to state this so blatantly is that the task is solvable in principle. When the unemployment problem is not solved in the short term, it is because society is not immediately willing to use the tools that the ruling elites actually have at hand. Because these tools imply taking from the rich (those with a job) and giving to the poor (those without a job).

For in the end the rulers can print paper money and pay unemployed people to do what society needs to get done, in return for the paper money.

For example, politicians can decide that society needs to build dikes to protect against rising sea levels, or remove litter from public places and highways, or paint all roofs white (in order to reflect more sunlight and reduce global warming), or create new pieces of art for public enjoyment. And they can print the necessary money to pay for this work. The new money will boost demand for everything that the workers need—food, shelter, energy, vacation—and have the traditional expansionary effect. The cost will be higher inflation, but that bothers the rich more than the poor. As long as there are underutilized resources in the economy, deficit financing of compulsory work for the state is sustainable. It is possible to lower unemployment by printing new money. But the rich will scream. Because they will see this for what it is: namely, a transfer of wealth and income from the rich to the poor.

If the elite is stupid enough not to solve the unemployment problem within reasonable time, revolution (or at least sufficient rattling of the system to get crisis work going) will result. Such disruption will lower incomes in the short term, but it will distribute the cards in new ways in the longer run and therefore provide new opportunity for the formerly unemployed. Disruption makes unemployment more bearable, and probably gets it back down into the 10% range.

So I see little reason why there should be higher levels of unemployment in the future. But that is not the same as saying there will be smooth sailing. Unemployment figures will continue to fluctuate between the barely acceptable and the totally unbearable. And all along there will be unnecessary suffering.

3. Will the Climate Problem Hurt Us?
Yes, but not critically before 2040.

My forecast shows in quantitative detail how I believe the global average temperature will increase over the next couple of generations. The average temperature will go from plus 0.8°C relative to preindustrial times in 2012 to plus 2.0°C in 2052, and a maximum of plus 2.8°C in 2080.

The forecast maximum in 2080 is above the threshold that world leaders agreed would place us in the danger zone for runaway climate change; but it is important to realize this is a politically negotiated goal. Views differed, and still differ, on what will be safe. Or in other words, what will hurt us.

There is a large body of literature about what will happen at plus 2°C. Science agrees on the broad lines—more drought in drought-prone areas, more rain in rainy areas, more extreme weather (strong winds, torrential rains, intense heat spells), more melting of glaciers and the Arctic sea ice, somewhat higher sea levels, and a more acidic ocean, in addition to the higher temperature and the higher CO_2 concentration in the atmosphere that will boost food and forest growth in higher northern latitudes. Ecosystems will move poleward and uphill.

But science cannot yet predict the detailed strength and regional distribution of these impacts. Thus it is impossible to forecast what will be the effect on your surroundings over the next generation. But you can get a strong indication if you start looking slightly beyond science. By asking locals in daily contact with nature, you will get to know what has changed over the last twenty or forty years. You can do worse than assuming that these changes will strengthen during the rest of your life.

Let me give a concrete example. The only rational reason to live in a cold, northern city like my hometown of Oslo during the dark subfreezing period from mid-November to mid-March is the great opportunity for cross-country skiing (ideally on moonlit white glades in the pine forests just north of the city) on the one meter or so of cold fluffy snow that covered the ground until the last real winter in 1986.

But over the last twenty-five years, the average winter temperature in Oslo has gone up by plus 2°C. This has shortened the period of stable cold weather from four to two months. Instead, we now have two months of good skiing and two months of wet, gray, and cold slush, which keeps the forest dark and makes it impossible to even go jogging there after work. One-half of the Oslo winter is gone, sacrificed on the altar of climate change. This is clearly visible in the eyes of someone who has been skiing regularly over the last fifty years. It is discernable in the snow statistics, but it is not yet an established fact in the urban public mind. And certainly not institutionalized in a strong Norwegian climate policy.

This loss of skiing is a nuisance, but not catastrophic. As is the prolongation of the dry period in the western United States, or the increased number of very hot days in Provence. But they do constitute a loss. And a longing, among the grown-ups, for the good old days. A little more problematic, to say the least, is the slow rise of the ocean level around those Pacific islands that will be submerged if the ocean actually rises by a meter—just twice the expected sea-level rise by 2052.

So if you want to find out how climate change will hurt you, ask a local elderly outdoorsman or old farmer what he believes is going on. And then try to answer the question "Will I be more satisfied?" under the conditions that he thinks are emerging. But please be aware how subjective the answers you get will be: Most Norwegian farmers living next to my moonlit skiing forest are delighted at the prospect of higher temperatures, better forest growth, and the opportunity to clear-cut more often, with less snow bothering the cutting operations.

4. *Will Energy Be More Expensive?*

Yes.

But once more, the precise answer depends on the detail in your question. Let us start by deciding what cost you are thinking about. Is it your total energy bill (in hard-earned dollars per year)? Or the national bill? Or the cost per unit of energy (in dollars per kWh of electricity or gallon of gasoline)? Or is it the share of the economy that is engaged in getting hold of all the energy that is needed to run the economy (measured as the percent of GDP in the energy sector—which should include those export sectors that are required to finance the importing of energy, if there is importing)?

I can answer only some of these questions, and the answers differ with the precise questions asked. The simplest answer follows directly from the Standard of Living part of figure 9-1 on page 233: the average per-person use of energy will increase. But only for a while—energy use per person peaks around 2040. So we will each have more energy available to us for some decades, until growth slows and growing energy efficiency leads to reduction in our annual use of energy.

So we will use more energy—more tonnes of oil equivalents of energy per person per year—until the 2040s. But will this cost more? I can't predict in detail. My spreadsheets tell me that the energy intensity of the economy will decline monotonically from 300 kilograms of oil equivalents per $1,000 of GDP in 1970 to 180 in 2010, and some 120 in 2050. This means that the value created per unit of energy used will increase dramatically, which also means that the share of total value creation that is expended on energy is likely to decline. But I can't say for sure, for it depends on whether the new forms of energy, replacing increasingly the old fossil sources, will prove to be very much more costly than power and heat based on coal, oil, and gas.

More simply put, after much empirical work, I have concluded that I think that future energy may be 30% more expensive than current fossil-based energy. During an initial introductory period the renewables will be even more costly, but in the long run I believe solar, wind, biomass, and CCS will be available at current prices plus 30%.

So in answer to your question: I believe energy prices will increase per unit of energy by one-third. But since the energy intensity will fall by 50% to 2052, your absolute bill per year may even decline. And the energy cost will be a declining share of the GDP, which will grow by more than 100%. But that is on a forty-year horizon; in the meantime, while society is increasing its investments in order to help the transition from a fossil-based toward a renewables-based economy, energy will be more expensive.

The percentage of the GDP that is in energy production gives a reasonable approximation to how energy prices will "feel" for you as a consumer. The percentage of the GDP in energy production translates (very roughly) to the percentage of the time you have to spend paying for your energy use. The Institute for Energy Research (IER)[2] in the United States has tried to estimate the share of energy in the world GDP. In 2005 some 8% of the US GDP was in the provision of energy. It means that (roughly) 8% of all labor and physical capital was used to obtain energy. The share has varied quite a bit over the last forty years. It started at 8% in 1970 and then rose to 14% after OPEC raised oil prices in the 1970s. It then declined over two decades to 6% during the years of recovery of the US economy after the oil shock. Since the year 2000 the share in energy increased once more, to 9% in 2006. The IER estimates that the equivalent number for the world economy is also 8%.

So this means very roughly that the average global citizen is spending one-twelfth of his or her time paying for energy, and that this could increase to one-eighth during the transition to a renewable future.

So energy will be more expensive, but not very much so, as I see it. The fundamental reason is the fact that one can even today produce clean power and heat from coal at a cost (using CCS) that exceeds the cost of conventional coal-based power and heat by only 50%. And coal with CCS will act as a near infinite backstop technology, keeping a lid on energy prices in the long run. I am obliged to stress that many informed people disagree with this estimate, which I base on engineering assessment of the (significant but finite) efficiency loss in CCS. My critics believe CCS will be much more costly. If they are right, it means that CCS will not be used, or at least not until later in the day. The effect will be to lower your energy bill in the short term and lengthen the period of transition to a low-carbon future.

In summary, the main reason why energy costs won't rise more in the short term is that humanity will be slow in making the transition to renewable energy. In 2052 a full 60% of the energy used will still be fossil. As a result climate damage will be growing fast, as will the unavoidable costs for repair of that damage. Paradoxically this means that humanity will choose to pay bills for repair after the crises, rather than paying the same amount of money for renewable energy ahead of time and avoiding the damage.

5. Will the Young Generation Calmly Accept the (Debt and Pension) Burden of the Old?
No.

I am now moving up the ladder of abstraction to look at some intangible issues beyond the more tangible questions of income, employment, climate damage, and energy costs.

The first issue concerns intergenerational equity, and it is particularly relevant in the industrial and emerging economies where the old ways of solving rights and obligations between the generations (and sexes) have been most dramatically changed over the last couple of generations. In the rich world, particularly, the first generation that has rung up a huge national debt and established a huge unfunded pension scheme is about to retire. The interesting, to say the least, question is whether the next generation will be willing to carry this burden and peacefully pay the debt and peacefully pay the pensions. I repeat my answer: I think not.

The simplest reason is they don't have to. They are legally obliged but can't be physically coerced. If they choose not to and stand shoulder to shoulder, there is little the elderly can do. The old will lose the intergenerational war if push comes to shove. The second reason is that we can already see that the burden is being shed. In forward-looking, well-organized countries, pension schemes have already been revised—in order to lower future payments. Greece was the first country to shed the sins of the fathers—and got the rest of the world to pay for one-half of the debt of the old generation. Former homeowners in the United States have started the struggle to get back some of the wealth that ended up in the financial institutions.

These processes will continue, I believe, although it is hard to tell what will be perceived as the equitable balance point in the distribution of well-being among the generations. But there is little doubt that the current situation (read: legislation) excessively benefits my post–World War II generation.

If we add impending climate damage into the intergenerational perspective, my generation looks even worse. Because then it is not only the current young but also the unborn future generation who are losing out. They have to live with the CO_2 emitted during my generation's partying during the last forty years. Many argue that this does not matter because we are leaving for future generations a whole lot of capital, infrastructure, and technology. But to paraphrase the World Business Council for Sustainable Development,[3] "People cannot succeed in ecosystems that fail."

In short, the current generation has tried to load too much onto the next generations. This will be undone. The young, I predict, will not take over the burden unabridged. Some debts won't be repaid, and part of my pension won't appear in my bank account.

Does it matter? It depends on who you are. Once more, you should try to decide how my answer is going to affect your own well-being.

6. Will the Passing of World Leadership from the United States to China Be Peaceful?

Yes.

The starting point here is my belief that China will be the world leader in 2052. This emerges with great clarity from my forecast, and especially from the regional split described in chapter 10. In 2052 China will have a population three and a half times bigger than that of the United States. The Chinese economy will be nearly two and a half times larger, and Chinese per capita production and consumption will be more than 70% of the US equivalents. China will be the premier driving force on the planet.

In some ways this is already the case. Current China is capable of acting in a manner that far exceeds the maneuverability of the two competitors for global supremacy: the European Union and the United States. The United States still has the biggest muscle (the US GDP equals 13 T$/yr, similar to that of the EU), but China is much more agile in the use of its somewhat smaller muscle (China's GDP is near 10 T$/yr). Militarily the United States is still more powerful outside US territory, but economically the Chinese influence is rising fast. It does not weaken the Chinese hand that it already owns 1 T$ of US federal debt, one-quarter of the US federal debt held by foreigners. This equals ownership of more than one month of the total output of the US economy.

Many believe that China won't reach hegemonic status because of lack of domestic resources or because of counterrevolution. My view is that China has sufficient coal and shale gas to run the economy in the transition stage, enough sun to fuel it in the long run, sufficient understanding of the climate threat to work up front to reduce the loss, and a sufficient tradition of Chinese independence to be willing to develop internally the resources it does not currently hold. But most important is the willingness and the ability of the Chinese to govern investment flows so as to achieve their goals. It should also be remembered that in the long run, China will no longer need all the energy and resources it currently uses for the production of export goods. In the long run it will suffice to have a sustainable interior supply of energy and resources sufficient to provide for the Chinese population, which will peak at 1.4 billion people around 2020 and be down to 1.2 billion in 2052.

Clearly things can go wrong for China, but I think this will take time. The alignment of the interests of the Chinese Communist Party and the great mass of Chinese is near perfect. Both need rapid growth in per capita consumption.

Both will applaud when it is achieved. Both will hurt when it fails, and try once more. There is, of course, at any time a group that would like to emphasize values other than material growth, but I believe they will be in the minority for a long time (just like in the United States), and their softer goals suppressed.

To do more with less will be the mantra of Chinese growth, in order to continue the goal of the last two thousand years, namely, to be a self-sufficient China independent of the barbarians from outside the Middle Kingdom. Increased energy and resource efficiency will be pursued with enthusiasm. Since both are achievable in principle, through the planned use of money and manpower, they will be achieved.

So what will the Americans do when the Chinese hegemon further exposes its full body? Not much. I believe in a friendly resolution of the potential conflict between China and the United States, because the United States also has enough resources inside its boundaries to run a self-sufficient shop for its inhabitants. It is true that the country currently depends on vast oil imports from abroad, but like China, the United States has enough coal and shale gas to run its economy for a long time (assuming little real GDP growth in the country over the next forty years, as I do). It has large agricultural muscle (more than sufficient for its domestic population—and if Americans decide to eat more healthily, also for quite a bit of biofuels). Furthermore the United States has some space that will be livable after climate change. Water may be a problem where it is currently needed, but activities can and will be moved if that is required to have enough water. And GMO crops will be used large-scale to reduce water scarcity, despite their drawback. If the American democracy finally decides to try to solve its obvious societal problems in a collaborative manner, the US investment capacity is huge and the problems solvable.

I think the latter sentence contains the essence of the US fate over the next forty years. The United States could maintain its hegemony if it decided to do so. But I don't think the American system of governance will be capable. Quick, bipartisan decision making is certainly not a US strength. And I see little that will change this fact on a forty-year horizon. Since the country is already rich, and the resources are there at least for living at a slightly lower footing, the United States can allow itself to slide into a secondary role, as a provincial and self-content country. Much like Europe smoothly moved down to second rank after the two World Wars.

Both China and the United States will be bothered by climate change. But both countries are big enough to include places that are relatively less affected. Their starting points are very different, the United States being rich and China much poorer (GDP per person today is one-sixth of the US rate). But their governance systems differ, will differ, and will help China move fast when the United States will be floundering. This won't create war since China's ambition is to be self-contained.

7. Will We Get a Stronger State?

In more places, but not everywhere.

Over the next couple of decades the world will be facing new problems (in addition to the well-known challenges of creating economic growth and maintaining social stability), some of which cannot be easily solved by the market.

The prime example is the climate challenge. It is a truly global problem: the temperature will rise everywhere, irrespective of who was the source of the emissions. And it is a truly long-term problem: the temperature will not react (that is, deviate from its current path) until thirty years after the initiation of the effort (as long as that effort is of realistic proportions).[4] Such truly global, truly long-term problems are hard to solve if one restricts oneself to using the powers of the "free" market only.

It's also likely that the state may need to intervene to address the increasingly uneven distribution of income and wealth that builds up over time as a natural consequence of the free market. Even the most diehard liberalists appear to agree that redistribution is something that is not automatically undertaken by the market by itself, but needs to be done via political action (such as through taxation). There is need for collectively agreed action in order to remove explosive inequity as a potentially destabilizing factor in the economy.

A third reason why the time might have come for stronger government is the historical fact that the world currently is a full twenty-five years into a period of increasing liberalization. This makes it likely that we have solved most of the problems that are easily solvable by the free market. If we try to extend the current era of liberalization, we will end up in a situation where the market has solved all the problems it can solve, so we are left facing only those problems that the market cannot solve. Sometime before this point, society will start exploring again societal solutions based on policy rather than relative prices.

So, in some nations, we will see a demand for a stronger state, capable of cutting through the democratic to-and-fro and making clear and effective policy, even if that implies less democracy and less market freedom. How fast will this happen? I think we are near a turning point in the slow societal oscillation between liberalism and a strong state. Over the next twenty years, we will see more frequent instances where the state intervenes and makes the necessary decisions rather than waiting for the market to lead the way.

It is hard to guess where stronger states will emerge first, but likely candidates are those nations that have pushed the liberalist thinking all the way to the brink, and those that have a tradition of successful government. Meanwhile, strong centralist authorities like that of Singapore will look increasingly good, as long as they manage to handle the tendency toward greater inequity. Curbing corruption is a first and very important step in that direction.

To avoid misunderstanding I would like to clarify what I mean by strong government, through a simple example. A strong government, for instance, would be able to shift a nation from cheap and dirty fossil energy to more expensive solar energy—*before* the latter is competitive. It is a government that would act in the long-term interest of the people, even if they do not agree in the short term. It is a government that is capable of withstanding not only the opposition from the enduring energy business but also the opposition from the voting majority who will want the cheapest possible energy in the short run. A strong government would also be capable of convincing the people to wait for a better solution and pay for its development while waiting. I agree that there is always the risk that the government may choose the wrong solution (and that the market might not have made the same mistake). But the risk can be reduced, for example, by letting the government define the goal and put up the money while allowing the market to choose the technique through a bidding process.

Will strong government come in time to solve the climate problem? As you have seen from my forecast, I think not. But by 2052 the acceptance and belief in strong government will far exceed that of today, and some of the obvious solutions will be well on their way.

8. Will the World of 2052 Be a Better World?

The answer depends on your age, profession, nationality, and, probably, family situation. And again, the answer does not rest solely on whether disposable income will be higher, but on whether your general satisfaction with life will have increased. There will be huge differences between people. To simplify, the average life satisfaction in 2052 will reflect the satisfaction level of some two billion people who will have moved from the farm to a decent apartment in a megacity during the last forty years, some two billion middle-class people who will hardly have had a wage rise in forty years, two billion who will have moved during their lifetime from $10/day (today's Vietnam) to $20/day (today's Ukraine), and two billion people who are still living a strenuous life in a semirural setting in a poor country.

All eight billion will have some level of Internet access, be much better informed, and be increasingly helped by local solar energy. They will have many fewer children. They will be largely urban (except for the minority still living off the land). They will grapple with overall effects of climate damage, but those in dense urban areas will likely have little firsthand experience with the damage caused by the erratic weather (though plenty of secondhand information via electronic media). They will live with the unpleasant knowledge that even more climate impacts lie ahead.

So, materially speaking the answer is probably yes—on average the world will be a better place. From a psychological perspective, probably no, because the future prospects in 2052 will be grim. That could change, though, if there is hope. If those experiencing the impacts of climate change have the comforting knowledge that, somewhere on the planet, some resourceful and well-run countries are putting tremendous effort into stopping global warming, they can maintain the hope of a better future world.

Again, it boils down to whether these groups will have more or less life satisfaction than they do today—a very subjective question, based on how they view their own well-being. It's important to note that people forty years from now will judge their circumstance more on how it has changed from their own recent past than from our vantage point of today.

Wild Cards

A number of unforeseen events can and will occur between now and 2052. In the following, I list a number of such "wild cards," to use the terminology of scenario professionals, and try to identify what impact they would have on my global forecast. I view them all as unlikely to occur, and this is why they are not integral parts of my global forecast.

Abundant Oil or Gas

What would happen if peak oil proves to be as untrue as many in the petroleum business think? What would happen if so much oil were found (and developed, and brought to market) that oil prices fell back to the good old value of $20 a barrel, the price throughout the 1990s? It would be a huge competitive advantage for oil, and it would (if allowed by government, which would happen only if the finds were so big that society was convinced oil would last for decades) slow the introduction of energy efficiency and renewable energy. But it would also steal market share from gas. The total effect would be to slow the reduction of CO_2 emissions and accelerate global warming. A larger share of the GDP would be consumption, so people would be materially better off, but they would live in a more threatening environment.

The same effect would result if one found even more supplies of abundant gas, as happened over the last ten years with the advent of cheap shale gas in the United States and elsewhere. Since gas emits much less CO_2 per unit of energy than both coal and oil, replacing these with gas leads to lower CO_2 emissions in the short term. But cheap gas will also make new renewables less competitive, and hence more gas will slow the long-term reduction in CO_2 emissions. So whereas cheap gas is a benefit in the short term, it does not solve the long-term problem—which is full transition to a solar era. Gas-fired utilities may, however, serve as a useful backup for intermittent wind power later in the transition.

In short, the total effect of finding more oil and gas is complex. One must quantify all the different effects and calculate the net impact, and accept that the net will vary over time. There does not exist a new and permanent equilibrium to simplify the answer.

Financial Meltdown

What would happen if there is total collapse in trust in the financial sector, which stops lending to the real economy and makes the world GDP contract, say by 20%, within a year? First of all I doubt that the world's central banks would let this scenario evolve, given that they have the authority to stop it (at least after some convincing in the parliaments) by printing more money and creating more demand, for example for more public goods and services—like road building during the Great Depression.

But assume they did not manage to stop this deep depression. The effect would be a dramatic fall in employment and income and a corresponding drop in energy use, CO_2 emissions, and the ecological footprint. There would be huge shifts in ownership and net asset values. But the main effect, over and beyond the decline in consumption and wealth and the associated suffering, would be a postponement of the human crash into the limits of the earth. But not by a great deal. If annual emissions were also cut by 20%, and this lasted for five years, it would reduce accumulated emissions by one year of normal emissions, and hence postpone self-reinforcing climate change from 2080 to 2081.

So a deep financial crisis wouldn't rescue the climate. But if the recession was used wisely to employ all the laid-off people in "green" projects funded by newly printed government cash, the downturn could be turned into a boon for the climate in the long run. But I am afraid this wouldn't happen.

Nuclear War

What would happen if someone drops a number of huge nuclear bombs, just to get a final solution to some irksome problem? Much less, I believe, than you might think. Nuclear war may cause insuperable pain and suffering in the moment of explosion, and the ensuing radioactivity will make life complicated for the affected people for a very long time.

But the direct impact on the world population and economy would be limited. If the bombs kill 100 million people, which I believe is ten times what would realistically happen, this would amount to 1.4% of the world's population and the same fraction of the world GDP (if we assume that the bombs kill the same fraction of all age groups). The bombs would set the world economy back by at most eight months (assuming a growth rate of 2% per year), and the population back by twelve months (assuming a growth rate of 1.4% per year). It would do even less to stop climate change than the deep recession discussed in the last section.

Once again, the suffering would be immense and totally unnecessary. And the inequity involved in someone being hit while the rest go free is unacceptable.

Disease

If a deadly disease were to "solve" the climate problem, it would have to reduce emissions from 2010 to 2050 by about one-third relative to my forecast. In broad terms, this would result if energy use was reduced by one-third, which in turn would result if the economy was reduced by one-third, which would result if the population was reduced by one-third. In other words, the climate problem would be solved if a pest killed some two billion people (one-third of the global population) and the die-off was evenly distributed among age groups and regions.

I can't imagine that anything like this could ever happen, and certainly hope not. But on the other hand, the bubonic plague in the years around 1350 killed that same fraction of European populations. A pest killing two billion people would be both a disaster beyond comprehension, and a solution to the climate problem.

Collapse in Ecological Services

What would happen if the ecological services on which we depend stopped working? If the bees stopped pollinating our fruit trees, if nature stopped distilling our drinking water, if trees stopped absorbing CO_2, if bacteria stopped breaking down our wastes, and so on? Scientists have calculated the value of the ecological services that humanity receives for free every year and concluded that the amount is of the same order of magnitude as the world GDP.

If nature stopped delivering these services, humanity would be facing collapse of society as we know it, because it would take us too much time to establish the man-made systems that could replace nature's supply of ecological services. To do so we would have to shift one-half of the workforce and one-half of all capital into the production of ecological services. This could possibly be done, but it would take a very long time, and in the end the consumable output of the economy would be one-half, because the other half would be producing something that formerly came for free. And since the population would still be the same, per capita consumption would decline to one-half. The total GDP would, however, still be the same, as would the ecological footprint. But as I said, I don't think humanity would be able to pull this one off.

Counterrevolution in China

What would happen if the Communist Party of China lost control, and economic growth fell to an average of 5% a year in the increasingly independent and disorganized regions of former China? The world GDP would grow more slowly, as would the CO_2 emissions and the ecological footprint. It would take a much longer time for the Chinese to get rich. And the advent of self-reinforcing climate change would be postponed by some years, giving humanity slightly more time to develop a climate-friendly world.

But most likely the disintegration of the authoritarian leadership would also reduce China's investment in forward-looking green technology, and this would work to increase emissions and counteract the beneficial effect.

Revolution in the United States

What would happen if there were revolution in the United States and a dramatic redistribution of income and wealth? This could conceivably be achieved through a citizens' rebellion that changed the tax laws fundamentally, thereby achieving a much more even distribution of income and wealth. I believe such revolution in the United States would have exactly the opposite effect of counterrevolution in China. It would accelerate GDP growth and increase the effort to make the country more climate-friendly. The redistribution would cause a huge increase in demand for consumer goods and services in the United States, and a huge wave of growth in the American economy. If the revolution were associated with the election of a strong government, one would get the additional advantage of an increase in the planned investments necessary to boost well-being and postpone climate change.

A Dedicated Global Effort to Stop Climate Change

What would happen if the world's leaders got together and decided to spend 5% of the world GDP every year for twenty years under an agreed plan to solve the climate problem? This would mean shifting 5% of the workforce and capital into the production of climate-friendly goods and services. This grand project would solve the climate problem. After twenty years of planned effort the world economy would be emissions free.[5]

A very simple way to do this would be to agree on a carbon tax of $100 per tonne of CO_2 levied at the coal face, oil well, and gas pipeline entry points. This would generate 3 T$/yr (namely $100 for each of the thirty-two billion tonnes of CO_2 that is currently emitted every year), which is close to 5% of the global GDP in 2010 of $67 billion per year. The money could be collected by the national government from the energy companies, which would have to pass the bill to their customers. And the government could pay the money back to all inhabitants—with the same amount per head. This would provide tremendous competitive strength for renewables and eliminate fossil-based energy. The government could speed the process further by using some of the money as temporary transition subsidies to projects that help reduce CO_2 emissions.

The Path to 2052

The path to 2052 will be tumultuous and full of conflict, like all other paradigm change. The believers in the old system—the "pro-growthers" working for a continuation of the fossil age—will put up a valiant fight to maintain what they view as the right solution, which also happens to defend their prerogatives. They will argue that more of the same will solve the problem. They will push the technological fix and argue that no behavior change is necessary. They will tend to forget that new technologies do not arise in a vacuum, nor instantaneously. If the initiative to solve the main problems of the era—scarcer oil, excessive greenhouse gas emissions, persistent poverty, and biodiversity destruction—is postponed until the problem is clearly visible, there is the risk that the problem will swell while we are still working on the solution.

As you have seen from my forecast, this is exactly what I believe will happen on the climate front. Humanity will put in place the solution to the energy and climate challenge—in this case by reducing the energy intensity and putting more renewable energy in the energy mix—much more slowly than if the problems had been addressed head-on by a willing society. The "pro-growthers" will contribute to the delay by clinging to the belief that the problem will solve itself through the combined working of technology and the market.

Opposing the "pro-growthers" will be a weird collection of people—the sustainability crowd—who have only one thing in common, namely, a longer-than-normal time horizon. The core will be the old-fashioned environmentalists, who constitute a small minority in modern democratic society. More surprisingly, perhaps, the group will include progressive heads of multinational corporations, who know that it takes ten years to change the positioning of the corporation and hence have the need to act long before voters and politicians agree that something is coming. The group will also include the farsighted leaders of those nations and institutions that are lucky enough to have chosen such people to guide them. And finally the coalition will include an increasing number of special-purpose NGOs and global institutions that are formed to fight for the long-term future of humanity, like the IPCC, UNEP, and WWF.

The sustainability crowd will win in the end, but not fast enough to avoid damage to the planet. They will win only after the destruction caused by climate change, resource depletion, biodiversity loss, and growing inequity can be easily seen and felt. They will win only when the future no longer looks promising. They will win only when the need for sustainability—the need for solutions that last longer than a decade or two—is no longer an academic topic, but totally obvious from looking out the window (or more precisely: from venturing outside the safe perimeter of the megacity to observe degraded ecosystems that have been exposed to extreme weather for a generation).

As you know from my forecast, the solution will be put in place so late that our children and grandchildren will inherit a world where the temperature will reach plus 2.8°C in the middle of the second half of the twenty-first century. This is, ironically, just late enough to make it unclear whether self-reinforcing climate change will be triggered or not.

"Glimpse 9-1: Sudden Rush to Solar" describes the bumpy and delayed road toward adoption of one of the central elements of the solution—namely, the widespread use of solar power and heat.

Sudden Rush to Solar

Paul Gilding

By 2052, installation of renewable energy, particularly solar, will have swept the world, will be powering one-half of our energy generation, and will be in explosive development, fundamentally changing the global economy and geopolitical landscape.

The process will be well under way by 2030. By then, the dramatic price reductions seen after 2010 will have accelerated sufficiently to enable renewable energy to overcome the powerful resistance to change by entrenched fossil-fuel interests.

In hindsight we will ask why not everyone saw that this was obviously going to happen. Solar energy and many other renewables are, after all, just another high-tech transformation—a process we have seen many times, and one we clearly understand.

Most proponents of new technologies, gripped by the excitement of what's possible, overpromise on price and performance and then, in the early stages, under-deliver. This results in the early forecasts of the demise of the relevant old industry or approach—such as we saw with the paperless office, the end of newspapers and books, and the death of film cameras, all proving to be overconfident forecasts. While at first those in the threatened industry panic at the forecasts of their demise, they soon decide that things are not so bad after all, as they observe, during the under-delivery phase, the new industry failing to produce effective technology that people will accept at the right price.

Then, with time and investment, the new technology—supported by eager investors, many of whom get burnt but some of whom see spectacular success—finally breaks through with good products at the right price, and the old industry is swept away. This generally occurs much later than first forecast, but then much faster than expected.

Consider the transition from printed to electronic books. Whereas the first efforts to move into digital books via computers began in the 1970s, it wasn't until 1998 that the first dedicated e-book readers were released. Take-up was still slow until mainstream products like the Sony and Kindle readers were released in 2006–7. It then took just four years before Amazon announced it was selling more e-books than printed books.

This explains how it has been and will be with renewable energy. Even before governments have decided to take serious action on climate, the new energy industry is taking off. Even though the old joke is true—that solar power has been just twenty years away from being competitive for forty years—we are now seeing genuinely dramatic price drops and growth rates. It is still true that no mainstream body agrees that half of all energy can be renewable by 2050. Bodies like the IEA and Shell still suggest renewables will at best power 20%–40% of total energy demand. But it is the nature of the old to dismiss the potential of the new, and that is what we've seen with other new technologies.

All of this transition could and would happen through market forces alone, once prices start dropping and industry scales up. But the markets won't have to do the job on their own. Some leading nations will provide helpful assistance through various forms of governmental intervention. A selection of progressive governments—including China—will make the change happen even faster than markets would otherwise deliver it.

From 2020 onward the scale of the threat posed to the global economy and society by climate impacts and resource constraints will become gradually clearer and more widely accepted. When denial that we have a system-wide problem ends, governments will be scrambling to accelerate the reduction of greenhouse gases.

One of their key responses will be to take strong measures to accelerate the elimination of old energy sources and replace them with renewable ones. This won't be limited to making *new* power supply renewable. Progressive nations will consider also closing down old but operating nuclear and coal plants. But this won't happen easily. Societies are loath to dump past investments, since they are, after all, cheaper and better known than new ones. So this won't immediately stop the momentum of climate change. But it will slow the slide toward an unmanageable future.

The economic and geopolitical implications of this economic and energy transition will be extraordinary. Some of these impacts will be unquestionably positive for all of society, but most will be chaotic and involve significant winners and losers.

One of the clear positives will be the broad availability of cheap and accessible energy in all countries. It may take a little longer than forty years, but in the end cheap solar power and heat will be available wherever the sun shines. While poor countries won't drive the change, they will be great beneficiaries of action by countries such as China, and possibly some in Europe. The countries that act in this area will take new energy technologies to scale in their own self-interest—because they want a secure and clean energy supply and seek the economic advantage from being producers of renewable-energy equipment. The result, however, will be global benefit, with all countries having freely available "fuel" from the sun, thus largely eliminating the issue of energy security and greatly reducing the financial burden of paying the ever-rising price for fossil-fuel imports.

However, some countries will be clear losers in this transition. Many countries in the Middle East and elsewhere will suffer dramatic loss of income as the world moves away from oil and coal. This will have considerable impact on geopolitical power and also on security issues, with countries changing governments as old regimes dependent on oil income fall from grace with their people for having managed the use of their countries' wealth so poorly.

The economic consequences for companies and investors will also be dramatic. The financial markets will not manage this transition smoothly. They will at first continue to put a high economic value on fossil-fuel assets, ignoring the clear evidence of a large unpriced risk. This risk is best understood by considering that to have an 80% chance of achieving 2°C of warming (the target agreed to by all major countries), around three-quarters of all proven reserves of fossil fuels can *never* be burnt, thus making them largely without value. Given that these reserves currently sit on company balance sheets as assets, the financial shock of this risk being priced in will be dramatic and will no doubt occur suddenly—like most re-ratings of risk in the financial markets.[6] Markets resist change just like people do, with no one wanting to be first to act, even if they can see it coming. Nor do they want to be last, and this is why the collapse in carbon-asset values will occur suddenly when it does, with wide-ranging economic consequences.

While I believe society will respond dramatically in the end, the run-up over the next forty years will be chaotic, confusing, and disruptive. For some time yet, at least one decade, perhaps even more, many will continue to deny the scale of the threat to the global economy posed by resource constraint and ecological impact. Despite the warnings of many eminent market participants such as Jeremy Grantham[7] that we have entered a new paradigm, the delusion that this will somehow "sort itself out" will be held on to tightly. But in the end, the laws of physics will determine that endless growth in the use of fossil energy cannot and will not continue.

Paul Gilding *(Australian, born 1959) is an independent writer and corporate advisor. He was previously executive director of Greenpeace International (1993) and CEO and owner of strategy consultancy Ecos Corporation (1995–2008) and energy-efficiency company Easy Being Green (2005–7). He wrote* The Great Disruption *(2011) and blogs at www.paulgilding.com.*

"Sudden Rush to Solar" makes the valid point that once the adoption of solar power starts, it will accelerate tremendously. In retrospect—from the perspective of the year 2100—it will seem like a sudden shift from a fossil- to a solar-based global society. The shift in the energy system will coincide in time with the shift of the overriding paradigm. In the solar age people will believe that a new road toward societal well-being is better than the old road toward continued "old-fashioned" economic growth. The majority will support the effort to make the world sustainable and find this task more engaging than creating another brand of hot dogs. Increased sustainability will be a prime value. Well-being will be more important than increased consumption. The public good will be more important than individual rights. Efforts will begin to repair some of the damage caused during overshoot. The new paradigm will be settling in alongside the distributed solar plants.

But it will require a lot to get there—and also to finance. "Glimpse 9-2: Financing the Future" tells the hopeful story about how this might be done, through the forward-looking perspective of one of the world's pension fund managers and other analysts of the same ideological inclination.

GLIMPSE 9-2

Financing the Future

Nick Robins

Long before 2052, I believe that the world's financial markets will have become one of the main driving forces for sustainable development.

The past forty years have become known as the era of financialization. During this time rising incomes, deregulation, and technological innovation delivered a massive growth in capital markets. But it also delivered widening inequality, increased market volatility, and facilitated the continued liquidation of natural assets.

The global financial crisis that started in 2007 has revealed that the world does not behave according to the stylized notions of conventional economics and finance. Individuals are not all-seeing, self-regarding "rational" automatons; fairness, for example, is a powerful motivator of human behavior, along with personal aggrandizement. Markets are also not the arena of efficiency and equilibrium that underpin modern financial practice and regulation. Income inequality—driven in part by the expansion of performance-related pay (e.g., bonuses), led by the financial sector—has emerged as a major source of financial fragility.[8] The spectacular growth in derivative markets is a case in point. Many had assumed that derivatives would bring greater market stability as complexity increased. In fact, derivatives acted as a risk magnifier in the crisis. Andrew Haldane, director of financial stability at the Bank of England, has said that finance has "shown itself to be neither self-regulating nor self-repairing. Like the rainforests, when faced with a big shock, the financial system has at times risked becoming non-renewable."

This inherent instability of the financial system is clearly problematic. But more worrying from a sustainability perspective is the "missing planet problem"—the disappearance of what was traditionally known as "land" and now termed "natural capital." Modern financial theory assumes away the resource base—and therefore implies that an inexhaustible stream of ecosystem services will continue to underpin economic growth. Natural capital is missing from both corporate and national balance sheets, making conventional investor projections of output and growth acutely vulnerable to the shock of the real. In spite of the growing awareness of the threat of climate change, for example, it is just dawning on financial markets that only a fraction of what is currently considered valuable assets—oil, gas, and coal reserves—can be exploited. The continuing (mis)allocation of capital into fossil-based assets potentially dwarfs the subprime housing bubble, with the looming prospect of stranded assets and further contractions in the value of pension funds.[9]

The net result is that financial markets are both a brake and an enabler on the road to sustainability. Financial short-termism is legendary. As John Maynard Keynes observed in 1936, "It is the long-term investor, he who most promotes the public interest, who will in practice come in for the most criticism wherever investment funds are managed by committees or boards or banks."[10] As a consequence, Keynes advised that "it is better for [one's] reputation to fail conventionally than to succeed unconventionally." Powerful institutional and intellectual forces for inertia remain in place. This does not bode well for a change that would make financial markets become one of the main drivers of sustainable development long before 2052—as I believe they will.

So why am I so confident that a shift will occur?

The first reason is that a growing minority of market practitioners recognize the limitations of twentieth-century conventional wisdom—and are implementing policies and systems to change how they operate. From almost nothing in 2006, over USD 25 trillion in assets now supports the UN Principles for Responsible Investment (UN PRI), a voluntary initiative that requires signatories to integrate environmental, social, and governance factors into their decision making. Real-world evidence already shows that sustainable investment is a better way of delivering risk-adjusted returns.

By nature, many institutional investors have to have a long-term outlook in order to deliver pensions and insurance far into the future. But the prevailing focus on short-term profits has masked this strategic perspective. The surge in commitment that led to initiatives such as the UN PRI arose from the failure of financial markets to succeed on their own terms. It was supported by rising acceptance that conventional risk analyses were unable to deal with new, long-term, system externalities such as climate change. The UN PRI and similar investor-led initiatives provide a latent support for more structural solutions, including regulation to confront the continued mis-pricing of natural capital.

The second reason why I think we will see a shift in financial practice flows from the dawning realization that the major constraint to the green economy is financial—and poses no insuperable obstacle. For instance, renewable energy operations are generally capital-intensive, requiring large injections of up-front investment in technology, but then they are considerably cheaper to operate. Energy efficiency invariably involves up-front costs, paid back through energy savings in the future. Until recently, the investment community was a missing stakeholder in sustainability negotiations. But this is changing as investors seek long-term assets that match their liabilities, and as governments look for injections of capital into the green economy that can replace loans from the overstretched banking sector. By 2020, I believe that new packages of policy support, regulation, and financial innovation will have become routine. For example, large-scale building-retrofit programs will be operating in all major cities, with investors receiving returns linked to the energy savings, most likely in the form of fixed-income bonds.

A much more difficult process will be how public policy and capital markets address the reality of unburnable carbon—fossil-fuel assets currently viewed as wealth. Financial crises occur when markets realize that what was previously regarded as a solid asset has dissolved. In the dot-com crash, the asset was overvalued technology stocks; in the credit crunch, the asset was overvalued property, particularly subprime housing. In the carbon transition, the asset will be overvalued fossil-based companies. The task for financial regulators charged with managing systemic risks to the markets will be to take away the punch bowl of fossil-fuel assets before the bubble bursts.

The third reason why change will occur is that governments and society will no longer be willing to give capital markets the benefit of the doubt. As with other fundamental sectors of the economy— such as agriculture and energy—the public now realizes that finance is heavily dependent on government regulation and subsidy for its continued existence. This subsidy includes not only the devastating cost of bailouts during crises, but also the routine underwriting of bank accounts and tax relief for individuals who save. At present, no sustainability requirements are attached to these transfers from the public purse. But that situation cannot and will not continue. In the UK, for example, the total government subsidy for pension savings is more than four times that for agriculture. By 2020, for example, I expect that pension subsidies will be provided only for funds that support the green economy. Other funds may well still exist but will no longer receive tax relief.

The vexing issue of remuneration and bonuses will also be resolved as a result of changing social expectations. The public is starting to realize that these are threat multipliers, increasing underlying financial volatility, and also perform a highly limited role in improved productivity and performance.

Foresight is not a particularly well-developed muscle in the human character. But apprehension about the future following from lived experience can overcome inertia. I believe that the convergence of the enlightened self-interest of long-term investors, the marriage of sustainability and financial policy via hard regulatory change, and the recasting of societal expectations will mean that capital markets will become a driving force for sustainable development long before 2052.

Nick Robins (British, born 1963) is a sustainable investor and business historian. He has worked on the policy, business, and financial dimensions of sustainable development for the past twenty years and is author of The Corporation That Changed the World: How the East India Company Shaped the Modern Multinational and coeditor of Sustainable Investing: The Art of Long-Term Performance.

The world will have to learn to live with economic growth rates lower than the current norm. To make this transition, we will need to learn how to redistribute without growth. In a stagnant economy it is not possible to rely on job creation to distribute the economic surplus. Unless something special is done, low economic growth rates will lead to high unemployment. History shows that high and growing unemployment rates cannot be sustained for decades, so sooner or later something will have to give.

Wise societies will find peaceful means to achieve more equitable sharing of the GDP; for example, through tax-based public jobs, job sharing, or limitations on the length of the work year. The latter was attempted by France during the 2000s. The French authorities tried to introduce a cap of thirty-five hours of work per week per person, in order to spread the same amount of work among more people. It did not work, because those who had jobs didn't want to share the available work. France might have had more success had it insisted on ten weeks of compulsory vacation per year, which would cut the same number of hours from the work year. A number of OECD countries have had better luck in their effort to revise generous pension systems, which would otherwise have required unacceptable and hence unsustainable transfers from the workforce to those who receive pensions.

But if the wise and farsighted do not lead the way toward more equity, the young and unemployed will be there to push them. I have already mentioned the naïve faith among most current Western grown-ups that today's young will pay the debt that grown-ups racked up during the last generation, while at the same time not having the money to live in the same style as their parents. Their frustration will coincide with an emerging understanding that life satisfaction lies not only in the material dimension. The result will be change—rebellion is probably a better term—perhaps not violent, but certainly strong enough to change the ownership of the numbers in the accounts of both the banks and the national economies.

CHAPTER 10

Five Regional Futures

So far, we have viewed the future through a worldwide lens. The forecast has been presented in global averages: average number of children, average productivity growth, and average willingness to invest in the future. But in the real future there will be huge deviations from the global averages. The path to 2052 will differ significantly from region to region.

The average sea level will rise some additional 36 centimeters by 2052, but that means that some areas will literally be underwater, while others won't even notice because of their rocky and steep shorelines. The global average per capita consumption will remain essentially stable from 2040 to 2052, but some regions (like China) will be growing while other regions experience decline in their purchasing power (like the United States). The same applies to energy use: global energy use stabilizes after 2030, but some regions will be increasing their energy use, while others decrease theirs. All regions will share the same worsening climate and the gradual disappearance of all things natural.

The simplest way to illustrate the fate of the regions is to split the world's 234 countries[1] into regions and apply the logical structure of my forecast to each of them. This task is simplified by the fact that are just 11 countries with more than 100 million inhabitants, and only 40 with more than 30 million each. These 40 nations include 80% of the global population, and a much larger share of the global economy.

I chose the regional split shown in the sidebar on page 266. The numbers are for 2010.[2]

Two of the countries on the sidebar—the United States and China—are individual countries that have been elevated to regional status because they are so big, in terms of either population or GDP.

The OECD includes the thirty-three countries of the old industrial world, and so the "OECD-less-US" in essence includes Europe—but also the nations of Japan, South Korea, Australia, New Zealand, Chile, and Canada.[3] The latter group constitutes a full third of OECD-less-US.

"BRISE" is my further development of the more common "BRICS" label. BRICS is Brazil, Russia, India, China, and South Africa. But since China is treated as a separate region, I chose to supplement the remaining four countries with

REGION	POPULATION (million people)	GDP (trillion dollars per year)
United States	310	13
China	1,350	10
OECD-less-US	740	22
BRISE	2,410	14
ROW (rest of the world)	2,100	8
SUM WORLD	6,910	67

the ten biggest emerging nations (Indonesia, Mexico, Vietnam, Turkey, Iran, Thailand, Ukraine, Argentina, Venezuela, and Saudi Arabia) and call the total the BRISE region, where the E stands for "emerging." BRISE has essentially the same population, some two billion people, as the rest of the world. It contains much of what is now viewed as the "poor world," but also exceptions (for example, many rich OPEC members). I ended using the more neutral term ROW.

The five double-page figures in this chapter show the result of applying my forecasting method to these five regions—using the same fifteen variables for the global graph presented in figure 9-1 on pages 232–33.

Toward 2052: The United States

The US future is illustrated in figure 10-1 on pages 268–69.

The US population will grow more or less in parallel with the world average and will peak at the same time, in the middle 2040s. Due to the aging of the population, the potential workforce in the United States, those aged fifteen to sixty-five years, will remain more or less stable at around 220 million persons. The support burden—defined as the total number of Americans divided by the potential workforce—will increase by a few percentage points, but not dramatically, because the growth in the number of old will be compensated for by a decrease in the number of young.

The economy will continue to grow for some decades, but not fast—only at an average growth rate of 0.6% per year over the next forty years. The rate of growth will decline and reach zero by the middle of the century. This is because the United States is already a mature economy—actually the most mature in the world, with the highest GDP per person on the planet (excepting some tiny special cases like Norway, Luxembourg, and Abu Dhabi). In other words, the gross labor productivity is already very high, and it will require substantial effort to make it grow further. In order to achieve higher growth, the United States must succeed in bringing a much larger part of those aged fifteen to sixty-five years into the workforce, or succeed in increasing labor productivity in services and care. Both are difficult and will not happen fast enough to avoid a continuation of the downward trend in productivity growth over the last forty years.

Furthermore, the United States has not been investing sufficiently over the last generation and needs to terminate its spending spree. US investment has been below 20% for most of the last generation and now is only 16%, less than two-thirds of the global average, which is 24% of the GDP. The United States will need to close this gap and make the extra investments necessary to meet its share of the coming problems of depletion, pollution, climate change, and biodiversity loss. My forecast is that the investment share of the GDP in the United States will grow from 16% in 2010 to more than twice that level in 2052. Through this extraordinary national effort, the country will be able to pay for substantial improvements in energy efficiency, make a significant shift toward a renewable energy supply, adapt to the higher sea level, (partly) protect itself against the increasingly extreme weather, and, finally, cover the unavoidable repair costs from hurricanes and climate-induced natural disasters.

As a consequence of the need for increased investment, aggregate consumption will grow very slowly, stagnate, peak (already in 2025), and then start a slow decline. Per capita consumption levels in 2052 will be some 10% lower than in 2010. The US consumer is about to experience a full generation where wages will not increase at all. In fact my forecast is that the US average per capita after-tax income will show a downward trend in real terms during all this time.

The combination of increasing energy efficiency and slow growth in GDP will allow US energy use to remain more or less constant over the next forty

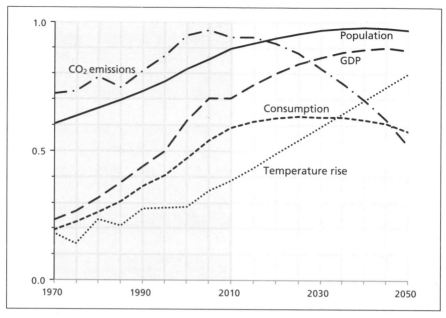

FIGURE 10-1a US State of Affairs, 1970–2050.

Scale: Population (0–350 million people); GDP and consumption ($0–$18 trillion per year); CO_2 emissions (0–6 billion tonnes CO_2 per year); temperature rise (0°C–2.5°C).

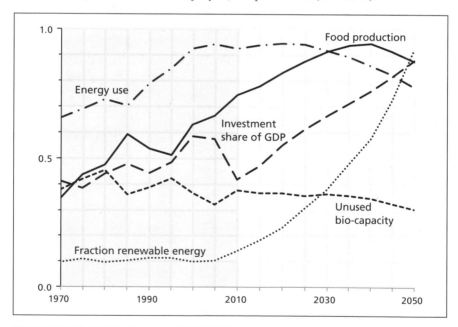

FIGURE 10-1b US Production, 1970–2050.

Scale: Food production (0–1.3 billion tonnes per year); energy use (0–2.5 billion tonnes of oil equivalents per year); fraction renewable energy (0%–40%); investment share of GDP (0%–40%); unused bio-capacity (0%–100%).

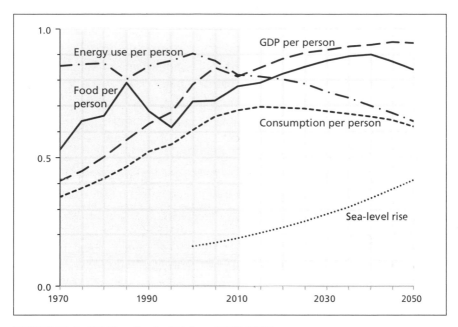

FIGURE 10-1c US Standard of Living, 1970–2050.
Scale: GDP per person and consumption per person ($0–$50,000 per person-year);
food per person (0–4 tonnes per person-year); energy use per person (0–9 tonnes of oil
equivalents per person-year); sea-level rise (0–1.4 meters).

years. The nation will make a huge shift from coal and oil to gas (including much
unconventional shale gas) over the next twenty years while renewable energy
(largely solar and wind) will be developed sufficiently to become the largest
sources of energy before 2052. During this time period most of America's
one hundred and ten nuclear reactors will gradually be closed down for age
reasons, and new ones won't be built because shale-gas power will be cheaper
than nuclear power. In 2052 there will be only forty reactors left, supplying a
mere 3% of the energy. As a result, CO_2 emissions from US energy use will
decline by nearly one-half by 2052, ending 35% below emissions levels in 1990.

Climate change will create problems for the United States, along the lines
predicted by science for a long time: a drying of the prairie and more violent
rains and winds. Some of the extra investment money will be used to limit the
damage to US agriculture and to pay for extra water. Still, some land currently
under cultivation will have to be abandoned during the next forty years because
of drought. The agricultural yield (tonnes produced per hectare-year) will continue up for a while, however, but then stagnate and decline some before 2052
because of the warmer temperatures. However, the US land mass is enormous

compared to the population, and the country will continue to be able to supply itself with natural resources and still have significant reserves left. The food production per person will remain very high by international standards, and although quite a bit of the surplus will be used for biofuels, some food may still be exported.

So all in all, the United States will experience material stagnation over the next forty years, stagnation partly because of the need to repay the debt run up over the last decades and partly because of the need to pay for the costs associated with more expensive energy and more aggressive climate damage. The US economy won't grow much, and by 2052 the Chinese GDP will outshine the US GDP by a factor of 2.5. The United States will be one-tenth of the global economy and no longer a superpower.

A central part of this forecast is the assumption that the US democratic and free-market-based system will not rise to the occasion and make the forward-looking policy revision that could easily change the American future in a positive direction. The tension among different societal and political groups will remain and hinder forceful collective action to improve the state of the United States of America.

"Glimpse 10-1: Bright Solar Future" gives an illustration of this phenomenon. It describes the manner in which solar energy will finally win its way into the American household—which is not through grand decisions in the US Congress, but via the back door of thousands of independent business and household decisions at the local level. So the obvious solar solution will be implemented in the end, but long after it could have if the conflict between different US interest groups had been less acrimonious.

GLIMPSE 10-1

Bright Solar Future

William W. Behrens

Between now and 2052, the world of energy will evolve more positively than many other aspects of human culture. And in that world, electrical energy will stand out, not just for replacing fuel energy in all sectors of the United States and the world, but also for doing it much more quickly than expected. The reason for this is simple: electrical energy will be produced with much less capital intensity than fuel energy.

Already, all fossil-based energy production requires heavy capital infrastructure. As the quality and quantity of fuel resources decline, the capital required to extract a gallon of fuel will increase dramatically (witness the intensity of capital required to develop the tar sands reserves). Yet, eventually, suppliers worldwide will be able to produce electricity with relatively small and modular hardware. As this trend develops, both transportation and space conditioning will turn toward increasingly efficient electricity-based hardware. By 2040, in the United States, electricity-supported transportation systems will be common in densely populated areas, and many homes and businesses will have been converted to air- and water-sourced heat pumps that operate on electricity from renewable sources, and will no longer rely on fuel-based boilers. The primary renewable electrical energy source will be solar.

The Rise of PV and Decentralized Energy

From 2012 to 2022, centralized utilities and corporations will still control the means of electricity production and will develop large-scale renewable energy plants to meet an increasing fraction of the electricity load. These plants will utilize all forms of renewable energy—whether produced by large-scale wind farms, photovoltaic (PV) farms, very large solar-thermal turbines, or even ocean energy. But as the second decade dawns, three influences will combine to create a rapid shift away from centralized electricity production and toward distributed production by micro-grids.[4]

One driver will be political. In the United States, democratic political institutions will finally recognize the stranglehold that fossil-energy companies exert on public decision making. After public and governmental backlash, lawmakers will enact legislation that levels the playing field, removing the financial and regulatory advantages currently extended to these huge players. The government will require fossil fuels to carry their full cost of production, including their waste stream, and will redirect the resulting revenues into balancing the government budgets (a necessary response to the economic collapses of the United States in the 2010s).

The second driver will be the solar industry itself, as China and other manufacturing powerhouses flood the world market with solar panels at prices far below current forecasts. As photovoltaic electricity becomes cheaper than fossil-based energy throughout all latitudes between 50° north and south, investment from all sectors will flow into PV.

The third and final driver will be in novel energy-storage technology. By 2020, we will begin to see on-site storage technologies that provide cost-effective, multiday reserves using low-grade silicon and other plentiful materials in battery-based, chemical, and mechanical storage contraptions.

Thus the decade 2022–32 will see experiments in all forms of solar power production, at a wide variety of implementation levels from the residential to the continental. By 2025, sights will be set on the first orbiting power station, with 1 MW capacity, and able to transmit power back to earth via wireless energy transfer. Such innovation will likely be the domain of a commercial-educational consortium. Just five years later, we could see a new prototype emerge: a 2,000-square-meter array that will deploy by robotics and beam over 4 TWh of electricity per year to a base receiver. The first will likely be located at a major university, powering the campus.

The distributed deployment of the new storage technologies in the early 2030s will form the backbone of micro-grids that will power campuses and cities and other localized networks. In 2038 the United States will follow the initiative of the European Union and will nationalize control of the electricity grid by placing operation of the increasingly "smart" grid into the hands of an independent public agency. While commercial entities will continue to own the transmission assets and will receive revenues for their deployment, this agency will make all supply-and-demand management choices. The smart-grid operators will welcome (and pay for) excess power fed back into their transmission lines from customers with extra production capacity, for temporary storage or for the use of other customers.

The New Solar Economy

Against this backdrop, the transition to a sun-based energy economy will be well under way—in the United States and in the world as a whole—with the United States and other countries reaching their solar targets (Thailand for example will reach its 20% solar goal by 2021). Developing nations will make electricity available through state-run networks powered by PV. Micro-grids will take hold in the old OECD world as an efficient means of generating power within a locality. And local grids will interface with the larger grid.

Centralized power-producing corporations will attempt to control solar with the concentrating solar arrays of the 2012–22 decade. But those will come to be seen as cumbersome and expensive, albeit effective. By 2052, the control of the energy economy by a very few large megacorporations, a characteristic of the fossil-fuel age, will be over. Solar power generation will be as close to the consumers as possible, sustainable, and stable for decades, freely exchanged at real-time market prices through the interconnection of micro-grids and national grids.

Although in 2052 much of southern Europe will continue to rely on power generated by large centralized plants in North Africa, individual European communities will create their own local solar farms, implement their own micro-grids, and further erode the control of the utility corporations. Elsewhere, many municipalities, schools, regions, and even individuals—rather than a few large utilities—will be in control of their own energy generation. PV is literally the only form of renewable energy with which this is possible, because the units of energy production are so small and so infinitely scalable.

In forty years, PV will provide 40% of the electricity consumed worldwide. Surprisingly, the fraction will be the same both in the old OECD countries and in the nations that will industrialize in the 2010s and 2020s. China will lead the transition to solar through very large-scale, centralized, government-owned and government-operated plants using Chinese hardware. In the United States, micro-grids with private ownership will interface through the publicly managed smart-grid infrastructure. In 2052 it will be abundantly clear that the old utility assertion that "renewables would never contribute more than a small percentage, because after all the sun doesn't shine at night" was a deliberate hoax. Renewables are indeed sufficient; in fact PV alone is enough to power the planet, not only today, but also in 2052, when total energy demand will already have peaked. Increasing energy efficiency and declining populations will allow sustainable increases in per capita use of energy and hence in the material standard of living.

PV infrastructure will be everywhere. Communities will use capped landfills and other commonly owned areas to implement solar "community gardens"; individual residents will each own enough PV in these common gardens or on rooftops to provide the electricity needs of their dwelling; their solar plot will be an asset of the dwelling that is purchased by a new owner, just like the garage. Building-integrated PV strategies, most notably PV-enabled curtain wall assemblies on urban high-rises, will turn most commercial structures into net-energy sources.

The evolution in PV between 2012 and 2052 will be nothing short of remarkable, even as the world's population will struggle with major environmental limitations, like freshwater shortage and global climate change. As the world looks forward to the second half of the twenty-first century, there will at last be widespread confidence that incoming sunlight is the most stable and reliable source of energy— the source with the most positive impact on our social structures and the lowest embodied waste stream.

William W. Behrens *(American, born 1949) coauthored* The Limits to Growth *while completing a PhD at MIT. He taught at Dartmouth College before changing careers to work hands-on to create sustainable communities. His company, ReVision Energy LLC, installs solar equipment throughout New England.*

I support the optimism of "Bright Solar Future," but I repeat that progress would have been much faster if the United States made a federal decision to succeed in solar power—as when it decided to put man on the moon in ten years.

Toward 2052: China

My forecast for China is illustrated in figure 10-2.

Surprising to many Westerners, the Chinese population will reach its maximum already in the 2020s—but it will be a flat and long peak. In this way the country will draw an early and huge advantage from the unpopular one-child policy of the last generation. China will be spared the extra burden of several hundred million people and will be able to use the released resources to create a better livelihood for the 1.4 billion people that will live in China in the 2020s.

The rapid slowdown in China's population growth rate will not come without difficulties. The potential workforce will decline dramatically, by a full

30% by 2052, and the support burden (the number of Chinese per worker) will go up from 1.4 to 1.7—reversing the similar lessening of the burden over the last forty years. This increase in the support burden by 20% in forty years will eat up half a percent of the annual growth in per capita consumption.

But this won't make much of a difference in the Chinese economy, which will maintain growth rates at a level that the rest of the world can only dream about. China is in the beginning of its process of catching up with the West. Its current GDP per person is one-fifth of the US equivalent. China is in the luxurious situation of being able to borrow concepts and solutions from the industrial world and introduce them in a setting with much lower wage levels. And it will be able to continue to do so until its labor productivity reaches US levels, and this won't happen until after the middle of the century. In 2052 China will have a GDP per person of some $34,000 per person-year, which will be three quarters of the US level at the time.

The Chinese economy will grow fast throughout the next forty years and will be four times bigger in 2052 than in 2012. This means an average growth rate of some 3.5% per year, but much higher during the next twenty years—before population decline puts a damper on GDP growth. In 2052, the Chinese GDP will be about as big as that of all the thirty-three OECD countries taken together.

China is well known for its tremendous savings rate (more than 40% of the national income), which made it possible for China to finance much of US imports during the 2000s. The high savings were mirrored by a high investment share in the GDP (more than 35%), and this will continue. Over the next twenty years *traditional* investment will decline toward the global norm (24%), but the Chinese government will compensate for this decline by spending freely to counter depletion and pollution, and by making the unavoidable investments to adapt to global warming, which will hit this landlocked country more than countries cooled by the oceans. Furthermore, there will be room for an impressive state-led effort to increase energy efficiency, double the energy supply, and make it much more renewable. The total effort will be simplified by the ability of the authorities to make rational national plans and implement them. China's long sequence of five-year plans, which systematically build the country toward its long-term goals for the nation, will prove useful when the challenge is to feed, clothe, house, and entertain a big population while simultaneously fighting the battle against climate change.

But the high investment share will not hinder consumption growth, since the economy will grow so fast. Amazingly, consumption per each Chinese will grow fivefold by 2052. The poor peasants who currently move into

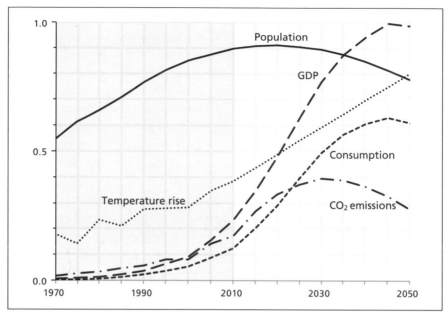

FIGURE 10-2a China State of Affairs, 1970–2050.
Scale: Population (0–1.5 billion people); GDP and consumption ($0–$40 trillion per year);
CO_2 emissions (0–40 billion tonnes CO_2 per year); temperature rise (0°C–2.5°C).

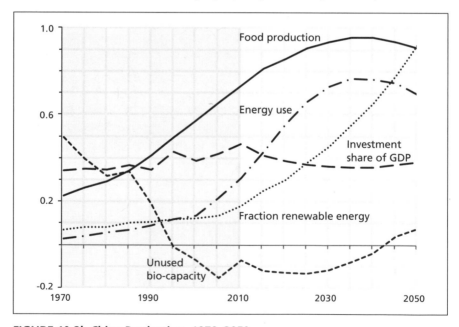

FIGURE 10-2b China Production, 1970–2050.
Scale: Food production (0–2.1 billion tonnes per year); energy use (0–8 billion tonnes of
oil equivalents per year); fraction renewable energy (0%–40%); investment share of GDP
(0%–100%); unused bio-capacity (minus 8%–40%).

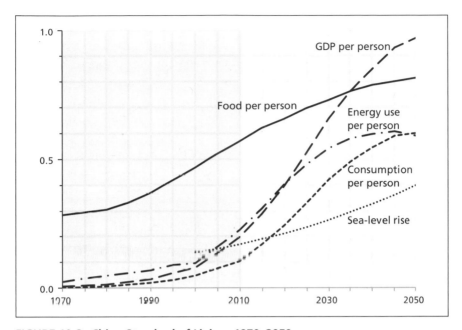

FIGURE 10-2c China Standard of Living, 1970–2050.
Scale: GDP per person and consumption per person ($0–$35,000 per person-year);
food per person (0–2 tonnes per person-year); energy use per person (0–8 tonnes of oil
equivalents per person-year); sea-level rise (0–1.4 meters).

Chinese megacities will look back forty years from now at a most spectacular rise in disposable income.

Energy use will more than double by the 2030s before it starts to decline as a result of rapidly rising energy efficiency. China's emissions of CO_2 will also double, before they peak in 2030 at fifteen billion tonnes of CO_2 per year. By 2052 they will have fallen some, to twelve billion tonnes per year, but this is still nearly five times China's emissions in 1990, and a full ten tonnes of CO_2 per Chinese per year. This is way above the sustainable level of emissions (which is estimated to be around one tonne per earthling per year), and about the same as the US per capita emissions at the time, which will be nine tonnes of CO_2 per American per year. Both countries will contribute significantly toward global emissions that may possibly trigger self-reinforcing climate change later in the twenty-first century.

The emissions from Chinese energy use in 2052 will be huge, even though China at that time will be getting as much energy from renewable sources as from its coal. The rest will come from a mixture of gas, oil, and nuclear. Nuclear power will supply 6% of the energy from more than two hundred reactors.

Chinese agriculture will increase output by another 25% before it peaks in the 2030s and starts to decline as a consequence of a beginning decline in average land yields, which in turn will be a consequence of higher temperatures and lack of water. But there will be more than enough food to feed the population: nearly 1.6 tonnes of food per person per year. This is way above the subsistence level and similar to per capita food availability in the OECD outside the United States.

But China will be in the uncomfortable situation of having its domestic resource base insufficient to cover its consumption. The biological capacity of the nation will be lower than its nonenergy footprint from 1995 to 2035, according to my forecast. China will have to rely on imports of natural resources for a generation or more, in painful conflict with its tradition and ambition of self-sufficiency. By 2052 the balance will be regained, but only barely, and as the balance of two falling entities: bio-capacity will fall because of climate change, and the footprint because of population decline.

Climate change will create significant problems for China during the next forty years. The rainfall will continue to move toward the southwest and away from where people live, and will need to be transported back, via canals. Desertification will occur in the interior, and the melting of the Tibetan glaciers will make summer water even more scarce. Along the coast, rising sea levels will cause further problems. But much will be done to reduce the (short-term) consequences, via huge infrastructure projects.

In summary, China will experience tremendous economic growth over the next forty years. More than a billion people will become much better off as a result of deft maneuvering by its strong government. The Chinese footprint on the planet will be substantial, both inside China and, for a while at least, outside. And China will contribute significantly to global warming, which is likely to become critical in the second half of the twenty-first century. But at that time the Chinese population will be in rapid decline, lessening its energy and nonenergy footprint every year.

"Glimpse 10-2: China—the New Hegemon" gives a lively description of what will happen in the Middle Kingdom as it once more takes its former role as the supreme power on planet Earth.

GLIMPSE 10-2

China—the New Hegemon

Rasmus Reinvang and Bjørn Brunstad

China in 2052 will not be a nation-state in a traditional sense. It will be a civilization-state, representing a modern incarnation of the Chinese dynasties that considered themselves the center of civilization in a world of barbarians. China in 2052 will be a country and a globalized ethnic identity with a strong sense of a glorious past, which after a 150-year project of tumultuous modernization from 1911 to 2052 again will be economically strong and sufficiently mature to act on the basis of its own history and instincts.

This huge nation will have a unique sense of exclusiveness and internal integration. Unlike the other main civilizations in the digitalized and globalized world of 2052, China will not be, for the most part, multicultural. The vast majority of people in China are Han Chinese—an ancestral lineage you are born into and cannot become.

In 2052, China will be a self-contained civilization linked to the geography of historic China and with no need to conquer new lands in the traditional sense. Efficient population-control policies on the mainland combined with steady emigration to both resource-rich and technologically advanced countries will ensure that the population in mainland China is falling, while the overall Chinese population globally will keep growing slowly. Mainland China will have a smaller population size (1.2 billion) than in 2012.

Another two hundred million Chinese will live outside of China, though their primary cultural identity will be Chinese. They will be found across the globe, driven by a strong tradition for investing in high-quality education and to engage in international trade at all levels. The Chinese thus will have access to, and be integrated in, all other main civilizations. Representatives of other civilizations will to a lesser extent have access to the Chinese civilization but by definition will never be able to become fully part of it—unless they are born of Han Chinese emigrants.

The Chinese economy will by far be the biggest national economy in the world, even if on a per capita basis it will still have some catching up to do. Owing to its size, China will dominate a large part of the global economy and will project economic and technological hard power as well as cultural soft power all over the planet.

We are not able to foresee what kind of political system China will have in 2052, but we are sure that the Chinese government in 2052 will be drawing actively on the long Chinese tradition for centralized government and meritocracy (Confucianism). This will have proven to be highly effective when addressing the main challenge of the twenty-first century: the inability of the resource-intensive and polluting modes of production, which currently dominate, to provide long-term welfare to the global population.

Driving the New Techno-Economic Paradigm

In 2052, low-carbon, ultra-resource-efficient solutions will have largely replaced the current inefficient use of fossil fuels in all sectors. Such solutions will have gained a dominant position in the global economy, akin to the position of the petroleum sector in the twentieth century. China will early on become a main force in the transition away from the fossil-based era—intrinsically motivated by its own development needs, a comparatively weak national resource base, and a keen eye for strategic positioning.

Building on years of ambitious top-down policies and large-scale investment, China will actively seek control of key "commanding heights" of resources and technology for the new techno-economic paradigm and will provide the bulk of the necessary market volume for scaling up and commercializing core technologies such as those that drive solar and wind energy or high-speed electrical mass transit.

Early on, Chinese companies will forge strong partnerships with technologically advanced Japanese and South Korean/Korean companies, while actively leveraging research and development carried out by overseas Chinese (especially on the initially techno-logically superior North American West Coast). A core strategic asset for China in the new techno-economic paradigm will be its early dominance in reserves and production of rare earth metals that are so vitally important in the production of new-paradigm mainstays like batteries, electric motors, and smartphones. China will gradually leave it to less developed countries to produce cheap, low-end goods for the global market. Instead China will sustain strong growth by increasing consumption internally and increasing its share of the global production of high-tech goods (especially, but not exclusively, related to smart, low-carbon, ultra-efficient solutions).

The attractiveness of the large internal Chinese market will ensure that production outside China increasingly will take into account the preferences of the Chinese customer and the product standards imposed by the Chinese government. In 2052, most countries will significantly depend on Chinese / east Asian technology and solutions for their energy systems, something that will be considered a potential security issue by many politicians in these dependent nations.

The Chinese worldview contains an implicit hierarchical understanding of the world. For more than a thousand years, the relationship between China and other nations was one of a tributary-state system with China in the center, and not a system where China engaged with other nations on an equal basis. In 2052, a large number of countries across the globe will have economies that are China-centered, as China will be their main trading partner. This will especially be the case for resource-rich and strategically located countries. China's relationship to these countries will be akin to the historical tributary-state system.

Countries with China-centered economies will be expected to align their foreign policy with China and respect their position in an economic ecosystem revolving around China. In the geographically defined inner circle we will find neighboring countries. The next sphere of influence will be countries that don't necessarily border on China but are closely integrated economically as they help China compensate for its comparatively weak natural-resource base through exports of commodities. This sphere will constitute the wider circle of "partner countries."

China will use a wide range of political and economic tools, including multiple forms of bilateral cooperation (such as cultural exchanges, grant programs, research programs, preferential trade agreements, overseas development aid), to maximize the integration of these countries and economies into a Sino-centric world order. In the various financial crises of the 2010s, China will use its unique financial surplus to refinance the massive public debt of many countries at better-than-market terms and with political strings attached. China will also make enormous investments overseas in public land and infrastructure that will be put up for sale at cutthroat prices in some countries—thus taking a swift giant leap in global power.

Coping with Climate Change

In 2052 China will be struggling with the effects of global warming. The average warming in China has been above the global average since the 1950s, and by 2052 severe droughts will be a permanent fixture in northern China. Increasingly frequent and intense rains will cause severe floods and erosion in the south. The production of staple crops will have shrunk, but China will not be dependent on food imports, because of its declining mainland population. Water supplies for the forty-five million people of the twin northern cities Beijing and Tianjin will come from huge water-transfer schemes from the Yangtze River basin as well as massive water desalinization projects on the coast. In Shanghai, dikes will be continuously strengthened in order to keep rising seawater levels at bay. The Chinese government will be working on plans for gradual relocation of the population in all "nonsustainable cities."

Even though China already now regularly experiences climate-related extreme weather events affecting millions of Chinese, by 2052 China will have proved (in spite of a few badly managed events) to be one of the most effective and structured countries in tackling effects of climate change in a systematic manner. China will have proved able to avoid large-scale instability and mobilize resources constructively and effectively toward adaptation. As a consequence, China in 2052 will be dominating the booming global market for climate adaptation engineering and planning competence. China will also actively provide bilateral climate adaptation aid to its "partner countries," but also to developing countries with weak governance structures.

In 2052, China will be strongly influencing the world in a distinct manner culturally, economically, and politically. Although China will not be alone, the Chinese civilization will remain particularly distinct and strongly driven by its own internal and historically founded sense of identity and logic.

Rasmus Reinvang *(Danish, born 1970) is an indologist who has lived and worked in China. He has a PhD from the University of Oslo (Norway), has previously taught at Copenhagen University (Denmark) and the University of Gdansk (Poland), and has more than ten years' experience with nonprofit and consultancy work related to sustainable development in an international context.*

Bjørn Brunstad *(Norwegian, born 1973) is a foresight specialist with twelve years of academic and practical experience with scenario planning, paradigm foresight, and other holistic and dynamic tools for strategy making and mobilization of collective action.*

I am convinced that the optimistic view of "China—the New Hegemon" is spot-on. During the next forty years China will soar, and for those of us who belong to neither the Chinese nor the US empire, it will be important to try to adapt to the major cultural change associated with a shift from US to Chinese supremacy.

Toward 2052: OECD-less-US

This region includes the old industrialized market economies of the world, except the United States (which is treated as a region by itself). OECD-less-US holds a population of 740 million people, which is more than twice as much as the United States, and its GDP is near twice that of the United States. So the OECD-less-US is a major player, and its future is illustrated in figure 10-3.

The population of the region is already stagnating as of this writing and will remain more or less constant until 2025, when it will start a slow decline, so that the population of OECD-less-US will be 10% lower in 2052 than it is today. The average age will increase and so will the crude death rate, but life expectancy at birth will continue to rise. So there will be an increasingly long-lived and healthy population, albeit with few children. The average family size will continue its downward trend from the last forty years.

The aging of the population will also lead to an increase in the support burden, but only after 2030 and only by some 10%. I believe society will respond to this challenge by a very gradual increase in the pension age, in order to limit the burden on the pension systems. This will also help stem the rather dramatic decline in the potential workforce, which will otherwise go down by one-quarter before 2052.

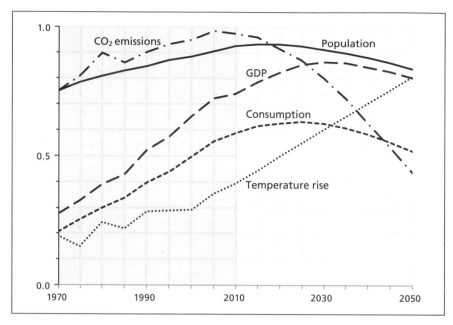

FIGURE 10-3a OECD-less-US State of Affairs, 1970–2050.
Scale: Population (0–800 million people); GDP and consumption ($0–$30 trillion per year); CO₂ emissions (0–7 billion tonnes CO₂ per year); temperature rise (0°C–2.5°C).

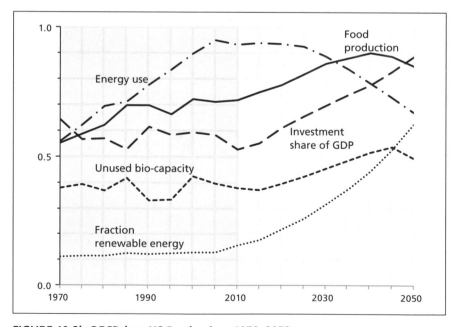

FIGURE 10-3b OECD-less-US Production, 1970–2050.
Scale: Food production (0–1.2 billion tonnes per year); energy use (0–3.2 billion tonnes of oil equivalents per year); fraction renewable energy (0%–70%); investment share of GDP (0%–40%); unused bio-capacity (0%–50%).

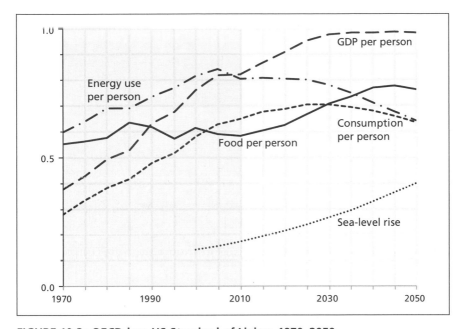

FIGURE 10-3c OECD-less-US Standard of Living, 1970–2050.
Scale: GDP per person and consumption per person ($0–$36,000 per person-year);
food per person (0–2 tonnes per person-year); energy use per person (0–5 tonnes of oil
equivalents per person-year); sea-level rise (0–1.4 meters).

The total GDP of the region will continue to grow, but not fast—and GDP will peak in the early 2030s some 15% above its current level. The slow growth will primarily be a consequence of population decline, but also an effect of slow productivity growth. Productivity will grow slowly because the region is already a mature economy, with most of its activity in services and care, which cannot easily be made much more effective. The main productivity reserve rests in the potential to get an even higher share of the potential workforce into employment. The current high unemployment levels in the OECD—over 10% of the potential workforce—is a golden opportunity when seen in this perspective. The region has all those hands that will be needed to take care of the aging population. But this will involve income transfer from those who are currently employed to the newcomers. Getting more people into work will require leadership and a willingness in the majority to invest in meeting the many challenges of the region, including those brought on by aging populations and a changing climate.

On this score the OECD-less-US region will have a better starting point than the United States. During the last couple of decades the OECD-less-US has maintained high investment rates, at about the global average of 24%

of GDP. This is a full 8 percentage points more than the United States and a good starting point toward increased extra investments to counter depletion, pollution, climate change, biodiversity loss, and the whole gamut of modern social problems. Funds will also be needed to repair damage caused by inclement weather; the recent long drought and the subsequent flooding in Australia is an example of what is in store.

GDP per person will stabilize at around $35,000 per person-year in 2035 and remain at that level. The GDP will consist of a growing share in investment goods and services, and a declining amount of consumption goods and services. By 2052 the Chinese will catch up with OECD-less-US, and at that time the two regions will have the same annual production of goods and services per person. Only the United States will (still) be ahead, by one-third.

As a very gross simplification of the big GDP picture, what will happen over the next forty years is that the United States will stagnate first at a high level. Then the rest of the OECD will stagnate at a somewhat lower level. And while this goes on, China will keep growing and catch up with OECD-less-US by the middle of the century. In the longer run, in the second half of the century, all three regions will probably approach a common level. Remember that this is in per capita terms: in 2052 the Chinese economy will be as big as the sum of all the thirty-three members of the OECD—including the United States.

The total amount of energy used in OECD-less-US will stay stable from now until 2030, and then it will start to decline. The use of oil and gas will fall throughout. The share of oil will decline to one-third, and this means that the use of oil in OECD-less-US will never be higher than it was around 2010. In other words, peak oil in that region is already behind us. Initially this peak will be compensated for by a significant and growing share of gas, but only until the very fast growth in renewable energy will make it possible to reduce gas use after 2035. The nuclear industry will be in steady decline; three-quarters of all reactors will be closed down by 2052, so there will be only some seventy left, providing less than 5% of the energy—mainly in France and Japan.

As a result of increased energy efficiency and changes in the energy mix, CO_2 emissions from OECD-less-US will decline at an accelerating pace from now until 2052. At that time emissions will be 55% below current emissions, and 50% below emissions in 1990. This will be within the ballpark of the IPCC's recommendation of a 50%–80% cut by 2052, made in 2007. But on the way there, for example, in 2020, the region will be way behind the EU's current ambition. This ambition, represented as the first number "20" in the EU's famous 20/20/20 legislation from 2009, is to cut emissions to 20% below 1990 levels already in 2020.

The OECD-less-US will have its share of climate problems over the next forty years. Increasing drought and sporadic flooding will affect much of its land mass, particularly in Australia and in the Mediterranean. But the northern land masses (in Europe and Canada) will be spared the worst climate excesses in the medium term, and even reap advantage in agriculture and forestry from warmer growing conditions and more fertilization from atmospheric CO_2. Local tourism in the Mediterranean summer will suffer as it gets too hot, but on the other hand, new opportunities will open in the far north as the ice melts. Australia will be subject to erratic weather—droughts and floods in a bewildering combination—and in sum the agricultural output of OECD-less-US will start to decline after 2040 due to the negative impacts of climate change. At the same time, the amount of unused land will increase some, as a consequence of a smaller population, further urbanization, and higher yields from land under cultivation. There may be room for new nature as the boreal forests grow back in the northern latitudes after the large-scale harvesting in the second half of the twentieth century.

So all in all, the OECD-less-US will experience gradual stagnation over the next forty years. There will be some growth, but it will feel like a gentle sideways glide. The population will contract slowly, and the region will eliminate a good deal of its CO_2 emissions. Climate change will at first help but later cause local damage and finally lead to reduction in agricultural output. There will be sporadic scarcity of some resources that the region needs to import, but none will last long enough to seriously perturb the peaceful status quo. There will be a solid supply of raw material and energy from the region's dumps, as recycling and reuse steadily win ground. And there will be enough sun and wind to run nearly half of the region's businesses and households.

The democratic traditions in the region will help ensure political stability and help constrain development of further inequity and limit its negative consequences. But the somewhat more relaxed attitude of the European nations (perhaps with the exception of Germany) will also lead to less aggressive utilization of the business opportunities that do emerge. The United States, and particularly China, will grab many of the inventions made in OECD-less-US. Hence the region will slide down in the hierarchy, but with a reasonably high level of life satisfaction among its inhabitants.

Toward 2052: BRISE

My fourth region, BRISE, consists of Brazil, Russia, India, South Africa, and ten big emerging economies, with a total of 2.4 billion people in 2010. The ten emerging nations are Indonesia, Mexico, Vietnam, Turkey, Iran, Thailand, Ukraine, Argentina, Venezuela, and Saudi Arabia—listed here by population size, from highest to lowest. Together the fourteen BRISE countries cover a huge land area in both tropical and temperate regions. They contain massive forests, both tropical and boreal; vast savannas and grasslands; and large, fertile plains spotted with agricultural villages. There is also significant industrial agriculture, huge manufacturing centers, and a number of megacities, but many people who remain in the countryside.

The region is so diverse that it is almost meaningless to talk about averages. It is for all purposes one-third of the world. The current GDP of BRISE exceeds that of China. The only good reason for grouping these countries together is that they are big countries (average population is 170 million people) and that they are well on their way on the road to industrialization. The average annual GDP per person in 2010 was $6,000 per person-year. That was some 15% below China. In the years ahead, while China is exploding, the BRISE countries will grow much more slowly, and they have been for a while. The future of BRISE is illustrated in figure 10-4.

The population, one-half of which is Indian, is growing. But the fertility rate is declining dramatically, and the population of BRISE will reach a flat peak long before 2052, and well below three billion people. The workforce will follow the same pattern.

The population is young, and the support ratio will stay relatively constant over the period.

But that will not be the case for productivity. The BRISE countries are in the ideal situation for borrowing technology and solutions from the industrial world (and increasingly China), and hence they will be able to show stellar growth if conditions remain right. That will be the case in a number of BRISE countries, while others, especially the huge, complex, and democratic India, will tend to hold the average back. As a result the collective GDP will treble by 2052, and the GDP per person will grow from $6,000 to $16,000 dollars per person-year, which will make the BRISE average in 2052 similar to the European average in the 1970s. That is a long delay: the material standard of BRISE will lag OECD-less-US by eighty years—that is, three generations.

Like all other countries, BRISE will need to increase its investment rate in order to handle the oncoming rush of modern problems—including climate change. But the countries are used to reasonably high investments, and since the GDP growth rate will remain high, aggregate consumption will rise impressively, as will the per capita bit.

Much investment will have to be put into expansion of the energy system, which will need to produce twice as much energy in 2052 as in 2010. The region has huge energy resources: oil and gas in Russia, Saudi Arabia, and Venezuela; coal in South Africa and Ukraine; biomass in Brazil and Indonesia; and nuclear technology in Russia and some other places. By the middle of the twenty-first century BRISE will have some seventy operational reactors (twice the number in the United States), providing 2% of the energy. Renewables, on the other hand, will cover nearly 40% of total energy. Much will be in the form of solar heat and power, but there will be a substantial contribution from biomass converted to biofuels and electricity. Brazil will be leading the way

The energy system will expand so fast that CO_2 emissions from fossil fuels will grow and not plateau until the 2040s, in spite of a respectable increase in energy efficiency partly through adoption of foreign technology.

Food production will keep growing, in spite of damage to some land, because of the huge unused areas of potentially arable lands in the region (for example in Brazil, Ukraine, and Siberia).

But the region also houses the scene for potential climate disasters following from a warmer earth. There will be the chance of insect infestations killing the boreal forest in Russia, fires releasing the methane from the bogs of Indonesia, the drying out of the rain forest in Brazil, and the inundation of Southeast Asian countries by water rushing down from melting glaciers in Tibet and from eroded, clear-cut hillsides devoid of the trees that used to absorb it. Not to speak about the impact of an extra 36-centimeter sea-level rise on India, directly, or more likely indirectly via immigration pressure from neighboring Bangladesh in the Ganges delta. Luckily these events won't all happen nor all at large scale (I think and hope!) during the next forty years. But there will be more than enough climate damage to slow progress and to absorb investment that could more beneficially have been used to improve life satisfaction for the people of BRISE.

BRISE has and will have a resource base that is so enormous that the nonenergy footprint will require only one-half of the available bio-capacity—primarily due to the uninhabited Siberia and the vast forests of the Amazon. So even in 2052 the average inhabitant of BRISE will have nearly as much unused area at hand (0.7 global hectare per person) as the average American (0.9). It is of course a problem that most of the resources will sit in Russia and Brazil, while the population will largely be located in southern and southeastern Asia.

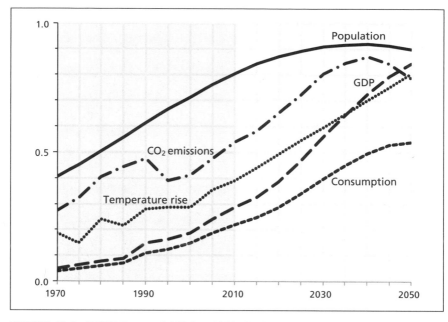

FIGURE 10-4a BRISE State of Affairs, 1970–2050.
Scale: Population (0–3 billion people); GDP and consumption ($0–$50 trillion per year); CO_2 emissions (0–13 billion tonnes CO_2 per year); temperature rise (0°C–2.5°C).

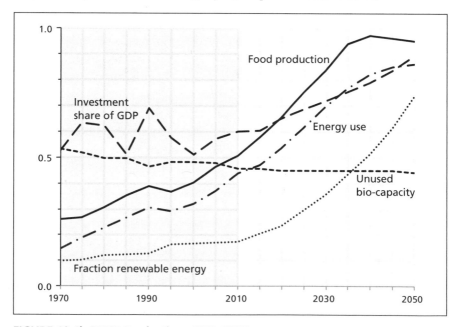

FIGURE 10-4b BRISE Production, 1970–2050.
Scale: Food production (0–3.7 billion tonnes per year); energy use (0–6.5 billion tonnes of oil equivalents per year); fraction renewable energy (0%–50%); investment share of GDP (0%–40%); unused bio-capacity (0%–100%).

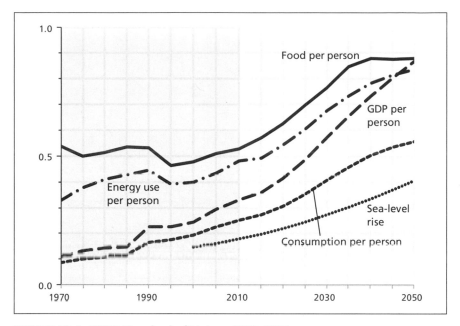

FIGURE 10-4c BRISE Standard of Living, 1970–2050.

Scale: GDP per person and consumption per person ($0–$18,000 per person-year); food per person (0–1.5 tonnes per person-year); energy use per person (0–2.5 tonnes of oil equivalents per person-year); sea-level rise (0–1.4 meters).

But at least it makes for a nice theoretical average, and one that could have been utilized for the common good in a world of perfect trade.

In sum, the BRISE region will be in lively development over the next forty years. There will be solid economic expansion, more people, and much more urban life. There will be enthusiasm, and widely varying quality in government. And there will be huge climate gas emissions and episodes of dramatic climate damage. All in all BRISE will do well, not as well as China, but much better than my fifth and final region: the rest of the world.

"Glimpse 10-3: Rich on Biofuels" gives an impression of what a progressive BRISE could achieve.

Rich on Biofuels

Jens Ulltveit-Moe

The current disenchantment with the environment in general and biofuels in particular represents a major business opportunity. Conventional first-generation biofuel from Brazil and southern Africa—in other words, sugarcane ethanol—is the most promising. Those investors who chose to enter the ethanol game in 2010–11 were able to invest at very attractive prices. On top of that, I believe, they will benefit from the aggressive investment in biofuels that will follow accelerating climate change and technological advance in the 2020s. As a consequence there will be in 2052 global fortunes made on sugarcane ethanol.

The Time Is Now

The essence of profitability is to acquire assets at low cost, preferably in a growing market. As I write this, the cost to enter the biofuels market is low. This can be traced in part to the setback for climate policy at the Copenhagen and Cancun climate summits, which stranded many projects initiated by unrealistic (as it turned out) optimism. But the inherent conservatism of the investment community and a disbelief in climate change have also kept investors at bay and prices down—creating a unique opportunity to both earn a profit and help save the climate at the same time.

The opportunity was further helped by the poor image of biofuels. It was in part richly deserved. At the peak, corn ethanol in the United States received USD 6 billion in annual subsidies—despite the fact that this type of biofuel gives next to no reduction in carbon emissions and increases the cost of food. Similarly in the EU, the farm lobby pushed through high import duties for corn ethanol, vegetable diesel, and sugar-beet ethanol, to protect their own dubious product. All helped to destroy the reputation of biofuels as an effective means to reduce climate emissions from transportation.

Investors got even more reticent after the financial crisis, since tighter public budgets meant a cut in subsidies to renewables. The shortage of public money—and in the absence of pressure for more climate policy from the electorate—investors saw sharp reduction in subsidies in Italy, Spain, and Germany. As a consequence there arose many good investment opportunities, primarily for those few renewables with lower (or at least similar) cost than the fossil alternative. I believe sugarcane ethanol was one of them.

Advantages of Sugarcane Ethanol

This biofuel does not need established agricultural land, is relatively cheap to produce, and is undergoing rapid technological advance. In addition it is truly carbon neutral: the CO_2 emitted from the use of sugarcane ethanol in one year is absorbed in the sugarcane growing the next year, and the production of sugarcane ethanol does not require much fossil fuel or fertilizer. It is also truly sustainable: rainfed sugarcane production has continued for decades in Brazil without destroying the soil.

Brazil is, in fact, the world's premier producer of sugarcane ethanol, and sugarcane is grown there on so little land that food production is not significantly impaired. Nor is such growth a cause of deforestation. While occupying only 0.9% of agricultural and pastureland in Brazil, sugarcane already powers more than half of Brazilian cars.

At the global level, IEA estimated that it will require 100 million hectares (Mha) or 6% of the available suitable land to provide 27% of transportation fuels in 2050.[5] In 2010, 30 Mha were used for energy crops. Of this some 20 Mha were in the United States and European Union. The negative attitude to energy crops in the United States and European Union will probably lead to the discontinuation of this land use, and thus there is a need for 120 Mha of new land for energy crops.

Fortunately the rest of the world has huge underutilized areas. Brazil alone has more than 200 Mha in pastureland. Much of this can be converted to sugarcane, because current meat production can be maintained on a substantially smaller area—through technological advance in grass and water. Eastern Europe has 40 Mha of underutilized land, and there is a similar potential in southern Africa. Providing 120 Mha of new land for biofuels, even after discontinuing the use of land for biofuels in the United States and European Union, is well within reach.

Today, sugarcane ethanol competes successfully with gasoline at the pump in Brazil without subsidies. The production cost is below USD 60 for the energy equivalent of a barrel of oil, and it is expected to fall toward USD 40 as technology advances. Brazil is easily the lowest-cost producer of biofuels in the world. The production cost of a tonne of its sugarcane ethanol is 35% of the cost of corn ethanol in the United States and 23% of the cost of sugar-beet ethanol in Germany.

Still the ramp-up on the global use of biofuels will be costly. IEA estimated an investment cost of 1%–2% of the total cost of transportation up to 2030, and in the ensuing twenty years a production cost equivalent to an oil price of USD 120 per barrel. For the period 2010 to 2030 seen as a whole, the IEA foresaw a net savings of about 1% of the total energy transportation cost. The societal benefit would be substantial, since this would reduce climate emissions from transportation by a quarter.

The technological advances in sugarcane ethanol production have been substantial and look likely to continue. Up to 2011 the yield per hectare doubled every twenty years, and even at half that rate of advance, yields will double again by 2052.

Next, the current technology focuses primarily on the sucrose content of the sugarcane, which means that only a third of the solar energy absorbed by sugarcane is utilized. By burning the leftover grass, the bagasse, another quarter of the solar energy can be converted to electricity, thus almost doubling the energy output from sugarcane production.

Finally, the fermentation process that creates the ethanol from sugarcane generates CO_2 emissions with a high concentration of CO_2. This CO_2 can be captured and stored more simply and cheaply than emissions from the combustion of fossil fuels. This could make some biofuels net carbon negative in the future.

Looking Ahead

So how will the human exploitation of the wonders of sugarcane ethanol play out over the next forty years?

A willingness to act, in spite of short-term costs, will result when dire scientific warnings finally emerge as observable reality for people in the rich world. This will happen already in the 2020s because global temperature will have risen notably, extreme weather will be frequent, and methane will start emerging from the previously frozen tundra of Siberia and Canada and scare the voter.

At that time China will have surpassed the EU leadership in fighting climate change. The Communist Party's prior sensitivity to the climate challenge, and a succession of floods and droughts, will ensure urgent action around 2020. The United States will be the bottleneck delaying global collaborative action for CO_2 reduction. But even American voters will eventually demand action against fossil emissions, albeit a decade after China and Europe.

The price of fuels will increase sharply in the 2020s because high carbon prices and mandatory blending of biofuels will be demanded by a scared majority of the voters.

The public image of biofuels will have shifted to the better, after the proven success of Brazil's large-scale use of sugarcane ethanol over the prior decades. This will ensure a healthy profit margin for a number of biofuels, and rapid expansion in their production and use.

The energy-crop sector will become increasingly high-tech, and the crop yield and the crop's resistance to adverse conditions will continue their dramatic increase. Genetic modification will be universally accepted—except in the EU—and will contribute significantly to increased yields in Brazil and Asia. Residuals from sugarcane, forestry, and agriculture will increasingly be valuable sources of electricity and heat.

By 2052, the sugarcane industry will make a contribution to transportation fuels on par with key OPEC states today. If Brazil by 2052 uses 7% of its agricultural and pastureland and ethanol yield increases by 1% per year during the next forty years, the Brazilian output of sugarcane ethanol will be fifteen times larger than today. The total energy content will be equivalent to some 2.5 million barrels of oil per day, or the current export of Iran or Nigeria. I believe this is a likely scenario.

In sum, sugarcane ethanol will have created substantial wealth for those early investors in Brazil and southern Africa, much to the disappointment of those who invested in the United States and Europe.

Jens Ulltveit-Moe *(Norwegian, born 1942) is founder and CEO of Umoe, www.umoe.no. The group has a turnover of USD 1 billion and 7,000 employees. The company invests counter-cyclically, proven lately by its switch from oil tankers and oil seismic to renewables including biofuels and solar PV.*

The vision of "Rich on Biofuels" is a wonderful example of green growth—that elusive ambition of many countries in the post (financial) crisis world.

Toward 2052: Rest of the World

My forecast for the rest of the world (ROW) is illustrated in figure 10-5.

ROW is an eclectic blend of 186 countries with a total population of 2.1 billion people in 2010. It is thus home for one-third of the world's population. Seventeen of those countries each have more than 30 million people and collectively have over one billion people. The most populous are Pakistan (168 million people), Nigeria (162), Bangladesh (142), Philippines (94), Ethiopia (82), Egypt (81), Congo (68), and Myanmar/Burma (48). The ROW region is the least industrialized third of the world and houses most of its poverty. The average GDP per person is about two-thirds that of the BRISE region.

The population is still rising fast—at 1.9% per year—compared to 2.4% per year forty years ago. The growth rate will continue to fall, however, and the population will peak in the 2050s (at 3.1 billion people), at much lower fertility rates than today. The fall will be driven by higher education levels, better contraception, and more urbanization, as elsewhere. But the effect of urbanization will occur later than in the other regions, because ROW will remain less industrialized, with more people on the land.

The potential workforce will almost double, and the population will stay relatively young. As a result the support ratio will continue its historical decline, lessening the burden on those who work.

Productivity developments have been erratic over the last forty years, and there is no reason to expect dramatic shifts from that general pattern. A couple of the countries in ROW will experience economic takeoff within the next forty years and copy the impressive growth of other emerging economies, but that won't significantly affect the average growth rate, which will remain low. Gross labor productivity will grow by 1.2% per year, which when combined with growth in the workforce of some 2% per year will give GDP growth in excess of 3% per year.

As a mathematical consequence the GDP will grow to three times its current size in 2052. GDP per person will grow from $4,000 to $8,000 per person-year. This amounts to some $20 a day, which is quite a bit higher than the infamous "$2 a day" that was used for decades to indicate the threshold of real poverty. That "$2" is around $3 a day expressed in the 2005 PPP dollars I am using. So in 2052 average income in ROW will be six times higher than subsistence, but much of the income will be in the urban agglomerations, so the rural areas will still house significant poverty.

ROW will also increase its investment rate in order to handle the oncoming rush of modern problems—including climate change. But the region will (as a gross generalization) remain poor and badly governed, so investment will be kept at its absolute minimum. Part of the minimum spending will be for the gradual expansion of the energy sector, and some of the extra investment will go into making energy supply less climate intensive. It is likely that part of the finance will be in the form of development assistance from the rich world, earmarked for climate purposes, possibly as a continuation of the Clean Development Mechanism.

The ROW energy system will grow gradually to 2052, and the CO_2 emissions will follow suit. But emissions will stagnate because of increasing energy efficiency and more renewable energy in the mix. This improvement will partly be a result of foreign technology—for example, in solar PV and electric vehicles. Still, in 2052 CO_2 emissons will be a meager 1 tonne of CO_2 per person-year. This happens to be equal to the annual per capita emissions allowable if a principle of sustainable and equal emissions for all earthlings were implemented. So in 2052 the inhabitants of the ROW region will still live sustainable lifestyles—from a narrow climate point of view. They will be emitting just one-seventh of the CO_2 emitted by their brothers and sisters in the United States. ROW will still be relatively unindustrialized.

Food production will outpace population growth; the amount of food available per person will grow gradually toward three times the subsistence level. This is because land yields will keep growing through the increased input of fertilizer, improved seed, and water. But this is again a regional average. Among its three billion people will be the majority of those who still starve in 2052. Furthermore, the area of cultivated land will start to decline around 2040, as a consequence of climate change, and because more land needs to be used to house increasing population numbers. And worse, near the end of the period, the ROW region will need imports in order to sustain its consumption of food, fiber, and fish. All the biologically productive land within the region will be in use. There will be no unused bio-capacity.

In conclusion, the rest of the world—ROW—will remain the poor cousin of the world family. There will be growth in per capita production and consumption, but by 2052 the three billion people of the region will still lag far behind the five billion living in the United States, OECD-less-US, China, and BRISE; and this in spite of the forty years of stagnation in the OECD.

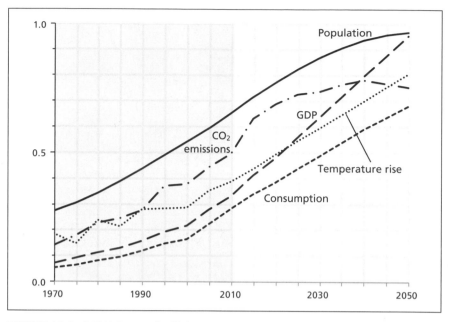

FIGURE 10-5a ROW State of Affairs, 1970–2050.
Scale: Population (0–3.2 billion people); GDP and consumption ($0–$25 trillion per year); CO_2 emissions (0–6 billion tonnes CO_2 per year); temperature rise (0°C–2.5°C).

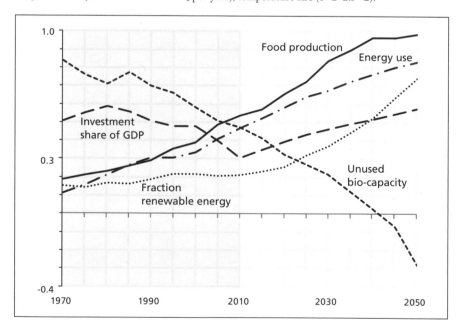

FIGURE 10-5b ROW Production, 1970–2050.
Scale: Food production (0–2.5 billion tonnes per year); energy use (0–3 billion tonnes of oil equivalents per year); fraction renewable energy (0%–40%); investment share of GDP (0%–40%); unused bio-capacity (minus 20%–50%).

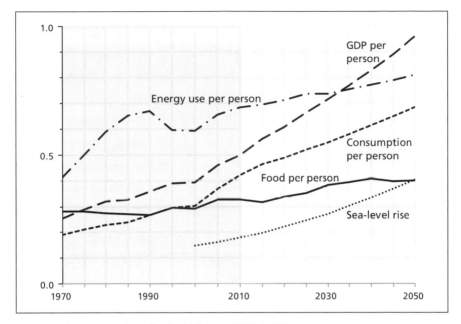

FIGURE 10-5c ROW Standard of Living, 1970–2050.

Scale: GDP per person and consumption per person ($0–$8,000 per person-year); food per person (0–2 tonnes per person-year); energy use per person (0–1 tonne of oil equivalents per person-year); sea-level rise (0–1.4 meters).

CHAPTER 11

Comparison with Other Futures

As part of the effort to improve the internal consistency of my global forecast, I have tried to compare the forecast with simulation runs from two of the few integrated, causal, dynamic world models that exist and have a sufficiently long time horizon. The comparison was made in order to find differences between the *2052* forecast and scenario runs from the models, explain their cause, and make modifications as necessary. Such testing cannot, of course, prove that my forecast is correct. But it does identify strengths and weaknesses in my thinking.

Testing against a Global Computer Model

The first model used was a revised version of the World3 model we used in 2003 to produce the simulation runs for the thirty-year update of *The Limits to Growth* study.[1] The revised model had added more detailed energy and climate sectors to the World3-03 model, based on the interesting hypothesis that man will use first those energy sources that have the highest energy return on energy investment (EROI).[2] We further modified the model structure on a couple of points in order to better reflect the causal structure described in figure 3-1 on page 57, and then we ran the model and identified the main differences between the computer run and my global forecast. The essential difference was that the revised model system tended to collapse around 2050 because renewable energy was not brought forth at sufficient speed in the model system. By forcing an accelerated introduction of renewables, it proved possible to postpone the crisis.

We did not push the effort further, because all I wanted was rough confirmation that it would be possible to re-create the essential characteristics of my global forecast using a computer model that treated all the relevant causal mechanisms endogenously. I also wanted confirmation that the timing within my forecast was defendable. On both scores, the results were corroborated. So, our comparison of the *2052* forecast with the revised World3-03 model did not lead to major change of my forecast, only to adjustment of some nuances.

As an example, it became obvious that the revised model is more pessimistic on the food and environment front than my forecast. This in turn was a result of its assuming that global bio-capacity is smaller than what I assume in my forecast, based on modern agricultural data. If the revised model is right, there will be less food available in the real world than my forecast projects over the next forty years. But if bio-capacity does indeed turn out to be smaller, the world will respond by allocating even more extra investment into agriculture and thereby compensate partly for the lack of food. But in doing so, the world will have to sacrifice some other worthy causes—for example, extra investment in energy efficiency or in repair of climate damage—and thus face stronger problems on that front. So, if the world truly is smaller than I assume in my forecast, the damage arising when humanity crashes into the world's limits will appear earlier.

The model's tendency to signal an early lack of food made us do an extra round of investigations into the current science on the effect of climate change on global food production over the next forty years. Interestingly, and as mentioned in an earlier chapter,[3] current thinking indicates that the effect of increased concentrations of CO_2 in the atmosphere will have a strong positive effect on agriculture—one that more than compensates for the negative effect of warming over the next forty years. In the longer term the total effect is likely to be net negative, and increasingly so, but that is again outside the horizon of my forecast. My forecast has been adjusted to reflect this view.

As a final point, the simulations run from the model tended to show uncontrolled collapse just after 2052. On this issue my forecast does not have a detailed opinion, since it goes only to 2052. My forecast does say that global warming may trigger self-reinforcing climate change in the second half of the twenty-first century, which would certainly qualify as a collapse. This matches the fact that the model runs indicated that humanity is pretty close to planetary limitations, and that although they may not be reached before 2052, they may be reached just after.

Comparison with *The Limits to Growth* Studies

Most analysts, when studying the long-term future, choose to develop potential scenarios versus making an actual forecast. That is, they limit themselves to conditional analyses of relatively limited scopes, trying to answer the question of what will happen if certain conditions are satisfied. What will happen to the global population if cancer is cured? What will happen to tourism if air fuel is included in a cap-and-trade system for CO_2? What will happen to economic growth in Europe if the EU is split? This tendency to keep within a reasonable topical area and shy away from forecasting makes it simpler to give defendable answers.

My global forecast is blatantly different. I have actively tried not to limit the scope, and I have actively steered toward an unconditional forecast. The reason is that I wanted to be able to answer my own question, which was: What will actually happen during the rest of my life? As you may remember from chapter 1, I was inspired by the hope that a clear answer would reduce my unending subconscious worrying about the future. I also made the forecast to help you answer the question, "How satisfied will I be in 2052?"

Now that my forecast exists, it is interesting to see how it compares with other forecasts. That is a legitimate question, but sadly, there aren't many forty-year forecasts to compare with. But there is the obvious opportunity to compare my forecast with that infamous 1972 study of the long-term global future, *The Limits to Growth* (*LTG*). Here I have the advantage of being an insider, as coauthor of the original book and of its follow-up studies in 1992 and 2004. Having been part of these studies does of course make me partial, but I will try as hard as possible to be neutral, or at the very least highlight my biases when they appear to influence my conclusions. My strongest biases probably come more from the fact that I am citizen of a wealthy industrialized country, with a hard-science education, and a deep respect for nature. Most of my disagreements with the conventional wisdom can be derived from that background.

A Forecast versus Scenarios

When using *LTG* as a comparison, one must start from the most central difference—namely, that *LTG* was not a forecast, but a scenario analysis. The original *LTG* sought to answer questions about what would happen to global population, industrialization, food production, resource use, and pollution up to the year 2100 in response to various sets of conceivable policy. What would happen if more money was put into population control? What would happen if agricultural techniques were changed in order to reduce land erosion? What would happen if there actually were less nonrenewable resources in the world than believed at the time? What would happen if people ended their romance with economic growth?

LTG provided the answer in the form of twelve different scenarios for the global future to year 2100. Some of these were clearly unattractive, showing humanity growing beyond the sustainable carrying capacity of the globe and collapsing into states of low quality of life after the overshoot. Others portrayed smoother trajectories, achieved through the implementation (in the model system) of forward-looking social policy that helped stabilize the system. One reason why the book was so much discussed, I believe, is that many found the stabilizing policies (like upper limits on per capita consumption) to be repugnant. The medicine was seen as worse than the disease.

Implicitly *LTG* gave support to those policies that help stabilize the world model system, but the main message of the book was at a higher level of aggregation. *LTG* stated that the growth of the global population and economy would crash into the physical constraints of the planet in the first half of the twenty-first century. The world would pass through these constraints—because of long reaction and decision delays—and move into overshoot, from which there would only be two ways back: "managed decline" or "collapse induced by nature." *LTG* recommended forward looking policy and rapid quick action, in order to avoid overshoot and to ensure a sustainable and just society below the carrying capacity.

LTG was very clear on the extreme limitations on the predictive strength of its statements. Data and knowledge were not sufficient to back concrete prediction within narrow uncertainty bands. All that could be expressed with credibility were statements concerning "behavior modes" involving broad trends and patterns of development. *LTG* was very clear that it could not predict when decline would occur, nor even what type of overshoot would be the most likely. But it did focus on the threat from physical limitations: resource scarcity and environmental damage. Softer threats, like accelerating inequity or cultural disintegration, were given a backseat.

In the following section I will discuss the *LTG* message in much greater detail, because it helps deepen the message of the current book.

2052 as a Further Elaboration

In the broadest sense, my forecast can be seen as an elaboration on one of the overshoot-and-decline scenarios in *LTG*. My forecast tells the story of a world that is moving briskly toward a climate crisis, caused by one very obvious global constraint: namely, the limited capacity of the earth's atmosphere to hold CO_2 without getting warmer. My forecast touches upon other constraints, such as finite reserves of fossil fuels, finite availability of arable land, finite amounts of wild fish, and finite space for biodiversity reserves, but basically says that the climate constraint is going to be the most pressing one over the next forty years. It makes the point that we have already overshot: Annual emissions of greenhouse gases are already some two times higher than what is absorbed in the world's oceans and forests. As a result the atmospheric concentration of these gases is rising. And as a result the temperature is increasing. And as a result living conditions for humanity (and nature) will become different, and in some ways more difficult, during the decades ahead.

But we have not only overshot. Humanity has embarked on the tedious effort to avoid "collapse induced by nature" and rather get on a path that could be described as "managed decline." Institutions like the IPCC and the United Nations Framework Convention on Climate Change have been built and negotiations have been conducted for decades already, in order to get in place a well-organized, effective, and fair reduction of climate gas emissions. There has been some progress, but current results are not sufficient to ensure that global warming will stay below plus 2°C.

The relation between LTG and my forecast can be stated as follows: My forecast picks one of the many scenarios in LTG and says that this is the most likely future. As I see it, in the 2004 edition of LTG this happens to be Scenario 3,[4] which is a scenario where both shortage of nonrenewable resources and dangerous pollution are postponed until the middle of the century through the application of technology. My forecast furthermore takes one resource—fossil fuels—and one pollutant—CO_2—and says that these are the critical substances. Then my forecast proceeds to add quantitative precision to the more general story told by Scenario 3 in LTG—the story of a "polution crisis."

LTG repeatedly made the valid point that the World3 computer model was unsuited for analysis of world developments after the onset of collapse/decline. This is because it was, and still is, hard to foresee the pattern of social tension and strife, institutional response, and the power games that will be released once a resource gets scarce or a pollutant reaches a critical level.

In my forecast I have tried to move one step beyond what we did in LTG. I have chosen climate as the arena of the first critical overshoot and pointed to the two main tools available to handle it: more energy efficiency and more renewable energy. And I tried to describe the likely evolution in their use. I have tried to guess what will happen when our current, largely democratic, institutions continue their effort to handle the emerging climate crisis—concluding that they will not act fast enough to solve the problem in time. I have made the point that the conflict is going to emanate from two "soft" arenas: insufficient productivity growth (which accelerates distributional problems) and excessive inequity (which will lead to social strife and conflict). And I have tried to quantify the resulting problems.

In LTG's "pollution crisis" scenario, the polluting emissions from a growing industrial sector finally overwhelm the absorptive capacity of the global ecosystem. As a consequence, pollution levels in the environment rise and in turn lead to reduced human life expectancy and lower agricultural yields.

Λ whole lot of capital is redirected from industrial investment to pollution control in order to reduce the pollution damage and fight further emissions, with the final result that the productive capacity of industry withers and leads to a decline in per capita availability of goods and services.

My forecast provides a similar trajectory on most points but is expressed in more conventional macroeconomic terms. I say that a necessary increase in investment to counter depletion, pollution, climate damage, biodiversity decline, and inequity will contribute to a decline in the average per capita consumption. I pinpoint the onset of consumption decline to the 2050s, but much earlier in the rich world. The poorer parts of the world will not experience much decline, because I do not expect that they will take off seriously before 2052.

Crash In Income versus Crash In Well-being

The story of the *2052* forecast is one of overshoot caused by delayed societal response to greenhouse gas emissions being allowed to increase beyond sustainable levels for generations. It is a story of lower consumption growth (and in the rich world, consumption decline) resulting partly from the costs of trying to mitigate the climate problem. And since it assumes an inadequate response, self-reinforcing warming in the second half of the twenty-first century may add to the consumption decline and make it feel much more like the future described by the emotional term "collapse."

Many will have read the *LTG* scenarios, and correctly, as telling a story wherein humanity crashes into global limitations so fast that the crash in itself reduces human longevity through starvation from overpopulation and toxic pollution. Furthermore, it is a crash with a whiplash effect, as the same toxic inputs also lower agricultural productivity and cause more starvation—and further loss of longevity—in a very Malthusian way. However, in the current globalized world of money and trade, it is more likely that the decline will take the form of reduced purchasing power, not increased mortality. In both cases—I would say—the effect is reduced quality of life. So what overshoots and collapses is "well-being," not population or GDP.

In overshoot-and-collapse scenarios there is a temporary period when the level of "well-being" exceeds what it proves possible to maintain in the long run. When faced with the threat of approaching decline, one possible human response would be to redefine the concept of "well-being" so it includes only those dimensions that can be supplied sustainably. Another solution would be to wait until the global population becomes small enough to allow everyone the privileges of the current few. I expect that in the twenty-first century we will see humanity do a bit of both. Thus if we avoid destroying the world in the process—if we avoid self-reinforcing climate change—there is hope: by the year 2100 the world population will be much smaller than it is today, and the energy system 100% solar. Humanity will be much closer to a sustainable state, particularly if some unsustainable values have changed in the process.

It is helpful to distinguish between the terms "overshoot and collapse" and "overshoot and decline." "Overshoot and collapse" refers to totally uncontrolled large-scale die-off, while "overshoot and decline" refers to a process in which humanity becomes increasingly deprived after a temporary period of relative glory.

Using this language, humanity may, I believe, experience overshoot and *collapse* in the twenty-first century. But not before 2052. The real test will come in the second half of the twenty-first century, when we know whether there will be self-reinforcing warming, and whether humanity will manage to adapt to this in a peaceful manner (by moving the remaining population into flood-proof and otherwise climate-proofed cities, and ensuring that the necessary production can take place in a steadily warming world).

I am equally convinced that the world will experience numerous cases of overshoot and *decline* before 2052. The main example will be the decline of the United States from its former role as the undisputed leader of the world. This decline will go along with an early peak (perhaps already behind us) and then long-drawn-out decline in US per capita consumption levels. The decline will not solely be due to physical limits to growth, as detailed in my forecast. But the increased cost of clean energy and the increasing need to handle extreme weather events caused by climate change will add to the burden from declining productivity growth made worse by unsustainable inequity.

Interestingly, even if overshoot and collapse does occur, the story of the twenty-first century may not be told in those terms. A collapse induced by overshooting the capacity of nature may instead be described as an evolution triggered and sustained by bad management at all levels—global, national, and corporate. Root causes are often described differently—much like the uprisings in the Arab Spring in 2011 that were seen by some as a yearning for democracy and freedom, while others saw them as the result of population pressure in a resource-poor environment. Similarly, some see the Iraq war as a consequence of the US need for oil at the turn of the twenty-first century, rather than as a US effort to promote the ideals of democracy. Or consider your own case: you have lived through the major part of the run-up to climate overshoot but may not ever have thought about it in those terms.[5]

Overshoot and Collapse in Some Detail

The forty years since the publication of *LTG* have proven how difficult it is to establish "overshoot and collapse" as a widely understood and used concept in global decision making. This is a pity. Being aware of the tendency toward overshoot and collapse, and sensitive to its consequences, is of tremendous use if the goal is to avoid unsustainability.

It is worthwhile to briefly summarize how the *LTG* book was received after it appeared in 1972. It led to a public debate that has lasted until this day, with strong views both for and against its alleged message. By its supporters, *LTG* was seen as a useful and constructive warning that global society ought to choose a different, more ecological road ahead. In their eyes *LTG* described the need for sustainable development—although that label was not invented until long after: *LTG* used the word "global equilibrium" to describe the same idea. For the critics, and they were in the majority, *LTG* was seen as misinformed and even dangerous hackwork predicting immediate collapse to the current social order because of resource depletion.

During the first twenty-five years after its publication, no one seemed to pick up the real message of the study, which is that overshoot is a likely consequence of slow societal decision making, and that once in overshoot, there is only one way out, namely, decline back down into sustainable territory. The general view was that *LTG* had been proven wrong, because oil had not in fact run out. The story of the public debate is well told by Italian scientist Ugo Bardi,[6] who reminds us that the treatment of *LTG* in this period resembled the more recent mistreatment of the IPCC by climate skeptics inside and outside the energy industry.

But in the year 2000 a revival of *LTG* as a respectable analysis began, initiated by a most surprising source, namely, Texas oilman and investment banker Matthew Simmons.[7] Simmons looked at rising energy prices since 1972 and concluded that they were early warnings of future bottlenecks in the production of oil and gas, and he was proven right four years later when gas prices in the United States exploded. In 2008 Australian scientist Graham Turner[8] helped the revival by showing that the world had actually followed the "standard run" (the business-as-usual scenario from 1972) of the *LTG* World3 computer model. And lately, in 2012, the well-regarded *New Scientist* crowned this process by bringing the story of the fall and revival of *LTG* to a broader scientific audience.[9]

But it was only the *New Scientist* paper that clearly pinpointed the connection between societal reaction delays and the risk of overshoot and collapse; or, in other words, long delays will make the quest for sustainable development even more difficult because they will tend to create a bumpy ride.

Sustainable development has emerged over the last twenty-five years as a good label, politically speaking, because it provides a goal but still gives room for all kinds of strategies. But therein lies its weakness: the goal of sustainable development is not particularly helpful in telling you what to do next. So instead of working *for* sustainable development, I suggest you should rather be working to *avoid* unsustainability. This is best done by identifying and removing unsustainabilities one at a time.

You should start with the least sustainable element in your surroundings—that is, you should identify what is going to blow up in your face first, if you do not change your ways. This might mean you start reducing your climate gas emissions before the local newspaper finds out you are not, or reduce your use of gasoline and heating oil before you are unable to pay your fuel bills, or find an alternative supplier of coffee if your current brand comes from a plantation not paying a living wage to its workers. This is sustainable development in practice.

The behavior mode of overshoot and collapse is important to understand because it signals that something is not sustainable. Through his book *Collapse*, Jared Diamond made the collapse part of this behavior mode well known.[10] But the core of the problem, from a policy point of view, is to be found in the first part of the behavior mode: the growth into overshoot. The core problem lies in the systems and policies that allow or drive expansion beyond what is sustainable—in growth beyond carrying capacity.

The concept of overshoot and collapse is more easily grasped and adopted by natural scientists, and particularly life scientists with practical experience from the dynamics of natural systems. They know well that animal populations routinely overshoot their food supply and then starve, sometimes destroying the food supply in the process. They also know well that the food supplies have to recover before those animal populations can revive. Think, for instance, about how a herd of deer might fare on a finite mountain plateau with no wolves or other predators to keep its population stable. The number of deer would increase as long as there was enough food. Eventually, a final wave of young deer would add just enough grazing pressure to make the herd eat up the available grassland and trample it to dust.

For people who buy the analogy that we are behaving like the deer in this scenario, the policy implications are obvious. It is important to know the carrying capacity of your environment. It is important to know what drives your expansion into this environment. It is important to avoid placing a burden on your environment that exceeds its carrying capacity. For if you do so, you may destroy its regenerative capacity—for a while or, in the worst cases, forever. In order to avoid inadvertent overshoot, it is important to have a forward-looking attitude and to act in time. If you do not, you increase the chance of unsustainability.

Let us go through the reasoning behind this in six detailed steps.[11]

1. Humanity Has an Ecological Footprint

The human ecological footprint is a measure of the burden humanity puts on the physical environment. It is a broad concept and includes in principle all human use of natural resources and all environmental impacts—irrespective of sort or kind. In very approximate terms it is the sum of human resource extraction and human pollution emissions, defined so as to include the destruction of biodiversity.

As discussed in chapter 6, one can measure the nonenergy ecological footprint as the land area necessary to produce the food, meat, wood, and fish we consume, and the land we cover with cities and infrastructure. I call this the nonenergy footprint because it excludes the land area necessary to mine the energy we use and the forest area we would need in order to absorb all the CO_2 emitted from our use of fossil energy.

The good news is that the nonenergy footprint per person is no longer growing much, and in some countries it is even declining. The bad news is that the total nonenergy footprint is still being pushed up by increases in the population: we do need ever more biologically productive land to feed and clothe humanity. And furthermore, the total ecological footprint, which also includes the energy aspects, is even bigger and now equals 1.4 planets.

Much confusion could have been avoided in the "growth vs. no-growth" debate over the last generation if one had used the concept of "ecological footprint" rather than imprecise constructs like "growth" or "physical growth" when trying to describe the negative impact of human activity on the planet. But the human ecological footprint did not really emerge as a credible label until the late 1990s, when the first regular reports tracking the footprint in quantitative terms emerged.[12] Prior to this, confusion dominated the debate, as most people interpreted the word "growth" as identical to "economic growth" or "growth in GDP," even when it was meant to describe "growth in the ecological footprint."

2. The Human Footprint Is Expanding

The human ecological footprint did expand continuously over the period for which we have data, and certainly since 1972. It became heavier both because human population expanded and because the amount of resources consumed and pollution generated per person per year expanded. But in parallel, technological advance did consistently lower the footprint, by reducing the area necessary to obtain a certain amount of resources or absorb a certain amount of pollution.

3. The Footprint Can Expand beyond Planetary Limits

It is possible for the human ecological footprint to expand beyond the carrying capacity of planet Earth, but only for a while. It is possible to exceed the maximum sustainable harvest, but only for a while.

For instance, you can cut more trees per year than what will grow back, as long as you start with a full forest. You can harvest more fish per year than will replenish, as long as you start with a big stock of fish. You can eat more food per year than is grown, as long as you start with a full storehouse of grain. But only for a while. The consumptive parts of the human footprint can only remain in unsustainable territory for a finite period of time, until whatever buffer that existed has been absorbed.

It is also possible to emit more pollution into a pond than is broken down by its bacteria, but only if you stop before you kill the bacteria. It is possible to reduce biodiversity by letting species go extinct, but only until the ecosystem collapses. It is possible to emit more CO_2 into the atmosphere than is absorbed by oceans and forests, but only until the global warming becomes unlivable. And again, only for a while. If the practice is continued, it will destroy the carrying capacity and force the practice to a halt.

4. Decision Delays Increase the Chance of Overshoot

When the human footprint is approaching a limit, society normally reacts, but only after some delay. First society spends time discussing the reality of the limit—and continues expanding while debating. It is only once the limit has been thoroughly exceeded that its position can be clearly established and the overshoot measured and documented. Only then does debate give way to a tentative decision to slow down. And while the debate and decisions linger on, growth continues and brings the footprint into unsustainable territory.

It will take time (decades?) to observe and agree that current global activity does indeed exceed the long-term carrying capacity of the planet. It will take time (decades?) for national and global institutions to pass the necessary legislation to stop overexploitation of the world's resources and ecosystems. And it will take time (decades?) to implement this legislation and make the necessary changes on the ground. So, growth in the footprint is unlikely to stop until long after global limits have been exceeded.

LTG's message of "overshoot caused by decision delays" is not generally understood. This was not surprising one generation ago, for in 1972 (when the human ecological footprint was around one half of today's) it was seen as rather inconceivable that global society would allow itself to grow beyond the sustainable carrying capacity of the globe. By today we know better. Currently the human demand on the biosphere exceeds the global bio-capacity by some 40%. Global greenhouse gas emissions are twice the sustainable levels. Many global fisheries have been overharvested to the point that commercial fish stocks have steeply declined. The tropical rain forests are still being cleared. The world of 2012 is "in overshoot."

5. Once in Overshoot, Contraction Is Unavoidable

Humanity cannot—in the long run—use more physical resources and generate more emissions every year than nature is capable of supplying or absorbing in a sustainable manner. Or, in other words: the human ecological footprint cannot continue to grow indefinitely because planet Earth is physically limited. Overshoot is a temporary phenomenon.

In each instance of overshoot, humanity has to move back into sustainable territory, either through "managed decline" or through "collapse induced by nature," the latter caused by the unmitigated working of "nature" or "the market." An example of managed decline would be to limit the annual catch of fish to a sustainable level through legislation and planned scrapping of fishing vessels and gear. An example of collapse would be the elimination of fishing communities through bankruptcies when there is no more income because the fish are gone (or to be precise: reduced to such low numbers that it no longer makes economic sense to continue the catch).

The world has not yet experienced large-scale environmental collapse. But there have been some instances of local overshoot, followed by contraction. The most famous case of "managed decline" is the effort to eliminate ozone-destroying chemicals through the Montreal protocol in 1987, upon discovery that the ozone layer over Antarctica was thinning. The measure seems to have worked in that at least the ozone hole is no longer growing. The most famous example of "collapse" is the collapse in the Canadian cod fisheries after 1992. Here the situation is less hopeful: after two decades without fishing, the fish stock has not yet recovered.

Some argue that contraction—forced or planned—is nothing but a normal element in the process of economic growth, and thus nothing to worry about. In this view overshoot and contraction is simply a process of one resource being replaced by another; or, more generally, one technology simply giving way to another. This view can be defended if the transition is smooth—if it occurs without temporary decline in human well-being. But if the transition to the new solution involves a temporary decline in human well-being when the old solution (for instance, cheap oil) is being phased out before the new solution (for instance, solar-based hydrogen) is in place, the transition must be said to involve an element of contraction, or welfare loss as the economists call it.

6. Overshoot Can Be Avoided through Forward-Looking Policy

By looking ahead, society will normally be able to tell that limits are approaching and to set in swing the proactive initiatives necessary to avoid crashing into the limits. The challenge of overshoot and collapse is solvable—at least in principle. But it is hard to solve in practice, because forward-looking policy normally requires sacrifice today to get a better tomorrow. Wise policy must ensure that the human footprint is not allowed to grow into unsustainable territory. That means refraining from expansion that would otherwise have given a short-term benefit. This is difficult in a democracy dominated by short-term voters and in markets dominated by short-term investors.

Many oppose the idea of forward-looking policy and would rather rely on the automatic "technological fix." In essence they oppose the idea that the world is finite—even in the physical interpretation. They believe instead that technology will remove the planetary limits faster than we approach them. In other words: technological advance will continue to push back limits and increase the carrying capacity of the planet.

I don't trust in such automatic technological optimism. I believe the world for all practical purposes is finite. And that overshoot is likely when there are significant reaction delays in a system: lags in the perception of and localization of limits; in the time-consuming, multi-stakeholder decisions to stop expansion; and in implementing the slowdown. Once in overshoot, contraction is the only way out. The way down to sustainability is longer if the underlying ecosystem has been damaged during the overshoot.

In recent decades, while the globe has been in overshoot, much discussion has taken place in various forums in order to find a path to sustainability through coordinated global action. The UN Millennium Development Goals[13] are probably the most concrete description of what needs to be done, and some progress has been achieved and measured. But we are far from having agreed decisions that when acted on will start to reduce the human ecological footprint.

The world might better understand the urgency of the challenge if it better understood the behavior mode—or the dynamics—of overshoot and collapse.

Perspectives on the Second Half of the Twenty-First Century

As you may remember from chapter 2, I chose a forty-year time horizon for my forecast for various reasons—primarily that it has been forty years since we did the first global outlooks.

It is ironic that by choosing forty years, I happened to stop the forecast just as the real action—the real contraction of the global system—is likely to start. As shown in my forecast, 2052 is more or less the exact time when the average per capita consumption level will peak, and a worldwide decline in material standards will start. The year 2052 is also the time when the global average temperature will surpass the danger threshold of plus 2°C. But by 2052 the global population will have started its decline, lessening the burden on the planet year by year. And we will be halfway through the transition from a fossil- to a solar-based economy. So the downturn may be short.

In order to get a more complete perspective on the future, it helps to look another fifty years ahead, toward the end of the twenty-first century. Only in this longer view can we consider the combined effect of declining population, stagnating GDP, significant warming, and decision makers who have learned that overshooting the climate limit is indeed dangerous and may trigger self-reinforcing climate change and pass judgment on whether we think they will achieve "managed decline" and avoid "uncontrolled collapse induced by nature."

It is harder to see further out, also because actions taken during the last part of the next forty years will influence developments in the second half of the twenty-first century. Our current generation of computer models and our mental models are not trustworthy in the period of contraction. So we must increasingly rely on art and conjecture, and I will end this chapter by having you read two thought-provoking examples of longer-term thinking. These may help your own speculation about what the long-term future might hold.

The first, "Glimpse 11-1: The Fifth Cultural Step," makes the important point that human culture will continue to evolve and that the next—the fifth—step might be far along by 2052. If this view is correct, humanity in the future will organize itself in a very different manner and rely on unconventional inputs in decision making. Complex networks of teams may set the course and lead partly based on perceptions that formerly were categorized as useless in the conduct of serious business.

The Fifth Cultural Step

Dag Andersen

The first half of the twenty-first century will be affected by huge numbers of people wishing to catch up, first with the standard of living of those in industrialized countries, and thereafter with their democracies. At the same time, the negative effects of the current system will become clearer. Nevertheless, I do not believe there will be a great conscious choice to change that system before 2052. Not even a total collapse of the current financial-capital system will lead to a deliberate decision in favor of transformational change. But what is already happening, and what will become clearer over the next forty years, is that the contours of the new will take shape. They are beginning to emerge on the creative periphery of current reality.

I am talking about a great shift of paradigm, perhaps even greater than the emergence of the modern era from the Middle Ages. In today's globalized society, without a globalized power structure, no one is in a position to stop such a shift. At the same time, however, no one is in a position to accelerate the shift at a time when it still could be done without great cost.

My belief in the coming system shift is based on simple extrapolation. The main characteristic of cultural history over the past 10,000 years has followed a path from the simple and unconscious to the complex and conscious. The rate of change has increased with the recent maturation of consciousness. Even though many will gradually come to understand that endless material growth is not possible on a small planet, the decision-making structures—whether economic or political—are not organized to decide on a fundamental paradigm change. The alternative must emerge, demonstrate its superiority, and take over gradually.

If one examines previous transitions from one cultural step to the next, they have four important characteristics in common. First, they have been shifts from a more restricted to a wider paradigm. Humanity has learned to relate to an increasing part of reality, both objectively and consciously. Second, the transitions have uncovered new skills and techniques that have enabled the use of this expanded understanding of reality. Third, the transition has involved a higher level of organization and, fourth, greater freedom.

Although I believe it will take more than forty years before the next—the fifth[14]—step in human evolution will have come into being, its emerging contours are already discernable and can be looked at through its three main pillars: the physical, the social, and the spiritual.

The Physical

Sooner or later the planet's ecological systems will enforce a transition from a growth-based to a closed-loop economy based on recycling and renewable energy—hopefully through high-tech, comfortable means but, if everything goes wrong, in a low-tech fashion. This shift involves purely physical phenomena that one can touch and feel.

From a technical point of view, the physical transition can already be performed in a relatively sophisticated way. Robotization, smarter machines, and nanotechnology will be well evolved before 2052 and will make it easier to reorganize into small-scale, high-tech units based on local raw materials and renewable energy sources. It means a transition from the simple mechanical models of industrialization to more complex organic models, where the whole life cycle is considered.

The shift may be introduced gradually and be financially profitable. All the same, it will constitute a radical break with the current economic wisdom of growth-based capitalism and is likely to be resisted by those currently earning fortunes of global proportions. For this reason, even the physical shift will emerge on the periphery of what is already established. It is only there that it will not be perceived as a threat. And it will be followed by more fundamental shifts.

The Social

One can already discern the emerging characteristics of the next cultural step in the field of human relations—a nonphysical phenomenon. A shift in this intangible world will be feared more than the technological/economic change. But the shift is already observable, and most visibly in the competitive spearhead of business.

The emerging phenomenon takes the form of what I call *the creative team*. In a system dominated by creative teams, the old, hierarchical, authoritarian control system is gone. The creative team is based on dialogue, where everyone submits his or her best in terms of ideas, insight, and experience to the group. If the team is wisely composed, it is more giving, more dynamic, creative, and adaptable, but also more demanding. Network organization at its best is a variant of the same construct. A higher level of consciousness is required, but the amount of energy liberated will outcompete the old systems in crucial areas in the long term.

Constructive dialogue, used in a conscious way, represents a radical break with competition—which is the basis of traditional economic thinking. It also represents a new way to resolve conflicting interests in democratic systems. In true dialogue you no longer seek security by controlling external factors. The energy in the relation lies in the pleasure of giving; the security is in yourself. The more you give, the more you get. Over the next couple of generations, positive experiences from such interaction will ensure that the old, antagonistic model is phased out.

The Spiritual

But the real core of the old paradigm that will be dying in 2052 is the idea that physical material—what we can see with our own eyes—is the only *real* reality.

Currently thoughts, feelings, and spiritual phenomena are considered side effects subordinated to the physical processes. Well into the next cultural step—once the new perception of reality has taken over—the core of the old paradigm will be expanded to include the nonphysical. Phenomena that have been left to religion from Descartes' time will once again become an integrated part of our perception of reality.

New religiosity, self-development, and healing are on the way in. Most people already believe in one form of god or another, and in life after death, so what will the practical consequences be? The next step is transformational change, not a question of more or less interest in religion. People will experience their own existence in a different way. The old paradigm will seem narrow and primitive—the representation of a lower cultural level to which almost none will want to return.

How we perceive ourselves and our surroundings is crucial. When that changes, everything changes. But perceptions do not shift overnight. A growing constituency has already started on the path toward self-development. They perceive self-development as important in order to have a good life and to perform well in various contexts. For this group, the development of consciousness has become a goal in itself. They consciously seek a continuing maturation after adulthood, because it provides meaning and a qualitative content to life.

Currently there is much methodological development, investigation, and experimentation in this area. All sorts of alternatives are being tried out, many of them from a paradigm well outside that of the established order. Consider alternative medicine—where the interaction between physical and mental aspects is a core issue. Alternative medicine is working within a holistic model, where the physical aspect is only one of several dimensions, and where things must not necessarily have a physical cause—quite to the contrary.

Most of this methodological development is taking place outside the established research institutions. Much of it has the character of kitchen-table experimentation, but this was also the case for technical revolutions up until the 1930s. How quickly things will evolve is difficult to tell, but it is worth remembering that it took no more than sixty-six years from when two bicycle-repair men, the Wright brothers, got the first aircraft to lift off until Neil Armstrong walked on the moon. A great deal will happen over the next forty years.

Dag Andersen (Norwegian, born 1947) is a political scientist, freelance advisor, lecturer, and author of The 5th Step: The Way to a New Society (2007).

"The Fifth Cultural Step" reminds us that humans won't always be doing the same things nor doing them in the same manner. During this century, the focus of human attention is likely to finally shift away from the material focus that dominated the past.

The second and final perspective on the longer-term future, "Glimpse 11-2: The Third Flowering of the Tree of Life," launches another provoking idea, namely, the rise of the self-programming robot: he who will look you in the eye in the same overbearing manner as you look into the empty eyes of your non-comprehending dog.

GLIMPSE 11-2

The Third Flowering of the Tree of Life

Jonathan Loh

Within the next forty years an event will take place that will alter not just the history of our species but the evolution of life itself. We may not know when exactly it occurs, but by 2052 we will be fully aware that it has happened. Such events have occurred twice before, but in different ways, and the third time will be different again.

To describe these past events, and the one to come, I will employ the analogy of the Tree of Life. This tree sporadically, suddenly, and spectacularly flowers[15] from one of its outer branches. It has done so twice, the last time at the tip of one of its myriad outer twigs. The first flowering was the start of the evolution of all multicellular organisms 550 million years ago, and the second marked the beginning of human cultural diversity some 70,000 to 80,000 years ago. A third flowering is about to begin on the outer edge of the tree, leading to a new evolutionary diversification.

Imagine the history of Earth condensed into a single year. The planet coalesced from hot dust and gases in the solar disk around 4.5 billion years ago; let us call this time 00:00 hours on January 1. Then it began to cool. Life first appeared sometime in March, but until November all living organisms were unicellular. Around mid-November single cells began grouping together into the first multicellular life forms, known as the Ediacaran fauna.

The First Flowering
The Ediacarans lasted only days before being blown away on November 18 by the Cambrian explosion: a sudden burst of evolutionary activity producing new life-forms at a rate unrepeated before or since. Bizarre organisms of enormous complexity appeared. Many had hard body armor and possessed formidable weaponry. The evolutionary arms race had begun. By the morning of November 20 it was all over. The first flowering had ended, but all organisms have since conformed to the basic blueprints that evolved at that time.

The Tree of Life continued to branch and grow, producing new species and losing old ones, for more than half a billion years. Then an extraordinary, unparalleled event occurred at the end of one of its branches in the late evening of December 31. That particular outer twig—one of millions—did not look exceptional, for although it represented a large mammalian species, it was by no means the biggest, or fastest, or the one with the most impressive body armor or weapons. But it began to talk. The species on that twig was our own, and as a result of our remarkable and unique innovation, language, the tree started its second exuberant flowering.

The Second Flowering

Modern humans first appeared around 200,000 years ago, well into the final hour of our year. Just how or when human language evolved is not known. It may have started with gestures rather than vocalizations. But once it had taken hold it enabled an entirely new mode of evolution—cultural evolution. Cultures evolve in a manner similar to species, through variation by mutation, hereditary transmission, and selection. The transmission of culture is mediated not through the passing of DNA from parent to offspring, but through the learning of behavior by one individual from another. The transmission rate is greatly facilitated by language.

About 7,000 languages are spoken in the world today, and each can be considered the expression of a different culture. These languages represent the outermost twigs of the cultural tree, but there are many more extinct languages whose branches ended before the present. Like species, some languages can be classified into families sharing a common ancestor, while others stand alone.

A big difference between biological and cultural evolution is speed. Biological evolution is slow, while cultural evolution is so rapid it can be observed within a lifetime. Another difference is that borrowing occurs between languages. Borrowing words is the equivalent of different species exchanging genetic material, something most organisms cannot do.

Athough the date of the origin of language is not known, it was almost certainly some 70,000 to 80,000 years ago. The population at that time was about 100,000 individuals, largely confined to the

African continent. At this time, in the middle of the last ice age, or around 23:52 on December 31, people began to migrate out of Africa, gradually spreading across Asia, following coastlines and moving up river valleys. Their descendants succeeded in crossing the straits between mainland Southeast Asia and Australia some 40,000 to 60,000 years ago. Others moved north into Europe or over the land-bridge into the Americas. The last great migration crossed not land but the Pacific Ocean, finally reaching New Zealand only 1,000 years ago, or seven seconds to midnight.

As they spread across the globe, living in small isolated groups, the migrants carried their languages and cultures with them. Cultural evolution gave rise to thousands of local variations, leading ultimately to the vast diversity of human languages and cultures. This was the second flowering of the Tree of Life, the cultural explosion.

Extinctions

Diversification has always been accompanied by extinction. There have been at least five mass extinctions in which global species diversity was suddenly reduced, on November 26 and December 2, 12, 15, and 26. On December 12, 245 million years ago, 96% of species went extinct. And on December 26, 65 million years ago, the last great extinction marked the demise of the dinosaurs. After each mass extinction, however, biodiversity recovered or exceeded its previous maximum.

Today, we stand on the brink of a sixth mass extinction. But this time we are losing cultural as well as biological diversity. Half of the world's population speaks one of about 25 languages. Of the remaining 7,000 languages, about half are spoken by fewer than 10,000 speakers.

Languages go extinct because the speakers either die out or, more usually, shift to a second language and within very few generations forget their mother tongue. And with their language, their culture declines. The root causes are globalization, migration, modern com-munications, or sometimes coercion.

It seems unlikely that bio-cultural diversity loss will reverse before 2052. And yet, as bio-cultural diversity declines, I believe that another rapid diversification will erupt from one linguistic twig at the edge of the Tree of Life. The language will not be English or Chinese, but a very recent, invented one. A *computer language* will initiate the third flowering.

The Third Flowering

This will not be a computer language used by programmers to write software. This will be a language used by *computers* to write their own programs. The programs will be written using the same evolutionary algorithm that led to biological and cultural diversity.

The underlying principle is that a computer can be given an objective and an initial program to work on. The computer then copies the program many times over, introducing random changes to the code. It runs the new generation of programs, selects the one that works best, and discards the rest. The cycle is repeated, again and again, until it produces a program that satisfactorily meets the objective. Of course, in biological or cultural evolution, there is no ultimate objective; nor will there be in digital evolution. The selection of programs will be determined by the prevailing market for applications.

Being more efficient, computer-written programs will begin to displace human-written programs, and then computer-designed computers will replace human-designed computers. Eventually, humans will not fully understand how computers work. By 2052, computers will have evolved artificial intelligence and even consciousness. Initially computers will depend on humans to manufacture them and feed them electricity, but this can increasingly be done by computers. Most humans will welcome this evolutionary burgeoning of computer technology, as it will provide extraordinary new applications that make their lives easier or richer.

The rapid diversification of computer-written programs will have begun but not matured by 2052. The new branches of the Tree of Life will consist of populations of programs, just as the older branches comprise populations of species or languages, but their form or function is not yet clear. Human culture is transmitted via memes: ideas that can be copied from one individual to another. A meme is the cultural analogue of a gene, but inhabiting minds rather than cells. Computer cultures will exist outside of human minds, transmitted from computer to computer. I suggest that the basic unit of transmission be called an *exeme*, an executable meme, the digital analogue of a meme or gene.

So we face a future in which the two ancient forms of evolutionary diversity diminish while a new one rises. It is not a path we consciously planned or wanted, any more than our hominin ancestors chose to speak, or our unicellular ancestors chose to form multicellular species. It will happen simply because a fundamentally new innovation allows massive evolutionary diversification. Where does it leave us? Will we be in control of computer culture? Or will computers come to view humans in the same way we view other species: interesting, useful, even necessary, but essentially a lower life-form?

Jonathan Loh (British, born 1963) is a zoologist specializing in the monitoring and conservation of biological and cultural diversity. He is an honorary research associate at the Zoological Society of London and consultant to WWF International.

The idea of the self-improving computer program is so obviously correct and so obviously influential for future development that once you hear it, you wonder why you didn't think about it before. "The Third Flowering of the Tree of Life" is a real trend breaker.

The two visions of the future presented in the preceding glimpses should help remind us not to get too fixated on our current problems and our current perspectives. It may take somewhat longer than another forty years to get there, but it is very likely that humanity in 2112 will be as dissimilar to us as we are to those who lived in 1912. Those were 1.7 billion individuals living in relatively isolated nations, with white spots on their global map, without electricity, women's rights, and the Internet. Subject to the joint evolutionary push from middle-class living, digital technology, and extensive climate damage, we are likely to see significant change over the next one hundred years—although this is but a blink in the 4.5-billion-year history of the earth.

CHAPTER 12

What Should You Do?

My forecast of global developments to 2052 is actually quite gloomy. Not catastrophic. But in a world that possesses all the tools it needs to redirect itself onto a sustainable path, the future outlook presented here is way below the ambitions and expectations of those few who truly worry about things like how humanity will fare between now and the middle of the twenty-first century.

First, my world of 2052 includes a large number of poor people. So although the world population at the time will be smaller than many now fear, it will still contain much misery. Some three billion people will still live below what I think is a satisfactory material standard of living, suffering inadequate food, housing, health, and security. Some effort will be made to solve the poverty problem over the next forty years, but not enough to remove poverty by 2052.

Second, my forecast also contains negative news for the one billion people who live in what is currently the rich world. For the average citizen of the rich world, the next forty years will be a long era without a real wage increase. Annual consumption per person, measured in inflation-adjusted dollars, will remain stable or even decline—in spite of continued hard work. This is because rich nations will have to use much more of their economic muscle to solve the onrush of modern problems that will hit them over the next forty years. They will have to build cleaner, and more expensive, energy systems; invest in making homes, cars, and factories energy efficient; and defend themselves against the emerging effects of climate change. They will have to repair the damage caused by increasingly extreme weather and perform research and development to find substitutes for scarce and expensive resources.

The list of additional work is very long. And if the rich world wants to keep the world livable in the long run, it will need to carry these costs not only for itself, but also for the poor world. At the very least, the rich world will have to pay for those side effects of poverty that directly affect its own well-being— for example, climate gas emissions from the poor world. The poor won't place first priority on solving a problem that will only hit them hard thirty years down the line. And, on the climate front, I think they are right to refuse to do so: they have the moral high ground, since the rich world actually created the climate problem by emitting most of the 770 billion tonnes of CO_2[1] of man-made pollution that currently sits in the earth's atmosphere.

Once more, I must stress that I do not like my forecast, because it is does not describe an attractive world, given my tastes. I would much rather have been able to forecast a world of increasing consumption that paralleled permanent solutions to the dual challenge of climate change and poverty. But I do not believe this will happen, not even in the rich industrialized world. These countries will not decline into anarchy—but they won't be able to engineer the rapid growth necessary to remove unemployment and inequity. They won't succeed in reviving their economies, not because it is impossible to do so, but because they will prove unable to make the necessary decisions. The industrial world, and particularly the United States, will not really rise to the occasion. True, these nations will do something. Some resources will be shifted away from the economic elite and transferred to the less privileged, but not enough to instill a sense of justice. Some traditional production will be shifted into the green sector, but not enough to keep global warming below plus 2°C. The rich world will move sideways for a generation while being caught up to by China and, to some extent, the big, emerging economies of BRISE. The mental shock will be worst for the Americans, who must get used to not being the global leader.

My forecast tells exactly how much, or how little, I expect the different regions will do. The sum total of the regional effort will not suffice. It will remove much poverty in China and in BRISE, but not in the rest of the world. It will reduce global greenhouse gas emissions, but not in time. As a result, in 2052 much of the world population—and particularly those living outside the relative safety of big cities—will live under conditions made worse by drought, flooding, insect infestations, sea-level rise, biodiversity loss, sporadic vicious storms, and so on.

To make things worse, the very real threat of self-reinforcing climate change in the second half of the twenty-first century will affect everyone, rich or poor, north or south, educated or not. Most likely the richer part of humanity will finally start a crash program to do something about the problem. And perhaps they will be pushed and joined by wise leaders of less democratic regimes further down on the income ladder. But a large part of the population will not be in a position to do anything extraordinary. Their time will be filled with work to make ends meet in their daily struggle for an acceptable life.

So, what to do? This is really two very different questions: What can society do to make my forecast not come true? And how can you live a better life in the world that I forecast? The first question involves societal action at the global level. The second can be handled by you—alone and independent of what others choose to do. Let us take the questions in sequence.

What Global Society Ideally Should Have Done

The first question is the simplest. What can global society do to remove the dual problems of poverty and climate change? As you probably are aware, the answer to these questions is well known, given time and again by several commissions and institutions.

On the poverty side, fifty years of development aid and fifty years of experimentation with different forms of economic organization have taught us that in order to achieve economic growth in the long run, it is essential to provide stable national institutions and education for all, especially women. And it has taught us that it is difficult for outsiders to deliver the solutions; that must be done by the citizens themselves. Outsiders can help by providing training, canceling excessive debt, and allowing imports. Many will argue that the free market is the best way to organize poor economies and position them for growth. Others will point to the recent Chinese experience and argue that the market need not be all that free; one can achieve great results even when capital flows are not governed by profitability. What seems to be essential are orderly, predictable conditions, little corruption, and sufficient investment in the future.

The economic challenge is to get such solutions in place. The last fifty years has taught us that this is easier said than done. The past has also taught us that it is much better if the resources of the developing nation are being used to build the country rather than being shipped off to international owners. And that simple and practical arrangements to reduce poverty—such as predictable income from the state in exchange for work that builds the nation, for a given number of days per year—work well. But that still does not make them simple to adopt in the practical—largely capitalistic and political—world.

So, removing poverty will require continued hard, traditional work for economic development; maximum learning from past experience, but without ideological blinders; and a greater willingness to redistribute income and wealth to the less privileged. Perhaps it would also help to make voters understand, and accept, that this effort won't provide immediate relief. My forecast shows how slow the process is likely to be.

What about your own personal responsibility on this score? As I see it, your only obligation is to provide moral and political support to the venture, to be in favor of knowledge-based efforts to get people out of poverty. Even if it hurts your ideological purity. And even when it requires you to pay more taxes than you would like.

Let me turn then to the problem of emerging climate change. Again the solution is well known. And in this case, not only at the aggregate level, but in fine detail. Anyone who is the least interested knows well what must be done if global warming is to be kept below plus 2°C. The actions have been repeated ad nauseam over the last five years. Global society needs to (*a*) increase energy efficiency; (*b*) shift to renewable energy; (*c*) stop destroying the forests; and (*d*) build carbon capture and storage (CCS) on a number of fossil-fired power and cement plants (those that can't be closed down in time, since society won't build renewable energy fast enough). All of these actions are technically feasible and not particularly expensive. If implemented now, they would lower per capita consumption by a couple of percentage points. And if properly executed, the effort would not reduce employment. People would work on building windmills instead of coal-fired utilities, making electric cars rather than gas guzzlers, forecasting quota prices rather than oil futures, and so on.

Thus, solving the climate problem amounts to a (minor) restructuring of the economy. This can be done without much difficulty—but only if the voters and rulers actually want to do it, which is rarely the case. Restructuring is relatively easy in an economy where investment flows are determined politically. It is much harder in a free market. The problem is that climate-friendly solutions normally are more costly than the cheapest solution, which is to do nothing and continue business as usual. In order to start the restructuring toward a climate-friendly economy, one needs legislation that helps the climate-friendly solutions compete in the marketplace. But in order to pass, such legislation needs a political majority, which rarely exists if the legislation means higher costs in the short term. So the free market is stuck in its old ways. We are unable to agree to do what we know needs to be done.

I am further irritated by the fact that climate-friendly solutions often are not, in fact, more expensive than the alternative. They only seem to be— simply because we do not include some hidden costs of the cheapest, "market" solution. If you use a lower discount rate and a slightly more realistic pricing of external effects of both the dirty and the clean solution, many climate-friendly solutions are competitive at current prices. But the powers that be do not allow for the use of such shadow prices, and hence the clean solutions are deselected. This problem has been identified, and many are working to put a real price on climate gas emissions. But to my great frustration this takes time, and it reveals the intense political opposition in many corners against solutions that involve higher taxes, a stronger government, or both.

And, so, what about your own personal responsibility on this matter? As I see it, your private obligation is to be publicly in favor of getting emissions down: to stress that the climate problem is real, that it requires rapid attention, that it can be solved technically and relatively cheaply, and that you are prepared to pay your part of the bill if a majority agrees to do so. If in addition to this you are willing to demonstrate in your daily life how simple it is to lower the greenhouse gas emissions resulting from your lifestyle, I think you have done more than your fair share. For in this case you will have helped along the political consensus that is necessary to trigger and sustain a strong and systematic move toward a climate-friendly future. But as you know from my forecast, I sadly do not think this mass move will occur until much later, only in the 2030s.

If you are irritated by my high-handed description of the situation, you might want to read a recent and more formal description of what is now the conventional wisdom on what ought to be done to solve the dual challenge of poverty and climate change. For example, there is a laudably clear list of actions in the recent *Resilient People, Resilient Planet* report of the UN secretary general's Special Commission on Sustainability,[2] which is intended as a supplement to, and extension of, the well-established and still somewhat elusive eight UN Millennium Development Goals agreed to by 189 nations in 2000.[3]

Seen from a conventional, rich-world perspective, the saddest aspect of my forecast is probably the fact that there will be no wage rise—and possibly a decline in real disposable income—in the rich world over the next forty years (give or take). This is not a problem for those of us at the top of both the global income and age pyramids. But for most who are younger and poorer, this will seem like an ominous future.

What to do? I think the answer here is to duck the issue and decide on a different success criterion. To accept the fact that consumption will decline and seek to increase well-being in other ways. It is an obvious fact that there is more to life than increased consumption (once you are above a minimum threshold that the average citizen in the rich world surpassed a generation ago). If we all got together and collectively espoused that well-being, not material gain, is the appropriate goal, then that goal would gain acceptance. I do, of course, get the point that more income tends to increase well-being, at all income levels, and that more income is the only thing that matters at low-income levels. But at the average income level of the rich world, it is fully possible to start a new process of increasing subjective well-being—within the constraints of stable consumption—rather than continue the one-eyed strife for higher pay.

So instead of celebrating New Year's Eve 2052 with the sad realization that your take-home pay the year before, when adjusted for inflation, was actually not much higher than that of your grandfather when he started collecting his pension in 2022, you should celebrate the fact that your life satisfaction (as measured by the well-developed instruments run on a monthly basis by the Global Bureau of Statistics since 2030) will show that your satisfaction level has in fact gone up by 1% or so every year since measurements started—in spite of your stagnant income.

When it comes to the development of new success measures, your personal obligation, as I see it, is to push the idea of the need for a reorientation toward new goals for society. Remind yourself and all around you that money isn't everything. Use any occasion to celebrate practical proof that this is true. Tell everyone that time is of the essence, that we need the new measures of success now! Remind them that it took a full thirty years from when the concept of the GDP—the current success measure—was invented in the 1930s until the GDP became regularly used by politicians for policy guidance in the 1960s. Thirty years is what it took for society to evolve practical measures of GDP in the 1940s, to build the institutional framework for regular measurement of GDP in the 1950s, and to achieve routine reporting of GDP and GDP change at the national level. Your private obligation is to help industrial society complete the process toward monthly measures of national well-being in much less than thirty years.

So there is more than enough for you, and others, to do to accelerate the global effort to end poverty, fight global warming, and create a new focus for social development. If something extraordinary happens—and I hope it will—then we can achieve a better future than the one I have forecasted.

Twenty Pieces of Personal Advice

Should you work to avoid the likely future forecast in this book or prepare for it? The answer is both. Work hard to change the future, but also start now to identify changes that will improve your personal well-being in a future world that does not get its act together and allows itself to live with a solid dose of poverty and an increasing element of climate change.

On this score, I have some advice: things that you can do as an individual who would like to live well, even in a situation where the political majority makes decisions that will make the world less attractive than it could otherwise have been. Much of this advice applies best to people like myself, now living in the comforts of the rich world, although it does not take much talent to disregard what is irrelevant and adapt the remaining to your own personal situation. For those caught in poverty, my advice is the same as it was forty years ago: work diligently and collectively for an equitable, productive, and well-organized society. This may involve breaking some distributional inequities/traditions/eggs in the short term.

Morally speaking, some of my advice is dubious, in the sense that if everyone did as I say, everyone would be worse off. But few listened to what I said during all the years I fought for sustainability, so I don't expect a mass stampede to follow in my footsteps now. Since the future, as I see it, is a creation of the majority view (except in the few remaining cases of autocracy—one of which, China, will be wildly successful), the majority will disagree not only with my advice but even with the backdrop that makes it rational.

That said, on to my twenty pieces of advice.

1. Focus on Satisfaction Rather Than Income

Remember that satisfaction is your core goal. Ask yourself what really makes you happy. What really makes you satisfied? What situation would you really like to be in? In other words, what would you like to happen during the next forty years? Or if you won't live that long, what would you like to be able to tell yourself when you are dying?

The answers to these questions are simple for those of you who genuinely and solely would like to make as much money as possible. Making money is a simple and practical goal and can help build life satisfaction. But giving it priority status assumes that you really do have financial advancement as your one and only goal. It gets more difficult if it matters how you made your money; or that your spouse left you in the process; or that your children or friends do not admire your goal; and so on.

When most alleged income maximizers refine their goal through such questioning (in private), the goal normally gets modified in the direction of making money subject to a number of constraints. For example, not in the cluster-bomb business and not after the third spouse said she or he was leaving because you were always in the office (or rather, on the smartphone). After much deep thinking, most balanced individuals conclude that their life goal is already quite complex and could be paraphrased to something like "maximizing life satisfaction—subject to the constraint that income keeps above a certain threshold."

Understanding that income is only part of the answer is a huge step in the right direction. It makes one aware of the fact that it is possible to increase one's well-being even if one cannot increase one's income. I agree this is more difficult if all your friends and neighbors judge you according to income. But it is not impossible. And many are already there, choosing careers that do not maximize income but provide other satisfactions. Just have a look in government, academia, and nongovernmental organizations. Many of their employees have effectively chosen my goal for life in postindustrial society:

"Satisfaction is working for something you believe in, with a certain degree of success." This means, among others things, that once you reach a goal, you must immediately establish a new one.

2. Do Not Acquire a Taste for Things That Will Disappear

It is an empirical fact that people end up liking to do what they have always done. People who have always played cards like to play cards. People who have always skied like to ski. The good thing is that this also works in reverse: if you would like to play cards when you are old, you can reach this goal by starting to play cards when you are young, and keep at it. It even works on much less attractive matters: if you want to jog as you age, nothing beats starting to jog when you're younger. After a decade or so you will see that your body craves the kick it gets from jogging.

So what does this have to do with the global future? You are capable of influencing your own future tastes, and so you should try to gear them toward what will fit the future. As you have seen from my forecast, future life will be very different from past life. If you do not take action, your preferences will be formed by your past life. As a result you may find the future disagreeable

Let me take an example. The future will be urban, dense, and crowded. Life there will be very different from life in the model cities of UK in the 1950s or the vast open tracts of a Californian suburb. The home for most will be an apartment in an urban tower in a megacity. And my simple point is that the apartment dweller will be happier if she prefers apartment living, which she is likely to prefer if she has always lived in an apartment. Thus my advice is: don't develop a taste for life in suburbia. Remind yourself about the lawns that need to be mowed, the insects that abound, the roofs that must be fixed, the gutters that clog, and the long boring commute to the city, the bar, and the shopping center. Learn to like your apartment better than any other home.

3. Invest in Great Electronic Entertainment and Learn to Prefer It

You don't need to be a visionary to see that electronic entertainment—entering your home via cable or wireless—will evolve spectacularly in the decades ahead. Already you can travel, via your TV or computer, to places formerly restricted to the intrepid explorer.

And you can experience things that happened long ago. Your experience with the sights and sounds of Egyptian pharaohs or the battle of Normandy comes from the screen. The same likely goes for your knowledge about climbing Mount Everest. As does mine. In most cases these digital experiences are already so lively that they substitute well for the real thing. They are much better than the descriptions early man chipped into stone or painted on grotto walls. They are more emotionally gripping than the stories written by hard-working monks on parchment some hundred years after the real thing happened.

And the electronic rendition will get even better as technology advances. There is little reason to doubt that the images will become three-dimensional; perhaps even smell will be added to the experience. Multimedia shows will be available everywhere, although you probably still will prefer to enjoy them from your home, along with someone. People are fundamentally social.

Another important development is the fact that the electronic content increasingly is not real but virtual—like the world of Harry Potter or most of the games played by computer aficionados. Virtual worlds will increasingly compete with the real world for our attention.

One may well ask whether anyone in the future will take the pain of a long plane trip in order to stand in the burning sun to see the real thing between the heads of a bunch of other tourists, when an ever fuller experience of the sightseeing spot can be had at the touch of your fingertip in your home edutainment center. I think the answer will be increasingly no. Except for the once-in-a-lifetime travel experience of, for example, seeing rare animals. But since this requires endless waiting in unpleasant positions at the break of day, some will opt to do this more simply, and cheaply, from the couch. This trend away from the real toward the virtual will be further helped by the fact that the ecological footprint of virtual trips is so much smaller. I agree that there will be many more people visiting sometimes rare and fragile places. There will also be an increased power requirement by the billions of home entertainment centers, upping the burden on the ecosystem. But the footprint of virtual tourism will be lower than if everyone traveled, and it leaves the animals in peace.

Current-day videoconferencing has already reduced business travel, and that trend will continue. And, with your mother in the room electronically in three dimensions and with smell, how often will you travel to see her? Both she and you should learn to like virtual communications.

Finally, it is interesting to note that the fascination with the real thing appears to be an acquired taste. I don't like electronic communications very much; I still prefer physical meetings. But I understand that this is a matter of taste. As you know, I believe tastes can be changed. And the taste in the preferred means of communication is already changing. Our children happily chat electronically via text and images on social media. They choose this channel over the telephone call that I prefer, but which in turn would have been perceived as a disrespectful gesture by my grandfather, who expected people to come by when they had something important to communicate.

So my advice is for you to go forth and buy the hardware and software you need for a great virtual night at home. After daily use for a decade you will like it much better. And while you are actively changing your tastes, virtual offerings will evolve beyond your wildest dreams.

4. Don't Teach Your Children to Love the Wilderness

Values are taught: transferred from parents to children under the helpful/ unhelpful influence of the society in which the upbringing takes place. So values are not a given. They change, much like your tastes. In the real world parents use much energy to get their children to value the local environment, the local religion, the local form of government, the local entertainment—be it bullfighting, cricket, gambling, or folk dance. If they can, parents try to teach their children to speak the local language, so they will fit in better and have a simpler life. In sum, this amounts to the traditional tendency of parents to perpetuate the local culture.

Such transfer of values is beneficial—in the sense that it teaches the children to enjoy the environment in which they live—but only if society evolves gradually. If society or its surroundings change too fast, the advice of the elderly becomes irrelevant. And in unlucky circumstances the careful inculcation of past values may cause incurable unhappiness.

An interesting example arises from the fact that humanity is in the process of eliminating wild nature from the surface of the planet. It hasn't gone all the way yet, but the amount of global land that is less than 10 kilometers away from the nearest village, highway, power line, or infrastructure development is going down—very fast. Even rarer is the good-looking wilderness spot not visited by a steady flow of people. As a result those people (like myself) who have been taught by parents to love the wilderness have fewer and fewer places to go, farther and farther away. These unlucky people are only deeply satisfied when there is no one else around so they can sense the silent presence of age-old undisturbed nature. This love of untouched nature is largely an acquired taste, along with our other preferences, although probably facilitated by our genetic disposition, since we evolved in the deep undisturbed forest.

So when you see your child sitting in front of the computer and think that she should rather be by the campfire in the great outdoors, you should constrain your temptation to interfere. By teaching your child to love the loneliness of the untouched wilderness, you are teaching her to love what will be increasingly difficult to find. And you will be increasing the chance of her being unhappy—because she won't be able to find what she desires in the future world of eight billion people and a GDP twice that of today. Much better then to rear a new generation that find peace, calm, and satisfaction in the bustling life of the megacity—and with never-ending music piped into their ears.

5. If You Like Great Biodiversity, Go See It Now

The human ecological footprint is growing. We already need 1.4 planets to produce the flow of ecological services that we consume, and by 2052 we will need a lot more. And as long as we use more than is produced, the global stocks are being worn down. On a per capita basis there is now only one-half of the unused land we had in 1970, and by 2050 it will be halved again. In seventy years we will lose three-quarters of all free space.

This fall in unused bio-capacity translates into a fall in the area of uncultivated arable land, uncut productive forests, unfished upwelling areas, ungrazed hillsides, unused turtle beaches, unregulated waterfalls, and undisturbed coral reefs. This tragic destruction of things natural will continue over the next forty years. There will of course be the continued effort to protect some of the pearls, the hot spots of biodiversity—the east African savannah, the very old tropical forests of Cameroon, the hilly, biodiverse expanses in the heart of Borneo, the colorful corals of the Great Barrier Reef, the rare fauna of the Galapagos, and so on—but climate change is beginning to take its toll even within the boundaries of nature parks. Coral reefs will increasingly bleach and lose their splendor as the ocean warms. Boreal forests will be damaged by bark beetles because winter will no longer be cold enough to kill them. Climate change will take its toll irrespective of whether the ecosystem is inside a park or not.

So, if you would like to see great biodiversity in the flesh, do it now. If you have already heeded my advice in number 2, above, and prefer electronic tourism, you can relax. Most great biodiversity has already been recorded electronically—and in detail. Future audiences will still be able to experience beautiful biodiversity after the original is gone. But the real firsthand experience of the staggering beauty and intrinsic harmony of undisturbed biodiversity is something different. See it now; soon it will be too late.

The fact that people who never experienced raw nature during their formative years find nature a little creepy and scary will reduce the number of people who take me up on my advice. That is good, because it will help reduce tourist pressure on fragile biodiversity and give you more time to follow number 6 on my advice list.

6. Visit World Attractions before They Are Ruined by the Crowd

The cultural diversity of the human race is disappearing even faster than the biological diversity, it seems. The decline is driven by what is called globalization, but it is in essence an explosion in the intensity of communications over the last fifty years or so. The homogenization, the leveling of cultural differences, was greatly helped by the advent of TV (making California beach life a visible dream in poor villages all over the globe) and more recently by the Internet (making absolutely everything visible more or less everywhere). As a consequence, much is becoming boringly similar across most of the traveled globe.

Despite this decline, there are still a great number of spots worth visiting for the one who likes to engulf herself in the variety of different lifestyles and local adaptations that still exist. Many of the real gems are gone, but some of the past cultures survive as museums. The Winter Palace, Versailles, and the Forbidden City are thought-provoking monuments to the incredible inequity that existed on Earth for millennia, and actually quite recently. They are all worth a visit. The problem here and in other pearls like the pyramids and Angkor Wat is the sheer number of tourists. Even today you must book months ahead if you want to see the artistic wonders of Florence without queuing. And if you think that is bad, wait until the Chinese middle class passes 500 million people. Then China will generate as many world travelers as the United States and Japan taken together. This will happen within decades. Some culture may be left, but it will be increasingly inaccessible because of the long lines. Unless one starts making copies—like the Disney Corporation did when the original Disneyland became too crowded.

In addition to the threat from crowding, there is the threat of increasing social unrest. A number of sightseeing spots will become unsafe because of local unrest. Or they may simply disappear—like the giant statues in Afghanistan that were bombed during their war—or become out of bounds—like the stone city of Petra that became inaccessible during the Syrian revolt.

All of this will continue: more homogenization, longer lines, and more social unrest in countries under bad management. My conclusion? Go while you can still get there. Don't let scalable obstacles—like the threat of terrorism, the need for early booking, or unpleasant coach-class seats—stop you. In 2052 it will be too late. By then the cultural world will be even flatter and the museums even fuller.

7. Live in a Place That Is Not Overly Exposed to Climate Change

Although science does not yet know exactly how the weather will change at the local level, the general picture is well known. The computer models of the Hadley Centre in the UK have already produced accessible weather forecasts at the national level for a decade.[4] They provide estimates of how the climate of your home country will be in 2050. So, if you are choosing where it is best to settle, the Hadley models can tell you how much warmer a given spot is likely to be, how much more or less it will rain there, and how high the storm surge will be along your coast. They can do so for the different seasons of the year.

The uncertainty in the estimates is big, but not so big that you cannot get a good idea of the general tendencies—if you want to. For us Norwegians it is helpful to know that it will rain more along our western coast; this will top off our reservoirs and increase the production of cheap hydropower. And that our Middle Ages cultural relics in the harbor town of Bergen are likely to be under a foot of water several days of the year, which signals a need to lift the buildings, or to protect them with dikes. And that the temperature increase in southeast Norway makes it inadvisable to buy skiing cabins below 400 meters above sea level.

The general advice is there if you want it. And if you need more detailed guidance at the local level, you could do worse than asking a local outdoorsman or farmer what he thinks is happening. You will choose best by using a mixture of computer-model forecasts and local advice. But I do recognize that this input will be but an addition to all the normal considerations of family, job, friends, cost, language, culture, and so on—which may make it unlikely that you move at all.

We already know that the sea level will rise by an additional foot by 2052. This alone tells you a lot about where you should not live (and also about which homes should be sold before everyone discovers the sad fact that they will be underwater—or will have fallen off the cliff). We know already which areas are destined to become warmer, and perhaps too hot to be livable during the warm season. Although global warming is a gradual process and it will take a long time before the heat in your hometown becomes excessive, I do suggest that if you do move, you avoid areas that border anything that is already too hot or too dry.

Another important consideration will be the future of any big river in the neighborhood. Living in the traditional flood zone will become a risky sport, particularly along rivers that come from glaciers that will melt and rivers that pass through forests that will be clear-cut. Both increase the chance of seasonal floods. Finally, it is not a good idea to locate just below mountains that are currently frozen and will give off landslides when the permafrost lifts two hundred vertical meters by 2052.

The art is to find a place where you are unlikely to be bothered by the new weather—including stronger winds, more torrential rains, more frequent drought, landslides—not to mention forest fires. Then make your choice. Hopefully you can find a suitable place inside your culture, that is, without moving too far. That may be difficult for some: the most obvious examples are the populations of low-lying islands in the Pacific, or Himalayan villagers depending on glacier melt for their summer crop.

Remember also that being protected against climate change does not only mean being defended against the direct physical change. It also means being protected against the indirect consequences of climate change, like the flow of climate refugees, the disappearance of protein imports from distant fisheries, or legislation that will ban livelihoods based on dynamite fishing in coral reefs or the harvest of tropical timber.

8. Move to a Country That Is Capable of Decision Making

A rational, fact-based, and forward-looking decision on where to live is not a simple matter. There are a large number of unknowns—both known and unknown. This is the basis for my eighth piece of advice: you should settle in a country that is capable of discovering problems when they arise and doing something about them.

The economic muscle of most industrialized and emerging economies is huge. So huge that if the decision was made to use it, the muscle would solve most problems. If one can manage to agree, one can throw enough labor and capital at any problem to make it go away. The exceptions are problems that cannot be solved in principle—like cost-free energy—or problems that have proved unsolvable for generations—like harmony between two religions with a missionary zeal. Luckily most of the obstacles between us and an attractive world are not of this nature. They are obstacles that can be removed, where there is a potential solution at hand. The real challenge is the widespread inability to agree to use the economic muscle to implement the solution.

For example, in the case of climate change, it would take no more than a tax increase of a few percentage points to bring in enough money to solve the climate problem within a generation. So the solution exists, but most societies seem unable to decide to use it, because they lack broad political support for short-term sacrifice and face fierce opposition from narrow interest groups that stand to lose a privilege.

In spite of this, democracy and the free market have solved a number of complex problems over the last couple of generations. But going forward, society will be facing problems that are not easily solved by these well-tested means. Global warming is a prime example, where more centralist actions seem necessary to achieve results. National governments can do much to defend against future climate damage: build dikes, move cities, strengthen buildings, shift roads, establish better storm sewers, build bigger reservoirs, and so on. If they can reach agreement and take action, the national government is capable of creating a much safer homeland, to use the US expression. And not only through tighter border controls and reduction of the rush of climate refugees, but through physical changes on the ground.

But such initiatives cost, and in the end it is the population that foots the bill, either in the form of higher prices for climate-friendly goods and services or through higher taxes. And here lies the problem, for as long as there appear to be cheaper ways out, both democracies and free markets tend to choose that cheaper route. Both are short term. Both are more than willing to disregard long-term costs. Both are strongly motivated by immediate savings. As a result wise action tends to be postponed. Action is achieved only after crisis has struck, not in preparation for future shock. It is simpler to reach agreement on the need to build higher levees after the water has broken through than when high water still remains a theoretical possibility.

So, I advise you choose as your new homeland a country that is capable of acting proactively in the decades ahead. This means a country that is capable of convincing its population to choose the narrow path. Or to be blunt, a country that does not rely solely on democracy and free markets. China certainly has the ability to act in a farsighted manner. The current capability of the United States is more questionable. But other examples exist. Germany has been able through democratic means to put in place a very expensive system of renewable energy long before its ample coal and steady imports of gas from three competing suppliers (Norway, Russia, and Algeria) ran out. The German parliament even managed to force the German consumer to pay the bill, through higher price for electricity.

When I tell you that central Europe is one of the places that is likely to be least influenced by climate change and mostly placed high above sea level, you might start to see one potential candidate in response to advice in numbers 7 and 8. But the weather is overcast, and the river Rhine may become even less useful for industrial cooling. And many others have the same goal for their migration.

9. Know the Unsustainabilities That Threaten Your Quality of Life

Once you have decided where to live (and my suspicion is that you have decided to remain where you already live, since we are all heavily influenced by tradition), I suggest that you proceed to map what kind of problems your location is going to face over the next decade or two—both physical threats (erratic weather, migration flows, brownouts) and nonmaterial threats (higher taxes, new legislation, cultural decline). Use my forecast as a guide to what will happen.

You may find it taxing to establish the list, requiring creativity and quite a bit of independent thinking. One help could be to ask friends and neighbors what they think will happen over the next ten years that would negatively influence local attractions and amenities. When foreigners ask me whether they should move to Oslo, I respond that this may well be a good idea, but that they must remember that the snow that formed the basis of high-quality winter living in the past will be replaced with slush. And that Norwegians live well with tax rates that surpass by a strong margin the worst nightmares of a Tea Party supporter in the United States.

Another procedure could be to start from a list of what you value (job in a certain sector, short commute, good schools, safe environment, available health care) and then ask about each of the elements: Given current trends, how long will this service/amenity survive? Will it last for five or fifteen years? Let me take an example. Assume that you put on your list that your well-being relies (at least partly) on a low pension age. In that case I suggest that you seriously consider moving away from all aging industrial countries of the world. There is only one effective, obvious, and easy-to-pass solution to the problem of the swelling number of old people (including me) in the rich countries, and that is to increase the pension age. When you know that these countries are democracies and that the vast majority of the voters are below pension age, you need not be a visionary to understand that the higher pension age will force its way to the surface. I agree it is hard to tell the exact timing. And you may choose to solve your desire for early pensioning by means other than moving. But if you want to retire on your own savings, be sure to place your money where it won't be lost when the climate worsens and tensions rise.

When you have finalized this list of future threats to your well-being, it has two obvious uses. It can be used for adaptation—moving outside the ageing OECD countries or establishing your own "climate-safe" pension fund, in order to protect yourself against a higher pension age. But second, the list can be used to modernize the upbringing of your children, so they are better adapted to their future life. In other words, if the annual snow is likely to disappear, teach your children to love golf. Or if you suspect that golf courses may become too crowded, suggest indoor martial arts.

10. If You Can't Stand a Job in Services or Care, Go into Energy Efficiency or Renewables

Once you have decided where to live and what threats you are likely to encounter there, it may be time to think about your future career. Or if you are beyond that stage, to think about what you should advise your children or grandchildren to do, when they grow up. My forecast does not provide details concerning future employment opportunities, but it does give some guidance.

First, some general advice. Get an education. It guarantees you a more interesting life and ensures greater choice. What you study does not matter much, so you may as well choose a topic that interests you. If that degree does not land you a job, it is simpler to change to a new topic than to start from scratch. Being both uneducated and unemployed is worse than being unemployed.

The economy will grow in the decades ahead, and so will the number of employed people. The rate of growth will be much higher in China and BRISE than in the OECD, which will make it simpler to find a job in the former. These less mature economies also sport the advantage that their industry sectors are still expanding, increasing the chance of landing a job in manufacturing.

But in the mature economies, both the primary (agriculture, forestry, and fishery) and the secondary (manufacturing) sectors will be declining. The significant job-growth opportunities will be in the tertiary sector (that is, in services and care). If you like a job in an office—this means in finance, retailing, education, health, or the care of old or young—the future is for you. If you are not among those who like work in front of a computer or with the needy and really would like to do something with your hands, energy efficiency and renewables will be attractive. As will of course be construction, particularly in adaptation and repair of climate damage.

The sector composition of national accounting reports gives the value added in the different sectors of the economy. By following them over time, you can see what is growing and what is not. A big sector has many jobs, and a growing sector has many new openings every year. Studying the accounts will remind you that many small and declining sectors also exist and could provide exotic opportunities for the risk lover.

Finally, if you remain unemployed, remember to fight for your rights. Lasting unemployment is a distributional issue. It can always be solved by changing national policy. The simplest technique is to tax the rich and use the money to create public employment. Needless to say, this will be opposed by the majority. A slightly more realistic approach is to devalue the national currency, which after a while will result in more export jobs. But devaluation will be vehemently opposed by those who don't want to pay higher prices for their imported goods and vacations overseas, and by the moneyed classes who worry that their savings will be eroded by inflation. Alternatively, the government can print money and use it to pay you for doing a job that needs to get done (like cleaning the streets or teaching children or caring for the elderly or building highways). This will benefit you and all those who benefit from the new spending. But again it will be opposed by the majority, for whom such policy is simply another way of eroding the purchasing power of their "hard-earned" wages.

If the unemployed do not put up a valiant fight for their right to a decent job—and I really mean in the form of a threatening physical presence if that is what it takes—no one else will.

So the future is no longer "plastics," as once was declared in the 1967 film *The Graduate.* The future is service and care, energy efficiency and renewable energy, and adaptation and repair, and if nothing helps—in intelligent and active protest.

11. Encourage Your Children to Learn Mandarin

This is simple advice for the more than 1.5 billion people who already know this Chinese language. It is much harder for the rest of us, who have been raised to learn that English is the preferred lingua franca—the one language that gives most international access to other people and foreign jobs. English may retain this leadership position, since (basic) English is such a simple language to learn and is already spoken (more or less) by one billion of the global population. But there is nothing like having direct access to the future hegemon—to its people, its corporations, and its culture.

And exactly because it is so difficult to learn Mandarin Chinese, the few who take the pain to do so will be in a preferential situation, especially in the job market. So if you are worried about your future income security and are in a situation where your children are sufficiently disposed to take some responsibility for your pension income, you should certainly try to convince them to learn Mandarin. Later this will most likely get them a job that will surf on the rapidly expanding wave of Chinese activity on Earth.

My similar advice to those speaking only Chinese is of course to learn English, in order to be able to communicate better with that majority of the world's population who will never make the effort to learn Mandarin. Good communications accelerate relationship building (*guanxi* in Chinese) even better than a good meal.

12. Stop Believing That All Growth Is Good

Let me now move on from physical satisfaction to more intangible values, still with the ambition of pointing you in directions that will increase your future well-being in a world that will make many wrong choices in the decades to come.

You are probably like me and most other humans. You are happy when something you believe in comes true. And like most, you think—even feel in your guts—that "growth is good." You unthinkingly consider growth as an advantage—better than stagnation, and certainly superior to no growth.

This tacit belief will give you subconscious satisfaction when things grow—when you read in the paper that GDP is up, employment is rising, trade is expanding—and give you discomfort when you learn that the population of Japan is going down, that sales of cheese are declining, and the number of new-car registrations is 7% less than last year. Like most, you intuitively feel that something is wrong if things decline. The slogan "growth is life"—proclaimed by the marketers of the growth paradigm—captures this emotion.

But here I fear your gut feelings will lead to unnecessary unhappiness. If you want to stay happy during the next forty years, I recommend that you refine and revise your thinking about growth. In the decades ahead, a number of things are going to decline. In some cases this decline will represent the fundamental solution to an underlying problem and should be celebrated, not grieved. In some cases continued growth will be disastrous, and certainly not the solution. So you need to teach yourself, and your heart, to distinguish between good growth and bad growth. And to celebrate with equal enthusiasm both good growth and good decline.

It is not surprising that we automatically assume that "growth is good." This results from our recent history and the endless barrage of pro-growth messages that hit us daily from all types of media. Furthermore, economic growth has indeed solved many problems over the last half century. It has helped increase income, helped remove poverty, created many new jobs, and given room for more public services. At the same time the restructuring that is a central element in economic growth has caused problems for many workers by making them superfluous and requiring them to move or retrain.

But in the future growth won't be generally good. One will need to be more discerning, and—interestingly—this process has already begun. Many are already skeptical about further growth in greenhouse gas emissions and were pleased in 2010 to read that the emissions of EU-27 fell by 7% from 2008 to 2009. And you shouldn't be surprised if you soon belong to the group who celebrates decline in national energy consumption because you have come to realize that what is important is to increase the standard of living, not to increase the annual energy use. A nation can increase its standard of living (read: achieve more pleasant indoor temperatures) by insulating its homes. It need not increase its use of electricity. For most of us managed decline in national energy use is an advantage—because it does not condemn us to an unpleasant indoor climate. The exception is the tiny minority working in the electricity business—but in a perfect world, they would get into the efficiency business.

Equally, unending population growth is not good on a finite planet. The Chinese elite understood this one generation ago and put in place policies that ensure that each Chinese will have a little more space, and a little more agricultural land, in 2052. Clearly, if China had been infinitely large, it would have been better to let people choose freely how many children they would like to have. But China is small compared to its population, and even though the forward-looking policies were put in place in the 1980s, China will depend on imports of food for the next several decades. That may be good for the pushers of free trade, but it is not according to the values of ancient China that placed independence as a central goal. For traditional China it is an unnecessary risk to rely on African agricultural land to feed its population. Better then to reduce the demand. Thus for China population growth is bad, and has been so for nearly forty years. Signals of slow growth or stagnation are received with content, and population decline will be celebrated when it occurs (possibly as soon as the early 2020s).

Parenthetically, it is a historical irony that the rapid urbanization that follows automatically from rapid economic growth also leads to a dramatic and voluntary decline in fertility—to such an extent that the mandatory one-child policy might actually one day be canceled without this leading to renewed population growth, simply because there is no desire for more children. The irony rests in the fact that the popular free will thus will prove to lag public policy by a generation or so. It is true, of course, that population decline will lead to challenges (the need to raise the pension age, and the need to have many more work in elderly care than in kindergartens). But these challenges are solvable, and the challenge is often smaller than expected, as shown by the slow rise in the variable called "support burden" in my forecast on page 65.

In sum, you need to replace the growth-is-good mantra with some hard thinking—not just to appear reasonably intelligent and well informed, but also to remain happy when central societal variables start to decline in the decades ahead.

This particularly applies to the coming peak and decline in national GDP, first in some rich industrial countries (led by Japan) and later in the whole world, in the second half of the twenty-first century, when the global population will be declining and productivity has reached its maximum. At that time it will be important to understand what is going on, reminding yourself that what matters is well-being and that well-being is more closely connected to growth in the GDP *per person* than to growth in the GDP.

So from now on, remind yourself that you are in favor of growth in A, B, and C and in favor of decline in D, E, and F. Celebrate growth and decline with equal fervor.

13. Remember That Your Fossil-Based Assets— Suddenly One Day—Will Lose Their Value

There is one important practical consequence of my twelfth piece of advice— which recommended a more nuanced perspective on growth. It follows from the fact that many things will not grow forever. Among them are the share prices in companies that produce and sell fossil-based energy. As shown by my forecast, global energy use will reach a peak around 2040 and decline thereafter—because of steady increase in energy efficiency and accelerating population decline. The use of fossil fuels will peak much earlier, as renewables gradually increase their market share.

This phenomenon is far out in time, especially as seen by the short-term analysts in the financial markets—for whom next year is inconceivably long into the future. These analysts still price shares in fossil-energy companies according to reserves: the higher the reserves of coal, oil, and gas the company controls, the higher the share value. They do not yet consider the fact that all energy companies taken together already have reserves that exceed by many times the amount of fossils that can be burned without heating the world way beyond plus 2°C, or what will be burned before 2052.

I agree with the analysts that it will take time before this realization dawns on the investors and causes a sudden drop in the valuations of energy companies. But that does not mean that the drop will never come. Sooner or later the share price of energy companies will reflect the fact that much of their projected future income from selling coal, oil, and gas will never materialize— either because humanity actively decides to phase out fossils or, more likely, because the gradual effort to increase efficiency and develop renewables will lead to peak and decline in the global use of fossils.

Isn't this irrelevant for someone who is going to use income from energy shares during the next decade? I am not so sure. It was interesting to note how quickly the share values of the German energy companies fell when Germany decided in 2011 to phase out nuclear energy by 2020. The anticipated positive cash flow from nuclear power was replaced overnight with a future cost stream associated with decommissioning the nuclear plants. It all happened well before the analysts had time to redo their spreadsheets and warn their customers.

It may be wise to de-emphaisize the fossil share in your pension fund. This may at least buy some additional peace of mind.

14. Invest in Things That Are Not Sensitive to Social Unrest

Since we are on the topic of safe havens for your pension fund, I want to add another piece of advice: do not invest in companies that will be negatively affected by the coming wave of social unrest. This piece of advice is really not very helpful, I am afraid, since I am unable to tell you exactly when and where tensions will build and explode into events that reduce the cash flow of your pet investments.

All I can say, as you have seen from my forecast, is that tensions will rise during the next several decades, because of mounting inequities in capitalist economies, because of the uneven distribution of scarce resources, and because of climate effects. In addition will come the unemployment effect of slower growth in productivity as economies mature.

I repeat that it is hard to say where this will come to a head. But I am sure it will help to be aware of the phenomenon, ahead of time, and at least consider the chance for, and possible impact of, social unrest before placing your bets.

15. Do More Than Your Fair Share—to Avoid a Bad Conscience in the Future

Once you have settled into your new climate-safe and well-governed location and invested your pension fund in companies that are likely to do well in the future, you should return to the question of your future mental well-being.

Your first priority should be to prepare the foundations for an unassailable answer to the question, "What did you do, (grand)father, when greenhouse gas emissions were allowed to grow out of control in the early 2000s?" You will need an answer that satisfies not just your (grand)children, but also all those who did not heed my advice and got trapped outside your safe haven and are now knocking on your door in order to be let in.

The answer is luckily very simple. All you have to do is to spend time— ideally in public, but at least at your personal, household, and community level—promoting sane perspective, policy, and practice. That means arguing in favor of the reality of the dual challenge of poverty and climate change, and obvious cooperative solutions that I described earlier in this chapter. Regretfully you must to do so in spite of the overwhelming opposition you will meet from short-term voters, politicians, and owners. It may be wise to leave a printed track, so it will remain beyond doubt that you actually did your fair share.

At the company level I have written elsewhere[5] about exactly what it means for a corporation to do its fair share in the effort to alleviate poverty and stabilize the climate. The answer is, briefly, that the company should keep growing but simultaneously reduce its "greenhouse gas emissions per unit of value added" by at least 5% per year. Value added is the company's contribution to GDP. Translated to the household, which does not contribute to the GDP according to the conventional national accounts, this means to cut greenhouse gas emissions by 1.7% per year. This goal can easily be achieved for the period to 2020 by insulating your home, shifting to a fuel-efficient car, and halving your air travel by making one two-week vacation trip per year rather than two one-week trips.

Once more, leave a written record—it is fun to measure the year-by-year reduction in one's climate impact, and the protocol may prove helpful in future disputes.

16. In Business, Explore the Business Potential in Current Unsustainabilities

Let me then turn now from personal to corporate advice on how to use my forecast for fun and profit.

My first advice would be to ask the corporation to repeat at the corporate level what I asked you to do at your personal level in my ninth piece of advice: get to know the factors that threaten the corporate profit stream—what I call the most urgent unsustainabilities on the corporate radar. This amounts to identifying the first things that will go seriously wrong if business is continued according to current corporate strategy—and the world evolves according to my forecast. I repeat that this process requires creativity and will benefit from outside views, for example, from your most aggressive critics in civil society. In all their unreasonable idealism, they probably see much more clearly what parts of your current corporate behavior will end up making negative headlines in the tabloids or on the Internet.

Once you know what wall you will hit first, you also know what problems most urgently need a solution. Sometimes a problem will be easy to solve, like when the fertilizer industry learned it could eliminate its huge N_2O emissions from its plants at essentially no cost, using the new Yara catalyst to do so.

More frequently the solution is hopelessly unprofitable. But then you know what to lobby for; namely, for those changes in taxes and regulations that will make your solution profitable. A great role model here is Philips, the lightbulb producer, who managed a profitable transition from producing cheap, old-fashioned, and energy-intensive lightbulbs to producing much more expensive low-watt bulbs. Philips did so by cooperating with civil society to achieve the suitable bans of the old stuff in the EU. The bans opened the way for high-volume sales of the new stuff and a rapid move down the learning curve for production costs. As a result much energy was, and is being, saved at reasonable cost.

A final option when you see one wall approaching is to be so unethical as to sell off the subsidiary to a buyer who has not yet seen the light—or more likely does not want to see the light—for ideological reasons.

17. In Business, Don't Confuse Growth in Volume with Growth in Profits

As you see from my forecast, the world is facing a period of tremendous change, not only in the geography of markets, but also in the energy system and in the products we use. The business landscape will shift accordingly. The art, from a business point of view, is to choose a winning horse, and the knee-jerk reaction is to look for markets that are growing fast, under the assumption that rapid growth will guarantee high profits. This is not necessarily so. Let me explain why.

Two sectors that are already showing rapid growth are windmills and photovoltaics. In the future we are likely to see similar growth in chargeable hybrid cars (cars that run the first 30–50 kilometers on an electric charge obtained in the garage during the night, and then use a conventional gasoline engine to fuel the rest of the trip). As I see it, windmills and photovoltaics are likely to be elements of the ultimate solution, while the chargeable hybrid car will prove to be a transition technology, on the way toward the future car that will run fully on electricity or hydrogen from CO_2-free power plants. My point here, however, is that although windmills, photovoltaics, and chargeable cars will represent fast-growing markets, none will guarantee a profit.

To see why, consider the underlying dynamics. Profits arise when there is a gap between the sales price and the cost of production using available technology. If such a gap exists, it signals a business opportunity and attracts investors. This is fine as long as the number of entrants is reasonable. But if the gap is big, the attraction is strong. As a result too many investors will pile into the profitable sector. The result will soon be excess capacity, downward pressure on prices, and low profitability. The result will also be rapid growth in capacity and sales. So we see how rapid growth does not necessarily go along with high profits.

The situation can be particularly bad for the early entrants, because the later entrants normally learn from the experience of the pioneers and achieve lower costs. Also the later entrants have the advantage of knowing that the market does indeed exist and roughly at what scale—the pioneers did indeed demonstrate this. Therefore the late entrants can enter at large scale, utilizing the economies of scale in production, and squeeze out the pioneers. Learning curves help lower costs and boost profitability, but the underlying knowledge is often available to both incumbent and newcomer alike.

My conclusion is not at all new. It is well known to most experienced investors. It is indeed hard to make money, even after one has found a potentially profitable niche. But it is worth stressing for the less experienced that high growth in volume is certainly no guarantee of high profitability. This was recently demonstrated by the price collapse in the PV market in 2010–11. A sudden fall in the market price for PV panels, caused by Chinese innovation and capacity, led to huge losses for a number of incumbents. But the price collapse at the same time catapulted installed capacity to even higher levels— supporting the forecast that solar PV will be one of the winners in the energy race, but not necessarily a financial winner for early investors.

18. In Politics, If You Want Reelection, Support Only Initiatives with Short-Term Benefits

Let me then turn to another arena, the world of politics. My underlying belief, as you know from my forecast, is that politicians are strongly limited in what they can do because of the short-term nature of the voter. The voters want improvement, but certainly not any form of improvement. They want improvement in the short term—which means in less than four years. It is difficult to win on a platform saying: "Let us sacrifice *x* today, in order to get 4*x* back in 2040." Politicians trying to lead in this manner tend to lose voters, influence, and finally their seat. The only high-profile leaders who have recently been able to force wise long-term policy onto their people seem to be the European Union (in climate matters) and the Communist Party of China (in matters of economic development). This most likely is due to the fact that both are further removed from democratic control than most politicians.

So what? The practical consequence is that if you want to be elected to public office, you must create a platform that is attractive in the short run. If you have ambitions for the nation in the long run, you may very well have to do some repackaging of your message. For example, let us assume you are in favor of electric cars because they reduce urban greenhouse gas emissions and will create a better life for our grandchildren. My suggestion is that you will win more votes for your view if you argue that electric cars are good because they will reduce noise level and air pollution levels in the city from day one. If your audience is extraordinarily sophisticated you may end your speech by saying that electric cars also "incidentally" lower greenhouse gas emissions and therefore will help solve the climate problem in the long run. But do not let the long-term effect be the foundation of your argument.

Or assume that you are in favor of better insulation of trailer homes because this will reduce power demand and greenhouse gas emissions from the local utility. Once again this should not be your basic argument. You will achieve more progress, I contend, if you choose to highlight the resulting decline in the monthly energy bill. And you can ensure that the savings will be fairly immediate if you are wise enough to implement your policy through regulatory change that allows the utility to split the profit from energy-efficiency investments with the owner of the trailer home. The utility will bring the investment money, do the construction job, and pass on one-half of the savings to the consumer as a deduction in the electricity bill.

Finally, assume you were President Obama. Assume you were in favor of a climate policy consisting of new wind farms on the US prairie and the retooling of Detroit to make electric cars that would run on the power of the prairie. Instead of promoting this as the "US Climate Law to Assist Future Generations" and thereby confronting the short-term nature of the US Congress and electorate, the exact same action on the ground could be promoted as "The Immediate Energy Independence Law," since the short-term effect of windmills and electric cars would be to reduce US dependence on oil imports from the Middle East.

Never underestimate the power of the short-term effect.

19. In Politics, Remember That the Future Will Be Dominated by Physical Limits

In the first decades after the end of World War II, resource constraints were not central in politics. What was missing was capital, real and financial. Progressive governments sought to increase investments at the cost of limiting consumption growth. The result was indeed an increase in the need for resources, but the geological abundance was rarely questioned. The challenge was to get access. Similarly, pollution of the environment was not seen as a significant factor—perhaps except within the smog-ridden urban agglomerations of the era, like London and Los Angeles. The world was still regarded as being infinitely big, for all practical purposes. Typical for the era, the historical resource limitation (L for land) was deleted from the equations of classical macroeconomics. As a result the intellectual underpinning of much economic policy making in the second half of the twentieth century was blind to the fact that the world is finite. It disregarded the fact that all resources are limited and that the capacity of the world to absorb pollution is also finite.

This will be different over the next forty years. There are limits in most countries to the amount of additional land available for cropping, grazing, and timber growth, and nowhere can more land be had for free. There are some land reserves in Brazil and Ukraine and elsewhere, but most arable land is already cultivated. Furthermore, the oceans are limited, as is the capacity to generate freshwater, maintain biodiversity, pollinate seed, bind CO_2, and so on. It is true that the technological capacity exists or will exist to lift limitations, and that this is feasible as long as there is enough energy at hand. But this will require thoughtful policy decision and implementation—and certainly won't happen by itself and without local opposition.

As a consequence future politicians will have to use much time on issues of depletion and pollution. These issues won't go away for a long time. There is no hope for a sudden, immense breakthrough that will solve in one go all the problems associated with the fact that the world is physically finite. Luckily for the politician there is a growing awareness in the population that resources are finite. The voters may show enough patience to let the politician spend time on this important issue. This was not the fact a generation ago.

Two precursors of this new focus are the issues of peak oil and climate change. Both illustrate the remarkably slow progress of policy making in the face of physical constraints. First, there were decades of discussion about the reality of the underlying phenomena, about whether there are in fact proximate physical limitations to conventional oil or to the capacity of the world's forests and oceans to absorb human CO_2. Then there were decades of discussion of what is the best response. And then finally there will be decades before policies actually bite and lead to a replacement for conventional oil or reduction in the concentration of CO_2.

For the politicians of the era it will be important to have a proper perspective on this glacial process, so as not to lose patience and faith, and to build their proposals on the short-term benefits, so they do not immediately get rejected by the voter.

Finally it may be of use to remind the budding politician that we are, after all, seeing signs of the emerging importance of physical constraints in the public debate. For decades labor productivity was the main focus: the overriding goal of economic policy was to increase the value added per hour worked. But in the new millennium we have seen increasing focus on both energy productivity and CO_2 productivity, which is the value created per unit of energy and CO_2, respectively. This makes sense when energy and CO_2 are more limiting than labor.

Terminology and conceptual challenges exist. It may prove useful to discuss these topics in terms of how much economic value is added, not per unit of manpower but per unit of energy or climate gas emissions. But if other limitations are more urgent, one may as well focus on the value added per unit of water, per unit of oil, per unit of land, per unit of fertilizer, or, ultimately, per unit of ecological footprint, highlighting the growing importance of physical constraints in an increasingly full world.

In the climate debate another approach could be to create two new public enemies, called "energy intensity" (i.e., the energy use per unit of GDP) and "climate intensity" (i.e., greenhouse gas emissions per unit of energy used). The long-term ambition should be to get them both as low as possible.

20. In Politics, Accept That Equal Access
to Limited Resources Will Trump Free Speech

Finally, future politicians are well advised to consider the impact on voter behavior and priorities of emerging resource constraints. Following the great revolutions of the 1700s people have been willing to support government, but largely on the condition that government remain small and keep out the way, leaving it to the individual to shape his or her own future. There have been variations on this theme, of course, with much stronger government being tried in places like the Scandinavian countries, China, and the Soviet Union. But the thought that the individual should ideally be free to pursue his or her own interest as long as it was not to the detriment of the majority has been a general guideline for generations. The institutionalization of human rights, including the right to free speech, has been one result.

This I believe will change in a resource-constrained world. It may take time, but gradually governments that allow scarce resources to end up in the hands of a minority will lose legitimacy—even if they allow people to talk and write about it. If water got scarce and a few wealthy individuals were allowed to buy what remained, leaving the rest with the options to use less or buy from the rich, I would expect enduring social unrest. This is particularly true because it is so simple to avoid the problem through rationing. The parliament can simply resolve that everyone will have access to a limited amount of water at a low price, and then leave it to the market to allocate the remaining supply and demand.

We already see this phenomenon at work in the field of energy. Many governments have found it necessary to subsidize oil use among its poor, to compensate for the fact that a few OPEC countries (and Norway) sit on most of the oil reserves and are able to lift prices above production costs. It is a sad fact that much of the subsidizing is done in an inefficient manner, but this does not preclude the efficient operation of a well-prepared system of rationing.

This also applies to the just distribution between generations. Over the next forty years politicians will increasingly be pushed to consider the rights of future generations. However, this issue will progress even more slowly than the effort to distribute equitably among those alive today—because there will be no effective spokesperson for the unborn. But hopefully by the end of the century there will be an international Court of Intergenerational Justice.

A government that can make sure that everyone gets his or her fair share of a limited resource supply will sit safer than one that solely promotes the right of each individual to argue why he or she should have a bigger share.

In an increasingly crowded world, collective well-being will be more important than individual rights.

Learn to Live with Impending Disaster without Losing Hope

So that is the limited advice I can provide. Now it's up to you to make the best of your future situation, optimize your well-being, and do so in a future world that will not play its cards as it should have.

Having been in your situation for some time, I do agree that the main challenge is mental. It is surprisingly difficult to maintain a happy outlook when you know deep in your heart that the world is on a path toward disaster. Even if your personal life is sound and satisfying, it is wearying to know that so much is being done systematically to destroy our common future.

Thus my final word of encouragement: Don't let the possibility of impending disaster crush your spirits. Don't let the prospect of a suboptimal long-term future kill your hope. Hope for the unlikely! Work for the unlikely!

Remember, too, that even if we do not succeed in our fight for a better world, there will still be a future world. And there will still be a world with a future—just less beautiful and less harmonious than it could have been.

Closing Words

There is only one more thing for me to say:
Please help make my forecast wrong.

Together we could create a much better world.

Appendices

1. Summary

2052: A Global Forecast for the Next Forty Years
The Limits to Growth study in 1972 addressed the grand question of how humanity would adapt to the physical limitations of planet Earth. Its authors, of whom I was one, offered these projections about the time period we have now entered:

- During the first half of the twenty-first century the ongoing growth in the human ecological footprint will stop.
- Humanity's resource use and environmental impact will be brought down to levels that can be sustained in the long run.

We wrote that these milestones would come to pass in one of many ways—for example through catastrophic "overshoot and collapse" or through well-managed "peak and decline."

In *2052*, I offer my status report after forty years—driven by curiosity, and a desire to understand whether, knowing what we know in 2012, humanity will rise to the occasion and effectively address the global unsustainabilities we still face. *2052* presents my forecast for the next forty years, based on the projections of other scientists, futurists, and thinkers. And here in a nutshell is what I expect will happen.

The process of adapting humanity to the limitations of the planet has indeed started. Over the next forty years, efforts to limit the ecological footprint will continue. Future growth in global population and GDP will be constrained not only by this effort, but also, by rapid fertility decline as a result of urbanization, productivity decline as a result of social unrest, and continuing poverty among the poorest two billion world citizens. At the same time there will be impressive advances in resource efficiency and climate-friendly solutions. There will also be a shift in focus toward human well-being rather than per capita income growth.

Still, based on the extensive database that underpins *2052*, it appears that the human response will be too slow. The most critical factor will be greenhouse gas emissions from human activities. These emissions will remain so high that our grandchildren most likely will have to live with self-reinforcing, and hence runaway, global warming in the second half of the twenty-first century.

Main Messages of 2052

- The global population will stagnate earlier than expected because fertility will fall dramatically in the increasingly urbanized population. Population will peak at 8.1 billion people just after 2040 and then decline.
- The global GDP will grow more slowly than expected because of the lower population growth and declining growth rates in (gross labor) productivity. Global GDP will reach 2.2 times current levels around 2050.
- Productivity growth will be slower than in the past because economies are maturing, because of increased social strife, and because of negative interference from extreme weather.
- The growth rate in global consumption will slow because a greater share of GDP will have to be allocated to investment—in order to solve the problems created by resource depletion, pollution, climate change, biodiversity loss, and inequity. Global consumption of goods and services will peak in 2045.
- As a consequence of increased social investment in the decades ahead (albeit often involuntary and in reaction to crisis), resource and climate problems will not become catastrophic before 2052. But there will be much unnecessary suffering from unabated climate damage around the middle of the century.
- The lack of a dedicated and forceful human response in the first half of the twenty-first century will put the world on a dangerous track toward self-reinforcing global warming in the second half of the twenty-first century.
- Slow growth in per capita consumption in much of the world (and stagnation in the rich world) will lead to increased social tension and conflict, which will further reduce orderly productivity growth.
- The short-term focus of capitalism and democracy will ensure that the wise decisions needed for long-term well-being will not be made in time.
- The global population will be increasingly urban and unwilling to protect nature for its own sake. Biodiversity will suffer.
- The impact will differ among the five regions analyzed in the book: the United States; the other OECD nations (including the European Union, Japan, and Canada, and most other industrialized nations); China; BRISE (Brazil, Russia, India, South Africa, and ten other big emerging economies); and the rest of the world (the 2.1 billion people at the bottom of the income ladder).
- The most surprising loser will be the current global economic elite, particularly the United States (which will experience stagnant per capita consumption for the next generation). China will be the winner. BRISE will make progress. The rest of the world will remain poor. All—and

particularly the poor—will live in an increasingly disorderly and climate-damaged world.

- The world in 2052 will certainly not be uniform or flat—the sentiment and conditions in the five regions will differ dramatically.

The Structure of 2052

The 2052 forecast is built around the cause-and-effect relationships described in figure 3-1 on page 57. The relationships are quantified in a spreadsheet that is available on the book's website, www.2052.info. The forecast is summarized graphically in figure 9-1 on pages 232–233, showing global developments from 1970 to 2050, and in figures 10-1 to 10-5 in chapter 10 for the five regions.

2. Definitions and Data Sources

Units Used

In this book most prices and costs are expressed in US dollars, and we use the symbol "$" whenever the value is expressed in 2005 money, using purchasing power parity (PPP) exchange rates to convert local currency to US dollars. When the international symbols for currencies (e.g., USD and NOK) occur in the text, it means that the precision level is lower, that the number may not be adjusted for inflation or has not been converted to US currency.

Notice that we use international terminology to signal orders of magnitude:

$$M = 1 \text{ million} = 10^6$$
$$G = 1 \text{ billion} = 10^9 = 1{,}000 \text{ million}$$
$$T = 1 \text{ trillion} = 10^{12} = 1{,}000 \text{ billion}$$

To help the reader grasp the magnitude of some of the money flows discussed in this book, we have introduced the special symbol "T$" as an abbreviation for "trillion 2005 PPP US dollars."

Regions Used

In this book we divide the world into five regions, called United States, OECD-less-US, China, BRISE, and ROW. The regions are defined below.

In addition to listing the countries in each region, we also include the regions' population size and annual production (GDP) for 2010. The population is given in millions of people and the GDP in trillions of 2005 PPP US dollars per year (abbreviated T$ per year).

The regions consist of the following countries:

UNITED STATES:
The United States, US Virgin Islands, and Puerto Rico.
Population 315 million people, and GDP 13 T$ per year in 2010.

OECD-LESS-US (MOST INDUSTRIALIZED COUNTRIES OUTSIDE THE US):
Austria, Belgium, Canada, Denmark, France, Germany, Greece, Iceland, Italy, Japan, Luxembourg, Netherlands, Norway, Portugal, Spain, Sweden, Switzerland, United Kingdom, Finland, Australia, New Zealand, Czech Republic, Hungary, Poland, South Korea, Slovakia, Chile, Slovenia, Israel, and Estonia.
Population 740 million, people and GDP 22 T$ per year in 2010.

CHINA:
China, Hong Kong, and Macau Special Administrative Areas.
Population 1,350 million people, and GDP 10 T$ per year in 2010.

BRISE (THE 14 BIGGEST EMERGING ECONOMIES):
Brazil, Russia, India, South Africa, Indonesia, Mexico, Vietnam, Turkey, Iran, Thailand, Ukraine, Argentina, Venezuela, and Saudi Arabia.
Population 2,400 million people, and GDP 14 T$ per year in 2010.

ROW (THE REST OF THE WORLD, INCLUDING THE LESS INDUSTRIALIZED COUNTRIES):
The 194 countries of the world, less those included in the four regions defined above (US, OECD-less-US, China, and BRISE).
Population 2,100 million people, and GDP 8 T$ per year in 2010.

Data Sources
The analysis in this book and the historical part of its illustrations are based on statistical data from many sources. The sources are listed below, in the sequence in which the variable occurs in the figures.

POPULATION, TOTAL AND AGE 15–64
United Nations, Department of Economic and Social Affairs, Population Division, 2011. *World Population Prospects: The 2010 Revision*, CD-ROM edition. http://esa.un.org/unpd/wpp/Excel-Data/population.htm.
Table: Population by Age Groups—Both Sexes: Total population (both sexes combined) by five-year age group, major area, region and country, 1950–2100 (thousands)

BIRTHS

United Nations, Department of Economic and Social Affairs, Population Division, 2011. *World Population Prospects: The 2010 Revision*, CD-ROM edition. http://esa.un.org/unpd/wpp/Excel-Data/fertility.htm.

Table: Births: Births (both sexes combined) by major area, region and country, 1950–2100 (thousands).

DEATHS

United Nations, Department of Economic and Social Affairs, Population Division, 2011. *World Population Prospects: The 2010 Revision*, CD-ROM edition. http://esa.un.org/unpd/wpp/Excel-Data/mortality.htm.

Table: Deaths—Both Sexes: Deaths (both sexes combined) by major area, region and country, 1950–2100 (thousands).

GDP, CONSUMPTION, AND INVESTMENT

Penn World Tables, Pennsylvania, 2011. Heston, Alan, Summers, Robert, and Aten, Bettina, Penn World Table Version 7.0, Center for International Comparisons of Production, Income and Prices at the University of Pennsylvania, May 2011. http://pwt.econ.upenn.edu/php_site/pwt70/pwt70_form.php.

ENERGY USE

BP Statistical Review of World Energy, 2011. http://www.bp.com/sectionbodycopy.do?categoryId=7500&contentId=7068481 or http://www.bp.com/statisticalreview.

CO$_2$ EMISSIONS

Institute for Energy Analysis, Oak Ridge Associated Universities, Oak Ridge, Tennessee, USA, 2011. http://cdiac.ornl.gov/trends/emis/meth_reg.html.

TEMPERATURE RISE

Met Office Hadley Centre observations datasets, Exeter, Devon, United Kingdom, 2011. http://www.metoffice.gov.uk/hadobs/hadcrut3/data/download.html.

Forecast from 2010 to 2050 from simulation run made by Siegel, L., Rice, P., and Jones, D., especially for this book, using their C-ROADS model driven by the forecast of CO$_2$ emissions in figure 5-3 on page 115 extended linearly to zero in 2100. Climate Interactive, Cambridge, Massachusetts, December 2011. http://climateinteractive.org/simulations/C-ROADS.

CO₂ CONCENTRATION

The nonprofit organization co2now.org, Pro Oxygen, Victoria, British Columbia, Canada, 2011, http://co2now.org/images/stories/data/co2-mlo-monthly-noaa-esrl.xls.

SEA-LEVEL RISE

History and forecast from simulation run made by Siegel, L., Rice, P., and Jones, D., especially for this book, using their C-ROADS model driven by the forecast of CO_2 emissions in figure 5-3 on page 115 extended linearly to zero in 2100. Climate Interactive, Cambridge, Massachusetts, December 2011. http://climateinteractive.org/simulations/C-ROADS.

FOOD PRODUCTION AND CULTIVATED LAND

UN Food and Agricultural Organization, Rome, Italy, 2011. http://faostat.fao.org/site/567/default.aspx#ancor.

NONENERGY ECOLOGICAL FOOTPRINT

Global Footprint Network, Oakland, California, USA, 2011. http://www.footprintnetwork.org/images/uploads/2010_NFA_data_tables.xls.

Historical data is available from the Network by request.

TOTAL FERTILITY

United Nations, Department of Economic and Social Affairs, Population Division, 2011. *World Population Prospects: The 2010 Revision*, CD-ROM edition. http://esa.un.org/unpd/wpp/Excel Data/population.htm .

Table: Population by Age Groups—Female: Female population by five-year age groups, major area, region and country, 1950–2100 (thousands).

3. Further Reading for the *2052* Glimpses

Glimpse 2-1: The Dark Decades by Carlos Joly

Hansen, J. J. (2007), "Global Warming, Tipping Point Near," *IPCC 4th Assessment Report*.

Stiglitz, J., et al. (2009), *Report on Economic Performance and Social Progress*, Paris.

Johnson, S. (May 2009), "The Quiet Coup," *Atlantic Monthly*.

Glimpse 2-2: Constraining Asian Consumption by Chandran Nair

Nair, C. (2011), *Consumptionomics: Asia's Role in Reshaping Capitalism and Saving the Planet*, Infinite Ideas Limited, Oxford, UK.

Gilding, P. (2011), *The Great Disruption: Why the Climate Crisis Will Bring on the End of Shopping and the Birth of a New World*, Bloomsbury Press, New York.

Glimpse 2-3: Shuffling toward Sustainability by Paul Hohnen

Hawken, P., Lovins, A. B., and Lovins, L. H. (2010), *Natural Capitalism: The Next Industrial Revolution* (10th anniversary edition), Earthscan, London.

Hardin, G. (1993), *Living within Limits: Ecology, Economics, and Population Taboos*, Oxford University Press, Oxford.

Glimpse 2-4: Intergenerational War for Equity by Karl Wagner

Margulis, L., and Sagan, D. (1987), *Microcosmos: Four Billion Years of Microbial Evolution*, Allen & Unwin, London.

Bakan, J. (2004), *The Corporation: The Pathological Pursuit of Profit and Power*, Free Press, New York.

Oreskes, N., and Conway, E. (2010), *Merchants of Doubt: How a Handful of Scientists Obscured the Truth on Issues from Tobacco Smoke to Global Warming*, Bloomsbury Press, New York.

Glimpse 2-5: Extreme Weather in 2052 by Robert W. Corell

Archer, D., and Rahmstorf, S. (2010), *The Climate Crisis: An Introductory Guide to Climate Change*, Cambridge University Press, Cambridge, UK.

Dessler, A., and Parsons, E. (2010), *The Science and Politics of Global Climate Change: A Guide to the Debate*, 2nd edition, Cambridge University Press, Cambridge, UK.

Stern, N. (2006), *The Global Deal: Climate Change and the Creation of a New Era of Progress and Prosperity*, HM Treasury, British Government, London.

Glimpse 4-1: The End of Uneconomic Growth by Herman Daly

Daly, H., and Farley, J. (2011), *Ecological Economics*, Island Press, Washington, DC.

Daly, H. (September 2005), "Economics in a Full World," *Scientific American*, pp. 100–107.

Glimpse 4-2: Light Green Growth by Thorvald Moe

OECD (2011), *Towards Green Growth: Green Growth Strategy Synthesis Report*, OECD, Paris.

Victor, D. (2011), *Global Warming Gridlock: Creating More Effective Strategies for Protecting the Planet*, Cambridge University Press, Cambridge, UK.

Glimpse 5-1: *The Road to PV* by Terje Osmundsen

IEA (2010), *Technology Roadmap: Solar Photovoltaic Energy*, IEA, Vienna.

IPCC (2011), *Special Report Renewable Energy Sources* (SRREN), IPCC.

The European Photovoltaic Industry Association and Greenpeace International (2011), *Solar Generation 6: Solar Photovoltaic Electricity Empowering the World*.

Glimpse 5-2: *The Death of Nuclear* by Jonathon Porritt

Schneider, M., Froggatt, A., and Thomas, S. (2011), *World Nuclear Status Report 2010–2011*, World Watch Institute, Washington, DC.

Roberts, P. (2004), *The End of Oil: On the Edge of a Perilous New World*, Houghton Mifflin, New York.

Brown, L. (2011), *World on the Edge: How to Prevent Environmental and Economic Collapse*, W. W. Norton, New York.

Glimpse 5-3: *Troubled Arctic Waters* by Dag O. Hessen

Key website on the ice situation is http://nsidc.org/arcticseaicenews.

UNESCO (2010), *Climate Change and Arctic Sustainable Development: Scientific, Social, Cultural and Educational challenges*, UNESCO, Paris.

Glimpse 5-4: *The Flight to the City* by Thomas N. Gladwin

Brugmann, J. (2010), *Welcome to the Urban Revolution: How Cities Are Changing the World*, Bloomsbury Press, New York.

Glaeser, E. (2011), *Triumph of the City: How Our Greatest Invention Makes Us Richer, Smarter, Greener, Healthier, and Happier*, Penguin Press, New York.

UN-Habitat (2011), *Cities and Climate Change: Policy Directions: Global Report on Human Settlements 2011*, Earthscan, London.

Glimpse 6-1: *Expensive Oil = Expensive Food* by Erling Moxnes

Sandvik, S., and Moxnes, E. (2009), "Peak Oil, Biofuels, and Long-Term Food Security," International System Dynamics Conference, Albuquerque, New Mexico.

Escobara, J. C., et al. (2009), "Biofuels: Environment, Technology and Food Security," *Renewable and Sustainable Energy Reviews*, vol. 13, pp. 1275–87.

Rajagopal, D., and Zilberman, D. (2007), *Review of Environmental, Economic and Policy Aspects of Biofuels*. Policy Research Working Paper 4341, The World Bank.

Glimpse 6-2: *The Limits to Protein* by David Butcher

Diamond, J. (2005), *Collapse: How Societies Choose to Fail or Succeed*, Viking Press, New York.

Jackson, J., et al. (July 2001), "Historical Overfishing and the Recent Collapse of Coastal Ecosystems," *Science*, vol. 293.

Glimpse 6-3: *The Race to Lose Last* by Mathis Wackernagel

WWF, Global Footprint Network, Zoological Society of London (2008), *Living Planet Report 2008*, WWF International, Gland, www.wwf.org/livingplanet.

Heinberg, R., and Lerch, D., eds. (2010), *The Post Carbon Reader: Managing the 21st Century's Sustainability Crises*, University of California Press, Berkeley.

Glimpse 6-4: *Urban Mining of Metals* by Chris Tuppen

http://www.chemistryinnovation.co.uk/roadmap/sustainable/roadmap .asp?previd=425&id=426.

US Geological Survey (2011), *Mineral Commodity Summaries 2011*.

UNEP (2010), *Metal Stocks in Society*.

Glimpse 6-5: *Nature Limited to Parks* by Stephan Harding

Flannery, T. (2011), *Here on Earth: A New Beginning,* Allen Lane, London.

Wilson, E. O. (2001), *The Diversity of Life,* Penguin Science Press, London.

Glimpse 7-1: *Megacity Living and Externalization of the Mind* by Per Arild sjordet and Lars Hem

Donald, M. (2001), *A Mind So Rare: The Evolution of Human Consciousness,* W. W. Norton, New York.

Dennet, D. C. (1991), *Consciousness Explained.* Little, Brown, Boston.

Diamond, J. (1997), *Guns, Germs, and Steel: The Fates of Human Societies,* W. W. Norton, New York.

Glimpse 7-2: *Individual Health from Public Care* by Harald Siem

Keep an eye on the agenda of www.who.int.

Glimpse 7-3: *The Future of War and the Rise of Robots* by Ugo Bardi

Singer, P. W. (2009), *Wired for War: The Robotics Revolution and Conflict in the 21st Century*, Penguin Books, New York.

Rosenbaum, Ron (2011), *How the End Begins*, Simon and Schuster, London.

Ferguson, Niall (2001), *The Cash Nexus*, Penguin Press, London.

Glimpse 7-4: *Military for Sustainability* by John Elkington

Anyone wanting a structured online glimpse of the future of conflict might want to start with this US Air Force Center for Strategy & Technology website, http://csat.au.af.mil/future-conflict.htm.

Glimpse 8-1: *Scotland Joins New Europe* by Catherine Cameron

The UK Climate Impacts Programme, high, medium, and low scenarios available to 2100, www.ukcip.org.uk/.

University College London Energy Institute, www.ucl.ac.uk/energy, including research on *The Revival of British Sea Power: Enough Wind to Power Europe.*

Smith, L. C. (2011), *The New North: The World in 2050,* Profile Books, London.

Glimpse 8-2: *The End of Mediterranean Disparity* by Thymio Papayannis

Norwich, J. J. (2010), *The Middle Sea: A History of the Mediterranean,* The Folio Society, London.

UNEP/MAP-Plan Bleu (2009), *State of the Environment and Development in the Mediterranean,* UNEP/MAP, Athens.

Ureta, I., and Lutterbeck, D. (2010), *Migration, Development and Diplomacy: Perspectives from the Southern Mediterranean,* Red Sea Press, Trenton.

Glimpse 8-3: *Slum Urbanism in Africa* by Edgar Pieterse

Cilliers, J., Hughes, B., and Moyers, J. (2011), *African Futures 2050: The Next Forty Years,* ISS Monograph 175, Institute for Security Studies, Pretoria.

Pieterse, E. (2008), *City Futures: Confronting the Crisis of Urban Development,* ZED Books, London.

Simone, A. (2010), *City Life from Jakarta to Dakar: Movements at the Crossorads,* Routledge, London.

Glimpse 8-4: *Valuing the Whole* by Peter Willis

Beck, D. E., and Cowan, C. C. (1996), *Spiral Dynamics: Mastering Values, Leadership and Change,* Blackwell Publishing, Oxford.

Hawken, P. (2007), *Blessed Unrest: How the Largest Movement in the World Came into Being and Why No One Saw It Coming,* Viking Press, New York.

Gilding, P. (2011), *The Great Disruption: Why the Climate Crisis Will Bring on the End of Shopping and the Birth of a New World,* Bloomsbury Press, New York.

Glimpse 8-5: *Systemic CSR, or CSR 2.0* by Wayne Visser

Anderson, R. (2009), *Confessions of a Radical Industrialist: Profits, People, Purpose—Doing Business by Respecting the Earth,* St. Martin's Press, New York.

Hollender, J., and Breen, B. (2010), *The Responsibility Revolution: How the Next Generation of Businesses Will Win*, Jossey-Bass, New York.

Visser, W. (2011), *The Age of Responsibility: CSR 2.0 and the New DNA of Business*, Wiley, London.

Glimpse 8-6: *Harnessing the Wisdom of the Crowd* by Elisabeth Laville

Here is a useful gateway to cooperative innovation: www.openinnovation.net.

Chesbrough, H. (2003), *Open Innovation: The New Imperative for Creating and Profiting from Technology*, Harvard Business Review Press, Boston.

Botsman, R., and Rogers, R. (2011), *What's Mine Is Yours: The Rise of Collaborative Consumption*, HarperCollins.

Glimpse 8-7: *Peak Youth Gaming for the Public Good* by Sarah Severn

Nugent, R. (2006), *Youth in a Global World*, Population Reference Bureau, available at www.prb.org/Publications/PolicyBriefs/YouthinaGlobalWorld.aspx.

The *EVOKE* social network website, www.urgentevoke.com.

Auberne, P. (2007), *Megatrends 2010: The Rise of Conscious Capitalism*, Hampton Roads Publishing, Charlottesville, Virginia.

Glimpse 9-1: *Sudden Rush to Solar* by Paul Gilding

Randers, J., and Gilding P. (2010), "The One Degree War Plan," *Journal of Global Responsibility*, vol. 1, issue 1, pp. 170–88.

Gilding, P. (2011), *The Great Disruption: Why the Climate Crisis Will Bring on the End of Shopping and the Birth of a New World*, Bloomsbury Press, New York.

Glimpse 9-2: *Financing the Future* by Nick Robins

Haldane, A. G. (2009), "Rethinking the Financial Network," speech at the Financial Student Association, Amsterdam, April 28, 2009.

Haldane, A. G., and May, R. M. (January 19, 2011), "Systemic Risk in Banking Ecosystems," *Nature*, vol. 469, pp. 351–55.

Kumhof, M., and Ranciere, R. (2010), *Inequality, Leverage and Crises*, IMF Working Paper.

Carbon Tracker Initiative (2011), *Unburnable Carbon: Are Financial Markets Carrying a Carbon Bubble?* available at www.carbontracker.org/carbonbubble.

Glimpse 10-1: *Bright Solar Future* by William W. Behrens

To follow the PV industry: *Photon International: The Solar Power Magazine*, Aachen, Germany.

Scheer, H. (2004), *The Solar Economy: Renewable Energy for a Sustainable Global Future,* Earthscan, London.

Glimpse 10-2: China—the New Hegemon by Rasmus Reinvang and Bjørn Brunstad

Dawson, R. (1978), *The Chinese Experience,* Phoenix Press, London.

Jaques, M. (2009), *When China Rules the World: The Rise of the Middle Kingdom and the End of the Western World,* Allen Lane, London.

Leonard, M. (2008), *What Does China Think?* Fourth Estate, London.

Magnus, G. (2010), *Uprising: Will Emerging Markets Shape or Shake the World Economy?* Wiley, London.

Glimpse 10-3: Rich on Biofuels by Jens Ulltveit-Moe

IEA (2011), *Technology Roadmap: Biofuels for Transport,* IEA, Vienna.

Goldemberg, J. (2008), *The Brazilian Biofuels Industry,* Biomed Central, Sao Paulo, available at http://www.biotechnologyforbiofuels.com/content /1/1/6.

Glimpse 11-1: The Fifth Cultural Step by Dag Andersen

Andersen, D. (2007), *The 5th Step: The Way to a New Society,* Kolofon, Oslo.

Kuhn, T. S. (1962), *The Structure of Scientific Revolutions,* University of Chicago Press, Chicago.

Lipton, B. H., and Bhaerman, S. (2011), *Spontaneous Evolution: Our Positive Future and a Way to Get There from Here,* Hay House, London.

Glimpse 11-2: The Third Flowering of the Tree of Life by Jonathan Loh

Dawkins, R. (1976), *The Selfish Gene,* Oxford University Press, Oxford.

Dennett, D. C. (1995), *Darwin's Dangerous Idea: Evolution and the Meanings of Life,* Penguin Books, London.

Mace, R., Holden, C. J., and Shennan, S., eds. (2005), *The Evolution of Cultural Diversity: A Phylogenetic Approach,* UCL Press, London.

4. Extra Data on Fertility and Productivity

Since the declines over time in total fertility (the number of children born to each woman on average through her fertile life) and gross labor productivity (the GDP divided by the number of people between fifteen and sixty-five years of age) play such an important role in the 2052 forecast, I include two extra graphs that illustrate the historical trends in these two variables. In both cases I have chosen data for a large leading region—the original fifteen members of the European Union (EU-15) for fertility trends, and the United States for productivity developments. The EU-15 are Belgium, Denmark, Germany, Finland, France, Greece, United Kingdom, Ireland, Italy, Luxembourg, Netherlands, Austria, Portugal, Sweden, and Spain.

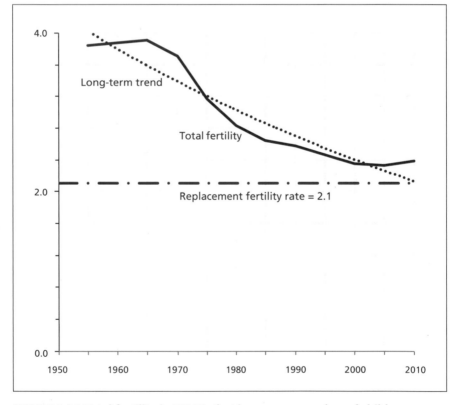

FIGURE A4-1 Total fertility in EU-15, that is, average number of children per woman during her fertile life, 1950–2010.

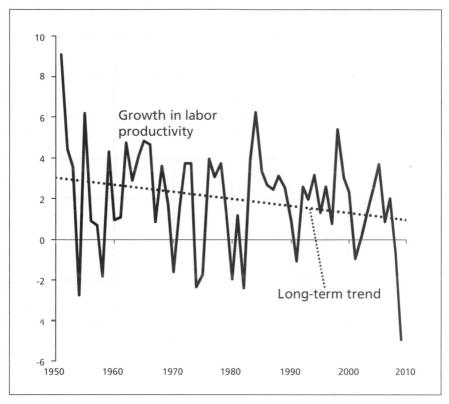

**FIGURE A4-2 Growth in US gross labor productivity,
in percent per year, 1950-2010.**

Notes

Preface: What Will the Future Bring?
1. Retold by former Foreign Minister Thorvald Stoltenberg of Norway, who helped negotiate peace in the former Yugoslavia in the 1990s.
2. Meadows, D. H., Meadows, D. L., Randers, J. and Behrens., W. W. (1972), *The Limits to Growth*, Universe Books, New York; Meadows, D. H., Meadows, D. L., Randers, J. (1992), *Beyond the Limits: Confronting Global Collapse, Envisioning a Sustainable Future*, Chelsea Green, White River Junction, Vermont; Meadows, D. H., Randers, J., Meadows, D. L. (2004), *Limits to Growth: The 30-Year Update*, Chelsea Green, White River Junction, Vermont.
3. *The Limits to Growth* in 1972 used two full pages to describe the climate issue (pp. 72–73), even though the book had only 167 pages and included 48 figures.
4. The UN Intergovernmental Panel on Climate Change; www.ipcc.org.
5. The Kyoto protocol was the first plan under the UN Framework Convention on Climate Change to reduce climate gas emissions, starting with the industrialized world; www.unfccc.org.

Chapter 1: Worrying about the Future
1. Randers, J. and Gilding, P. (2010), "The One Degree War Plan," *Journal of Global Responsibility*, vol. 1, no. 1; Randers, J. (2008), "Global Collapse—Fact or Fiction?" *Futures*, vol. 40, no. 10, December; Randers, J. and Alfsen, K. H. (2007), "How Can Norway Become a Climate-Friendly Society?" *World Economics*, vol. 8, no. 1, January–March; Wackernagel, M., et al. (including Randers, J.) (2002), "Tracking the Ecological Overshoot of the Human Economy," *Proceedings of the National Academy of Sciences of the United States of America*, vol. 99, no. 14, July; Randers, J. (1996), "Depressing Trends" in de Mattos-Shipley, H. (ed), *WWF Changing Worlds*, Banson, London; Randers, J. (1994), "The Quest for a Sustainable Society—A Global Perspective" in Skirbekk, G. (ed), *The Notion of Sustainability*, Scandinavian University Press, Oslo.
2. Another social scientist has recently chosen to write books on the longer time horizons. See Friedman, G. (2010), *The Next 100 Years: A Forecast for the 21st Century*, Anchor Books, New York.

Chapter 2: Five Big Issues toward 2052
1. The World Business Council for Sustainable Development (2011), *Vision 2050: The New Agenda for Business*, Geneva, available at www.wbcsd.org/vision2050.aspx.
2. Meadows, D. H. and Robinson, J. M. (1985), *The Electronic Oracle: Computer Models and Social Decisions*, Wiley, New York.
3. Carson, R. (1962), *Silent Spring*, Houghton Mifflin Company, Boston.
4. Stiglitz, J., et al. (2009), *Report by the Commission on the Measurement of Economic Performance and Social Progress*, Paris.
5. The 2010 US Supreme Court ruling in Citizens United v. Federal Election Commission, reaffirming the freedom of corporations to spend unlimited funds on lobbying and electoral politics, is the icing on the cake.
6. Joly, C. and Olsen, P. I. (2011), *The Nordics, the Welfare State and the Eurozone Crisis*, Center for Development and Environment, University of Oslo, Norway; summary version in *Social Europe Journal*, www.social-europe.eu/author/carlos-joly-and-per-ingvar-olsen/.
7. Jacobson, M. Z. and Delluchi, M. A. (November 2009), "A Plan to Power 100 Percent of the Planet with Renewables," *Scientific American*.

8. CIA (2010), *World Factbook*, Washington, DC.

9. The figure is from Grantham, J. (2011), "Time to Wake Up: Days of Abundant Resources Are Over," *GMO Quarterly Letter*, April 2011.

10. The time series for PV costs are collected from data in *PV News* (1982), vol. 1 through vol. 22 (2003), and data in Bloomberg's New Energy Finance service for the years 2003 to 2010 (see http://bnef.com/markets/renewable-energy/solar). Used by permission from Terje Osmundsen, Scatec Solar AS, Oslo, Norway.

11. The figure is based on data in the spreadsheet available on the *2052* website, www.2052.info.

12. The figure is based on data from Global Carbon Project (2011), *Carbon Budget 2009*, available at www.globalcarbonproject.org.

13. See http://unfccc.int/essential_background/items/2877.php.

14. This is an express agreement under international law entered into by sovereign states and international organizations, under the Vienna Convention on the Law of Treaties of 1969; see www.public international law.net/.

15. See the UN Framework Convention on Climate Change, Article 2, "Objective," at http://unfccc.int/resource/docs/convkp/conveng.pdf.

16. See Climate Action Tracker at www.climateactiontracker.org; Climate Action Network at www.climatenetwork.org; United Nations Evironment Programme at www.unep.org/climatechange; Project Catalyst at www.project-catalyst.info/index.php?option=com_content&view=article&id=52&Itemid=60; World Resources Institute at www.wri.org/climate; the Pew Center at www.pewclimate.org; CO_2 Scorecard at http://co2scorecard.org; and ClimateInteractive at http://climateinteractive.org/scoreboard.

17. An excellent overall summary is available at http://en.wikipedia.org/wiki/Global_climate_model.

18. Nakicenovic, N. (ed) (2000), *Special Report on Emissions Scenarios: A Special Report of Working Group III of the Intergovernmental Panel on Climate Change*, Cambridge University Press, Cambridge, UK. This volume is out of print but available from http://www.grida.no/publications/other/ipcc_sr/?src=/climate/ipcc/emission/index.htm.

19. Intergovernmental Panel on Climate Change (2007), *Climate Change 2007: The Physical Science Basis*, Working Group I Contribution to the Fourth Assessment Report of the IPCC, Cambridge University Press, p. 16, Cambridge, UK.

20. See a description of C-ROADS simulator at http://climateinteractive.org.

21. The Global Carbon Project was formed to assist the international science community to establish a common, mutually agreed knowledge base supporting policy debate and action to slow the rate of increase of greenhouse gases in the atmosphere. The Global Carbon Project is responding to this challenge through a shared partnership with the International Geosphere-Biosphere Programme (IGBP), the International Human Dimensions Programme on Global Environmental Change (IHDP), the World Climate Research Programme (WCRP) and Diversitas. This partnership constitutes the Earth Systems Science Partnership (ESSP). See www.globalcarbonproject.org.

22. General circulation models (GCMs) depict the climate using a three-dimensional grid over the globe, typically having a horizontal resolution of between 250 and 600 km, 10 to 20 vertical layers in the atmosphere, and sometimes as many as 30 layers in the oceans.

23. Intergovernmental Panel on Climate Change (2007), see note 19 above.

24. Available at www.europeanclimate.org/index.php?option=com_content&task=view&id=72&Itemid=79; See www.iiasa.ac.at/Research/ENE/GEA/index_gea.html; see www.unido.org/index.php?id=1001185&sb=12; see Grubler, A. (2008), "Energy Transitions," in Cleveland, C. J. (ed), *Encyclopedia of Earth*, Environmental Information, Washington, DC, available at www.eoearth.org/article/Energy_transitions.

25. The figure shows data from model simulations for the A1FI scenario for the period 2010 to 2050, as presented by Ganguly, A. R., et al in *Proceedings of the National Academy of Sciences (PNAS)*, September 15, 2009, vol. 106, no 37, p. 1555, and available via www.pnas.org /content/106/37/15555.abstract. A1FI leads to a warming of +2.4°C in 2050 relative to preindustrial times, while my forecast—with its lower emissions—leads to +2.0°C, both according to the C-ROADS computer model (see appendix 2 for details). To be exact, the numbers in the map should have been corrected for the temperature increase before 2000 (+0.7°) and for the lower emissions in my forecast (–0.4°), that is, by a total of +0.3°C. The uncertainty in the numbers is so big that I have not made this correction. The data has been used with permission of *PNAS*.

Chapter 3: The Logic behind My Forecast

1. See Randers, J. (ed) (1980), *Elements of the System Dynamics Method*, Pegasus Communications, Waltham, MA, Chapter 6.
2. See appendix 2 for exact definitions.
3. See appendix 2 for the exact definition of the symbol "$", which means 2005 PPP US dollars.
4. The biological capacity of a land area is defined as its ability to produce biomass (measured in tonnes per year). It depends on the fertility of the land and the input of solar energy, rain, and man-made agricultural inputs.
5. Jones, A., et al. (2012), *Resource Constraints: Sharing a Finite World. Implications of* Limits to Growth *for the Actuarial Profession*, report for Institute and Faculty of Actuaries, Anglia Ruskin University, to be published fall 2012.

Chapter 4: Population and Consumption to 2052

1. This is shown in figure 4-1 in the form of the crude death rate, which is annual deaths as a percentage of the current population. The reason why the death rate does not decline after 2010 is that the age structure of the population changes from 2010 to 2050. Gradually there is a larger fraction of old people.
2. Since the decline in fertility is so central to my forecast, I have added in appendix 4 an extra graph showing the detailed development of fertility in the rich industrial world, exemplified by EU-15 since 1950.
3. Austria, Australia, Benelux, Canada, Denmark, France, Germany, Greece, Iceland, Ireland, Norway, Spain, Sweden, Switzerland, UK, and US.
4. Notice that in the graphs I use the more technical format: $56,000 per person-year.
5. Since the long-term decline in gross productivity is so central to my forecast, I have added in appendix 4 an extra graph showing the detailed rate of change of gross productivity from 1950 to 2010 in the richest big country throughout this period, namely the US.
6. Appendix 2 lists the data sources used.
7. Stern Review (2007), *The Economics of Climate Change: The Stern Review*, Cambridge University Press, Cambridge.
8. Nordhaus, W. (2007), *The Challenge of Global Warming: Economic Models and Environmental Policy*, White Paper, Yale University, New Haven, Connecticut, July 24, p. 231.
9. McKinsey & Company (2009), *Pathways to a Low-Carbon Economy*, available at www.mckinsey .com/globalGHGcostcurve.
10. OECD (2009), *The Economics of Climate Change Mitigation: Policies and Options for Global Action Beyond 2012*, OECD, Paris.
11. Sitariz, D. (ed) (1993), *Agenda 21: The Earth Summit Strategy to Save Our Planet*, EarthPress, Boulder, Colorado, p. 310.

12. Nordhaus, *The Challenge of Global Warming*, p. 171, see note 8 above.

13. IEA (2009), *World Energy Outlook*, Vienna.

14. IEA (2011), *World Energy Outlook*, Vienna.

15. United Nations Evironment Programme (2011), *Towards a Green Economy: Pathways to Sustainable Development and Poverty Eradication*, UNEP, Green Economy Initiative, Nairobi.

16. Calculated as an approximate oil price ($100 per barrel) times the annual consumption of oil (4,000 million tonnes of oil per year × 7 barrels per tonne of oil).

17. The data is from the reinsurance company Munich Re, via *The Economist* (2011), "Counting the Cost of Calamities," January 14, 2011, p. 54.

18. OECD (2011), *Towards Green Growth: Green Growth Strategy Synthesis Report*, OECD, Paris, p. 6.

19. OECD (2009), *The Economics of Climate Change Mitigation*, OECD, Paris.

20. Which means overall greenhouse gas concentration at about 550 ppm CO_2e.

21. Victor, D. (2011), *Global Warming Gridlock: Creating More Effective Strategies for Protecting the Planet*, Cambridge University Press, Cambridge.

22. The situation has been further confused by spells of deflation, which made the numerical value of consumption decline, even in times when its real value remained stable.

23. Production (down 0.5%/yr) equals workforce (down 1.5%/yr) times productivity (up 1%/yr).

Chapter 5: Energy and Co_2 to 2052

1. Here I follow the totally illogical, but prevalent, custom of viewing heat and electricity as one product and add the amount of heat in fuels to the amount of electricity arising from nonfossil sources like hydro, wind, solar, and nuclear, using the formula 1 kWh = 1 kWh$_{heat}$ = 1 kWh$_{electricity}$. This is truly mixing apples and pears, but it does not seem to bother non-physicists.

2. The exception is the future use of carbon capture and storage (CCS) as discussed later in the chapter.

3. Carbon Tracker Initiative, *Unburnable Carbon: Are Financial Markets Carrying a Carbon Bubble?* available at www.carbontracker.org/carbonbubble.

4. To convert gas prices from US to metric units, use $3 per million BTU = 1 Norwegian krone per standard cubic meter of gas. Or in technical jargon 3 USD/MBTU = 1 NOK/Sm3.

5. IEA (2010), *Energy Technology Perspectives*, Vienna.

6. Inferred from the increase in CO_2 emissions in A1FI from 10 to 24 GtC/year from 2010 to 2050.

7. IPCC (2011), *Special Report Renewable Energy Sources (SRREN)*, IPCC, Working Group III.

8. 10 T$ is approximately 15% of world GDP in 2010.

9. Lovins, A. (2011), "Reinventing Fire," presentation, http://www.rmi.org/rmi/Reinventing Fire. See also Lovins, A. B., and Rocky Mountain Institute (2011), *Reinventing Fire: Bold Solutions for the New Energy Era*, Chelsea Green, White River Juction, Vermont.

10. Monbiot, G. (2011), "The Nuclear Industry Stinks," *The Guardian*, July 5, 2011.

11. Porritt, J. (May 3, 2006), *Is Nuclear the Answer?* Sustainable Development Commission, London.

12. Lovins, *Reinventing Fire*, see note 9 above.

13. WWF International (2007), *Climate Solutions: The WWF Vision for 2050*, Gland, Switzerland.

14. IEA (2010), *Energy Technology Perspectives*, Vienna, p. 90.

15. The factors used (expressed in tons of CO_2 per ton of oil equivalents of energy) are 1.06 for coal, 0.8 for oil, 0.57 for gas, and 0 for nuclear and all renewables.

16. Thanks to Drew Jones, Lori Siegel, and Phil Rice at www.climateinteractive.org.

17. In order to make their estimate, Climate Interactive first had to add their own estimates for CO_2 from sources other than energy (mainly cement and deforestation, as shown in figure 2-4 on page 42). They then had to add the emissions of the other important greenhouse gases. The dotted top curve in figure 5-4 on page 119 shows the total effect of these additions. It shows the

total concentration of greenhouse gases measured as CO_2 equivalents. The lower dashed curve shows the concentration of CO_2 in the atmosphere. The parallel development of the two curves explains why most of the climate debate focuses solely on CO_2, which is simpler to measure.

Chapter 6: Food and Footprint to 2052

1. For an overview, see Lobell, D. (2011), "Impacts in the Next Few Decades and Coming Centuries," *Climate Stabilization Targets: Emissions, Concentrations, and Impacts over Decades to Millennia*, National Academies Press, Washington, DC, chapter 5. Also available at http://www.nap.edu/catalog/12877.html.

2. Worm, B., et al. (2009), "Rebuilding Global Fisheries," *Science*, vol. 325, p. 578.

3. Gutierrez, N., Hilborn R. and Defeo, O. (2011), "Leadership, Social Capital and Incentives Promote Successful Fisheries." *Nature*, vol. 470, pp. 386–89.

4. A more complete introduction to footprint science can be found at http://www.footprint network.org/en/index.php/GFN/page/methodology/.

5. Bio-capacity is the regenerative capacity of an ecosystem that provides for resources, absorbs waste, and provides for urban space. It is measured in surface area of biologically productive space. The measurement unit is global hectares, or hectares with world average biological productivity. In 2007, there were 1.8 global hectares of bio-capacity available per person, worldwide. See www.footprintnetwork.org.

6. See www.footprintnetwork.org/overshoot.

7. See www.footprintnetwork.org.

8. The world's lands vary tremendously in their capacity to produce a crop. In order to calculate the total carrying capacity of the world, one starts from the capacity of each piece of land to produce biomass. Highly productive land produces more than ten tonnes of biomass per year (in the form of plant or tree material), and other land much less. By summing all land areas times their productivity one gets the global biological capacity—or *bio-capacity* for short. Since the growth of an individual piece is influenced by technology—for example, fertilization or irrigation—bio-capacity depends on the technology used. But this latter effect is included in the unit used to measure acreage, which is called *global hectares*, which is short for "hectares of land at average productivity in the year of measurement." For more detail see www.footprintnetwork.org.

9. *The Millennium Ecosystem Assessment* (2005), Island Press, Washington, DC. Also see www.maweb.org.

10. Kenison Falkner, K., and Edmond, J. (1990), "Gold in Seawater," *Earth and Planetary Science Letters*, vol. 98, no. 2, pp. 208–21.

11. The Silver Institute (2010), *World Silver Survey*, the Silver Institute, Washington, DC.

12. International Panel for Sustainable Resource Management (2010), *Metal Stocks in Society*, United Nations Environment Programme.

13. International Resource Panel (2011), *Recycling Rates of Metals*, United Nations Environment Programme.

14. Miranda, M., and Sauer, A. (2010), *Mine the Gap: Connecting Water Risks and Disclosure in the Mining Sector*, World Resources Institute, working paper, Washington, DC.

15. European Commission (2008), *Press Release on Critical Raw Materials*, Brussels.

16. European Commission (2011), *Tackling the Challenges in Commodity Markets and on Raw Materials*, COM, Brussels, p. 25. Also see www.chemistryinnovation.co.uk/stroadmap/.

17. Based on current consumption rates plus 4% per year growth.

18. Mikolajczak C. (2009), Indium Corporation, private communication on availability of indium and gallium.

19. Report from the workshop organized by Nanoforum and the Institute for Environment and Sustainability, JRC Ispra, 30 and 31 March 2006.
20. US Geological Survey (2011), *Mineral Commodity Summaries 2011*, US Geological Survey, Washington, DC.
21. See www.soamsilver.com/innovation.asp.
22. See note 14 above.
23. Parmesan, C., and Yohe, G. (2003), "A Globally Coherent Fingerprint," *Nature*, vol. 421, pp. 37–42. Notice that species move poleward more slowly than climatic zones, because of slow adaptation. The climate zones may move poleward at some 10 km per year in the twenty-first century.

Chapter 7: The Nonmaterial Future to 2052

1. Meadows, D. H., et al. (1972), *The Limits to Growth*, Universe Books, New York.
2. Eloranta, J., "Military Spending Patterns in History," EH.Net, February 5, 2010. Available at eh.net/encyclopedia/article/eloranta.military (accessed 12 May 2011).
3. See www.dw-world.de/dw/article/0,,14981853,00.html.
4. See http://en.wikipedia.org/wiki/Eisenhower's_farewell_address.
5. See www.trumanproject.org/about/mission/thrust
6. See www.gci.ch.
7. See www.thisisecocide.com/general/465/.
8. See http://blog.gathminternational.co.uk/2011/04/26/the-united-states-army's-net-zero-initiative/.
9. See http://en.wikipedia.org/wiki/Skunk_Works.
10. See www.centri.net/smartbunker/.
11. See www.foia.cia.gov/2020/2020.pdf.
12. Gilbert, S. (2004), *Environmental Warfare and US Foreign Policy: The Ultimate Weapon of Mass Destruction*, Center for Research on Globalization. See also www.globalresearch.ca/articles/GIL401A.html.
13. Quote from Walt Kelly's Pogo, on an American poster for the first Earth Day, in 1970.

Chapter 8: The Zeitgeist in 2052

1. See www.metoffice.gov.uk/climate/uk/2011/; Manley, G. (1974), "Central England Temperatures: Monthly Means 1659 to 1973," *Quarterly Journal of the Royal Meteorological Society*, vol. 100, pp. 389–405, available at www.rmets.org/pdf/qj74manley.pdf.
2. Train delays into London Liverpool Street from most parts of the East due to repairs to power lines affected by hot weather. Speed restrictions also in place. BBC News online June 27, 2011.
3. UK Met Office (2011), http://www.metoffice.gov.uk/climate/uk/2011.
4. Department for Environment, Food and Rural Affairs (July 2008), *Ensuring the UK's Food Security in a Changing World*, DEFRA, London.
5. British Gas announced gas and electricity price increases on July 8, 2011.
6. See www.statistics.gov.uk.
7. This follows referendums in 1974, 1979, and 1997.
8. Department for Environment, Food and Rural Affairs, *Ensuring the UK's Food Security*.
9. In April 2011 France closed its border with Italy, and stopped the trains running, in order to prevent French-speaking Tunisian migrants from entering France. The Tunisians had traveled across the Mediterranean and then through Italy, escaping unrest and riots in Tunisia.
10. Stott, P., et al. (2004), "Human Contribution to the European Heatwave of 2003," *Nature*, vol. 432, pp 610–14.

11. There is some discussion about extending this into other areas, including linking it to developments taking place under the auspices of the United Nations Convention on the Law of the Sea (UNCLOS), which is playing a leading role in the Arctic.

12. According to the UK Climate Impacts Programme (UKCIP) the maximum increase in mean temperature in any part of Scotland is very unlikely to be more than 3 °C in winter, 3.8 °C the mean in summer, mean daily maximum in summer 5.4 °C. In southeast England maximum increase in mean temperature is 3.4 °C, 4.6 °C the mean in summer, mean daily maximum in summer 6.5 °C. Source: UKCIP.

13. Changes in annual mean precipitation in any part of Scotland are very unlikely to be more than 5%. Winter mean precipitation up to +28%, summer precipitation +1%. In southeast England changes in annual mean precipitation are very unlikely to be greater than 6%. Winter mean precipitation +36% and summer mean precipitation +7%. Source: UKCIP.

14. The New North is Canada, Russia, the northern US, Iceland, Finland, Greenland, Norway, and Sweden, as identified in Smith, L. C. (2010), *The World in 2050: Four Forces Shaping Civilization's Northern Future,* Dutton, New York.

15. Cilliers, J., Hughes, B. and Moyers, J. (2011), *African Futures 2050: The Next Forty Years,* ISS Monograph 175, Institute for Security Studies, Pretoria, p. 30.

16. UN-Habitat (2010), *State of the World's Cities 2010/2011: Bridging the Urban Divide,* Earthscan, London; Ravallion M., Chen S. and Sangraula, P. (2007), *New Evidence of the Globalization of Poverty,* World Bank, Washington, DC.

17. In my forecast, Africa is even bigger, 28%, because I assume lower population growth in the rest of the world. (Note from Jorgen Randers on January 26, 2012.)

18. Cilliers, J., Hughes, B. and Moyers, J. (2011), *African Futures 2050,* p. 60.

19. Foster, V., and Briceño-Garmendia, C. (eds) (2010), *Africa's Infrastructure: A Time for Transformation,* World Bank, Washington, DC.

20. Sudeshna, B., et al. (2009), *Access, Affordability, and Alternatives: Modern Infrastructure Services in Africa,* World Bank, Washington, DC, pp. 4–5.

21. Friedman, T. L. (2008), *Hot, Flat and Crowded: Why We Need a Green Revolution and How It Can Renew America,* Farrar, Straus & Giroux, New York.

22. Hawken, P. (2007), *Blessed Unrest: How the Largest Movement in the World Came into Being and Why No One Saw It Coming,* Viking Press, New York, gives a compelling account of the emergence of this trend.

23. PWC (2011), Global CEO Survey. Available at www.pwc.com/gx/en/ceo-survey/index.jhtml.

24. Means "peace" in English.

25. Pew Research Center (2010), *Millennials—A Portrait of Generation Next,* Washington, DC.

26. The Spiral Dynamics framework is based on the original research of Dr. Clare W. Graves and is carried on primarily by two practitioners, Don Beck and Chris Cowan, whose approaches have diverged somewhat. Don Beck framed a new and modified version of SD and called it Spiral Dynamics Integral (SDi).

27. See www.ted.com/talks/jane_mcgonigal_gaming_can_make_a_better_world.html.

Chapter 9: Reflections on the Future

1. The least unrealistic method would be to extract CO_2 from the atmosphere by growing trees, and then this use wood to run power stations with CCS, which sends the carbon back into the ground (and the electricity to the consumer). But it would have to be done at sufficient scale to overwhelm the effect of the methane from the tundra.

2. Institute for Energy Research (2010), *A Primer on Energy and the Economy,* Washington, DC, February 16.

3. The World Business Council for Sustainable Development has become famous for promoting sustainability and the slogan "Business cannot succeed in societies that fail."

4. In principle it is possible to do much more and have a strong and faster effect. See Randers, J., and Gilding, P. (June 2010), "The One Degree War Plan," *Journal of Social Responsibility*, vol. 1, no. 1, pp. 170–88.

5. See ibid., for more detailed calculations along these lines.

6. Carbon Tracker Initiative (2011): *Are Financial Markets Carrying a Carbon Bubble?* available at www.carbontracker.org/carbonbubble.

7. Grantham, J. (2011), "Time to Wake Up: Days of Abundant Resources Are Over," GMO Quarterly Letter, April 2011, www.gmo.com.

8. See Kumhof, M., and Ranciere, R., (2010), *Inequality, Leverage and Crises*, IMF Working Paper.

9. Carbon Tracker Initiative (2011): *Are Financial Markets Carrying a Carbon Bubble?* available at www.carbontracker.org/carbonbubble.

10. Keynes, J. M. (1936), *General Theory of Employment, Interest, and Money*, Macmillan, London.

Chapter 10: Five Regional Futures

1 See http://en.wikipedia.org/wiki/List_of_countries_by_population.

2. More detail in appendix 2.

3. I have also removed two members of the OECD, Mexico and Turkey, from the OECD category, in order to ensure that the OECD category is more uniformly industrialized.

4. A microgrid is a localized (for instance, to a campus, city, or region) electrical infrastructure supported by its own power generation and energy storage equipment, serving the needs of its consumers and interfacing at its boundaries with the larger grid, to either supply or demand excess energy.

5. International Energy Agency (2011), *Technology Roadmap: Biofuels for Transport*, IEA, Vienna.

Chapter 11: Comparison with Other Futures

1. The initial work was done by Dolores Garcia, then an independent researcher in Brighton UK, and described in Garcia, D. (2009), "A New World Model Including Energy and Climate Change Data," available at http://europe.theoildrum.com/node/5145.

2. See Garcia, D. (2011), "New World Model—EROEI issues," available at http://europe.the oildrum.com/node/5688; Murphy, D. J., and Hall, C. A. S. (February 2011), "Energy Return on Investment, Peak Oil, and the End of Economic Growth," *Annals of the New York Academy of Sciences*, vol. 1219, pp. 52–72, available at http://onlinelibrary.wiley.com/doi/10.1111/j.1749-6632.2010.05940.x/abstract.

3. Lobell, D. (2011), "Impacts in the Next Few Decades and Coming Centuries," *Climate Stabilization Targets: Emissions, Concentrations, and Impacts over Decades to Millennia*, National Academies Press, Washington, DC, chapter 5. Also available at http://www.nap.edu/catalog/12877.html.

4. See Meadows, D. H., Randers, J., and Meadows, D. L. (2004), *Limits to Growth: The 30-Year Update*, figure 6-1, p. 210.

5. See further discussion of this point in Randers, J. (2008), "Global Collapse—Fact or Fiction?" *Futures*, vol. 40, no. 10, December.

6. Bardi, U. (2011), *The Limits to Growth Revisited*, Springer, New York.

7. Simmons, M. R. (2000), "Revisiting *The Limits to Growth*. Could the Club of Rome Have Been Right, After All?" September 15, 2000. Available at http://www.greatchange.org/ov-simmons,club_of_rome_revisted.pdf.

8. Turner, G. (2008), "A Comparison of *The Limits to Growth* with 30 Years of History," *Global Environmental Change*, vol. 18.
9. MacKenzie, D. (2012), "Doomsday Book," *New Scientist*, January 7, p. 38.
10. Diamond, J. (2005), *Collapse: How Societies Choose to Fail or Succeed*, Viking Press, New York.
11. The following analysis rests heavily on Randers, J., "What Was the Message of *The Limits to Growth?*" scheduled for publication in *Gaia* (Verlag) in 2012.
12. WWF International (2010), *The Living Planet Report 2010*, Gland, Switzerland.
13. See www.un.org/millenniumgoals/bkgd.shtml.
14. See Andersen, D. (2007), *The 5th Step: The Way to a New Society*, Kolofon, Oslo.
15. I use the word "flowering" to enhance readability. A technically more accurate description would be rapid and prolific branching.

Chapter 12: What Should You Do?

1. The atmosphere weighs 5,100 trillion tonnes and humans have increased the concentration of CO_2 by about 100 ppmv from the preindustrial level of 280 ppmv. CO_2 has a molecular weight of 44 versus air at 29.
2. The UN Secretary-General's High-Level Panel on Sustainability (2012), *Resilient People, Resilient Planet: A Future Worth Choosing*, New York, February. Available at www.un.org/gsp/.
3. Available at www.un.org/millenniumgoals/bkgd.shtml.
4. Available at www.metoffice.gov.uk/climate-change/resources/hadley.
5. Randers, J. (2012), "Greenhouse Gas Emissions per Unit of Value Added (GEVA)— a Corporate Guide to Voluntary Climate Policy," accepted for publication in *EnergyPolicy*.

Index

About the Author

Jorgen Randers is professor of climate strategy at the BI Norwegian Business School, where he works on climate issues and scenario analysis. He was previously president of BI and deputy director general of WWF International (World Wildlife Fund) in Switzerland. He lectures internationally on sustainable development and especially climate, and is a nonexecutive member of a number of corporate boards. He sits on the sustainability councils of British Telecom in the UK and the Dow Chemical Company in the United States. In 2006 he chaired the cabinet-appointed Commission on Low Greenhouse Gas Emissions, which reported on how Norway can cut its climate gas emissions by two-thirds by 2050. Randers has written numerous books and scientific papers and was coauthor of *The Limits to Growth* in 1972, *Beyond the Limits* in 1992, and *Limits to Growth: The 30-Year Update* in 2004.

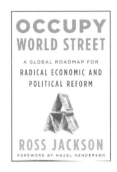
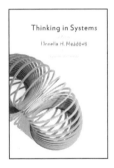

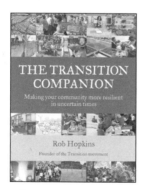
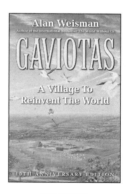